Miracle Girls

1

by Nami Akimoto

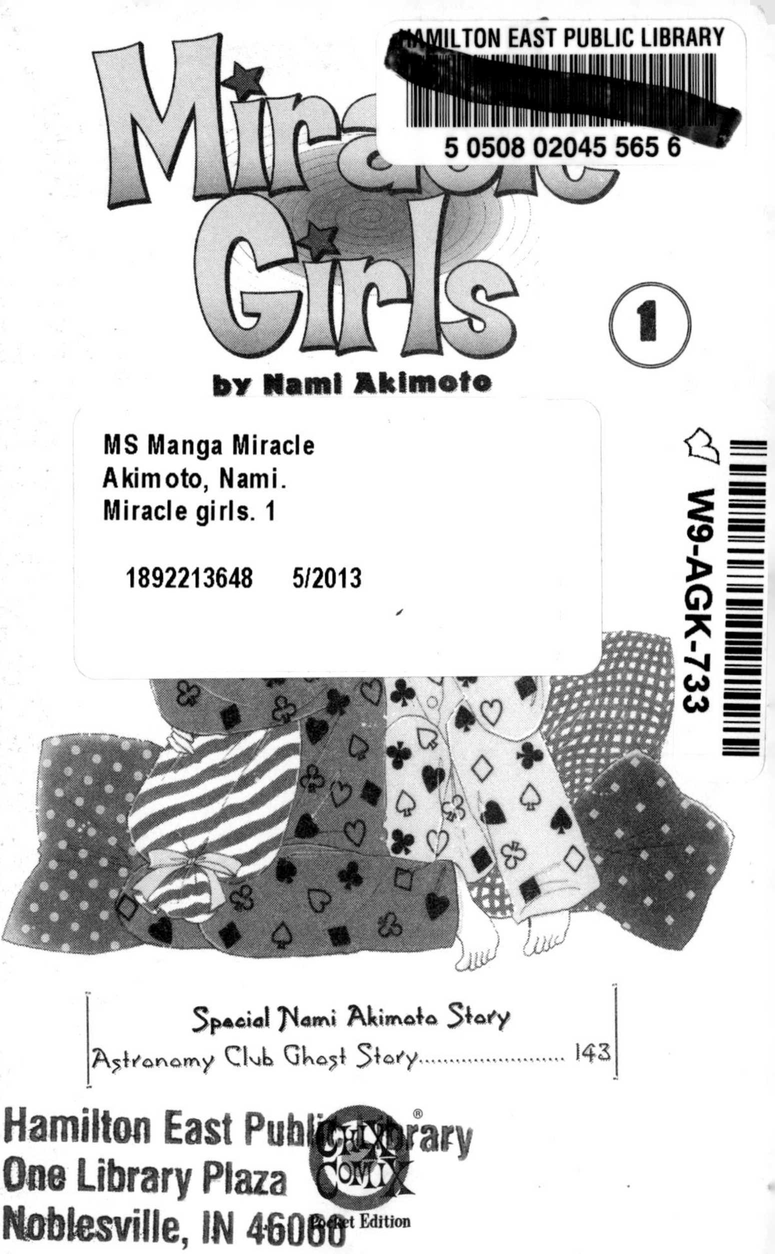

Special Nami Akimoto Story

CHLX COMIX® Pocket Edition

TOKYOPOP Press Presents
Miracle Girls 1 by Nami Akimoto
Chix Comix Pocket Edition is an imprint of Mixx Entertainment, Inc.
ISBN: 1-892213-64-8
First Printing January 2001

10   9   8   7   6   5   4   3   2   1

This volume contains the Miracle Girls installments from
Miracle Girls Chix Comix No.1 through No.3 in their entirety.

Translator - Anita Sengupta. Retouch Artists - Wilbert Lacuna & Romualdo Viray II.
Graphics Assistant - Steven Kindernay. Graphic Designer - Akemi Imafuku.
Editors - Jake Forbes, Mary Coco & Michael Schuster. Editorial Intern -Trong Ta.
Production Manager - Fred Lui. Vice President, Publishing - Henry Kornman.

Email: editor@Press.Tokyopop.com
Come visit us at www.TOKYOPOP.com.

TOKYOPOP
Los Angeles - Tokyo

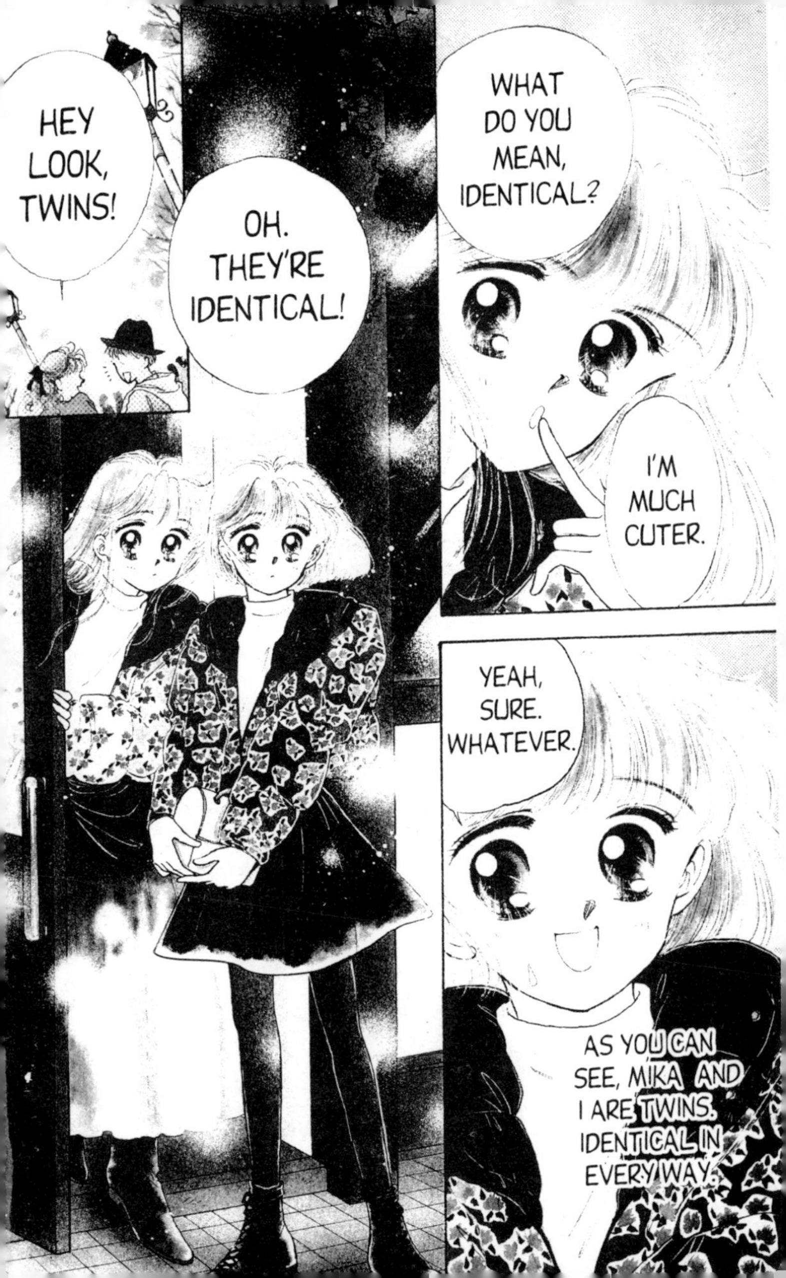
HEY LOOK, TWINS!
OH. THEY'RE IDENTICAL!
WHAT DO YOU MEAN, IDENTICAL?
I'M MUCH CUTER.
YEAH, SURE. WHATEVER.
AS YOU CAN SEE, MIKA AND I ARE TWINS. IDENTICAL IN EVERY WAY.

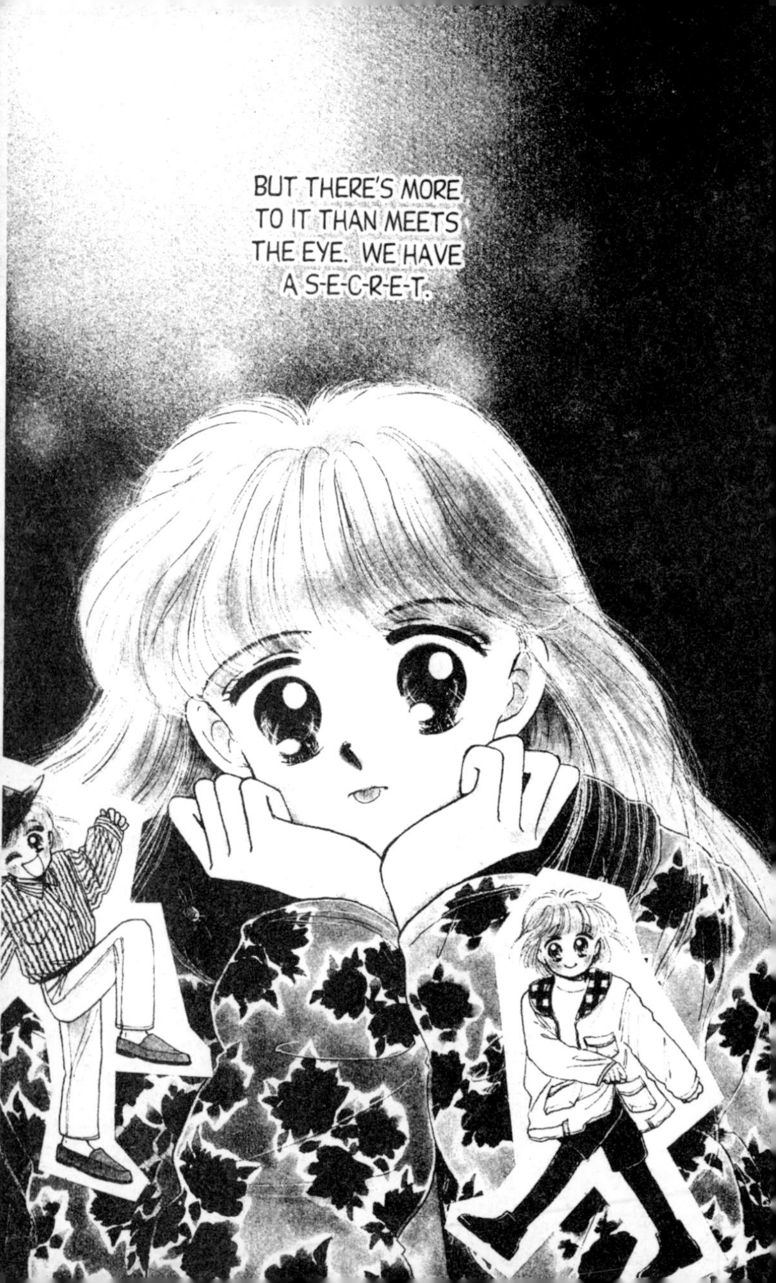
BUT THERE'S MORE TO IT THAN MEETS THE EYE. WE HAVE A S-E-C-R-E-T.

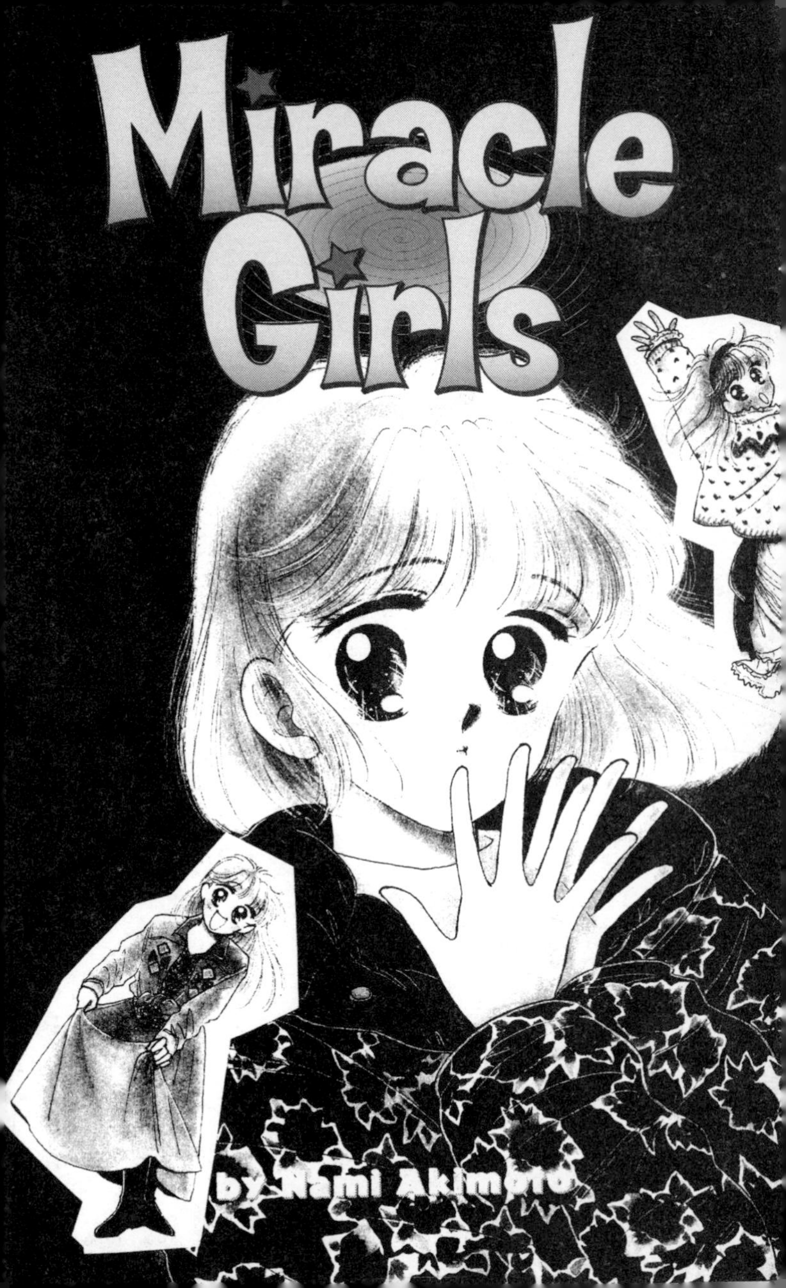
Miracle Girls
by Nami Akimoto

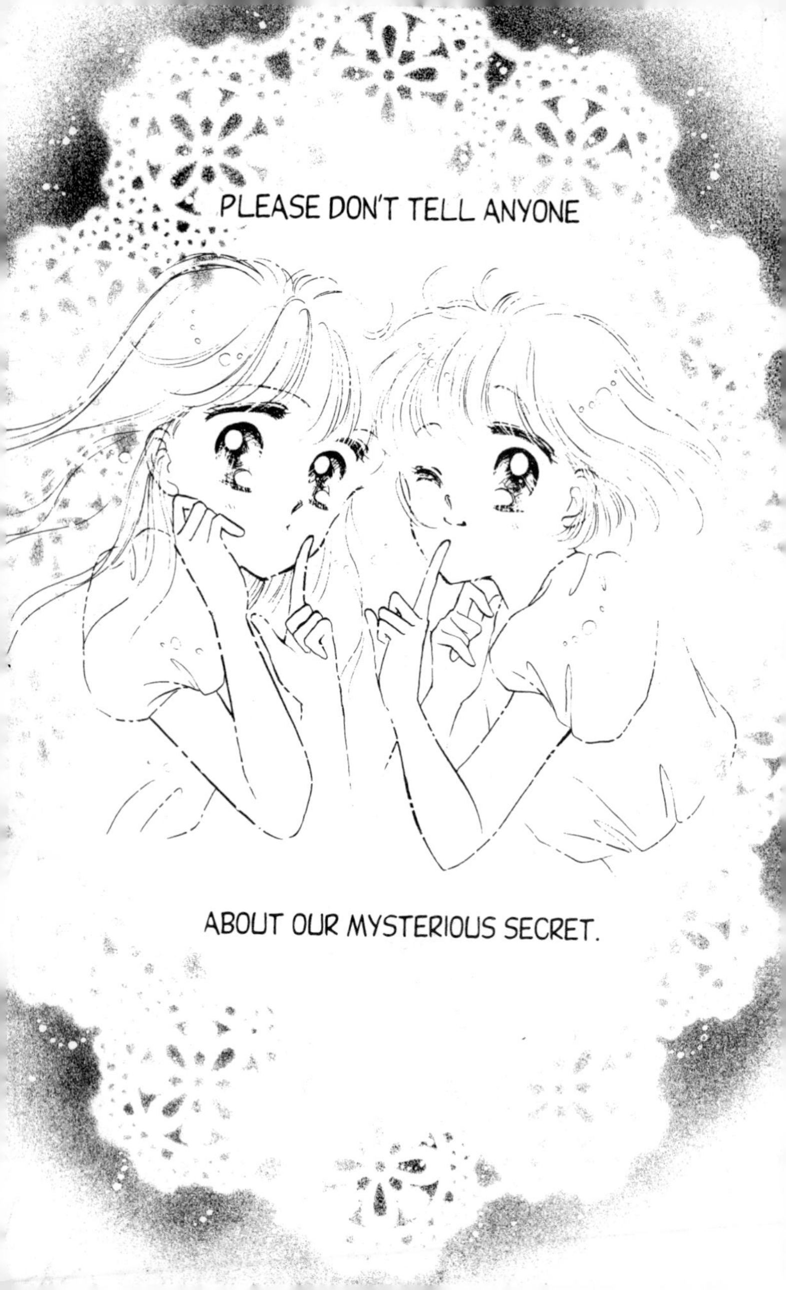
PLEASE DON'T TELL ANYONE
ABOUT OUR MYSTERIOUS SECRET.

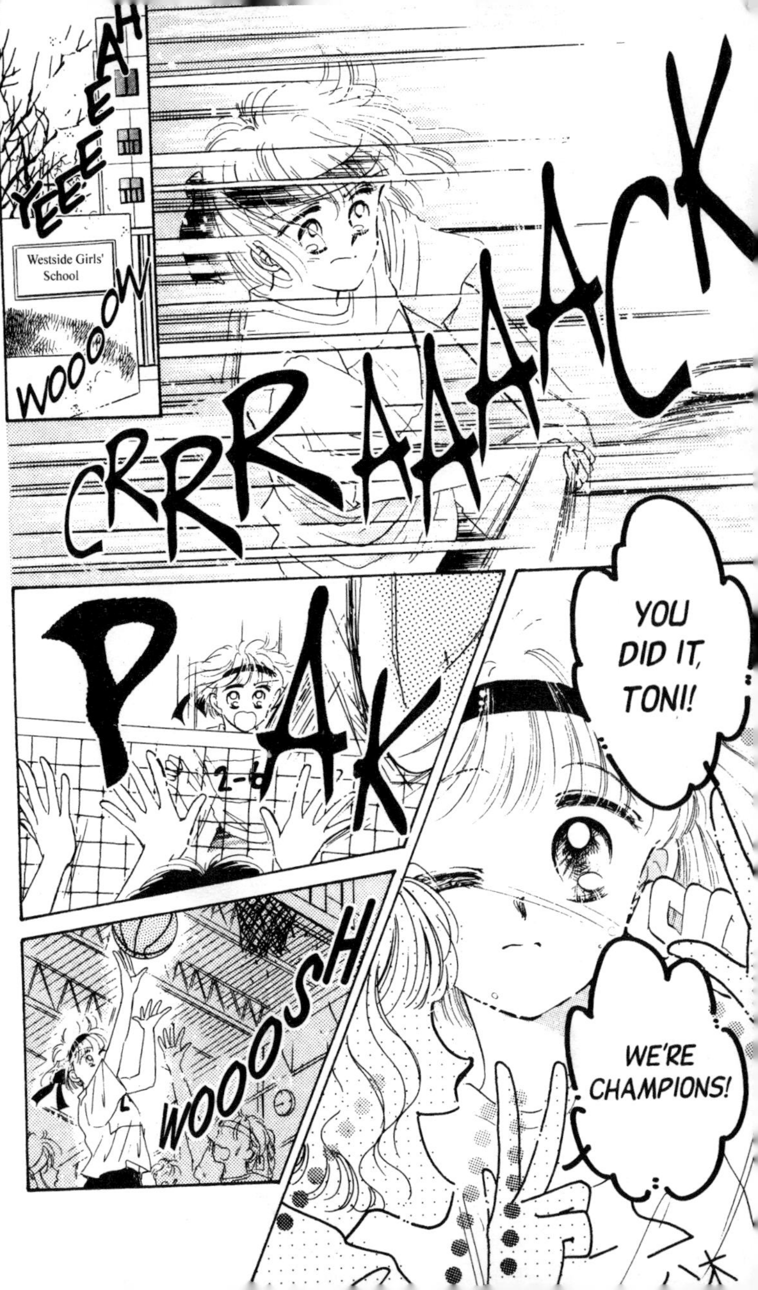
Westside Girls' School
YEEEEAH
WOOOOOW
CRRRAAAACK
PAK
WOOOSH
YOU DID IT, TONI!
WE'RE CHAMPIONS!

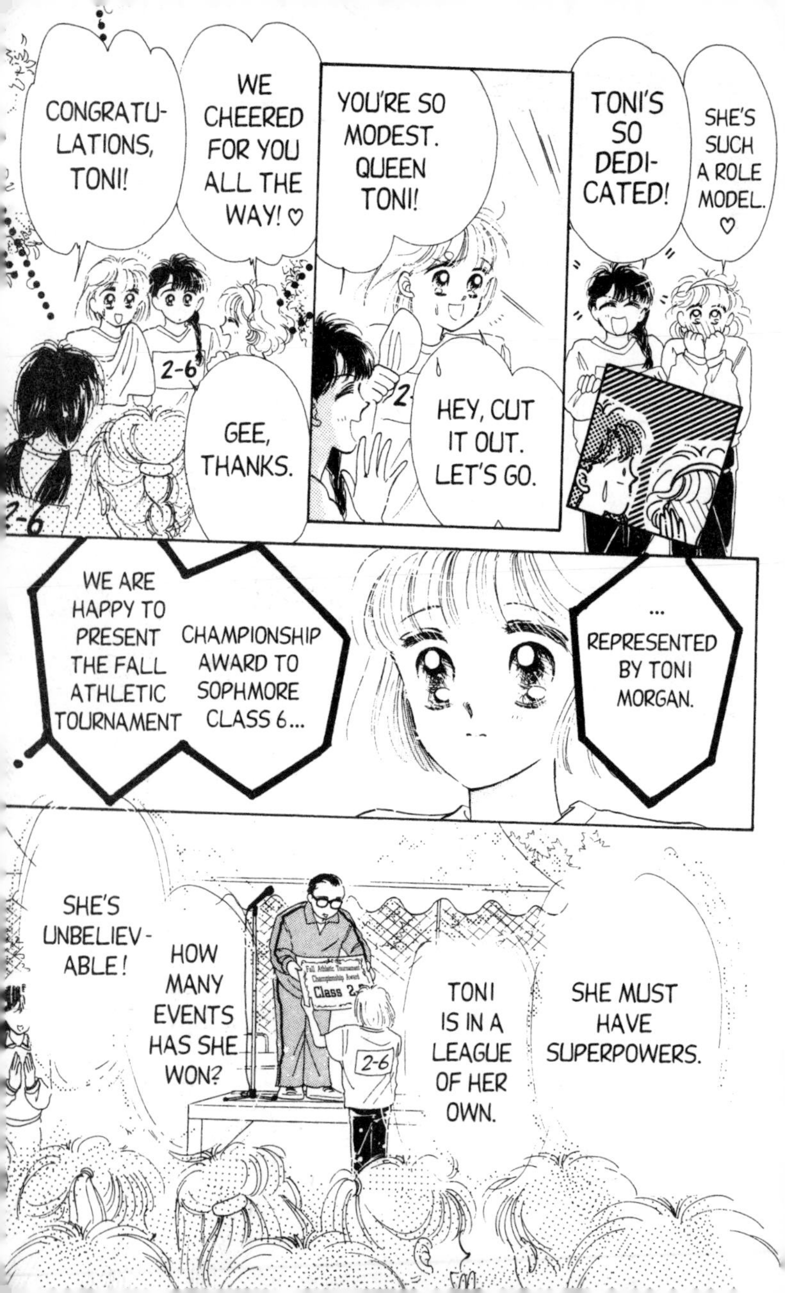

CONGRATULATIONS, TONI!
WE CHEERED FOR YOU ALL THE WAY! ♡
GEE, THANKS.
YOU'RE SO MODEST. QUEEN TONI!
HEY, CUT IT OUT. LET'S GO.
TONI'S SO DEDICATED!
SHE'S SUCH A ROLE MODEL. ♡
WE ARE HAPPY TO PRESENT THE FALL ATHLETIC TOURNAMENT CHAMPIONSHIP AWARD TO SOPHMORE CLASS 6...
...REPRESENTED BY TONI MORGAN.
SHE'S UNBELIEVABLE!
HOW MANY EVENTS HAS SHE WON?
Fall Athletic Tournament Championship Award Class 2
TONI IS IN A LEAGUE OF HER OWN.
SHE MUST HAVE SUPERPOWERS.

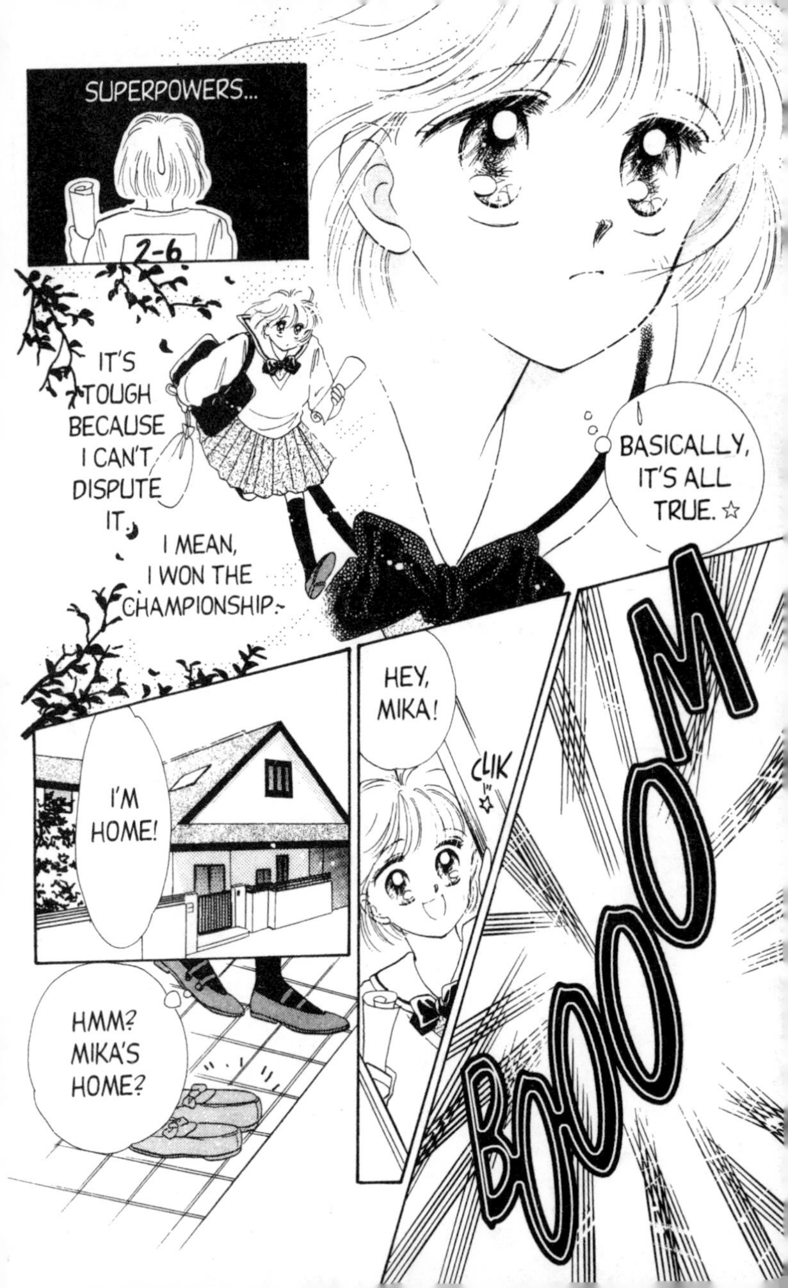

SUPERPOWERS...
2-6
IT'S TOUGH BECAUSE I CAN'T DISPUTE IT.
I MEAN, I WON THE CHAMPIONSHIP~
BASICALLY, IT'S ALL TRUE. ☆
I'M HOME!
HMM? MIKA'S HOME?
HEY, MIKA!
CLIK ☆
BOOOOM

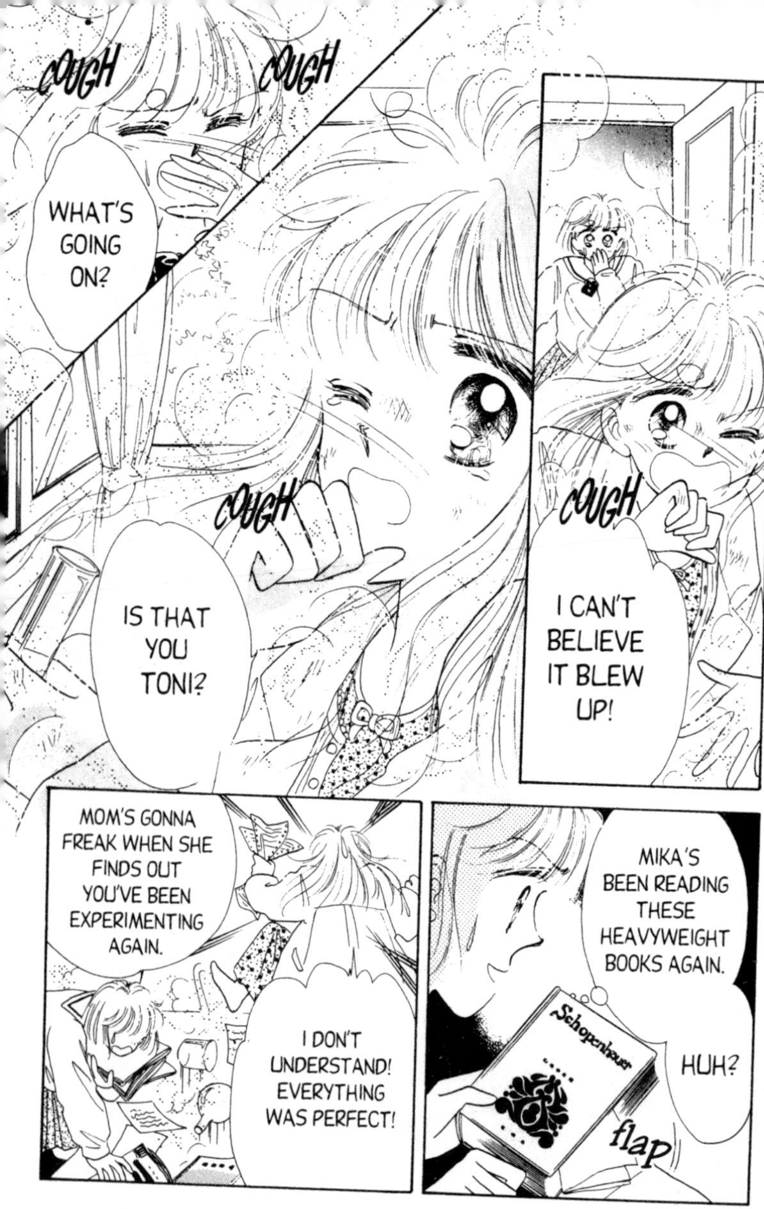
COUGH
COUGH
WHAT'S GOING ON?
COUGH
IS THAT YOU TONI?
COUGH
I CAN'T BELIEVE IT BLEW UP!
MOM'S GONNA FREAK WHEN SHE FINDS OUT YOU'VE BEEN EXPERIMENTING AGAIN.
I DON'T UNDERSTAND! EVERYTHING WAS PERFECT!
MIKA'S BEEN READING THESE HEAVYWEIGHT BOOKS AGAIN.
Schopenhauer
HUH?
flap

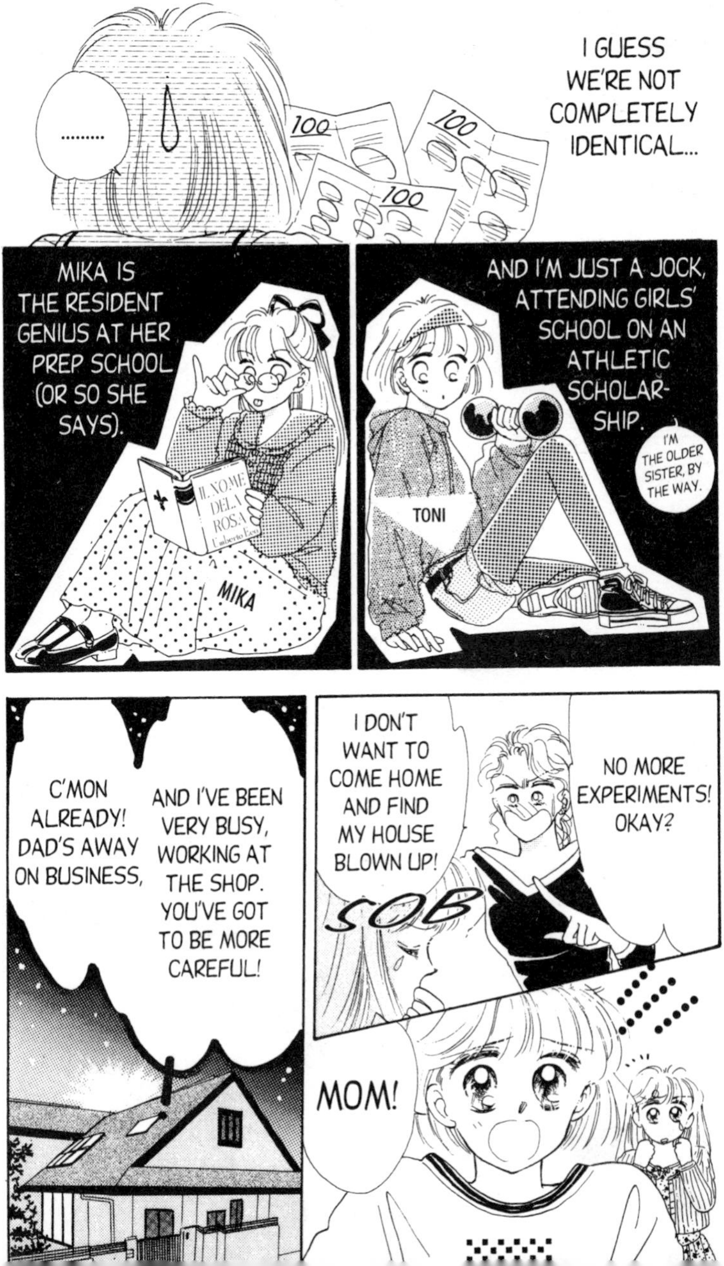
....
100
100
100
I GUESS WE'RE NOT COMPLETELY IDENTICAL...
MIKA IS THE RESIDENT GENIUS AT HER PREP SCHOOL (OR SO SHE SAYS).
IL NOME DELA ROSA Umberto Eco
MIKA
AND I'M JUST A JOCK, ATTENDING GIRLS' SCHOOL ON AN ATHLETIC SCHOLAR-SHIP.
I'M THE OLDER SISTER, BY THE WAY.
TONI
C'MON ALREADY! DAD'S AWAY ON BUSINESS,
AND I'VE BEEN VERY BUSY, WORKING AT THE SHOP. YOU'VE GOT TO BE MORE CAREFUL!
I DON'T WANT TO COME HOME AND FIND MY HOUSE BLOWN UP!
NO MORE EXPERIMENTS! OKAY?
SOB
MOM!

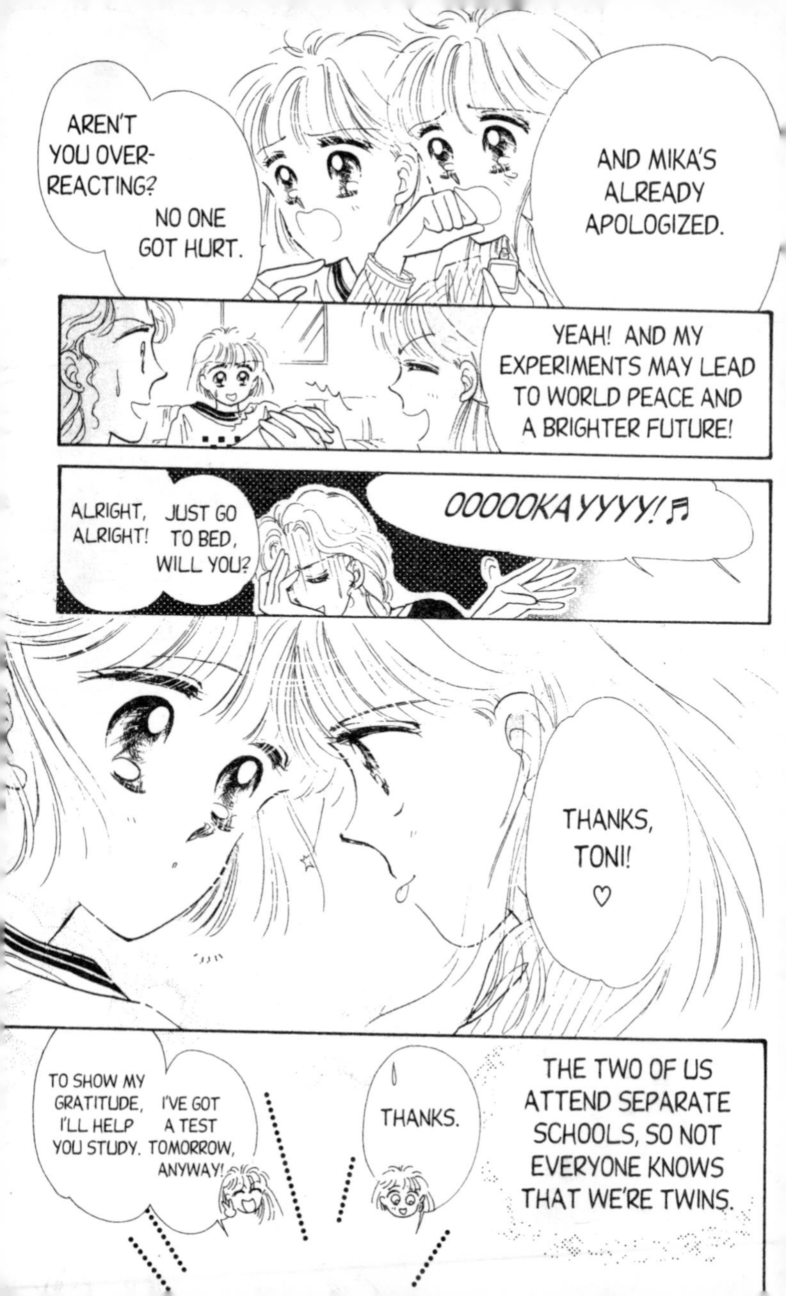
AREN'T YOU OVER-REACTING?
NO ONE GOT HURT.
AND MIKA'S ALREADY APOLOGIZED.
YEAH! AND MY EXPERIMENTS MAY LEAD TO WORLD PEACE AND A BRIGHTER FUTURE!
ALRIGHT, ALRIGHT!
JUST GO TO BED, WILL YOU?
OOOOOKAYYYY! ♬
THANKS, TONI! ♡
TO SHOW MY GRATITUDE, I'LL HELP YOU STUDY.
I'VE GOT A TEST TOMORROW, ANYWAY!
THANKS.
THE TWO OF US ATTEND SEPARATE SCHOOLS, SO NOT EVERYONE KNOWS THAT WE'RE TWINS.

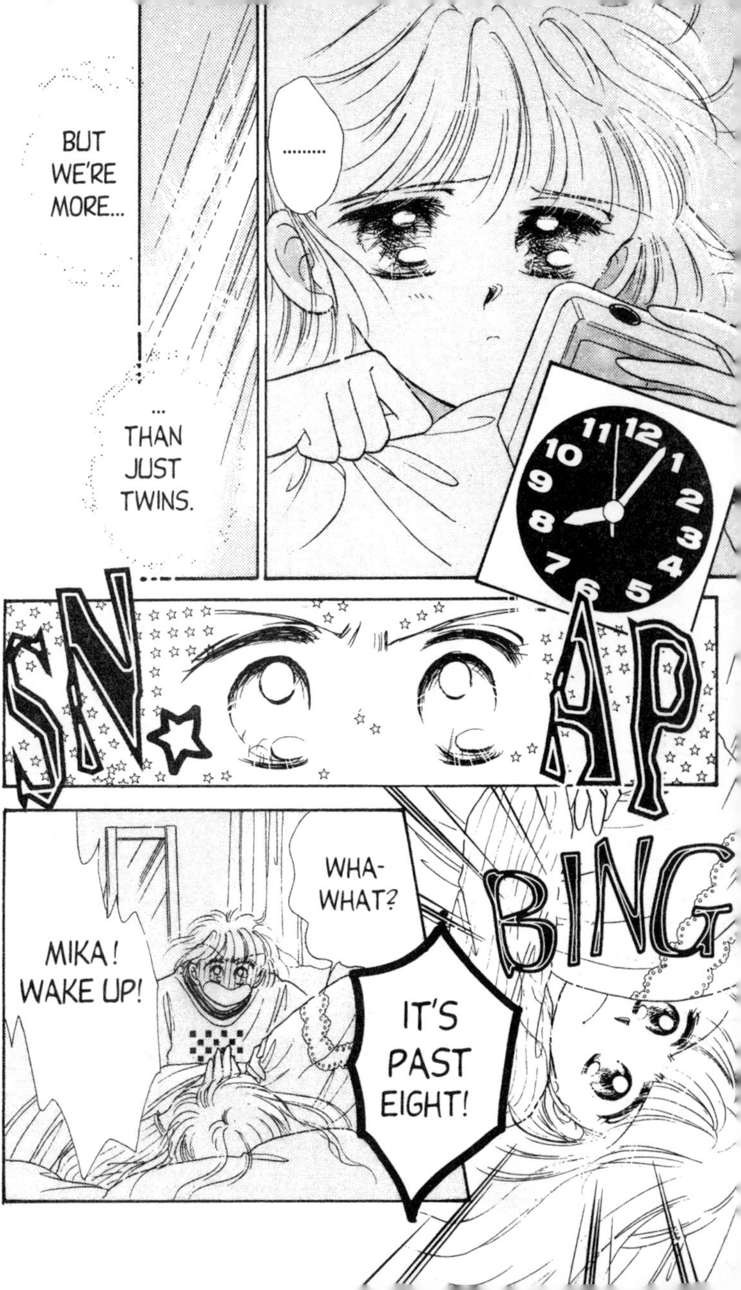
BUT WE'RE MORE...
... THAN JUST TWINS.
....
SN☆AP
MIKA! WAKE UP!
WHA-WHAT?
BING
IT'S PAST EIGHT!

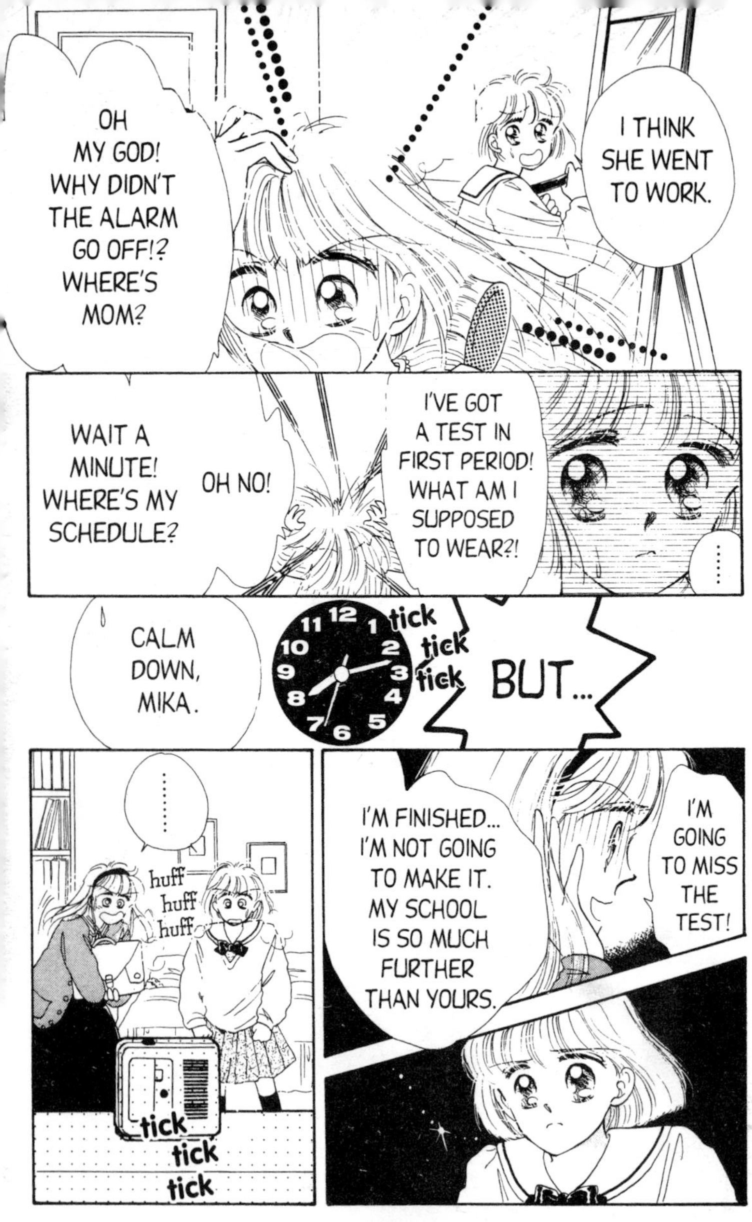
OH MY GOD! WHY DIDN'T THE ALARM GO OFF!? WHERE'S MOM?
I THINK SHE WENT TO WORK.
WAIT A MINUTE! WHERE'S MY SCHEDULE?
OH NO!
I'VE GOT A TEST IN FIRST PERIOD! WHAT AM I SUPPOSED TO WEAR?!
......
CALM DOWN, MIKA.
tick tick tick
BUT...
....
huff huff huff
tick tick tick
I'M FINISHED... I'M NOT GOING TO MAKE IT. MY SCHOOL IS SO MUCH FURTHER THAN YOURS.
I'M GOING TO MISS THE TEST!

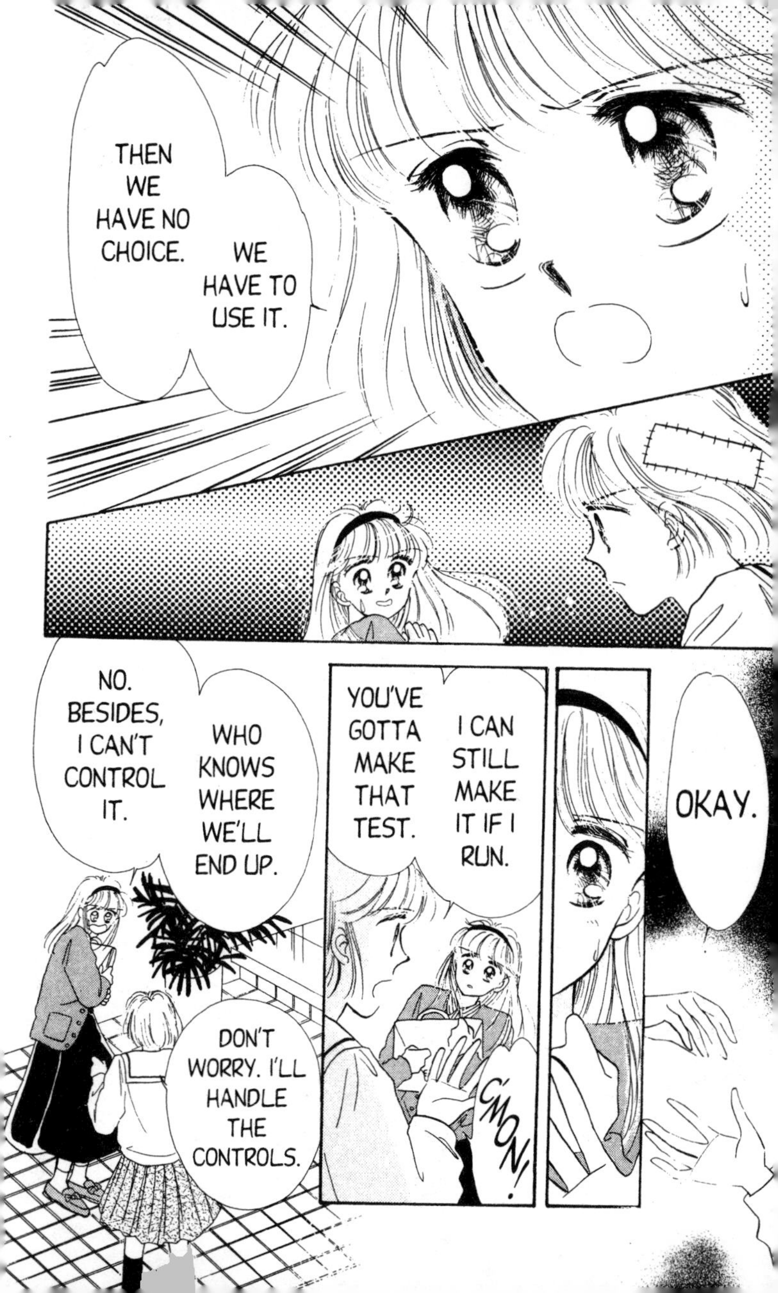
THEN WE HAVE NO CHOICE.
WE HAVE TO USE IT.
NO. BESIDES, I CAN'T CONTROL IT.
WHO KNOWS WHERE WE'LL END UP.
DON'T WORRY. I'LL HANDLE THE CONTROLS.
YOU'VE GOTTA MAKE THAT TEST.
I CAN STILL MAKE IT IF I RUN.
C'MON!
OKAY.

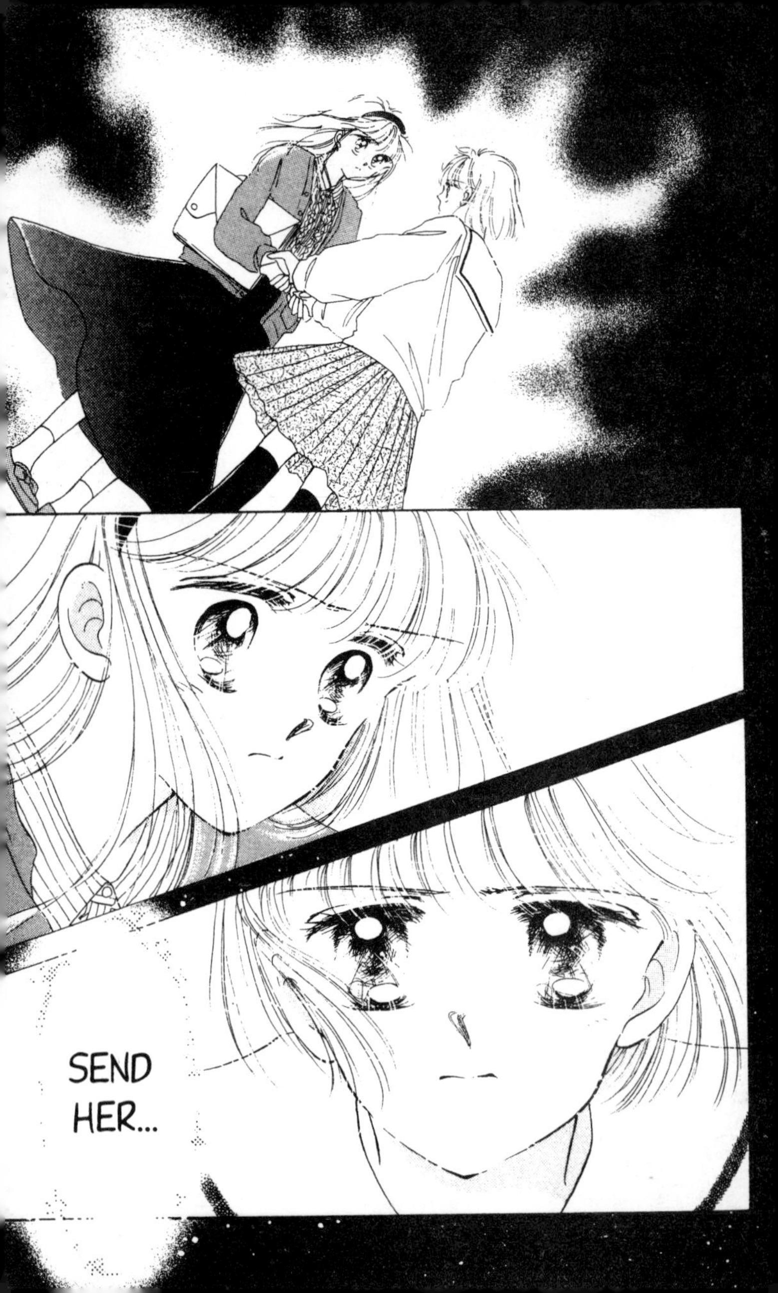
SEND HER...

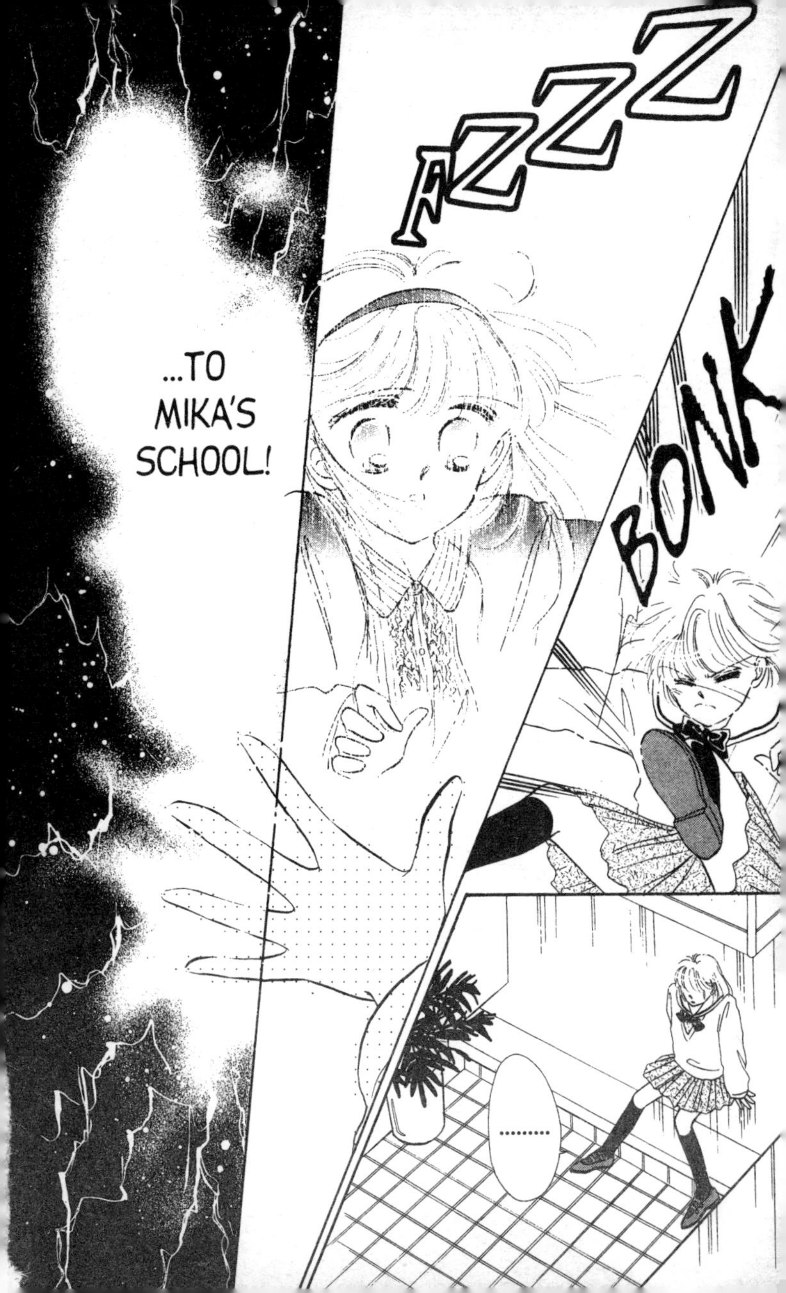
...TO MIKA'S SCHOOL!
FZZZZ
BONK
....

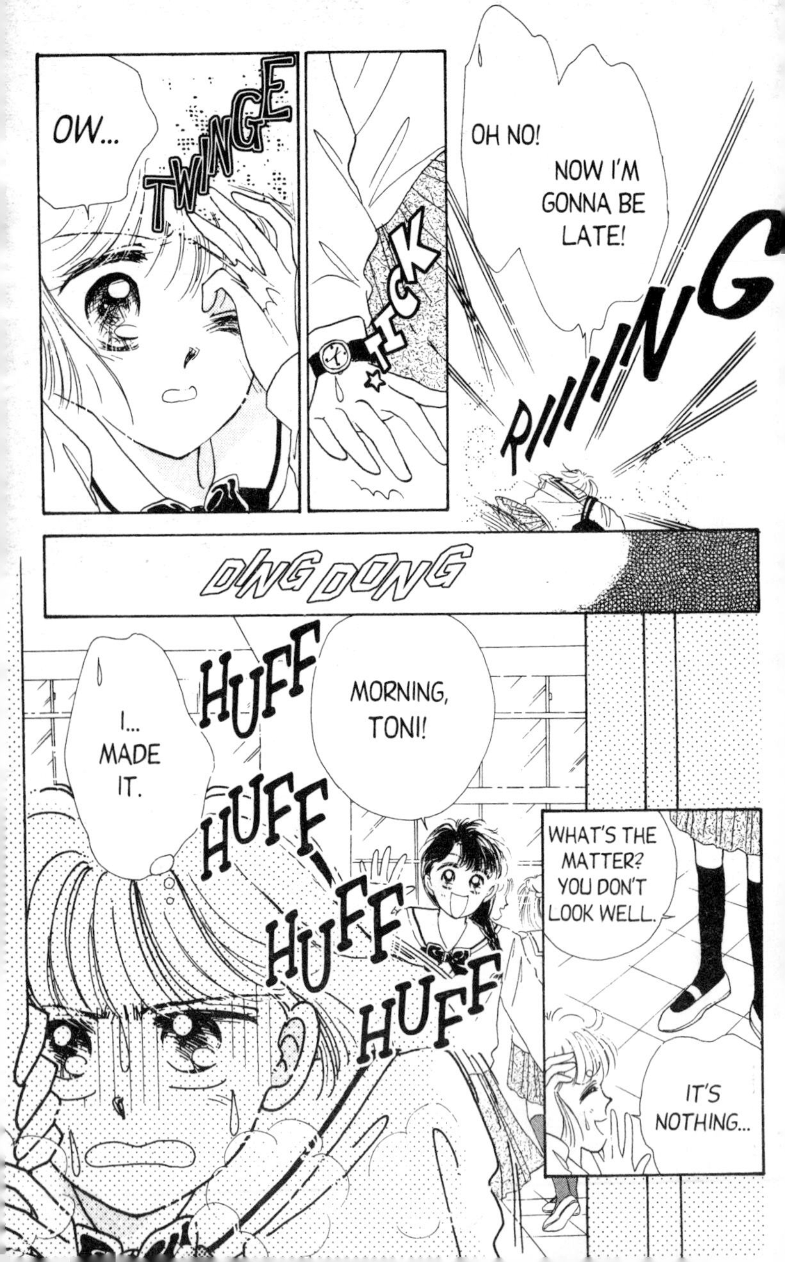
OW...
TWINGE
TICK
OH NO!
NOW I'M GONNA BE LATE!
RIIIIING
DING DONG
I... MADE IT.
HUFF
MORNING, TONI!
HUFF
HUFF
HUFF
WHAT'S THE MATTER? YOU DON'T LOOK WELL.
IT'S NOTHING...

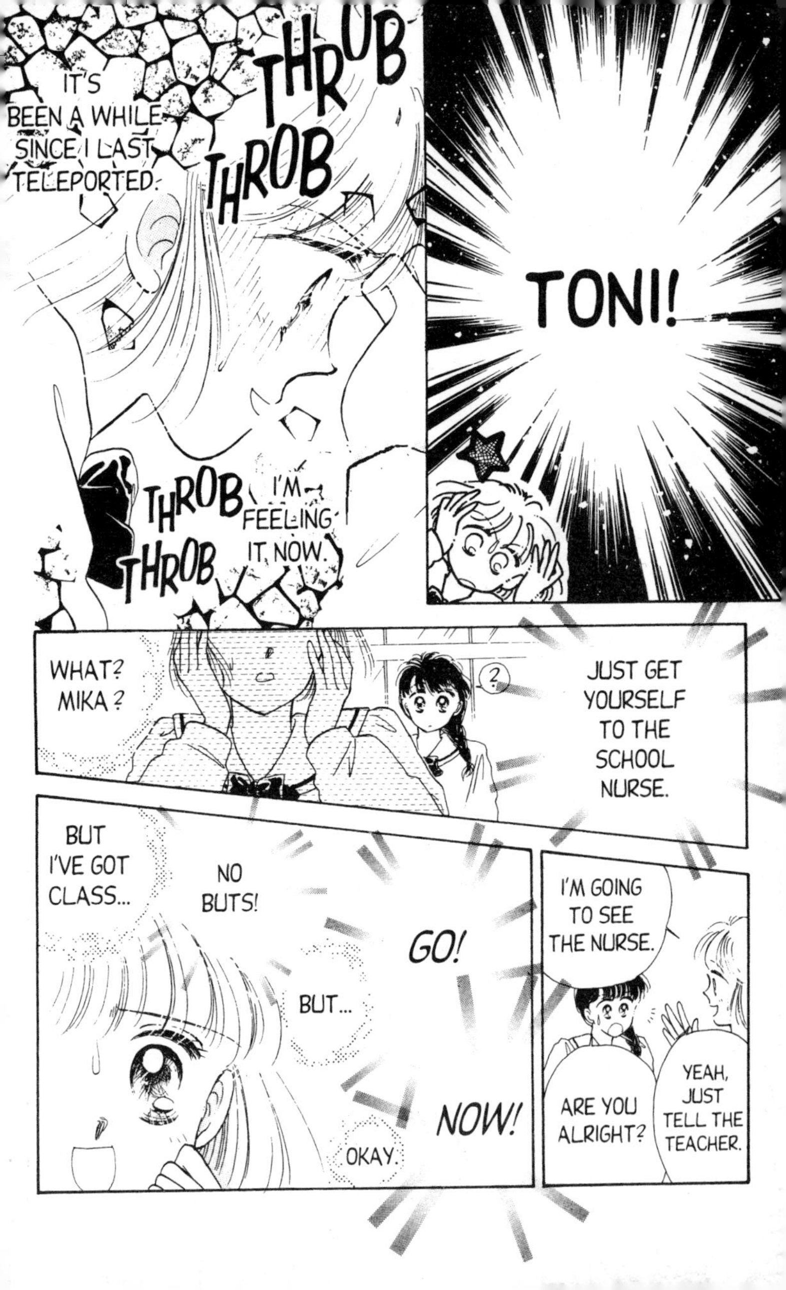
IT'S BEEN A WHILE SINCE I LAST TELEPORTED.
THRUB THROB
THROB THROB
I'M FEELING IT NOW.
TONI!
WHAT? MIKA?
JUST GET YOURSELF TO THE SCHOOL NURSE.
BUT I'VE GOT CLASS...
NO BUTS!
GO!
BUT...
NOW!
OKAY.
I'M GOING TO SEE THE NURSE.
ARE YOU ALRIGHT?
YEAH, JUST TELL THE TEACHER.

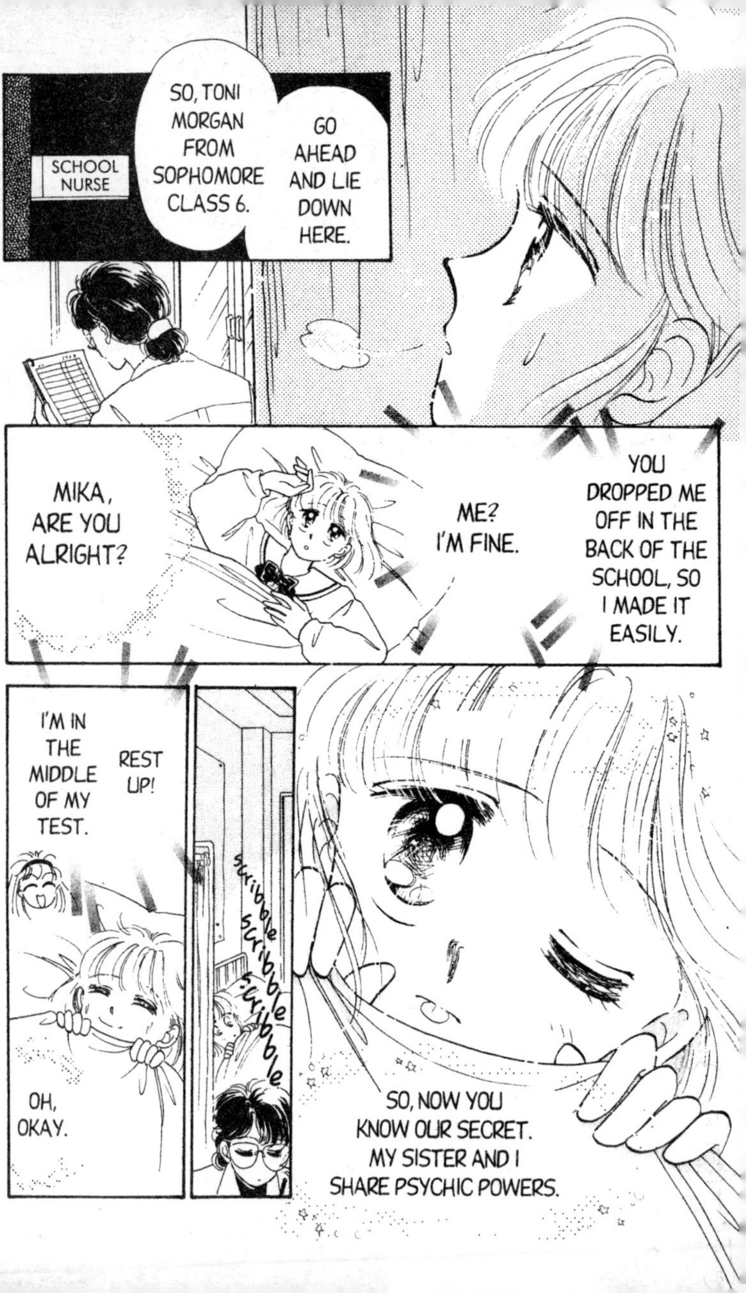
SCHOOL NURSE
SO, TONI MORGAN FROM SOPHOMORE CLASS 6.
GO AHEAD AND LIE DOWN HERE.
MIKA, ARE YOU ALRIGHT?
ME? I'M FINE.
YOU DROPPED ME OFF IN THE BACK OF THE SCHOOL, SO I MADE IT EASILY.
I'M IN THE MIDDLE OF MY TEST.
REST UP!
OH, OKAY.
scribble scribble scribble scribble
SO, NOW YOU KNOW OUR SECRET. MY SISTER AND I SHARE PSYCHIC POWERS.

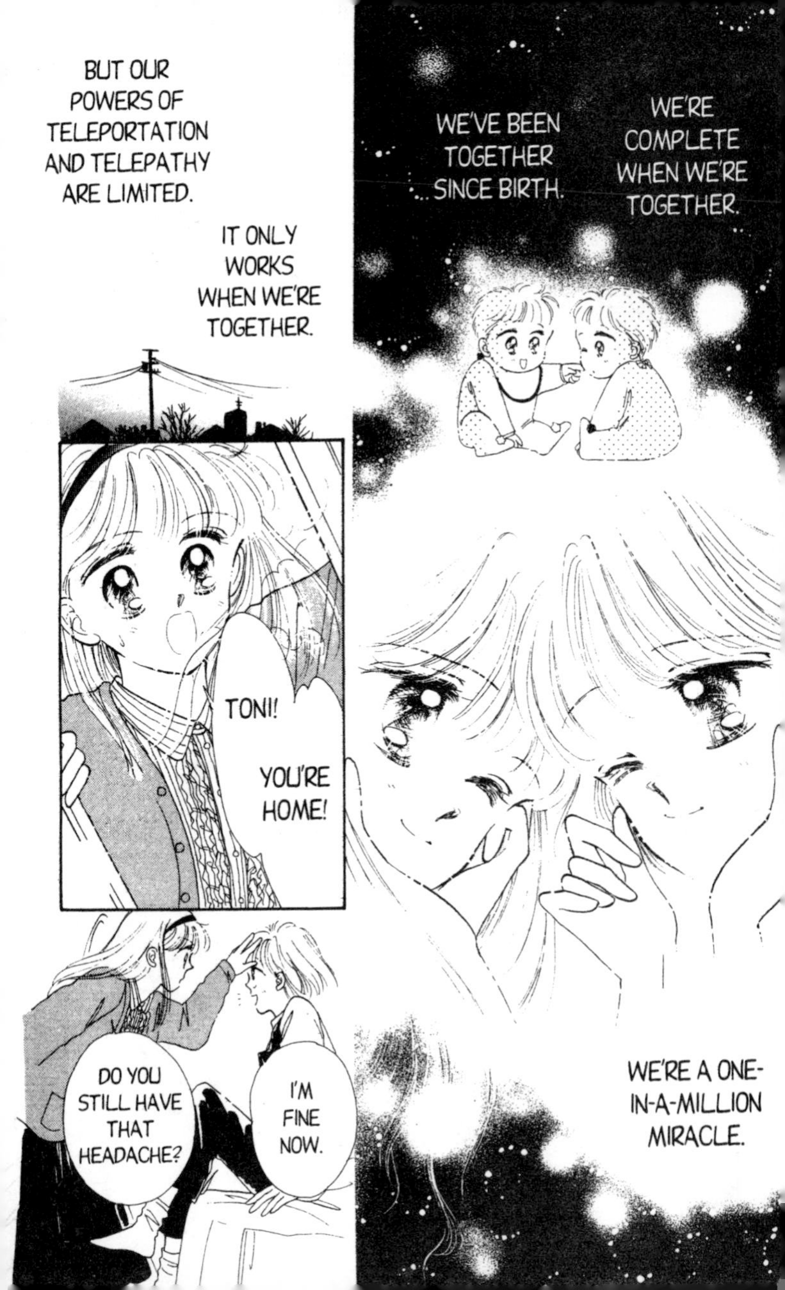
BUT OUR POWERS OF TELEPORTATION AND TELEPATHY ARE LIMITED.
IT ONLY WORKS WHEN WE'RE TOGETHER.
TONI!
YOU'RE HOME!
DO YOU STILL HAVE THAT HEADACHE?
I'M FINE NOW.
WE'VE BEEN TOGETHER SINCE BIRTH.
WE'RE COMPLETE WHEN WE'RE TOGETHER.
WE'RE A ONE-IN-A-MILLION MIRACLE.

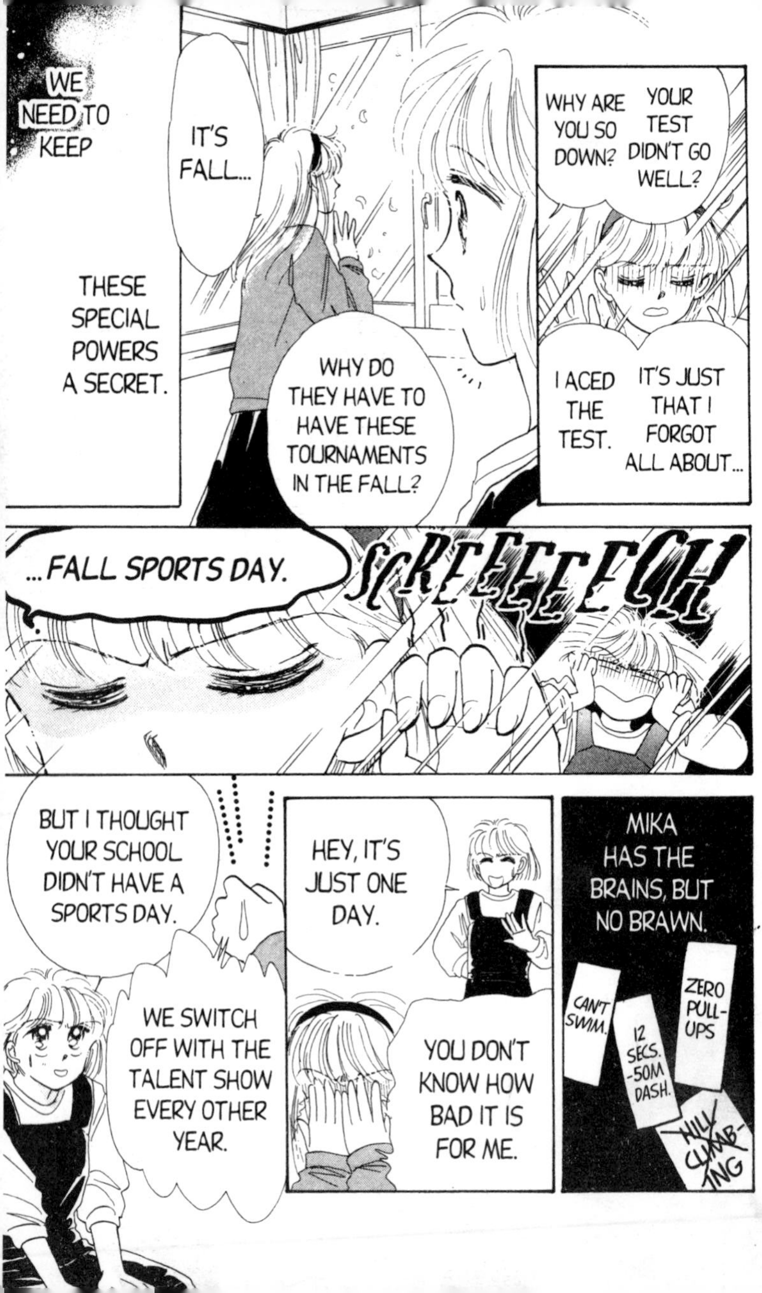
WE NEED TO KEEP THESE SPECIAL POWERS A SECRET.
IT'S FALL...
WHY DO THEY HAVE TO HAVE THESE TOURNAMENTS IN THE FALL?
WHY ARE YOU SO DOWN?
YOUR TEST DIDN'T GO WELL?
I ACED THE TEST.
IT'S JUST THAT I FORGOT ALL ABOUT...
...FALL SPORTS DAY.
SCREEEEECH
BUT I THOUGHT YOUR SCHOOL DIDN'T HAVE A SPORTS DAY.
WE SWITCH OFF WITH THE TALENT SHOW EVERY OTHER YEAR.
HEY, IT'S JUST ONE DAY.
YOU DON'T KNOW HOW BAD IT IS FOR ME.
MIKA HAS THE BRAINS, BUT NO BRAWN.
CAN'T SWIM.
12 SECS. -50M DASH.
ZERO PULL-UPS
HILL CLIMBING

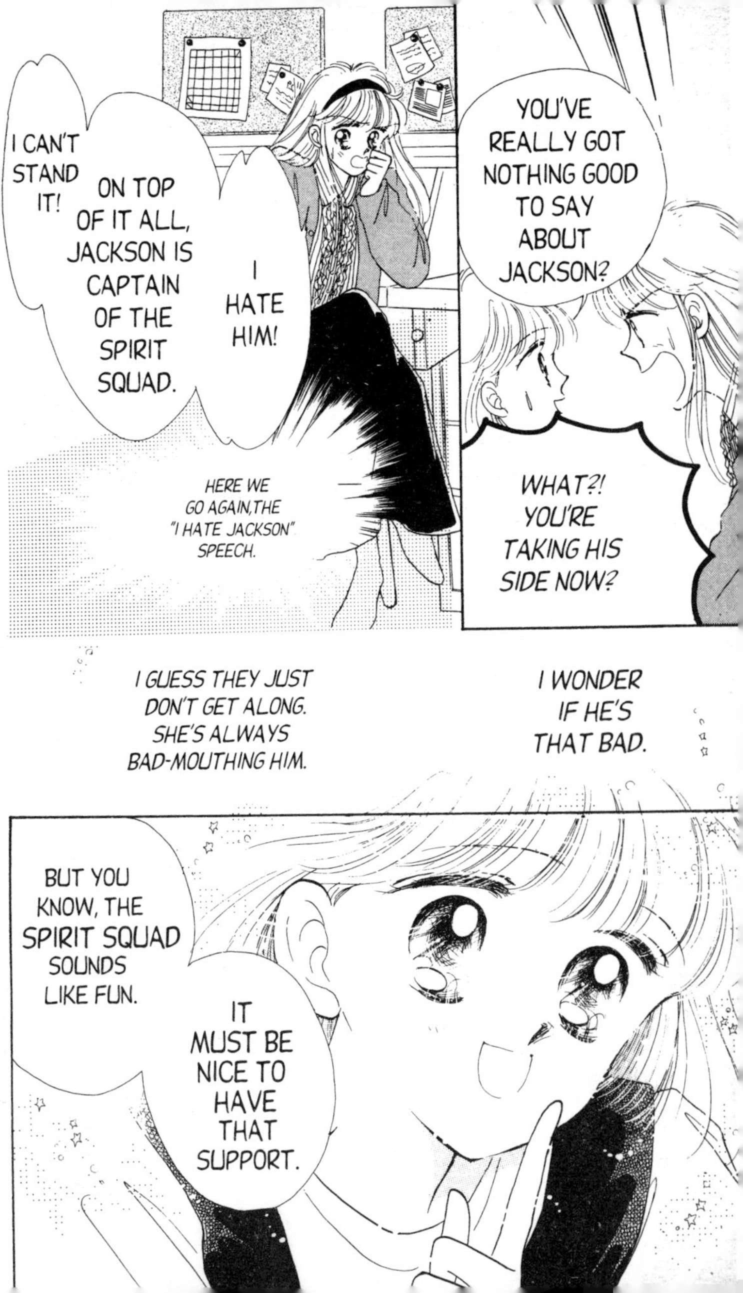
I CAN'T STAND IT!
ON TOP OF IT ALL, JACKSON IS CAPTAIN OF THE SPIRIT SQUAD.
I HATE HIM!
HERE WE GO AGAIN, THE "I HATE JACKSON" SPEECH.
YOU'VE REALLY GOT NOTHING GOOD TO SAY ABOUT JACKSON?
WHAT?! YOU'RE TAKING HIS SIDE NOW?
I GUESS THEY JUST DON'T GET ALONG. SHE'S ALWAYS BAD-MOUTHING HIM.
I WONDER IF HE'S THAT BAD.
BUT YOU KNOW, THE SPIRIT SQUAD SOUNDS LIKE FUN.
IT MUST BE NICE TO HAVE THAT SUPPORT.

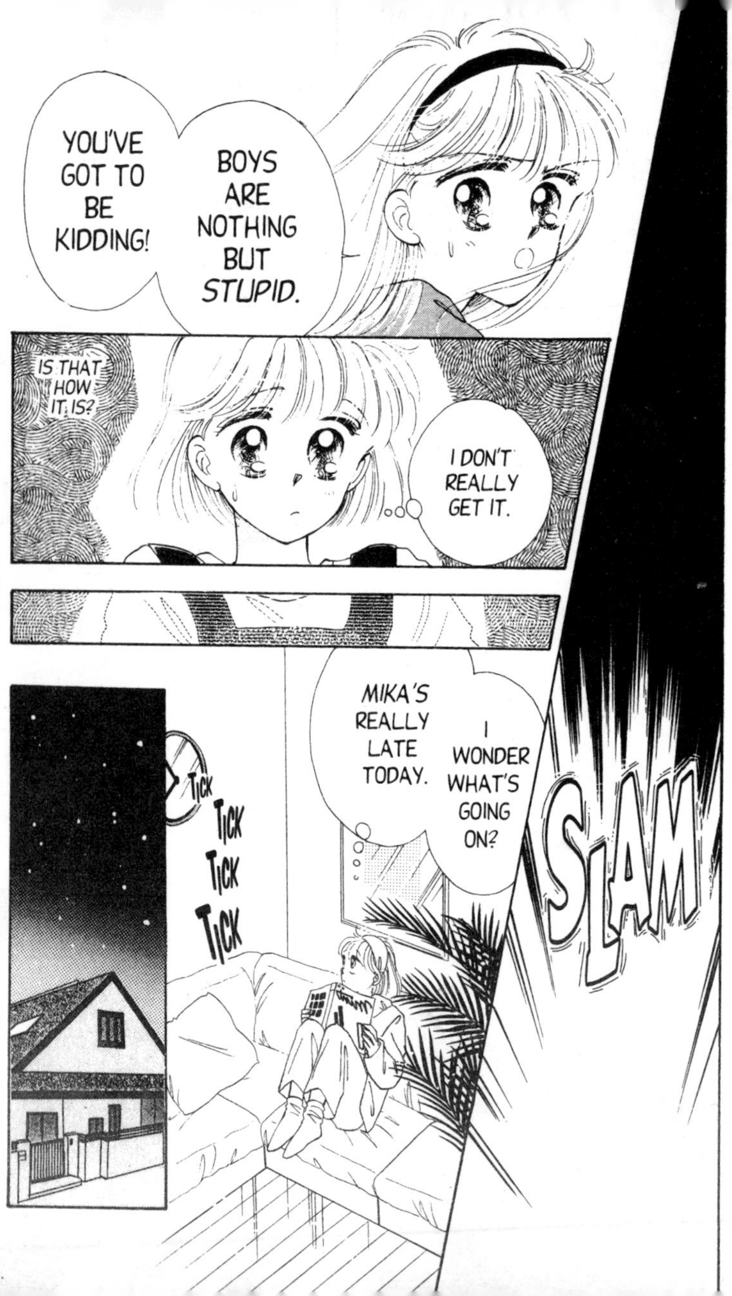
YOU'VE GOT TO BE KIDDING!
BOYS ARE NOTHING BUT STUPID.
IS THAT HOW IT IS?
I DON'T REALLY GET IT.
MIKA'S REALLY LATE TODAY.
I WONDER WHAT'S GOING ON?
TICK
TICK
TICK
TICK
SLAM

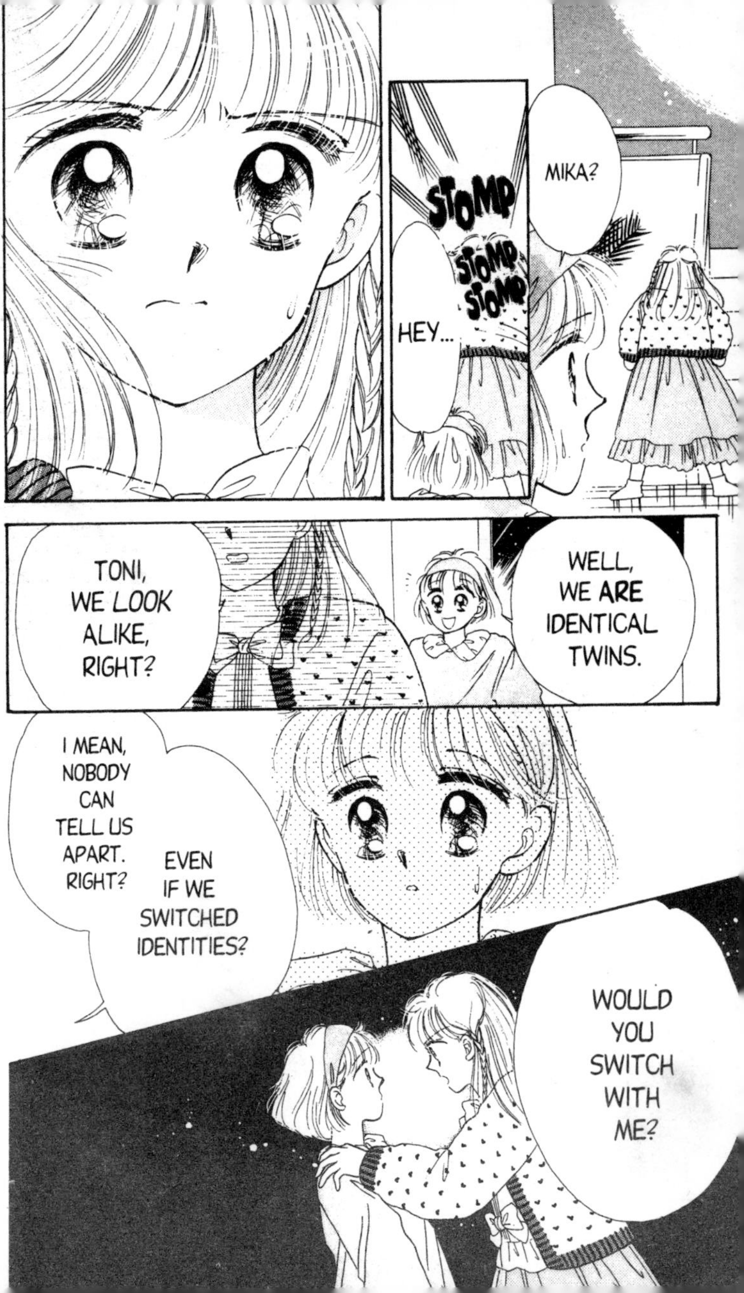
HEY...
STOMP
STOMP STOMP
MIKA?
TONI, WE LOOK ALIKE, RIGHT?
WELL, WE ARE IDENTICAL TWINS.
I MEAN, NOBODY CAN TELL US APART. RIGHT?
EVEN IF WE SWITCHED IDENTITIES?
WOULD YOU SWITCH WITH ME?

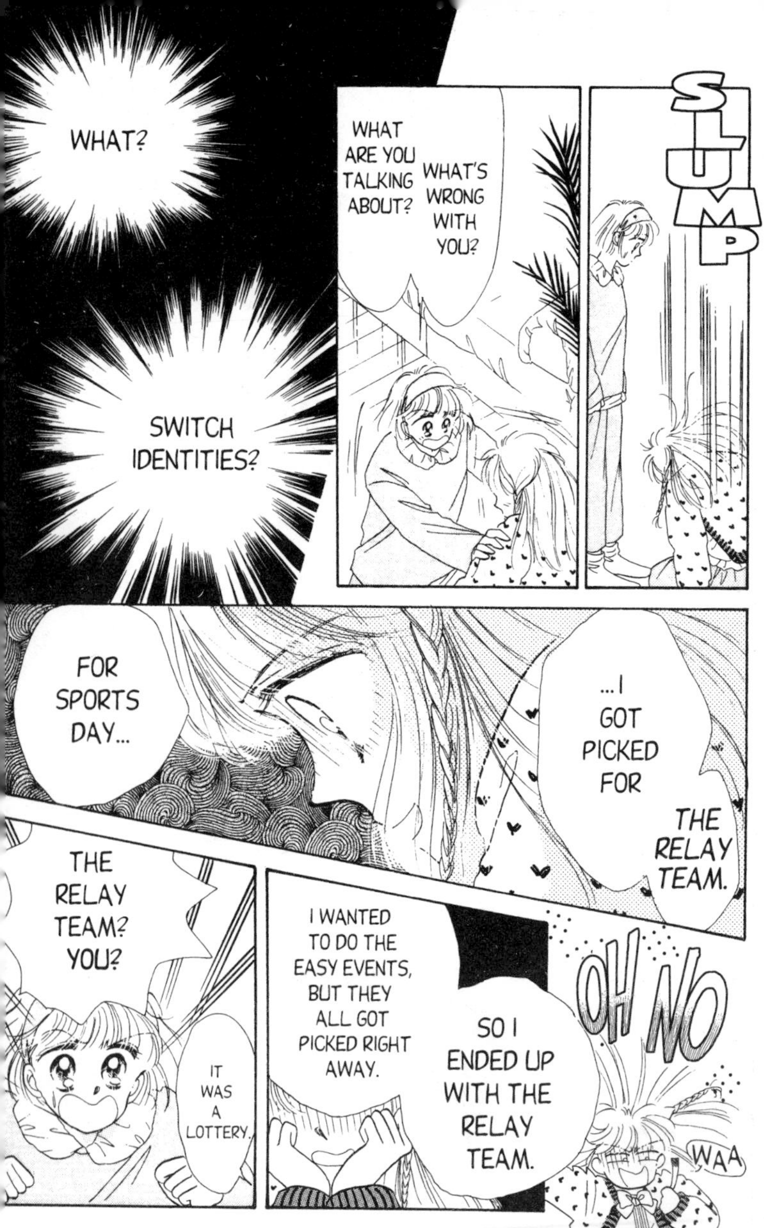
WHAT?
SWITCH IDENTITIES?
WHAT ARE YOU TALKING ABOUT?
WHAT'S WRONG WITH YOU?
SLUMP
FOR SPORTS DAY...
...I GOT PICKED FOR
THE RELAY TEAM.
THE RELAY TEAM? YOU?
IT WAS A LOTTERY.
I WANTED TO DO THE EASY EVENTS, BUT THEY ALL GOT PICKED RIGHT AWAY.
SO I ENDED UP WITH THE RELAY TEAM.
OH NO
WAA

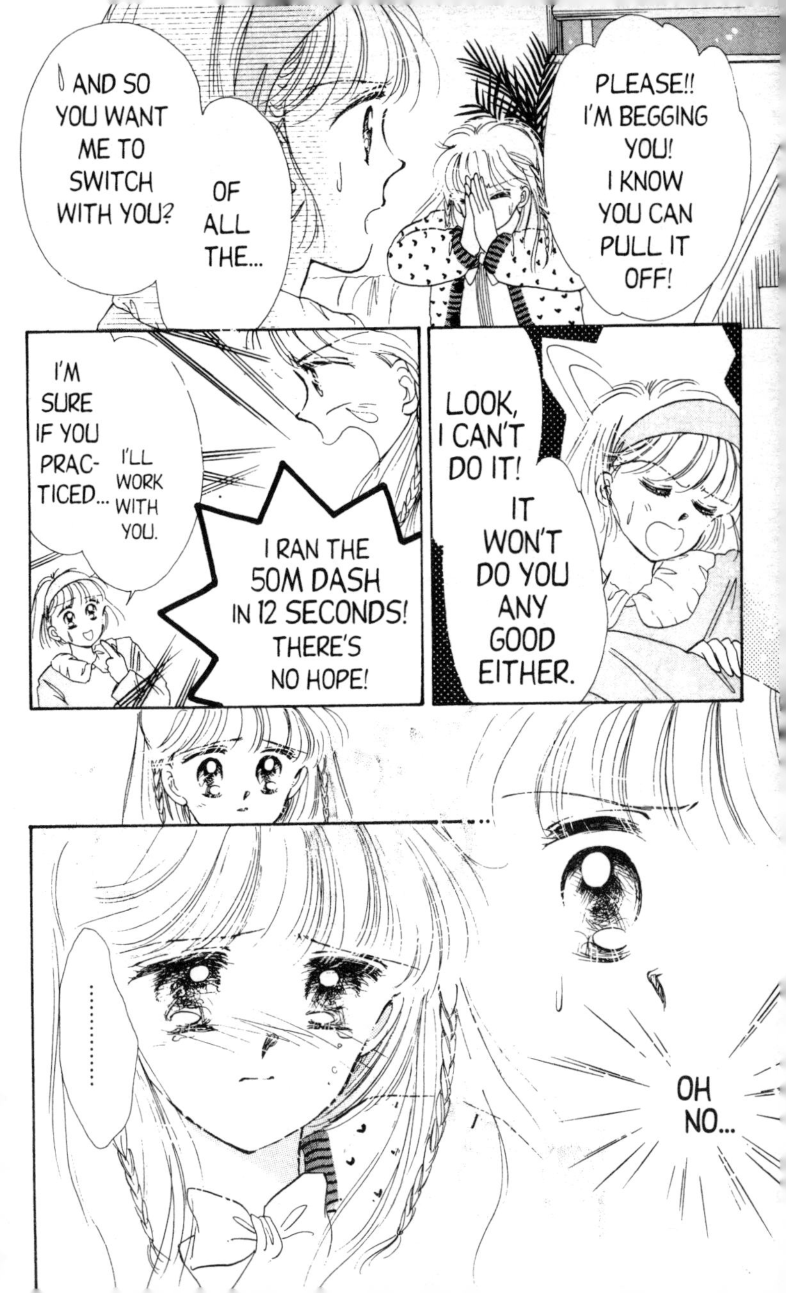
AND SO YOU WANT ME TO SWITCH WITH YOU?
OF ALL THE...
PLEASE!! I'M BEGGING YOU! I KNOW YOU CAN PULL IT OFF!
I'M SURE IF YOU PRAC-TICED...
I'LL WORK WITH YOU.
I RAN THE 50M DASH IN 12 SECONDS! THERE'S NO HOPE!
LOOK, I CAN'T DO IT!
IT WON'T DO YOU ANY GOOD EITHER.
....
OH NO...

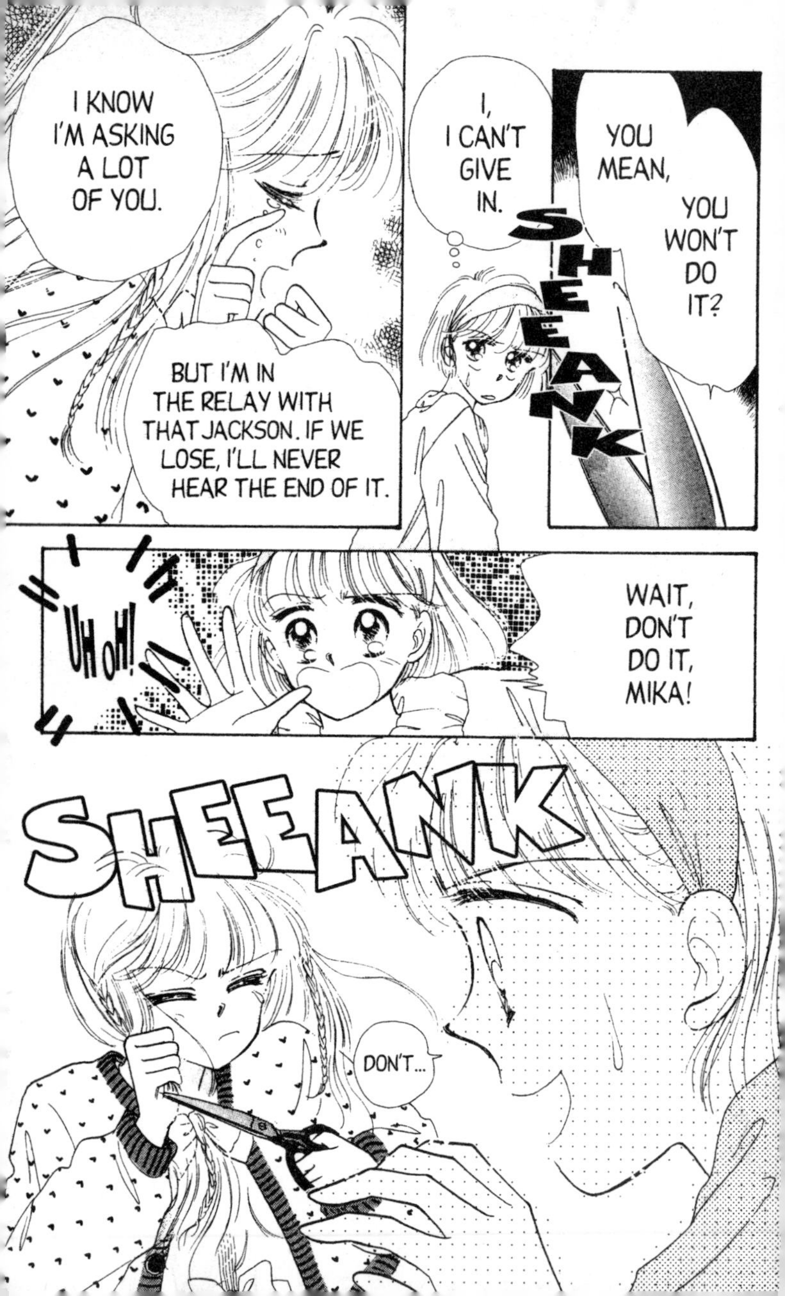

I KNOW I'M ASKING A LOT OF YOU.
BUT I'M IN THE RELAY WITH THAT JACKSON. IF WE LOSE, I'LL NEVER HEAR THE END OF IT.
I, I CAN'T GIVE IN.
SHEEANK
YOU MEAN, YOU WON'T DO IT?
UH OH!
WAIT, DON'T DO IT, MIKA!
SHEEANK
DON'T...

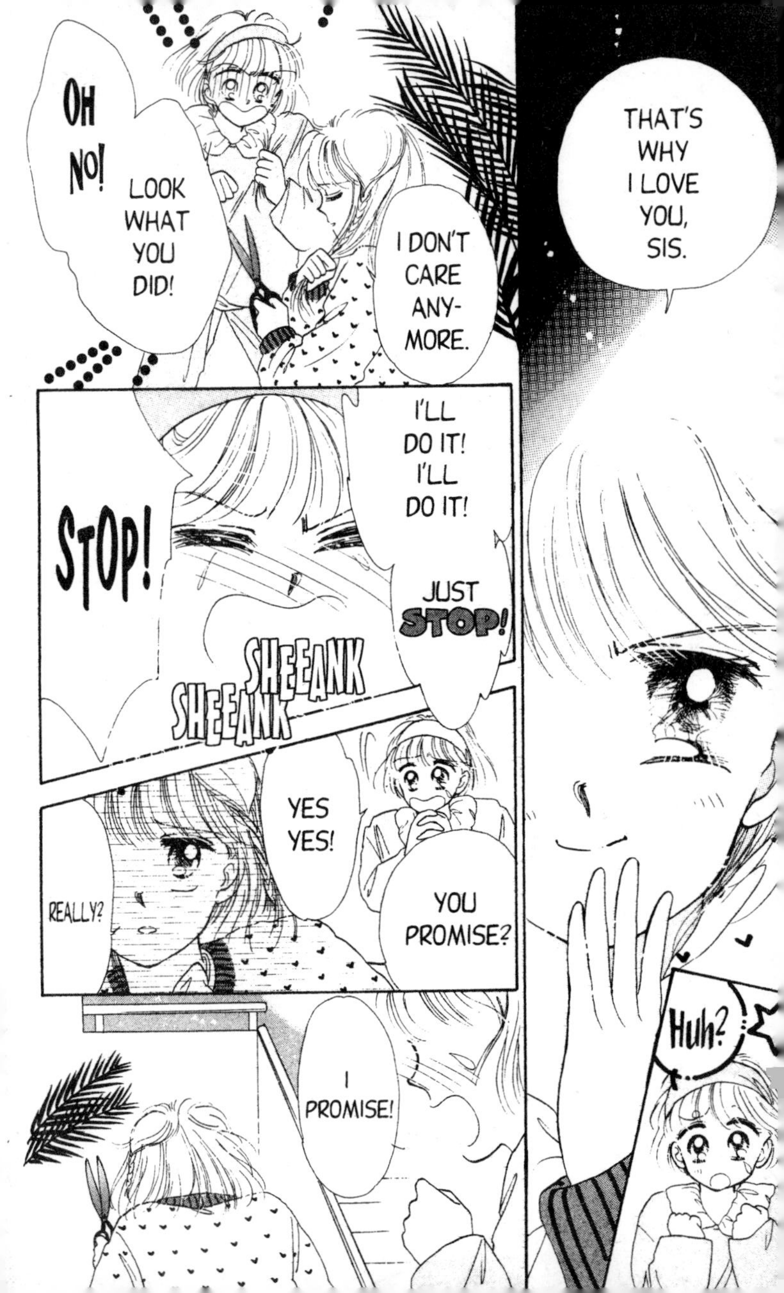

OH NO!
LOOK WHAT YOU DID!
I DON'T CARE ANYMORE.
STOP!
I'LL DO IT! I'LL DO IT!
JUST STOP!
SHEEANK
SHEEANK
REALLY?
YES YES!
YOU PROMISE?
I PROMISE!
THAT'S WHY I LOVE YOU, SIS.
Huh?

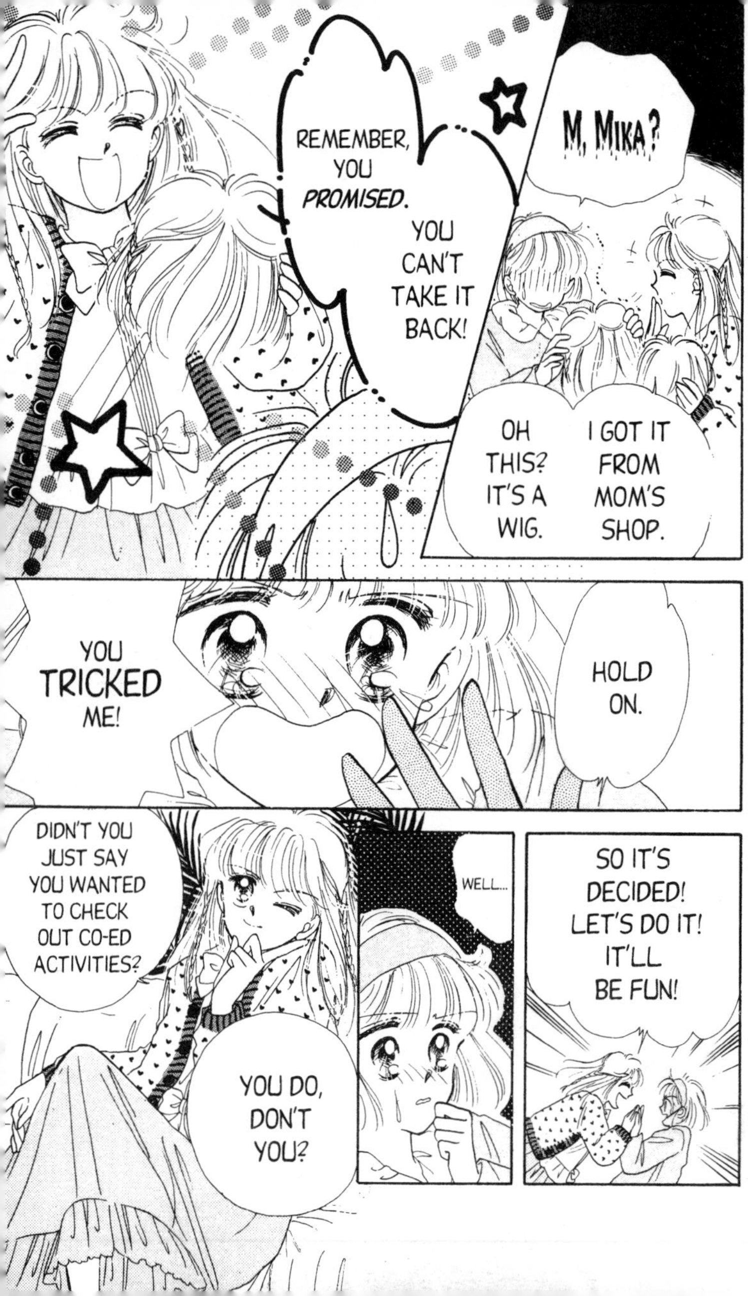
REMEMBER, YOU *PROMISED*.
YOU CAN'T TAKE IT BACK!
M, MIKA?
OH THIS? IT'S A WIG.
I GOT IT FROM MOM'S SHOP.
YOU **TRICKED** ME!
HOLD ON.
DIDN'T YOU JUST SAY YOU WANTED TO CHECK OUT CO-ED ACTIVITIES?
YOU DO, DON'T YOU?
WELL...
SO IT'S DECIDED! LET'S DO IT! IT'LL BE FUN!

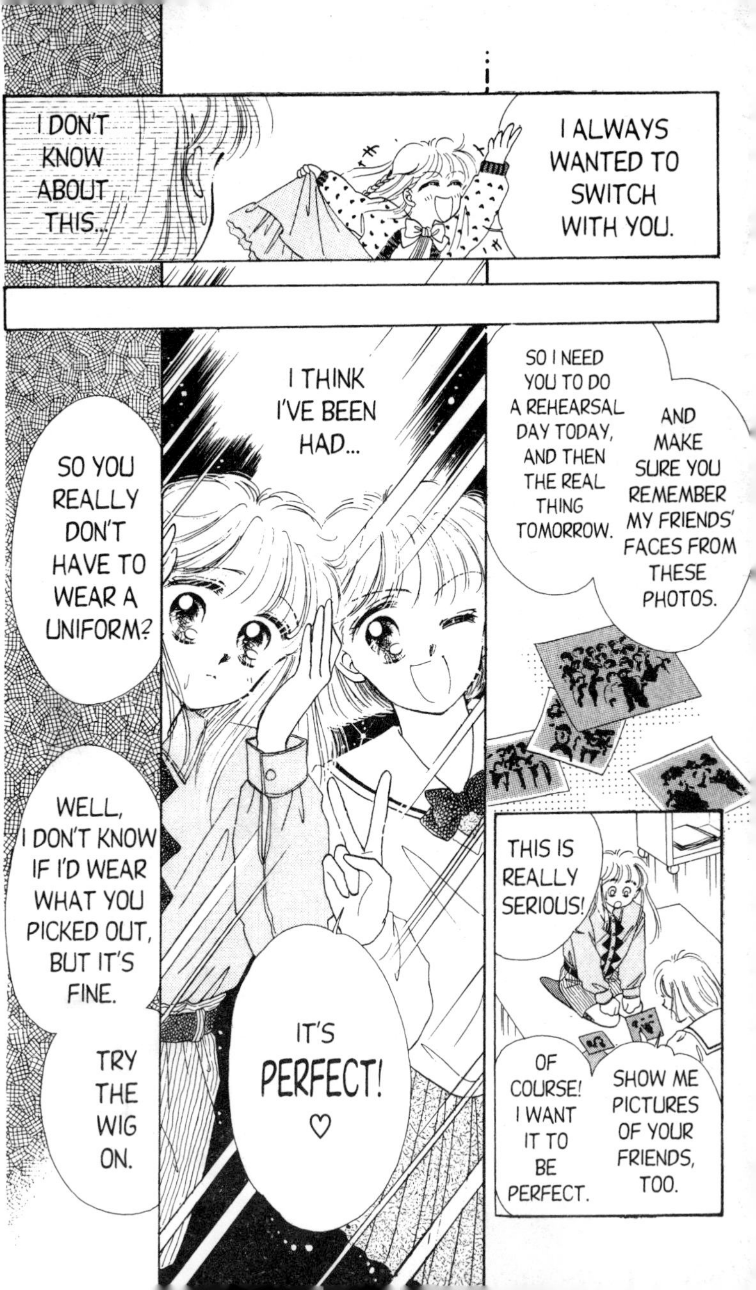
I DON'T KNOW ABOUT THIS...
I ALWAYS WANTED TO SWITCH WITH YOU.
I THINK I'VE BEEN HAD...
SO YOU REALLY DON'T HAVE TO WEAR A UNIFORM?
WELL, I DON'T KNOW IF I'D WEAR WHAT YOU PICKED OUT, BUT IT'S FINE.
TRY THE WIG ON.
IT'S PERFECT! ♡
SO I NEED YOU TO DO A REHEARSAL DAY TODAY, AND THEN THE REAL THING TOMORROW.
AND MAKE SURE YOU REMEMBER MY FRIENDS' FACES FROM THESE PHOTOS.
THIS IS REALLY SERIOUS!
OF COURSE! I WANT IT TO BE PERFECT.
SHOW ME PICTURES OF YOUR FRIENDS, TOO.

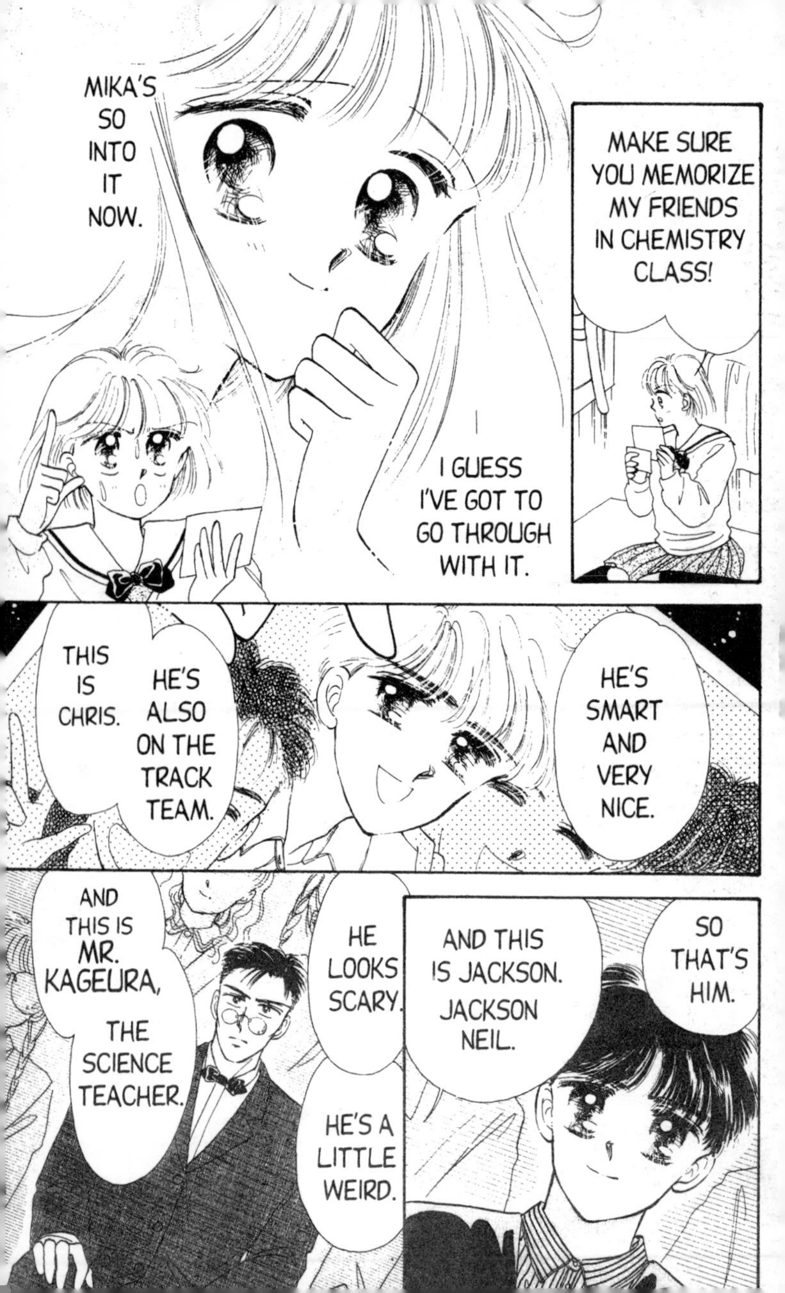
MIKA'S SO INTO IT NOW.
I GUESS I'VE GOT TO GO THROUGH WITH IT.
MAKE SURE YOU MEMORIZE MY FRIENDS IN CHEMISTRY CLASS!
THIS IS CHRIS.
HE'S ALSO ON THE TRACK TEAM.
HE'S SMART AND VERY NICE.
AND THIS IS MR. KAGEURA,
HE LOOKS SCARY.
THE SCIENCE TEACHER.
HE'S A LITTLE WEIRD.
AND THIS IS JACKSON.
JACKSON NEIL.
SO THAT'S HIM.

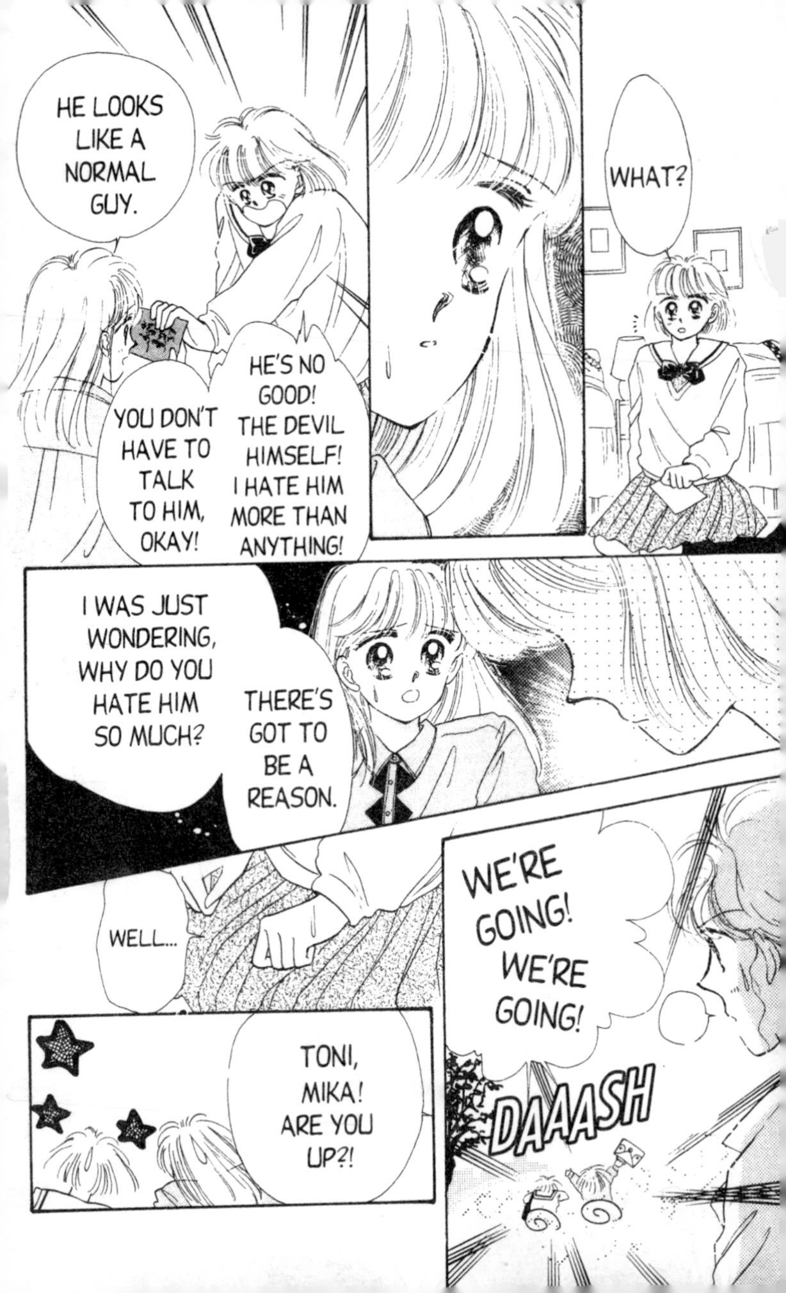
HE LOOKS LIKE A NORMAL GUY.
YOU DON'T HAVE TO TALK TO HIM, OKAY!
HE'S NO GOOD! THE DEVIL HIMSELF! I HATE HIM MORE THAN ANYTHING!
WHAT?
I WAS JUST WONDERING, WHY DO YOU HATE HIM SO MUCH?
THERE'S GOT TO BE A REASON.
WELL...
TONI, MIKA! ARE YOU UP?!
WE'RE GOING! WE'RE GOING!
DAAASH

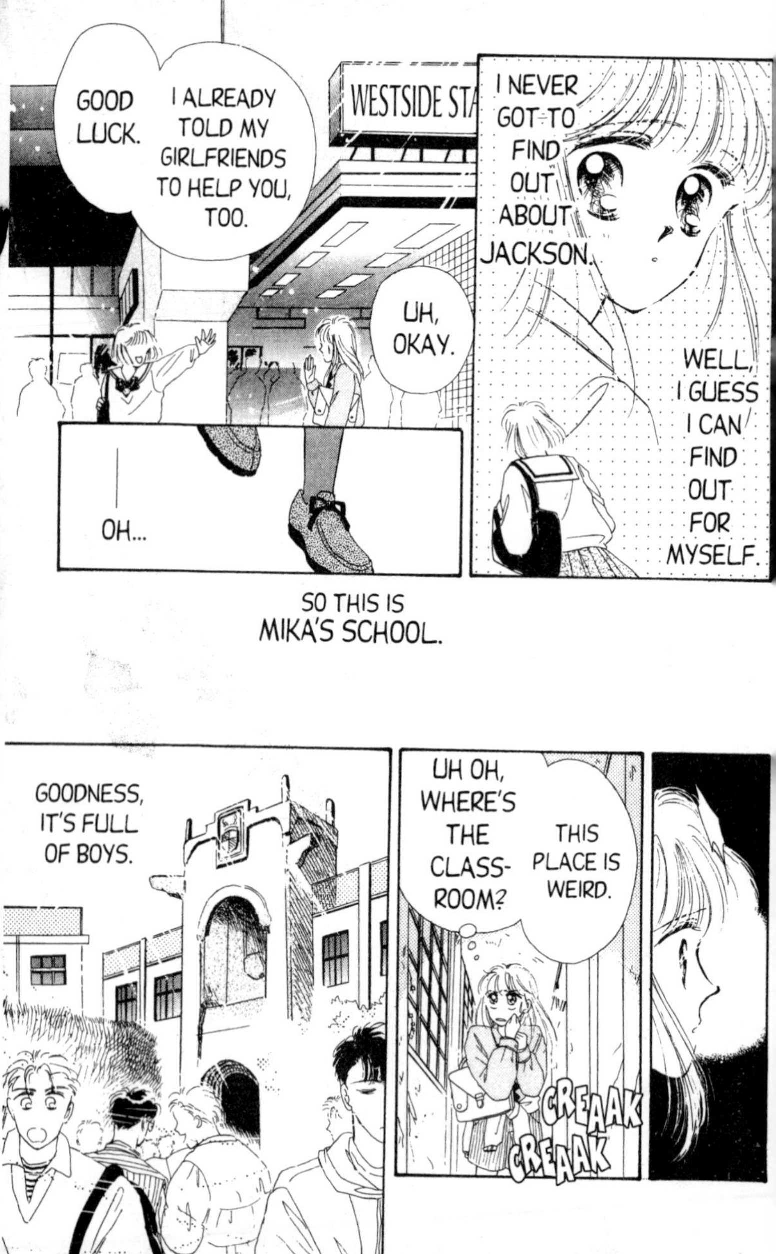
WESTSIDE STA
GOOD LUCK.
I ALREADY TOLD MY GIRLFRIENDS TO HELP YOU, TOO.
UH, OKAY.
OH...
I NEVER GOT TO FIND OUT ABOUT JACKSON.
WELL, I GUESS I CAN FIND OUT FOR MYSELF.
SO THIS IS MIKA'S SCHOOL.
GOODNESS, IT'S FULL OF BOYS.
UH OH, WHERE'S THE CLASS-ROOM?
THIS PLACE IS WEIRD.
CREAAK
CREAAK

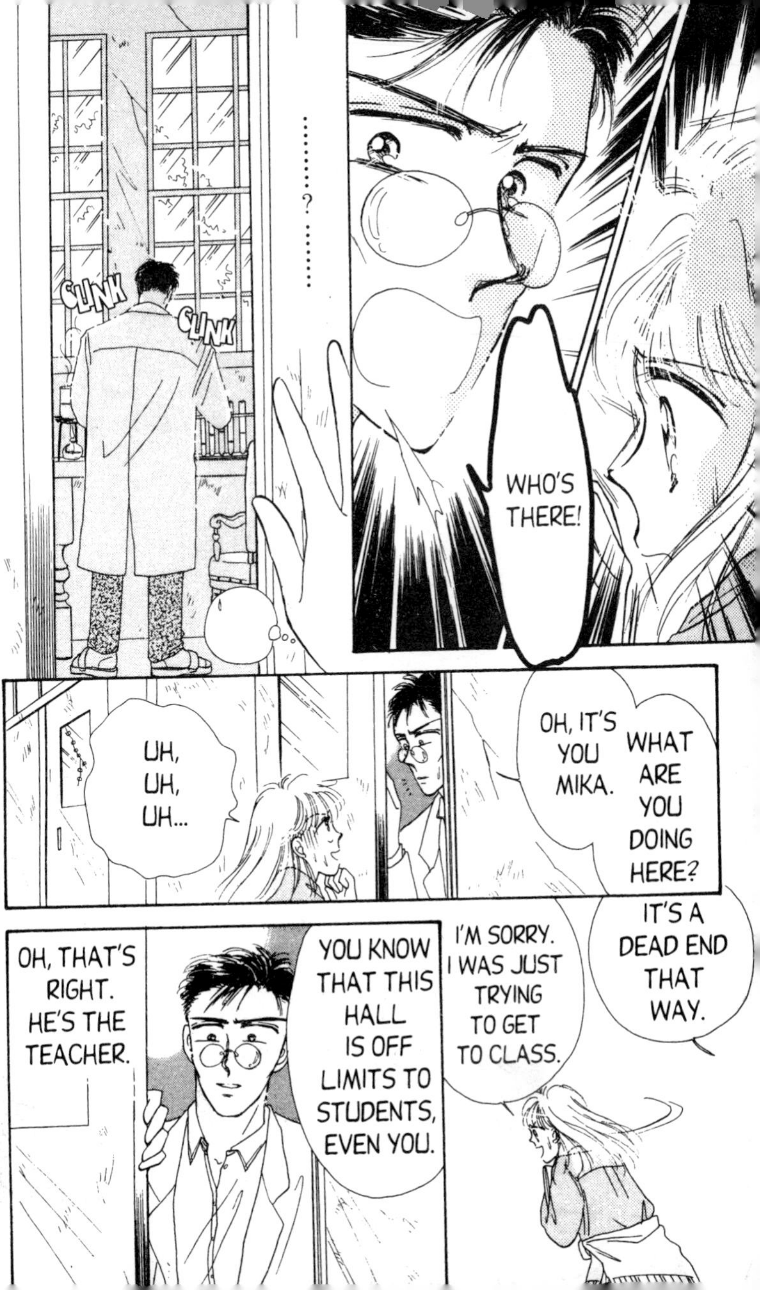
CLINK
CLINK
......?......
WHO'S THERE!
UH, UH, UH...
OH, IT'S YOU MIKA.
WHAT ARE YOU DOING HERE?
OH, THAT'S RIGHT. HE'S THE TEACHER.
YOU KNOW THAT THIS HALL IS OFF LIMITS TO STUDENTS, EVEN YOU.
I'M SORRY. I WAS JUST TRYING TO GET TO CLASS.
IT'S A DEAD END THAT WAY.

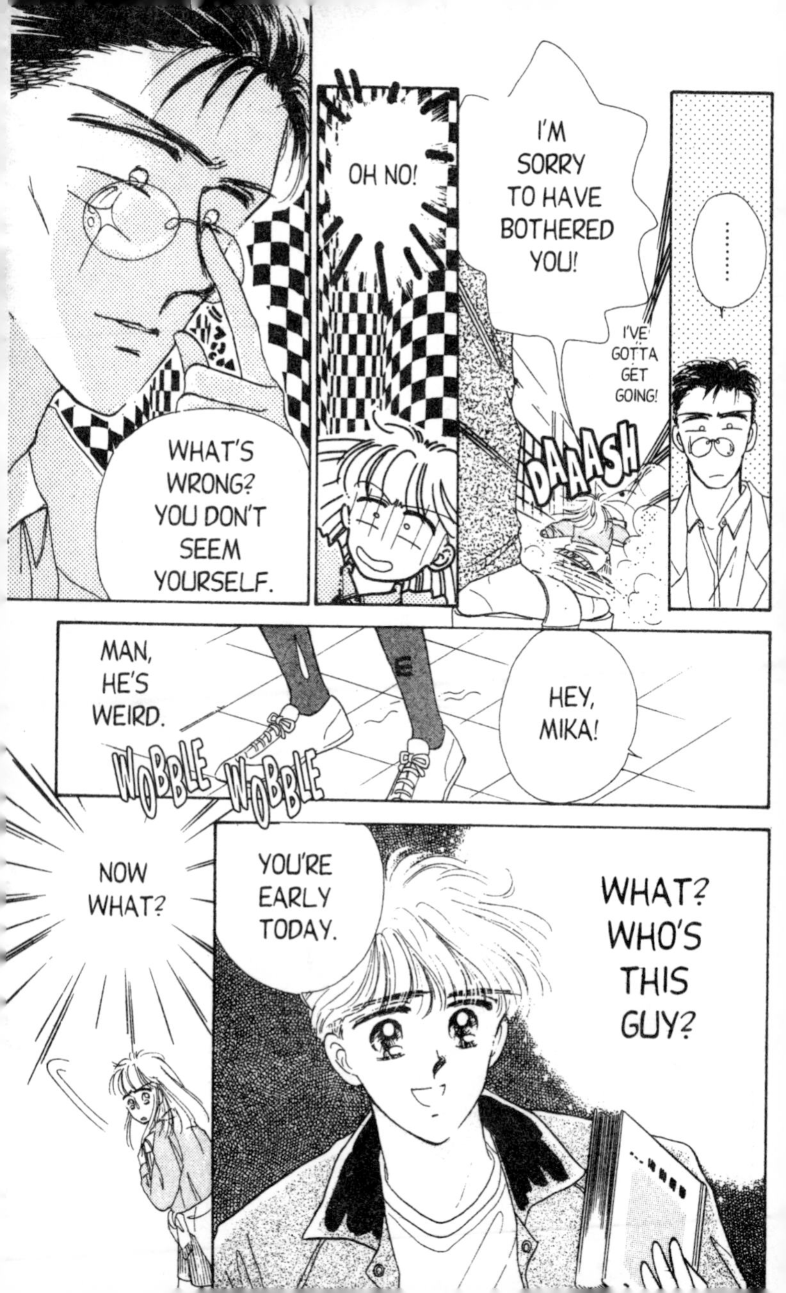
WHAT'S WRONG? YOU DON'T SEEM YOURSELF.
OH NO!
I'M SORRY TO HAVE BOTHERED YOU!
I'VE GOTTA GET GOING!
DAAASH
......
MAN, HE'S WEIRD.
WOBBLE WOBBLE
HEY, MIKA!
NOW WHAT?
YOU'RE EARLY TODAY.
WHAT? WHO'S THIS GUY?

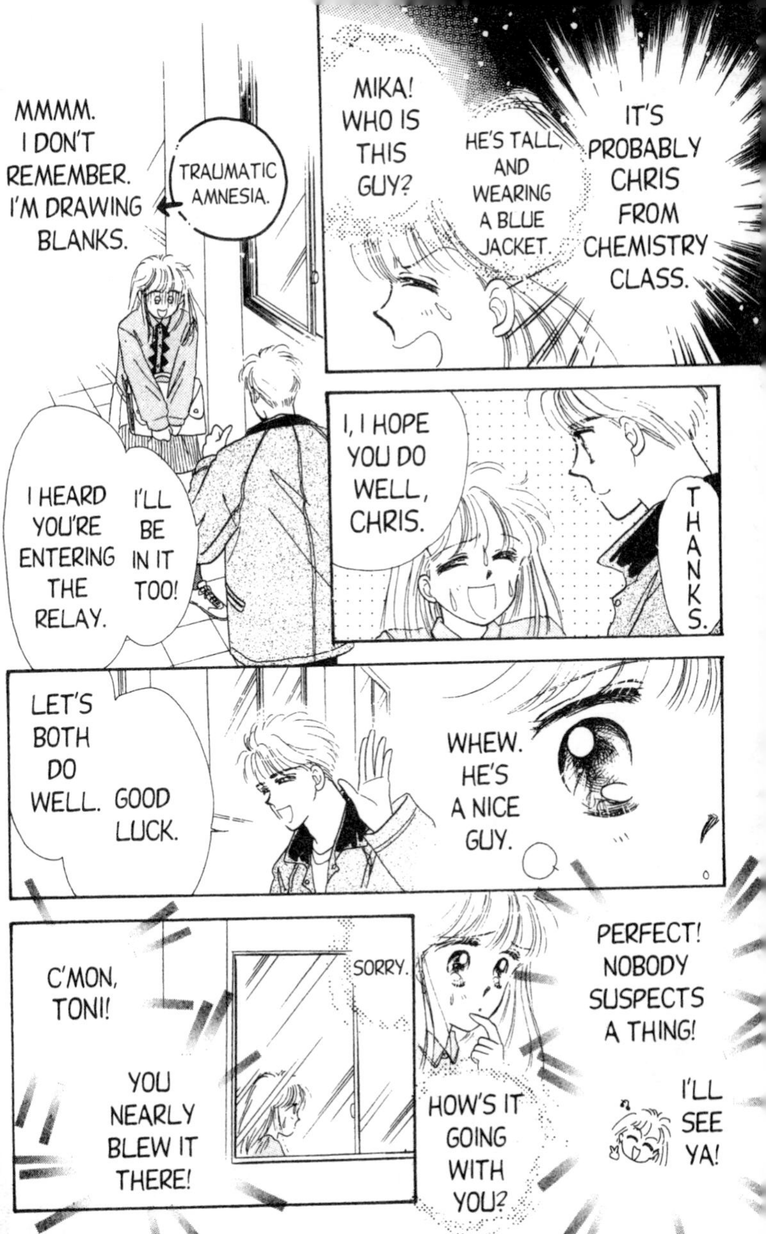
MMMM. I DON'T REMEMBER. I'M DRAWING BLANKS.
TRAUMATIC AMNESIA.
I HEARD YOU'RE ENTERING THE RELAY.
I'LL BE IN IT TOO!
MIKA! WHO IS THIS GUY?
HE'S TALL, AND WEARING A BLUE JACKET.
IT'S PROBABLY CHRIS FROM CHEMISTRY CLASS.
I, I HOPE YOU DO WELL, CHRIS.
THANKS.
LET'S BOTH DO WELL.
GOOD LUCK.
WHEW. HE'S A NICE GUY.
C'MON, TONI!
YOU NEARLY BLEW IT THERE!
SORRY.
PERFECT! NOBODY SUSPECTS A THING!
HOW'S IT GOING WITH YOU?
I'LL SEE YA!

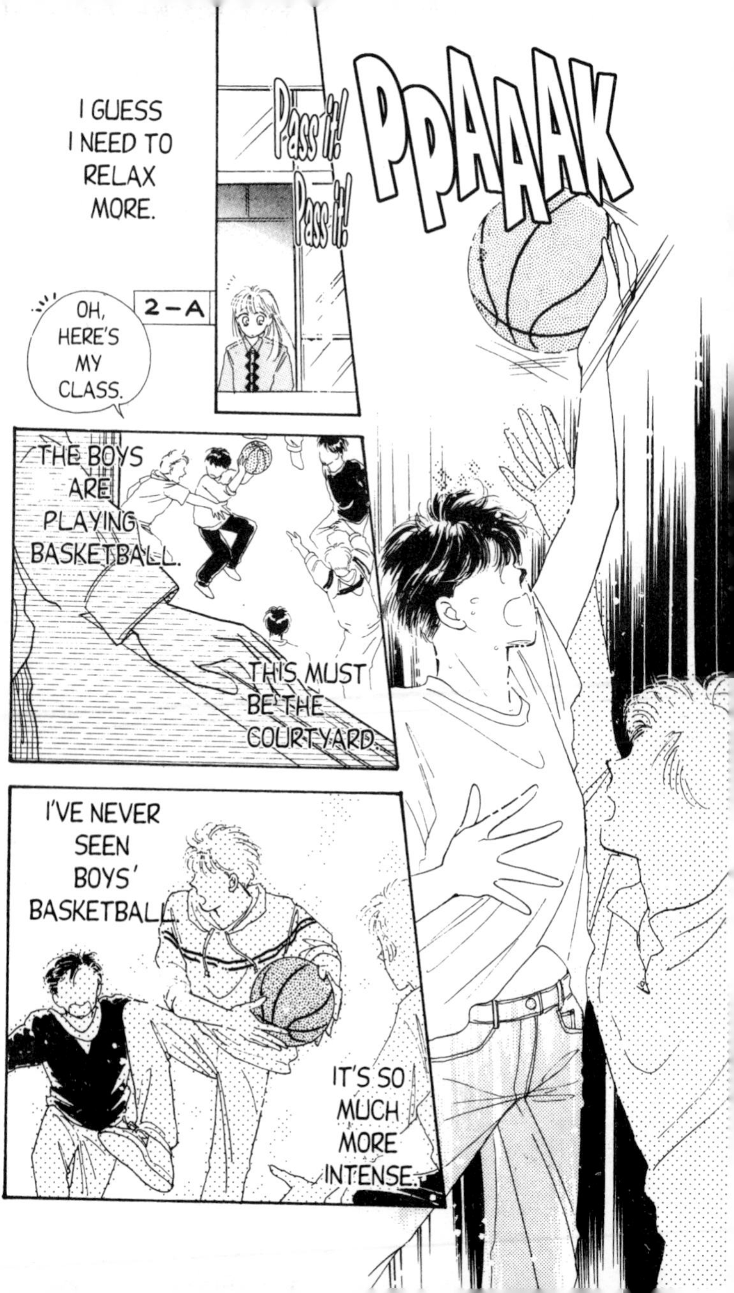
I GUESS I NEED TO RELAX MORE.
Pass it! Pass it!
OH, HERE'S MY CLASS.
2-A
THE BOYS ARE PLAYING BASKETBALL.
THIS MUST BE THE COURTYARD.
I'VE NEVER SEEN BOYS' BASKETBALL.
IT'S SO MUCH MORE INTENSE.
PPAAAK

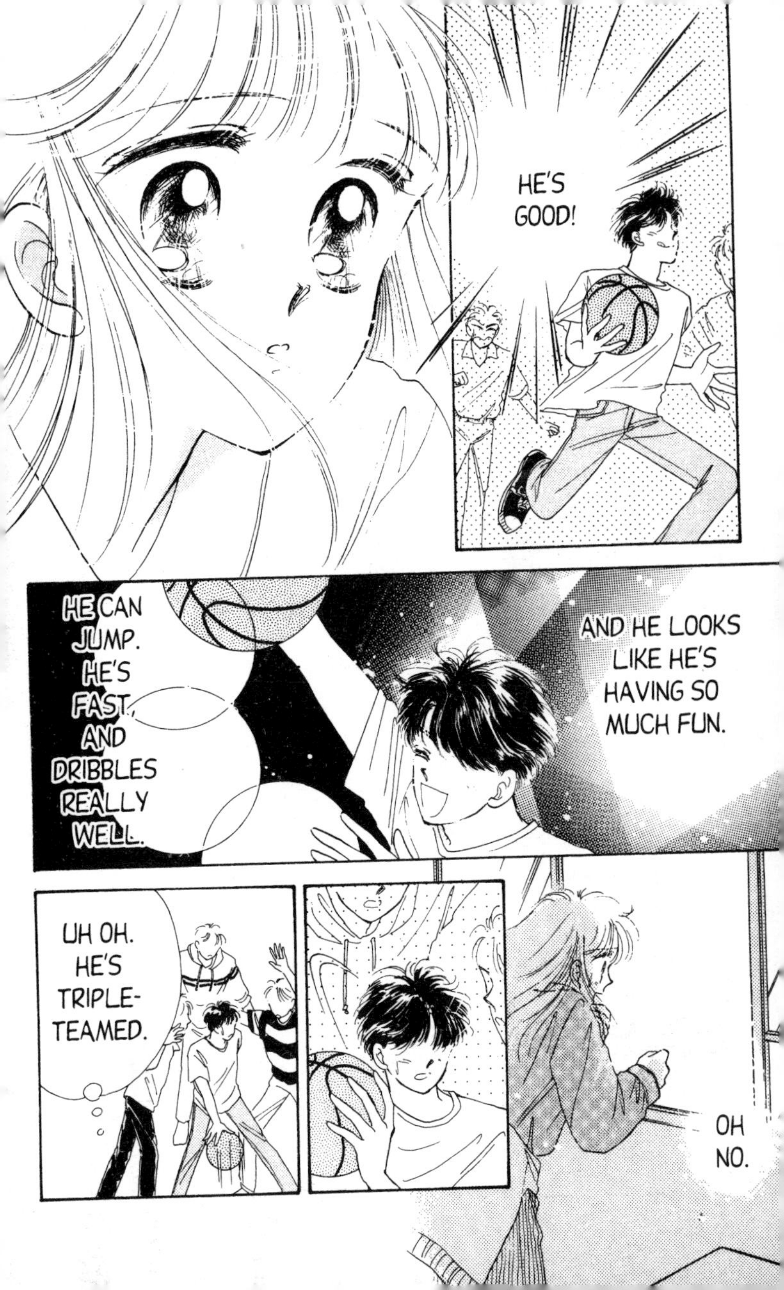
HE'S GOOD!
HE CAN JUMP. HE'S FAST, AND DRIBBLES REALLY WELL.
AND HE LOOKS LIKE HE'S HAVING SO MUCH FUN.
UH OH. HE'S TRIPLE-TEAMED.
OH NO.

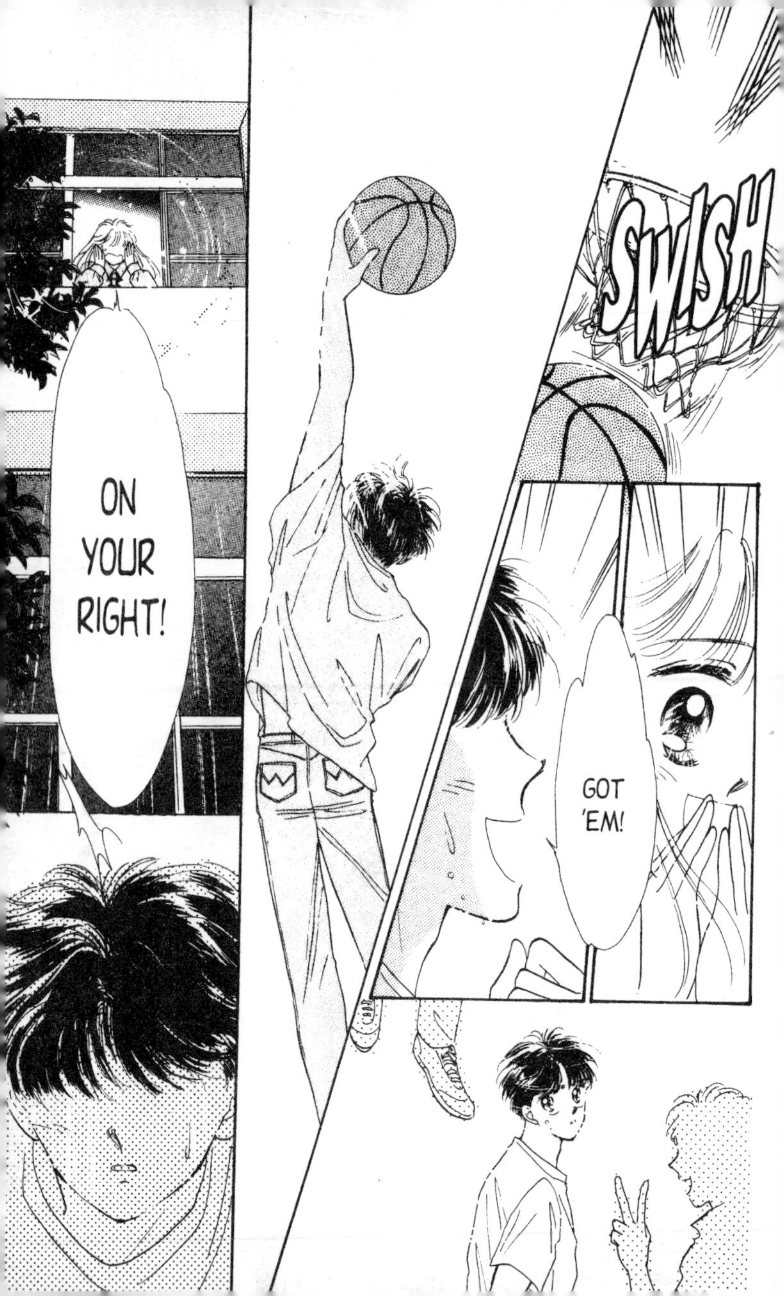
ON YOUR RIGHT!
SWISH
GOT 'EM!

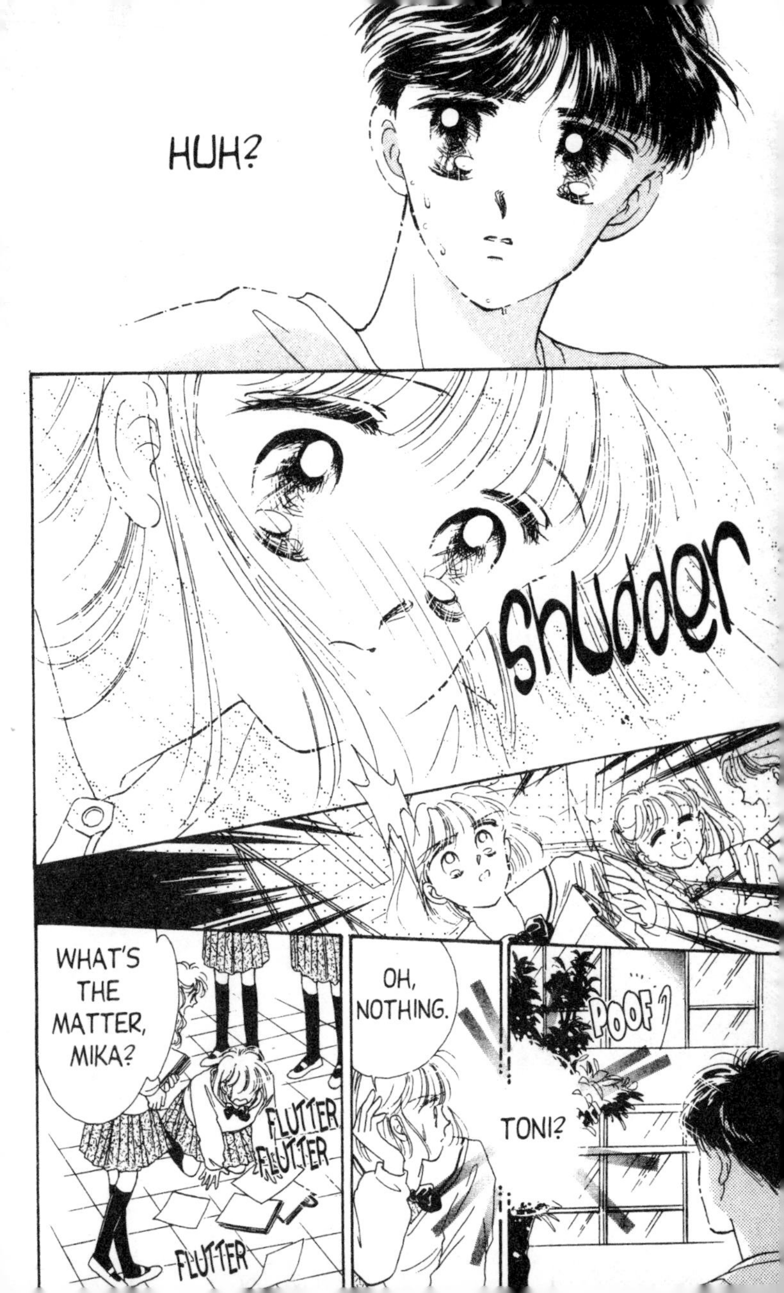
HUH?
SHUDDER
WHAT'S THE MATTER, MIKA?
FLUTTER FLUTTER
FLUTTER
OH, NOTHING.
...
POOF
TONI?

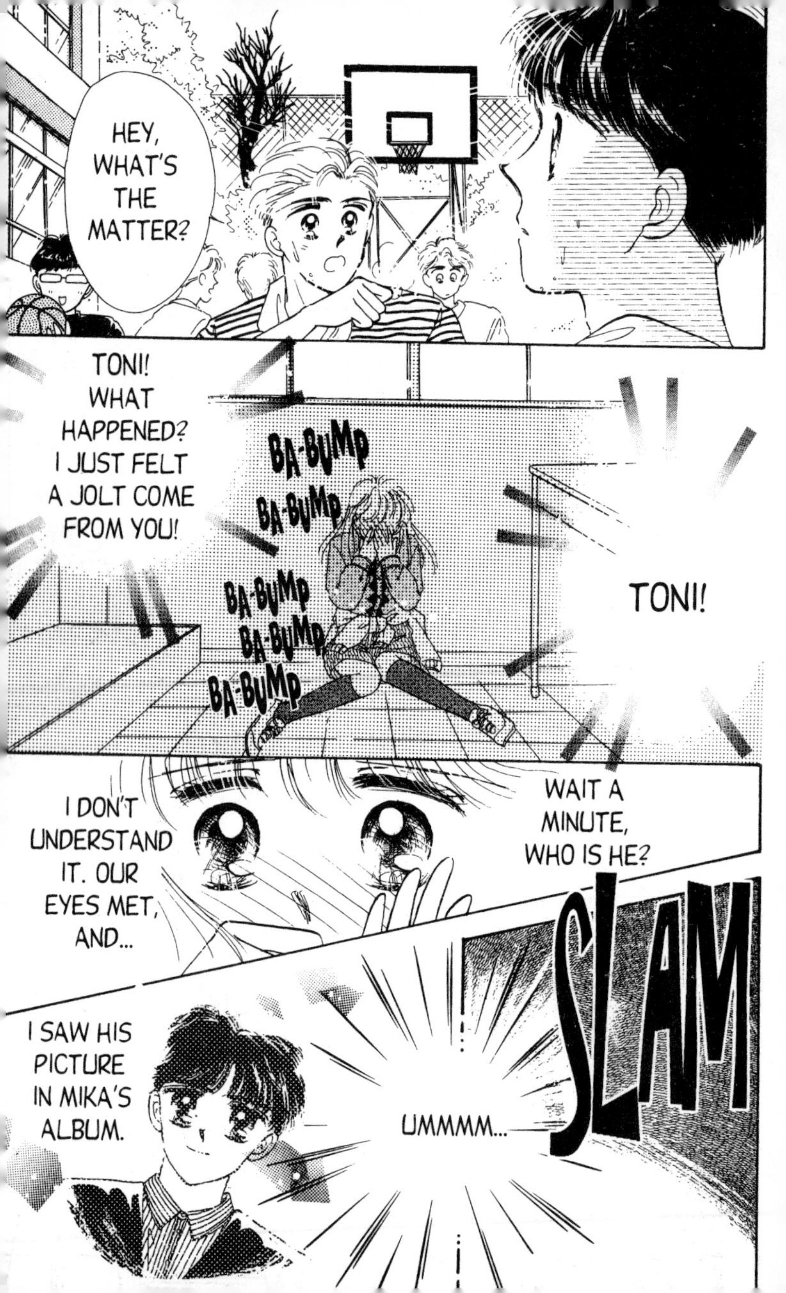
HEY, WHAT'S THE MATTER?
TONI! WHAT HAPPENED? I JUST FELT A JOLT COME FROM YOU!
BA-BUMP
BA-BUMP
BA-BUMP
BA-BUMP
BA-BUMP
TONI!
I DON'T UNDERSTAND IT. OUR EYES MET, AND...
WAIT A MINUTE, WHO IS HE?
I SAW HIS PICTURE IN MIKA'S ALBUM.
UMMMM...
SLAM

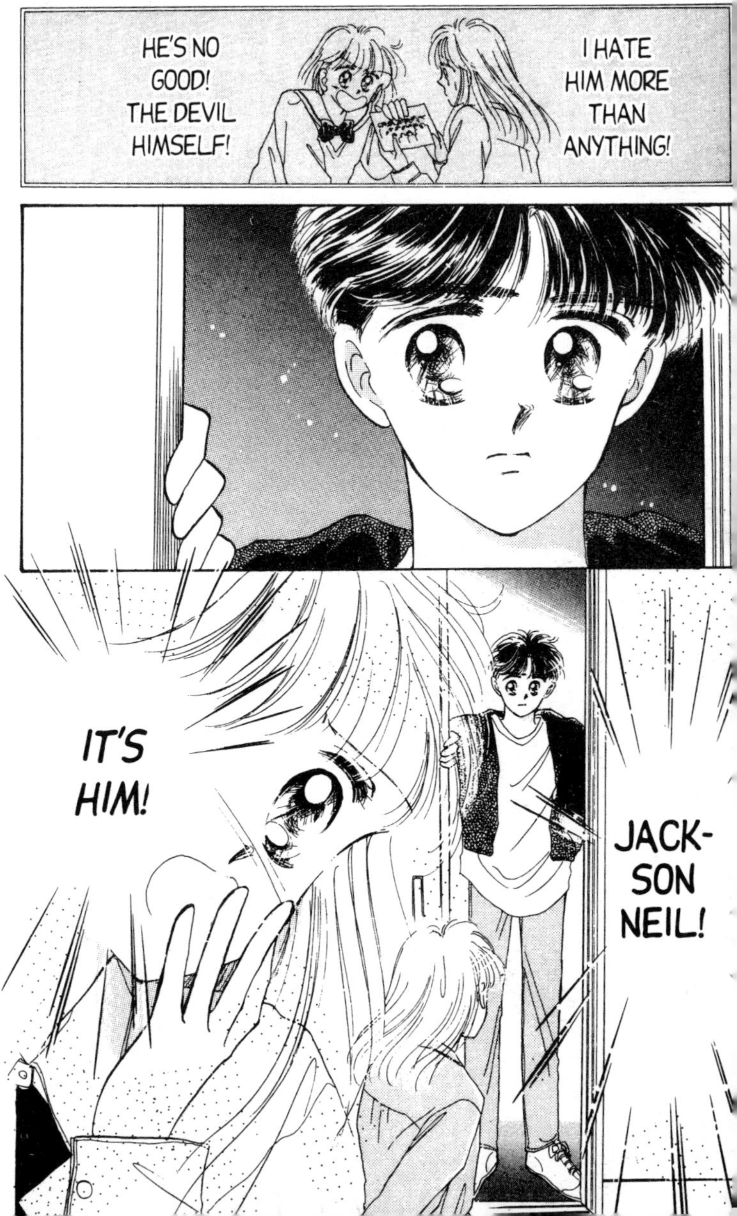
HE'S NO GOOD! THE DEVIL HIMSELF!
I HATE HIM MORE THAN ANYTHING!
IT'S HIM!
JACK-SON NEIL!

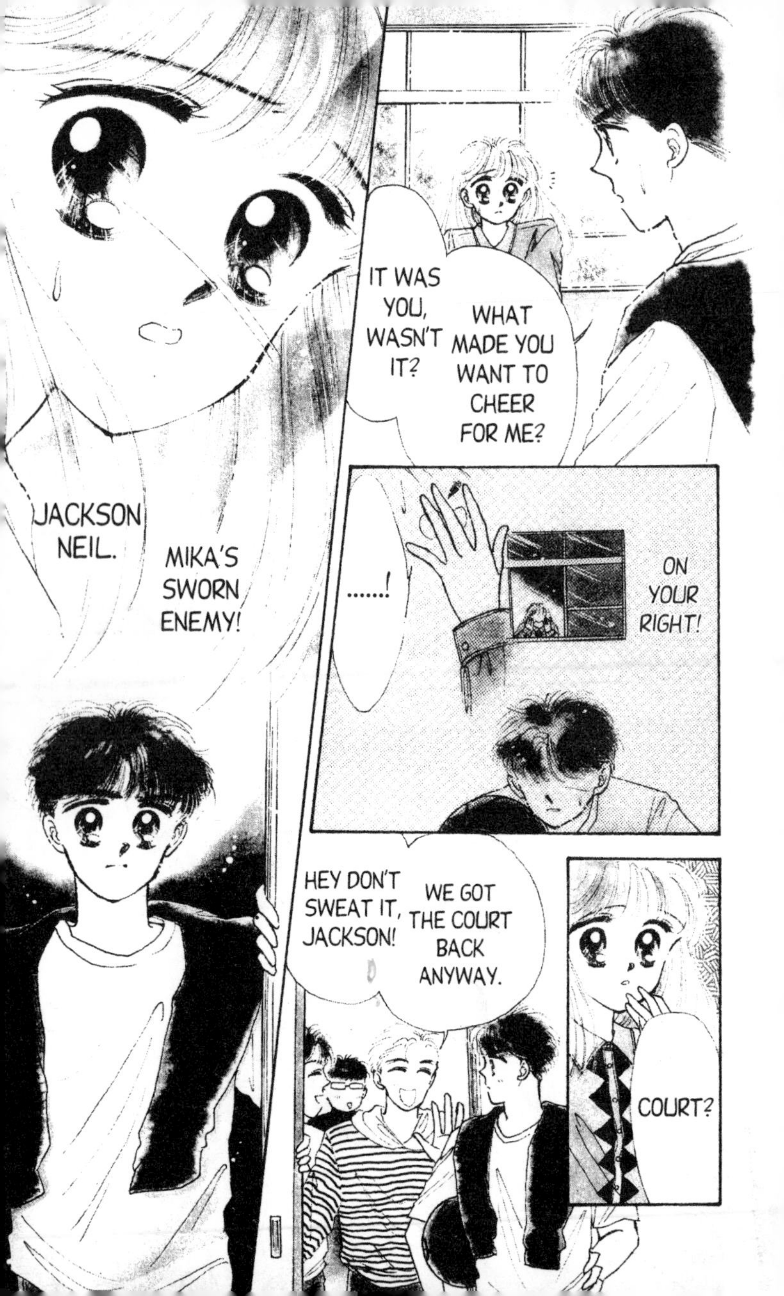
JACKSON NEIL.
MIKA'S SWORN ENEMY!
IT WAS YOU, WASN'T IT?
WHAT MADE YOU WANT TO CHEER FOR ME?
......!
ON YOUR RIGHT!
HEY DON'T SWEAT IT, JACKSON!
WE GOT THE COURT BACK ANYWAY.
COURT?

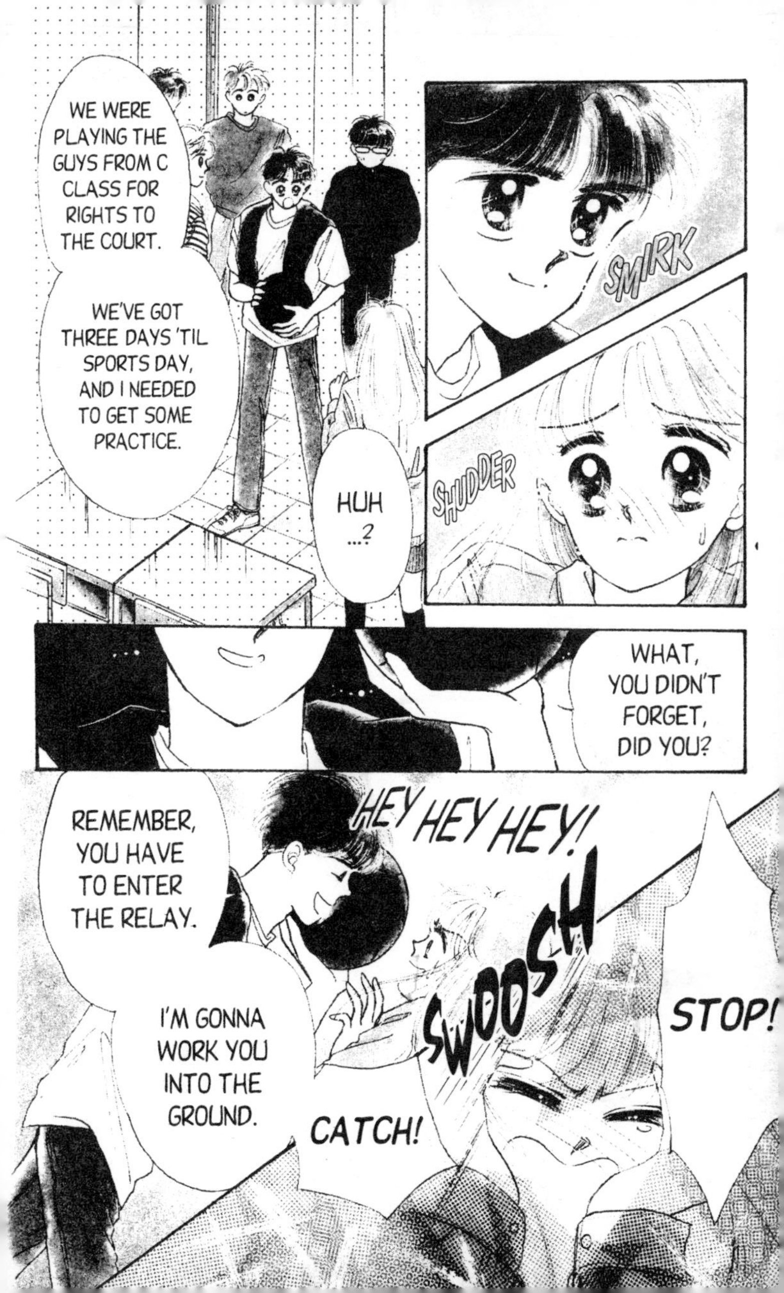
WE WERE PLAYING THE GUYS FROM C CLASS FOR RIGHTS TO THE COURT.
WE'VE GOT THREE DAYS 'TIL SPORTS DAY, AND I NEEDED TO GET SOME PRACTICE.
HUH ...?
SMIRK
SHUDDER
WHAT, YOU DIDN'T FORGET, DID YOU?
REMEMBER, YOU HAVE TO ENTER THE RELAY.
I'M GONNA WORK YOU INTO THE GROUND.
HEY HEY HEY!
SWOOSH
CATCH!
STOP!

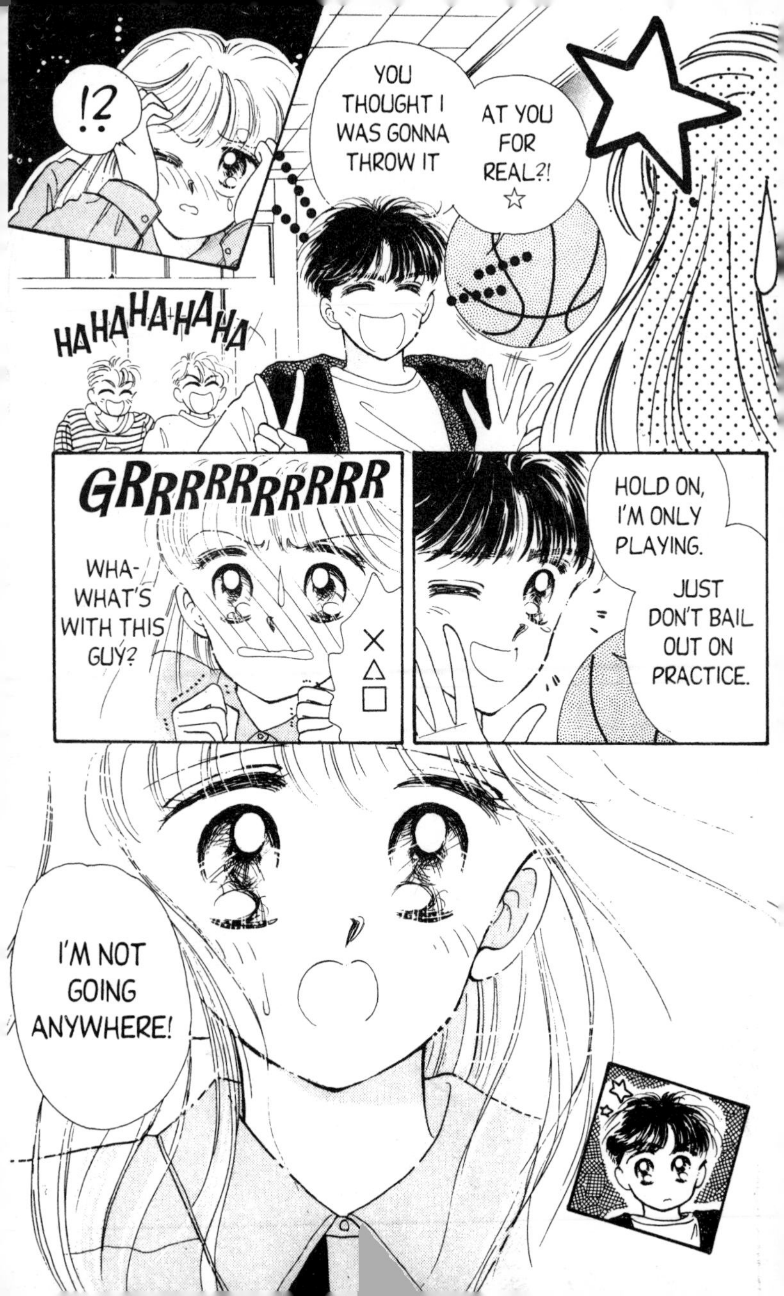
!?
YOU THOUGHT I WAS GONNA THROW IT
AT YOU FOR REAL?! ☆
HAHAHAHAHAHA
GRRRRRRRRRR
WHA- WHAT'S WITH THIS GUY?
×
△
□
HOLD ON, I'M ONLY PLAYING.
JUST DON'T BAIL OUT ON PRACTICE.
I'M NOT GOING ANYWHERE!

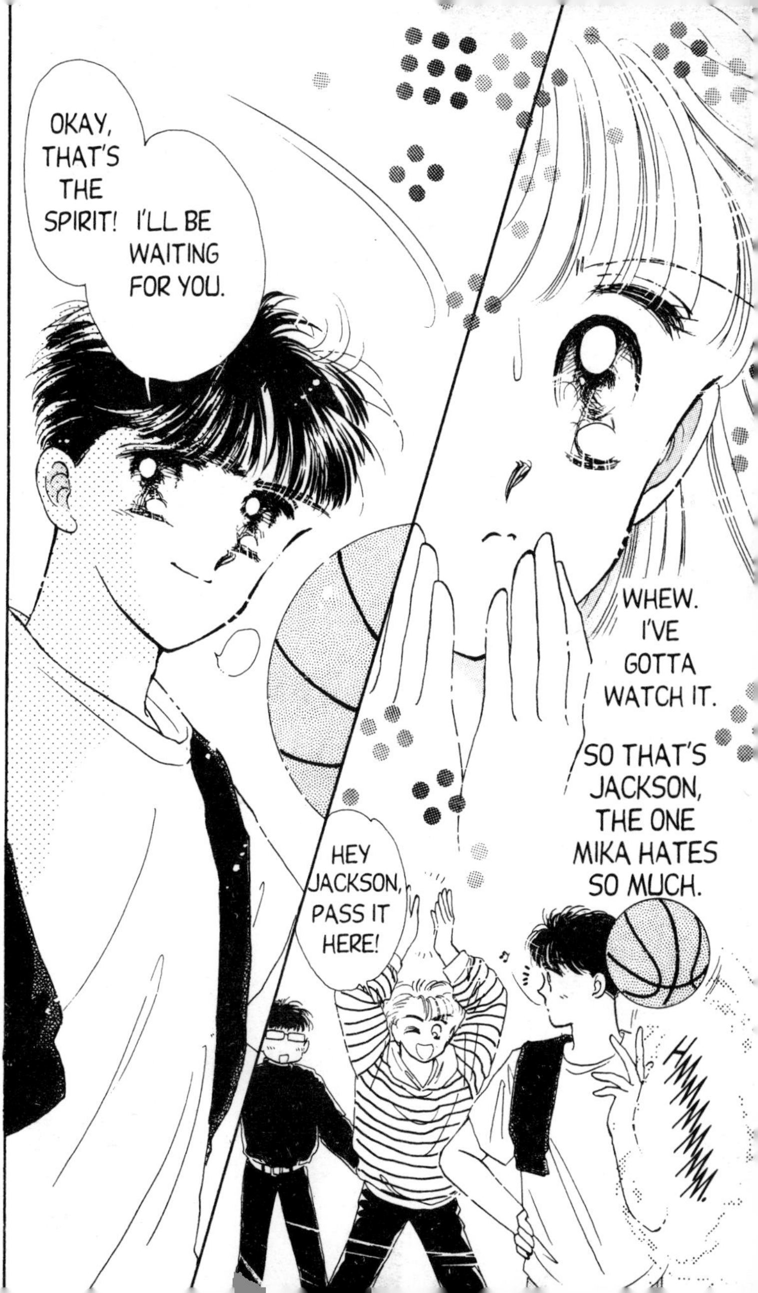
OKAY, THAT'S THE SPIRIT! I'LL BE WAITING FOR YOU.
WHEW. I'VE GOTTA WATCH IT.
SO THAT'S JACKSON, THE ONE MIKA HATES SO MUCH.
HEY JACKSON, PASS IT HERE!
HMMMMM.

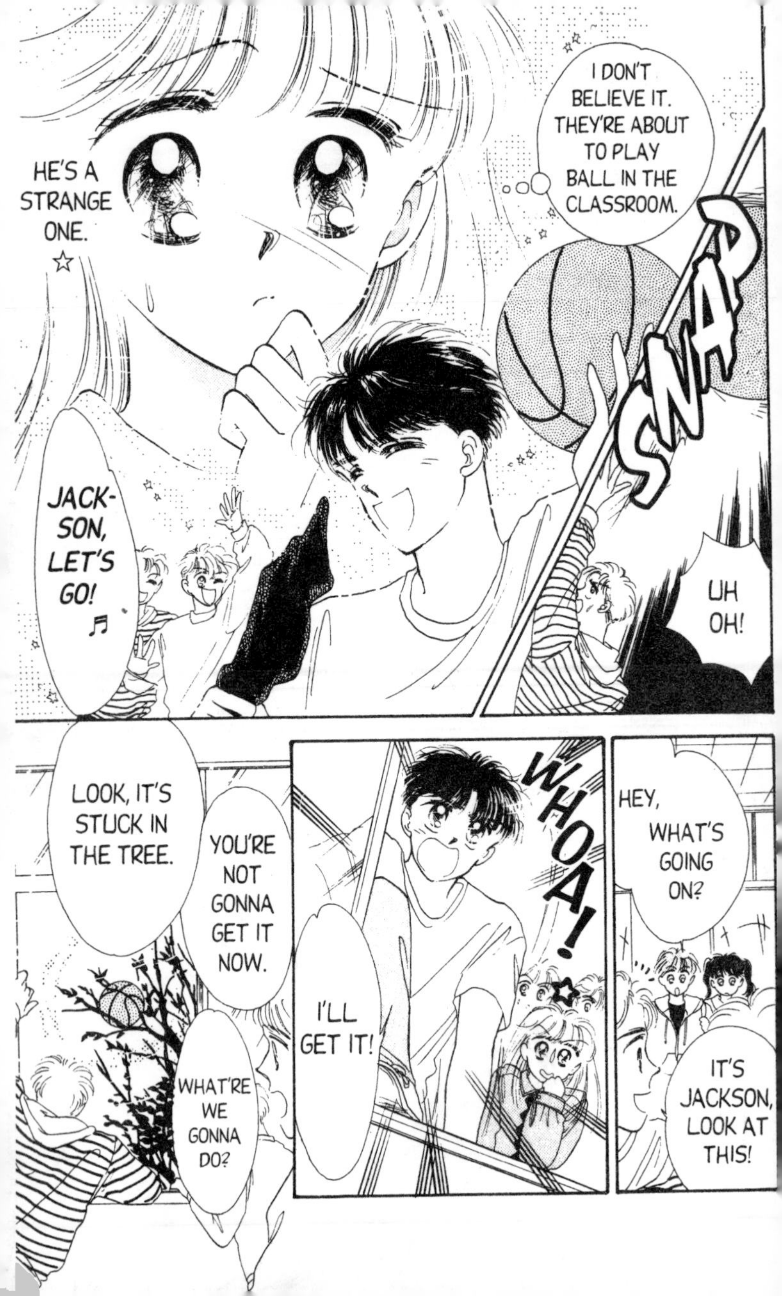
HE'S A STRANGE ONE. ☆
I DON'T BELIEVE IT. THEY'RE ABOUT TO PLAY BALL IN THE CLASSROOM.
JACK-SON, LET'S GO! ♫
SNAP
UH OH!
LOOK, IT'S STUCK IN THE TREE.
YOU'RE NOT GONNA GET IT NOW.
WHAT'RE WE GONNA DO?
WHOA!
I'LL GET IT!
HEY, WHAT'S GOING ON?
IT'S JACKSON, LOOK AT THIS!

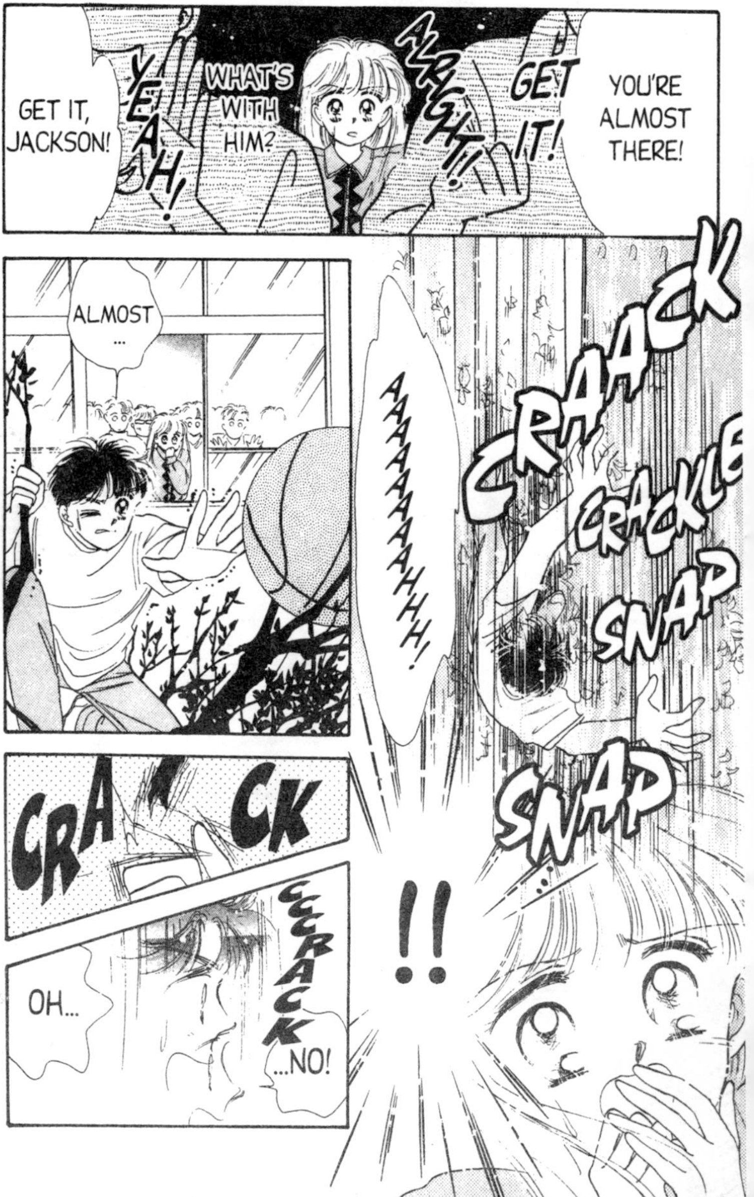
GET IT, JACKSON!
YEAH!
WHAT'S WITH HIM?
ALRIGHT!!
GET IT!
YOU'RE ALMOST THERE!
ALMOST ...
AAAAAAAAAAAAHHH!
CRAACK
CRACKLE
SNAP
SNAP
CRA CK
OH...
CCCRACK
...NO!
!!

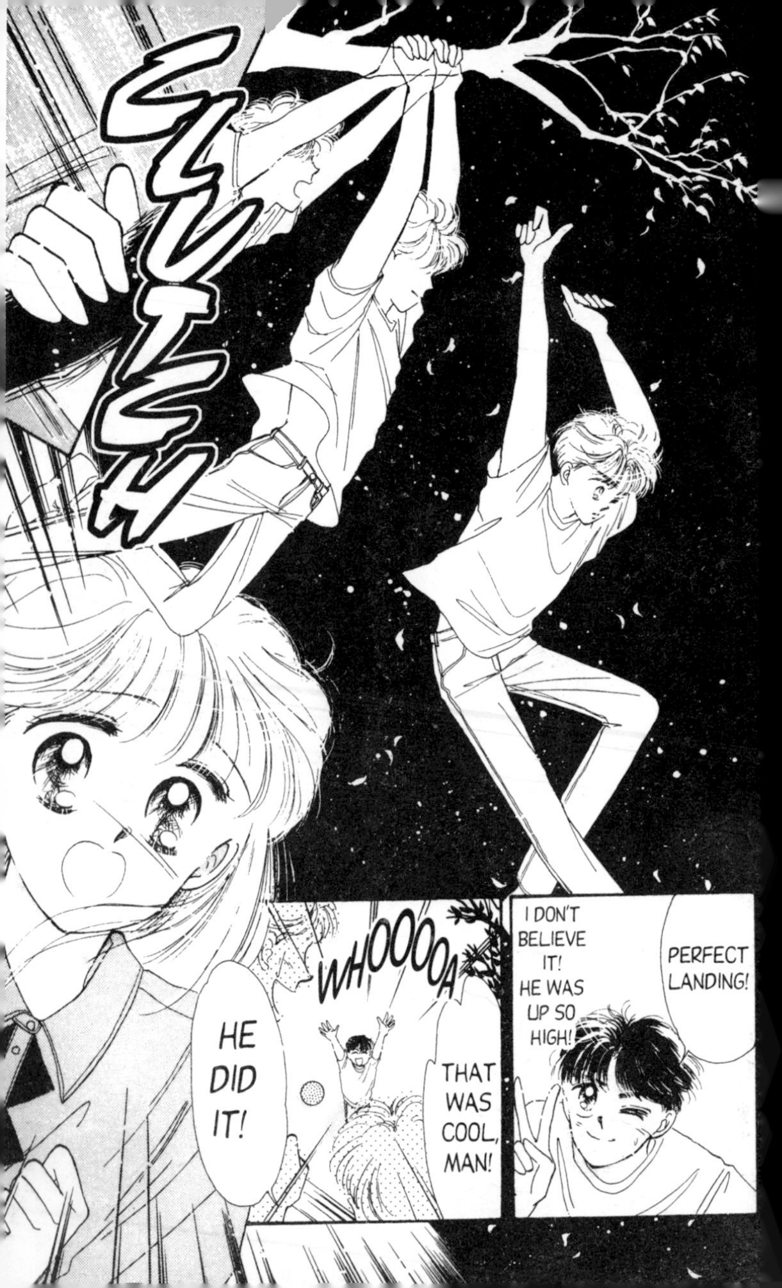
CLUTCH
HE DID IT!
WHOOOOA
THAT WAS COOL, MAN!
I DON'T BELIEVE IT! HE WAS UP SO HIGH!
PERFECT LANDING!

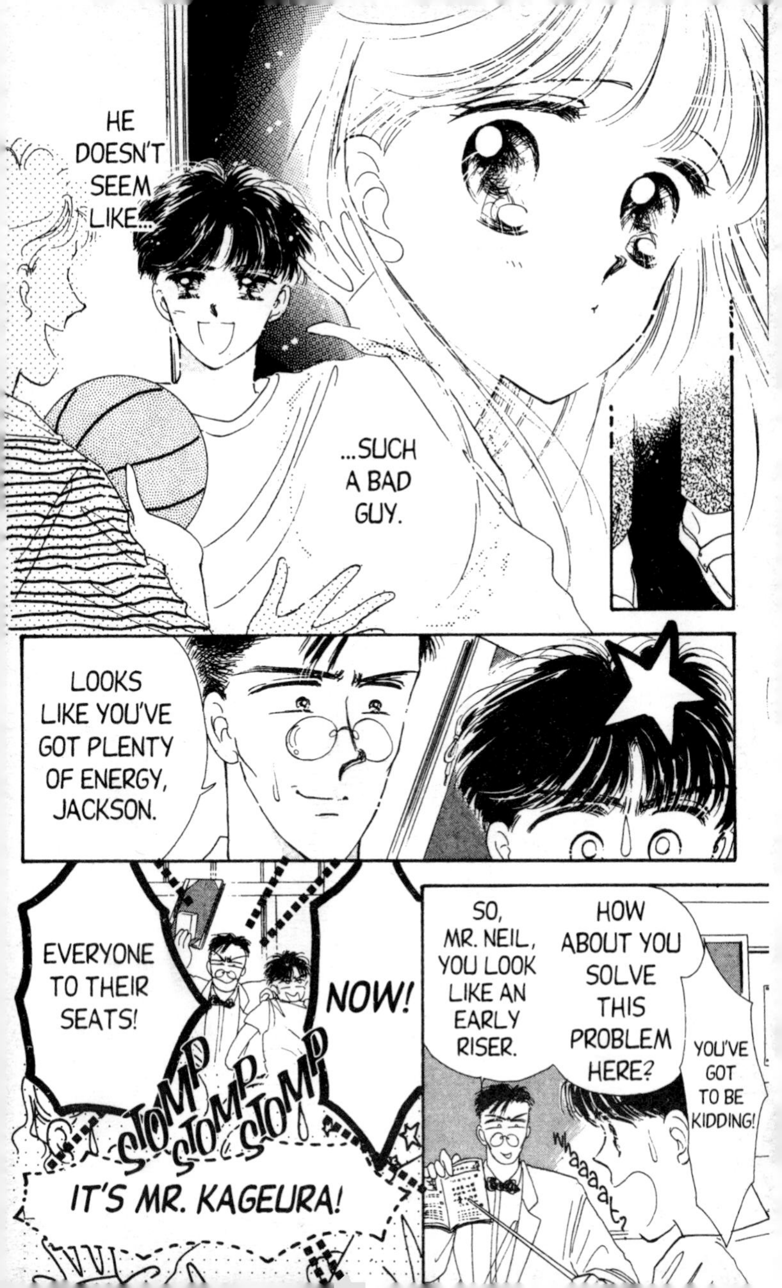

HE DOESN'T SEEM LIKE...
...SUCH A BAD GUY.
LOOKS LIKE YOU'VE GOT PLENTY OF ENERGY, JACKSON.
EVERYONE TO THEIR SEATS!
NOW!
STOMP STOMP STOMP
IT'S MR. KAGEURA!
SO, MR. NEIL, YOU LOOK LIKE AN EARLY RISER.
HOW ABOUT YOU SOLVE THIS PROBLEM HERE?
YOU'VE GOT TO BE KIDDING!
Whaaaaat?

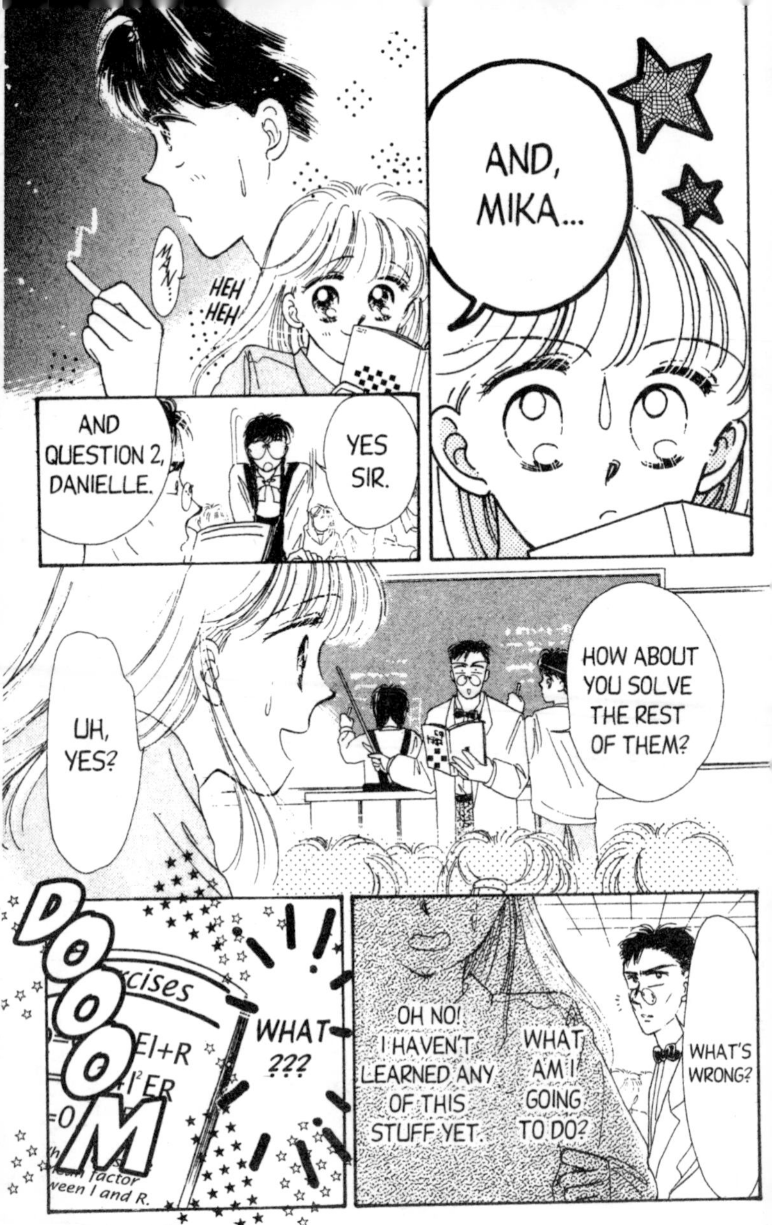
MAN...
HEH HEH
AND QUESTION 2, DANIELLE.
YES SIR.
AND, MIKA...
UH, YES?
HOW ABOUT YOU SOLVE THE REST OF THEM?
DOOOOM
WHAT ???
OH NO! I HAVEN'T LEARNED ANY OF THIS STUFF YET.
WHAT AM I GOING TO DO?
WHAT'S WRONG?

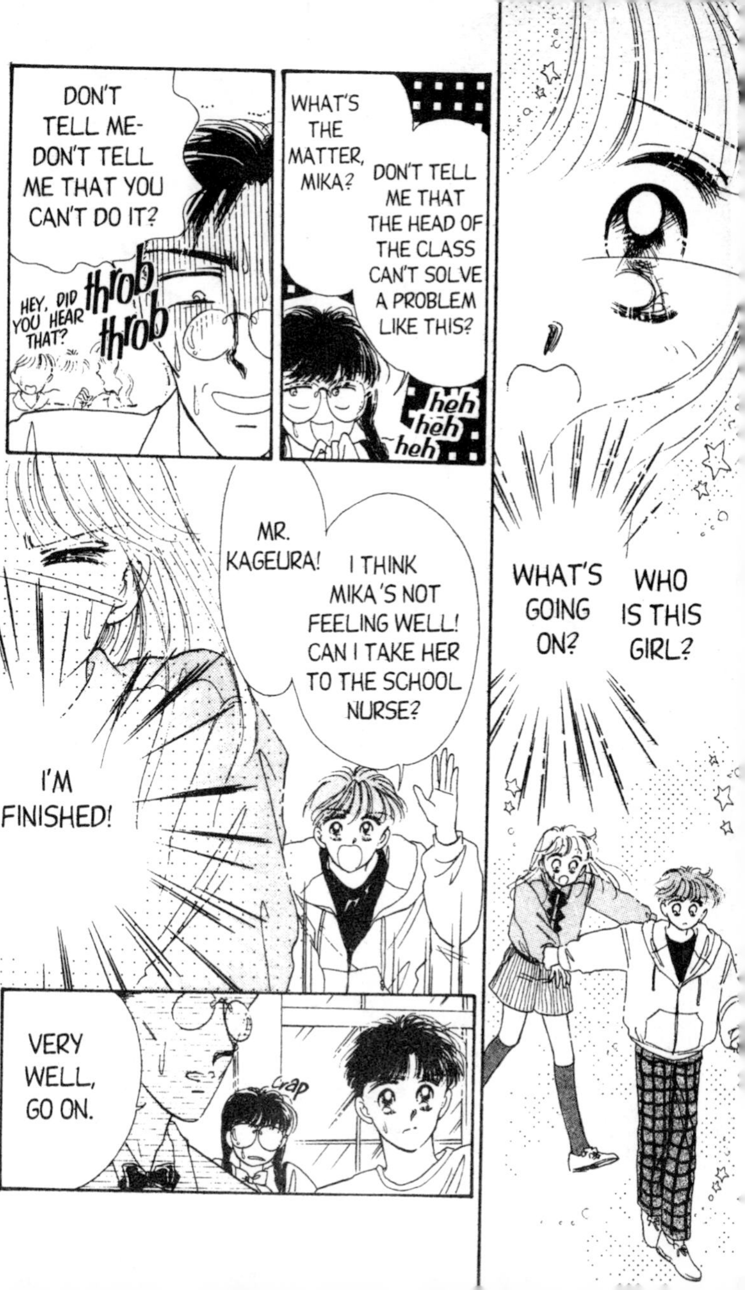
DON'T TELL ME- DON'T TELL ME THAT YOU CAN'T DO IT?
HEY, DID YOU HEAR THAT?
throb throb
WHAT'S THE MATTER, MIKA?
DON'T TELL ME THAT THE HEAD OF THE CLASS CAN'T SOLVE A PROBLEM LIKE THIS?
heh heh heh
I'M FINISHED!
MR. KAGEURA!
I THINK MIKA'S NOT FEELING WELL! CAN I TAKE HER TO THE SCHOOL NURSE?
VERY WELL, GO ON.
Crap
WHAT'S GOING ON?
WHO IS THIS GIRL?

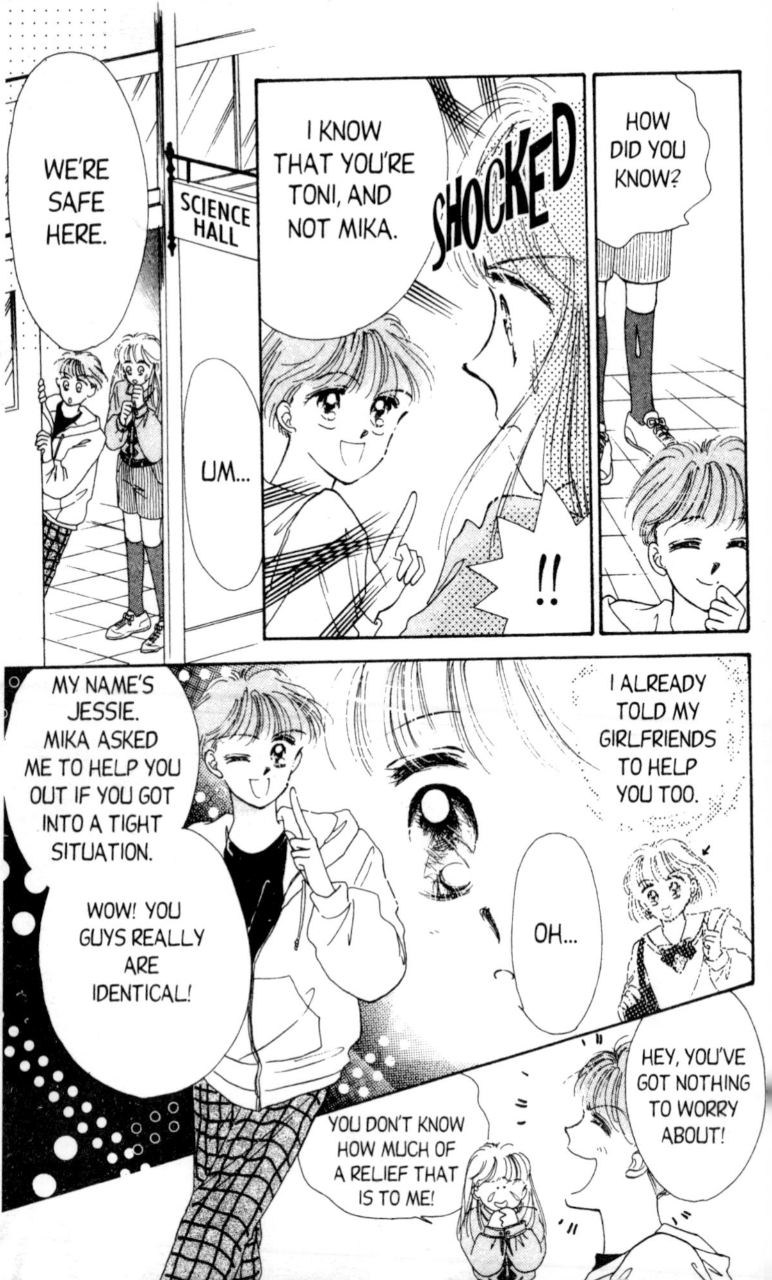

WE'RE SAFE HERE.
SCIENCE HALL
UM...
I KNOW THAT YOU'RE TONI, AND NOT MIKA.
SHOCKED
!!
HOW DID YOU KNOW?
MY NAME'S JESSIE. MIKA ASKED ME TO HELP YOU OUT IF YOU GOT INTO A TIGHT SITUATION.
WOW! YOU GUYS REALLY ARE IDENTICAL!
OH...
I ALREADY TOLD MY GIRLFRIENDS TO HELP YOU TOO.
YOU DON'T KNOW HOW MUCH OF A RELIEF THAT IS TO ME!
HEY, YOU'VE GOT NOTHING TO WORRY ABOUT!

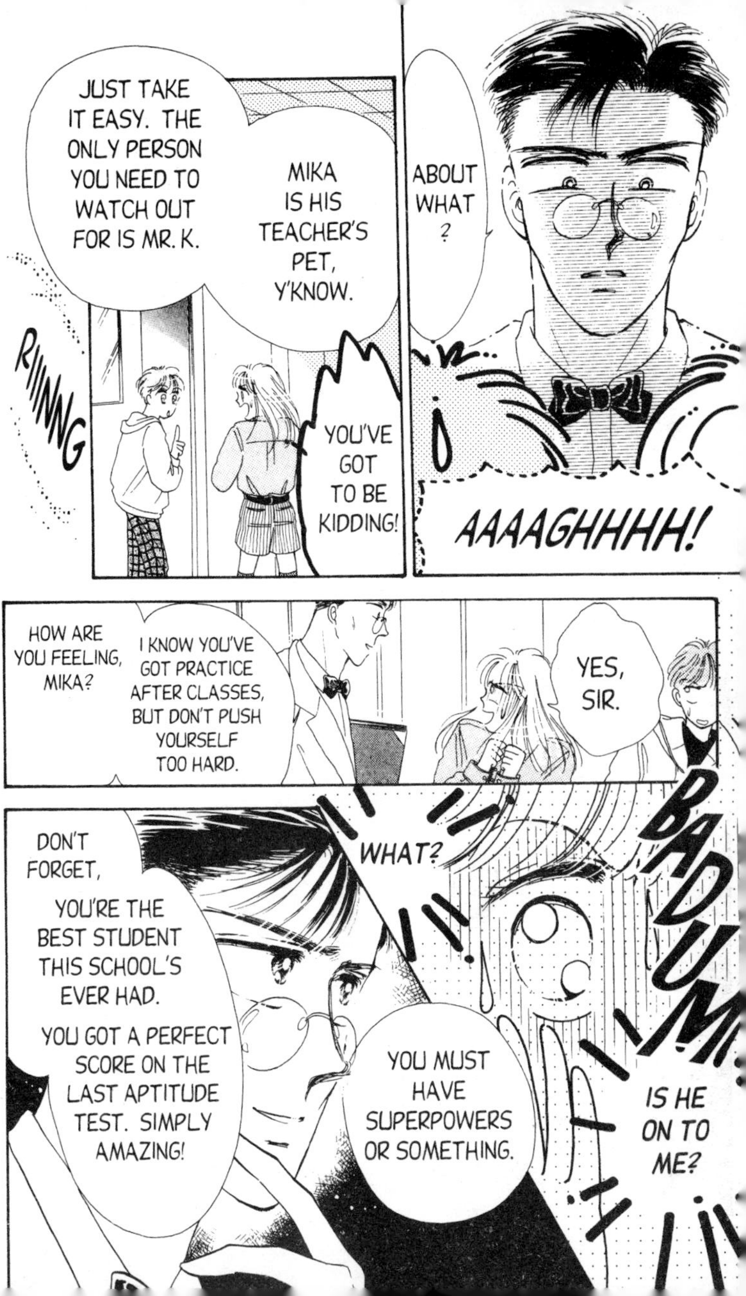
JUST TAKE IT EASY. THE ONLY PERSON YOU NEED TO WATCH OUT FOR IS MR. K.
MIKA IS HIS TEACHER'S PET, Y'KNOW.
RIIINNG
YOU'VE GOT TO BE KIDDING!
ABOUT WHAT?
AAAAGHHHH!
HOW ARE YOU FEELING, MIKA?
I KNOW YOU'VE GOT PRACTICE AFTER CLASSES, BUT DON'T PUSH YOURSELF TOO HARD.
YES, SIR.
DON'T FORGET,
YOU'RE THE BEST STUDENT THIS SCHOOL'S EVER HAD.
YOU GOT A PERFECT SCORE ON THE LAST APTITUDE TEST. SIMPLY AMAZING!
WHAT?
YOU MUST HAVE SUPERPOWERS OR SOMETHING.
BADUM!
IS HE ON TO ME?

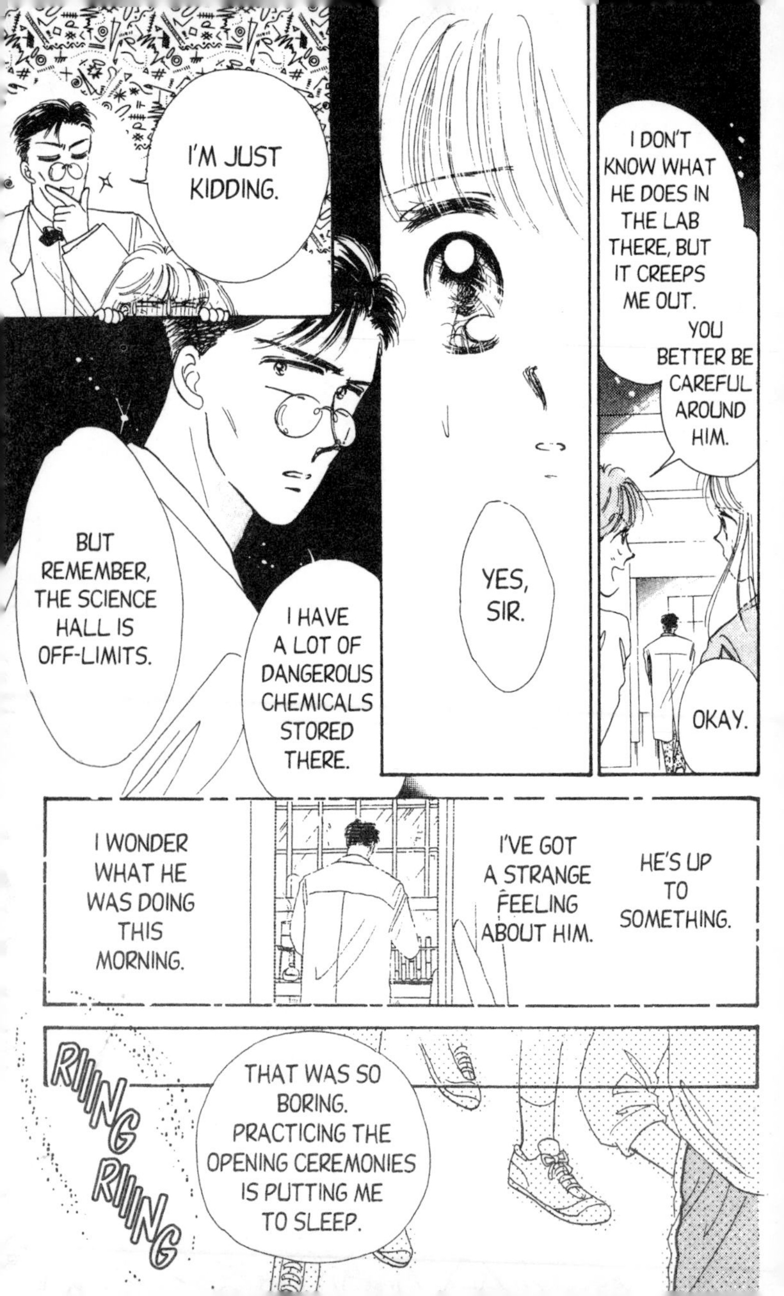
I'M JUST KIDDING.
BUT REMEMBER, THE SCIENCE HALL IS OFF-LIMITS.
I HAVE A LOT OF DANGEROUS CHEMICALS STORED THERE.
YES, SIR.
I DON'T KNOW WHAT HE DOES IN THE LAB THERE, BUT IT CREEPS ME OUT.
YOU BETTER BE CAREFUL AROUND HIM.
OKAY.
I WONDER WHAT HE WAS DOING THIS MORNING.
I'VE GOT A STRANGE FEELING ABOUT HIM.
HE'S UP TO SOMETHING.
RIIING
RIIING
THAT WAS SO BORING. PRACTICING THE OPENING CEREMONIES IS PUTTING ME TO SLEEP.

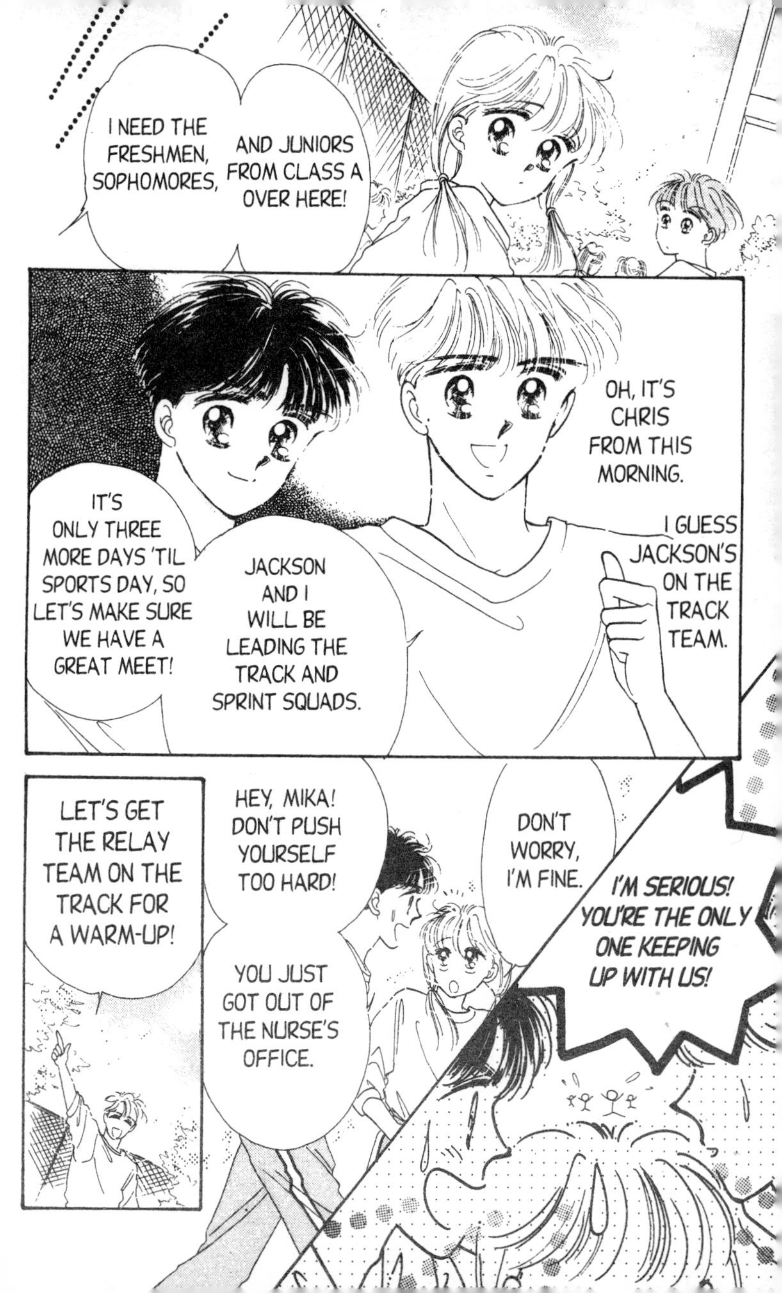
I NEED THE FRESHMEN, SOPHOMORES,
AND JUNIORS FROM CLASS A OVER HERE!
IT'S ONLY THREE MORE DAYS 'TIL SPORTS DAY, SO LET'S MAKE SURE WE HAVE A GREAT MEET!
JACKSON AND I WILL BE LEADING THE TRACK AND SPRINT SQUADS.
OH, IT'S CHRIS FROM THIS MORNING.
I GUESS JACKSON'S ON THE TRACK TEAM.
LET'S GET THE RELAY TEAM ON THE TRACK FOR A WARM-UP!
HEY, MIKA! DON'T PUSH YOURSELF TOO HARD!
YOU JUST GOT OUT OF THE NURSE'S OFFICE.
DON'T WORRY, I'M FINE.
I'M SERIOUS! YOU'RE THE ONLY ONE KEEPING UP WITH US!

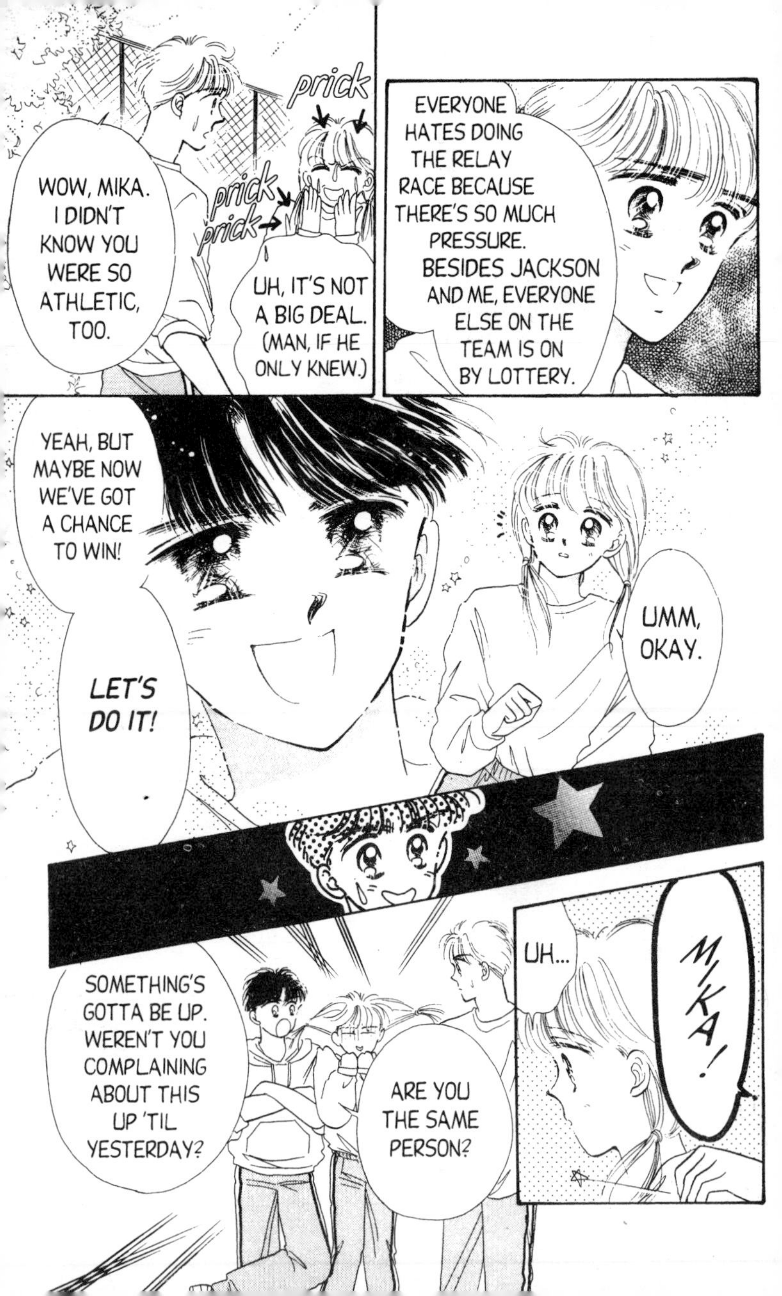

WOW, MIKA. I DIDN'T KNOW YOU WERE SO ATHLETIC, TOO.
prick
prick
prick
UH, IT'S NOT A BIG DEAL. (MAN, IF HE ONLY KNEW.)
EVERYONE HATES DOING THE RELAY RACE BECAUSE THERE'S SO MUCH PRESSURE. BESIDES JACKSON AND ME, EVERYONE ELSE ON THE TEAM IS ON BY LOTTERY.
YEAH, BUT MAYBE NOW WE'VE GOT A CHANCE TO WIN!
LET'S DO IT!
UMM, OKAY.
SOMETHING'S GOTTA BE UP. WEREN'T YOU COMPLAINING ABOUT THIS UP 'TIL YESTERDAY?
ARE YOU THE SAME PERSON?
UH...
MIKA!

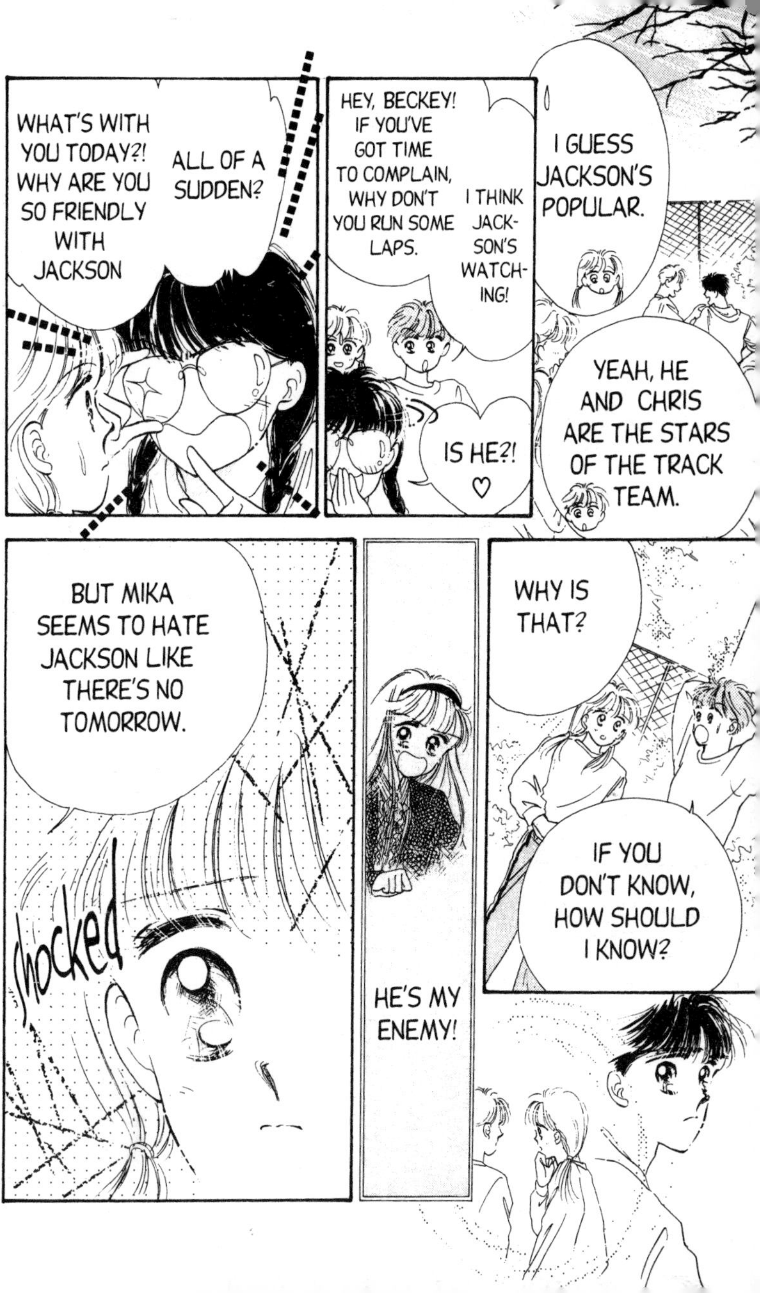
WHAT'S WITH YOU TODAY?! WHY ARE YOU SO FRIENDLY WITH JACKSON
ALL OF A SUDDEN?
HEY, BECKEY! IF YOU'VE GOT TIME TO COMPLAIN, WHY DON'T YOU RUN SOME LAPS.
I THINK JACK-SON'S WATCH-ING!
IS HE?! ♡
I GUESS JACKSON'S POPULAR.
YEAH, HE AND CHRIS ARE THE STARS OF THE TRACK TEAM.
BUT MIKA SEEMS TO HATE JACKSON LIKE THERE'S NO TOMORROW.
shocked
HE'S MY ENEMY!
WHY IS THAT?
IF YOU DON'T KNOW, HOW SHOULD I KNOW?

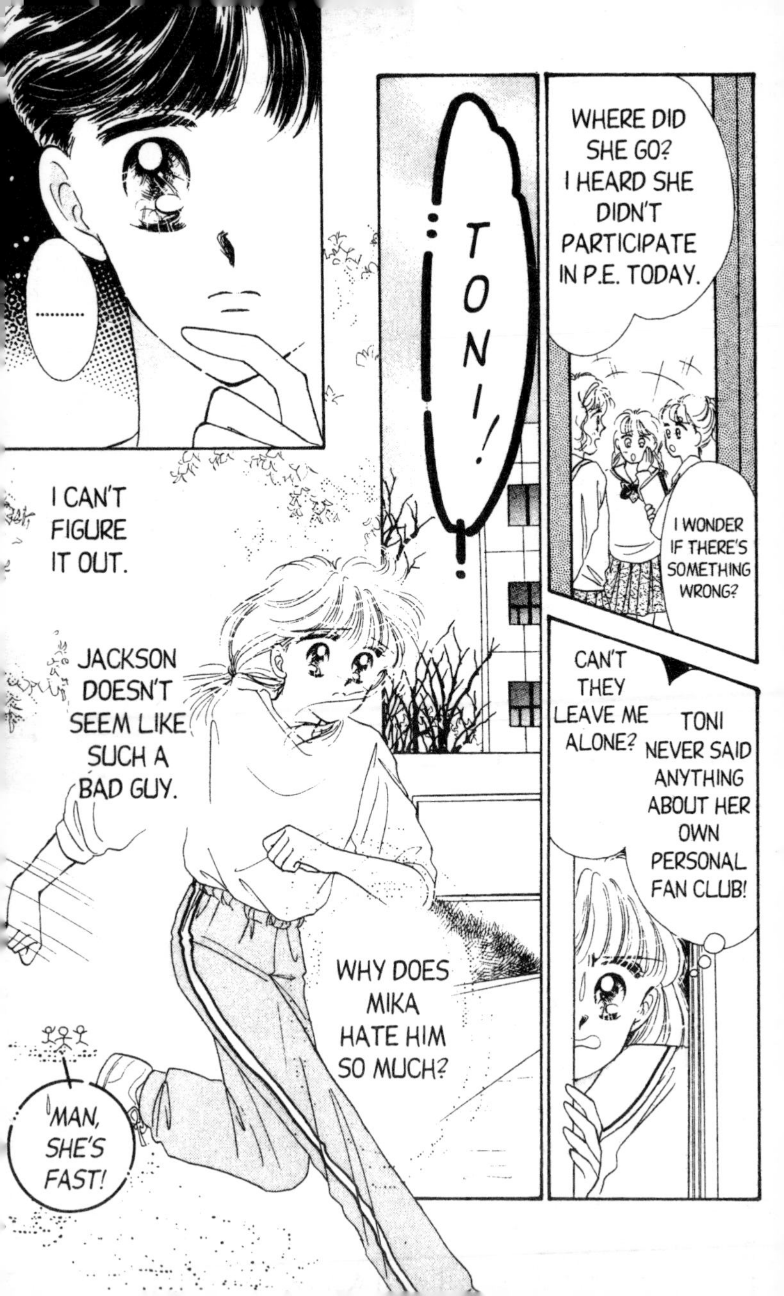
....
I CAN'T FIGURE IT OUT.
JACKSON DOESN'T SEEM LIKE SUCH A BAD GUY.
WHY DOES MIKA HATE HIM SO MUCH?
MAN, SHE'S FAST!
TONI!!
WHERE DID SHE GO? I HEARD SHE DIDN'T PARTICIPATE IN P.E. TODAY.
I WONDER IF THERE'S SOMETHING WRONG?
CAN'T THEY LEAVE ME ALONE?
TONI NEVER SAID ANYTHING ABOUT HER OWN PERSONAL FAN CLUB!

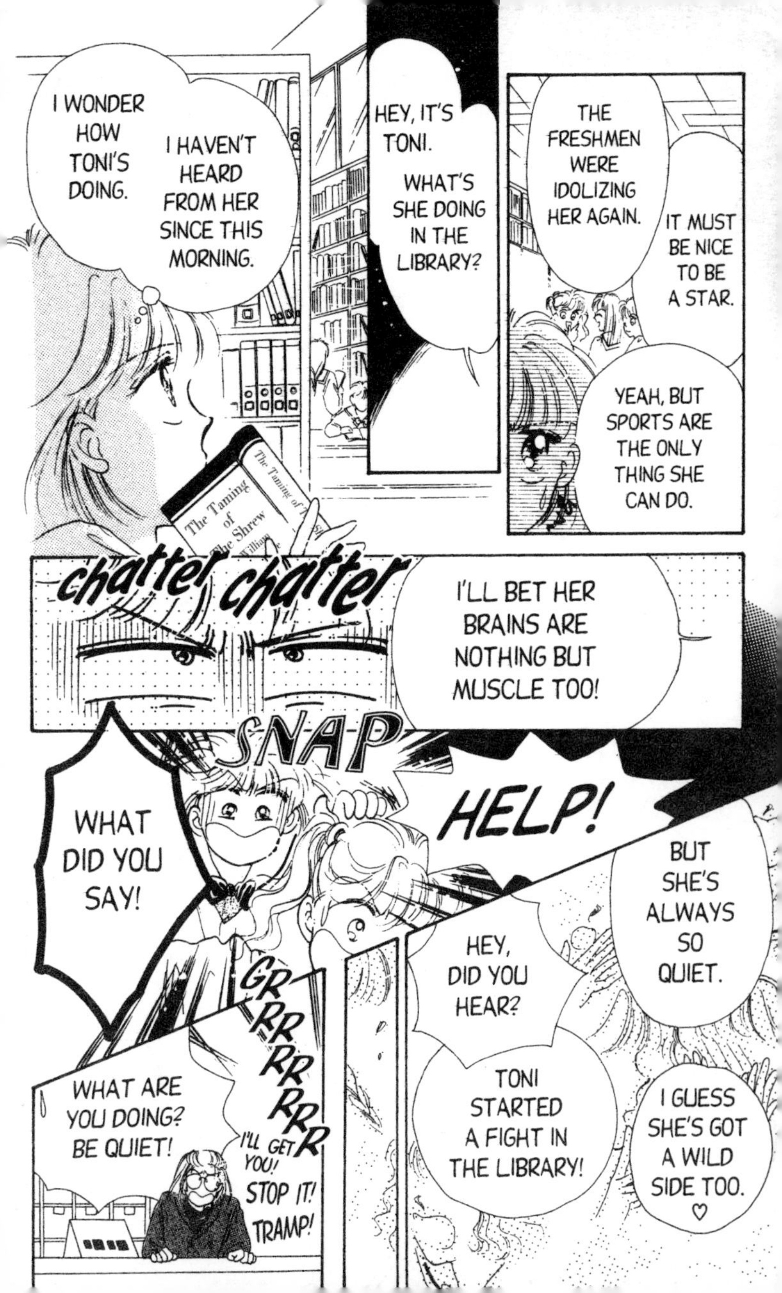
I WONDER HOW TONI'S DOING.
I HAVEN'T HEARD FROM HER SINCE THIS MORNING.
The Taming of The Shrew
HEY, IT'S TONI.
WHAT'S SHE DOING IN THE LIBRARY?
THE FRESHMEN WERE IDOLIZING HER AGAIN.
IT MUST BE NICE TO BE A STAR.
YEAH, BUT SPORTS ARE THE ONLY THING SHE CAN DO.
chatter chatter
I'LL BET HER BRAINS ARE NOTHING BUT MUSCLE TOO!
SNAP
WHAT DID YOU SAY!
HELP!
GRRRRRRRR
WHAT ARE YOU DOING? BE QUIET!
I'LL GET YOU!
STOP IT!
TRAMP!
BUT SHE'S ALWAYS SO QUIET.
HEY, DID YOU HEAR?
TONI STARTED A FIGHT IN THE LIBRARY!
I GUESS SHE'S GOT A WILD SIDE TOO. ♡

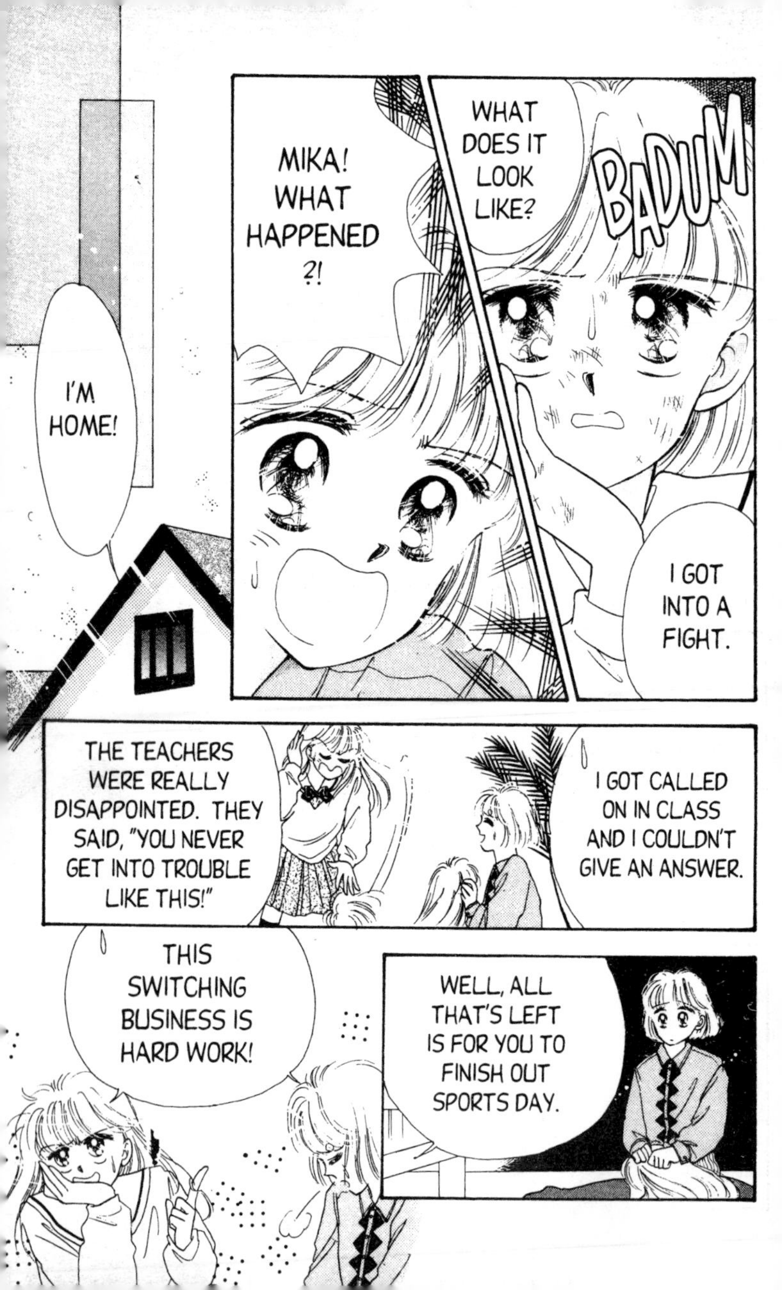
I'M HOME!
MIKA! WHAT HAPPENED ?!
WHAT DOES IT LOOK LIKE?
BADUM
I GOT INTO A FIGHT.
THE TEACHERS WERE REALLY DISAPPOINTED. THEY SAID, "YOU NEVER GET INTO TROUBLE LIKE THIS!"
I GOT CALLED ON IN CLASS AND I COULDN'T GIVE AN ANSWER.
THIS SWITCHING BUSINESS IS HARD WORK!
WELL, ALL THAT'S LEFT IS FOR YOU TO FINISH OUT SPORTS DAY.

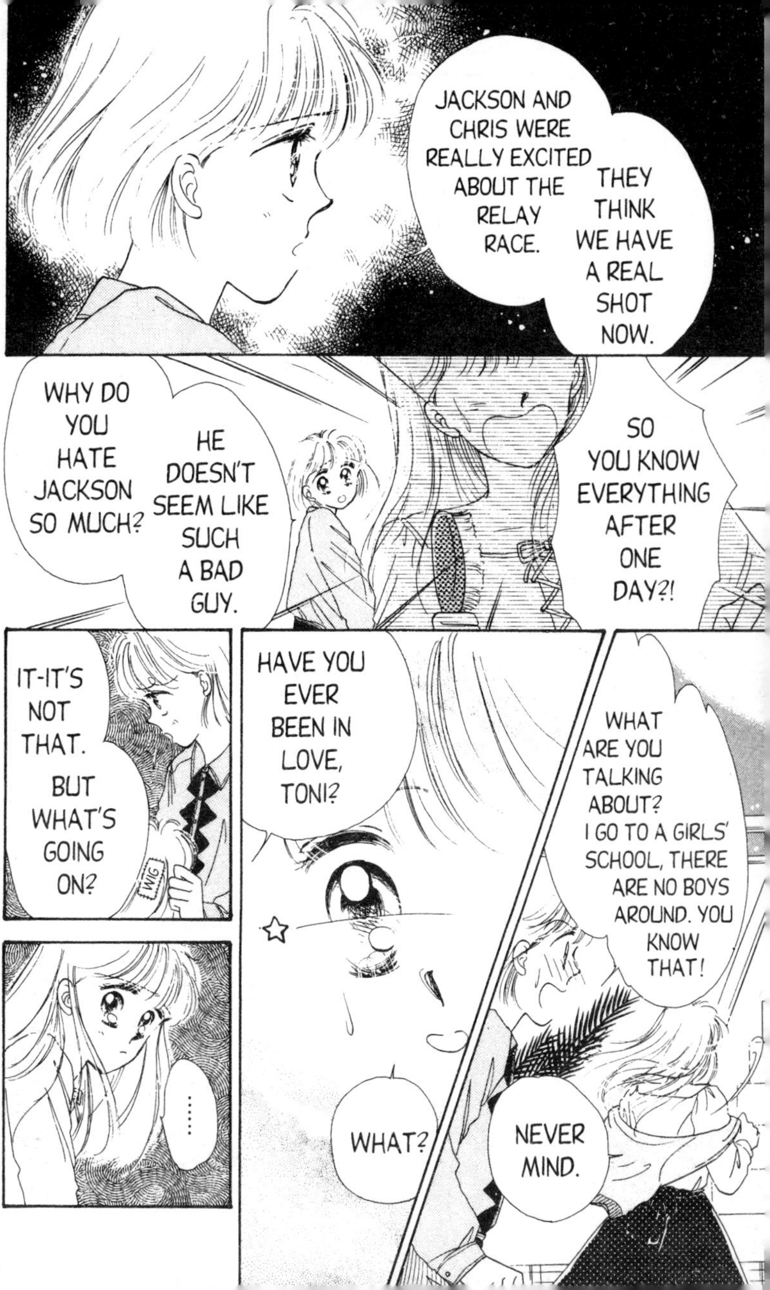
JACKSON AND CHRIS WERE REALLY EXCITED ABOUT THE RELAY RACE.
THEY THINK WE HAVE A REAL SHOT NOW.
WHY DO YOU HATE JACKSON SO MUCH?
HE DOESN'T SEEM LIKE SUCH A BAD GUY.
SO YOU KNOW EVERYTHING AFTER ONE DAY?!
IT-IT'S NOT THAT.
BUT WHAT'S GOING ON?
WIG
HAVE YOU EVER BEEN IN LOVE, TONI?
WHAT ARE YOU TALKING ABOUT? I GO TO A GIRLS' SCHOOL, THERE ARE NO BOYS AROUND. YOU KNOW THAT!
......
WHAT?
NEVER MIND.

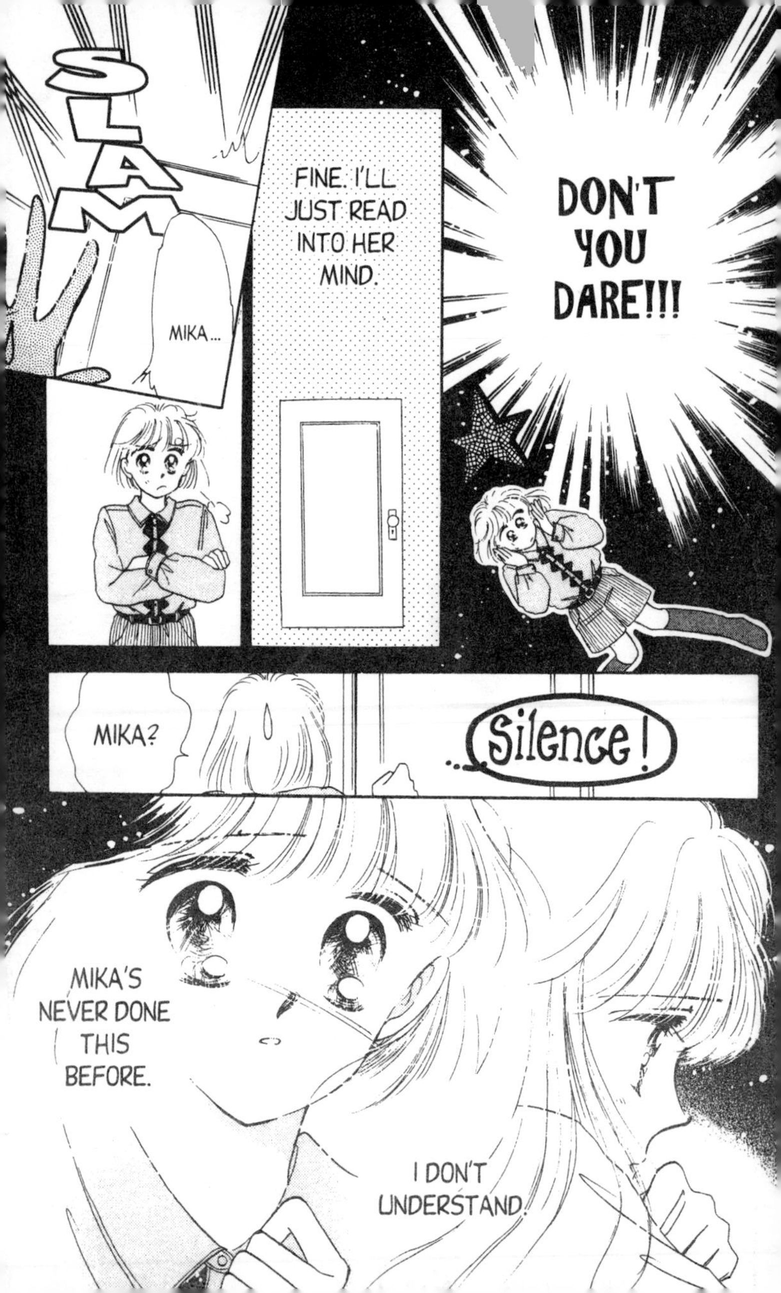
SLAM
MIKA...
FINE. I'LL JUST READ INTO HER MIND.
DON'T YOU DARE!!!
MIKA?
...Silence!
MIKA'S NEVER DONE THIS BEFORE.
I DON'T UNDERSTAND.

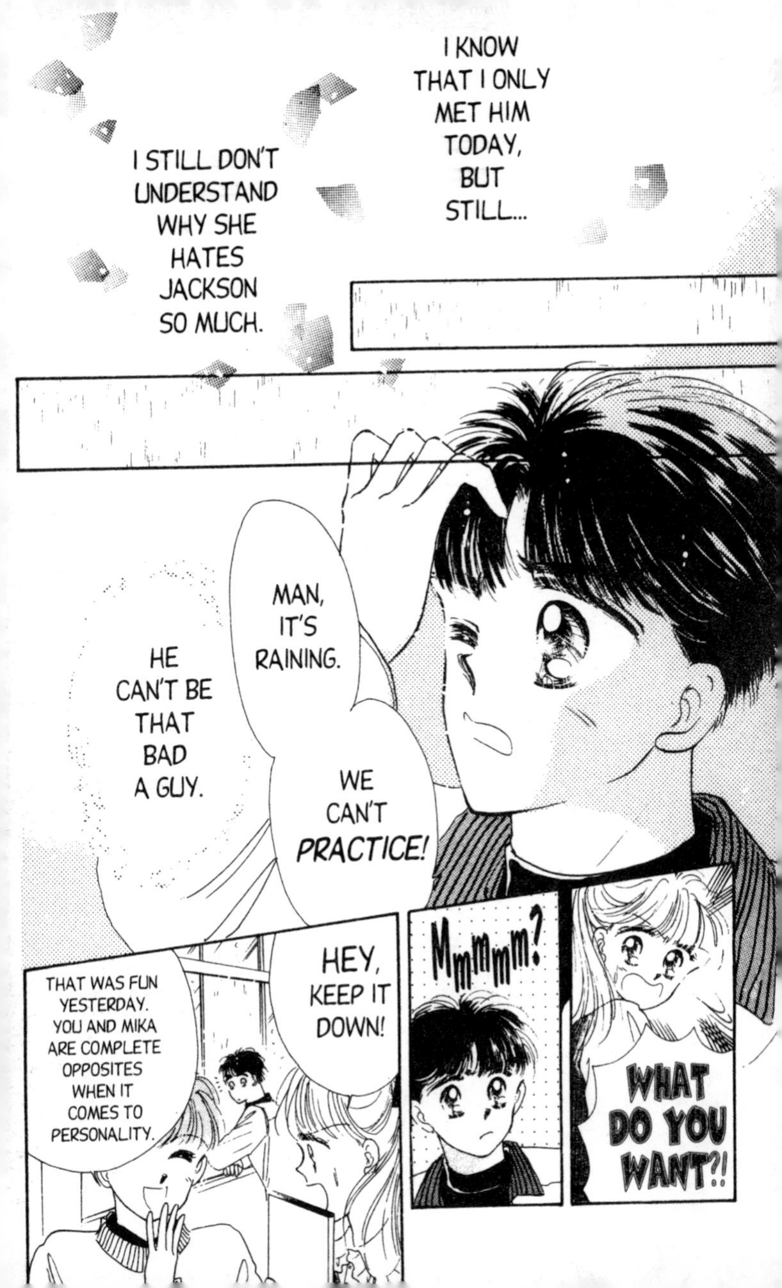
I STILL DON'T UNDERSTAND WHY SHE HATES JACKSON SO MUCH.
I KNOW THAT I ONLY MET HIM TODAY, BUT STILL...
HE CAN'T BE THAT BAD A GUY.
MAN, IT'S RAINING.
WE CAN'T PRACTICE!
THAT WAS FUN YESTERDAY. YOU AND MIKA ARE COMPLETE OPPOSITES WHEN IT COMES TO PERSONALITY.
HEY, KEEP IT DOWN!
Mmmmm?
WHAT DO YOU WANT?!

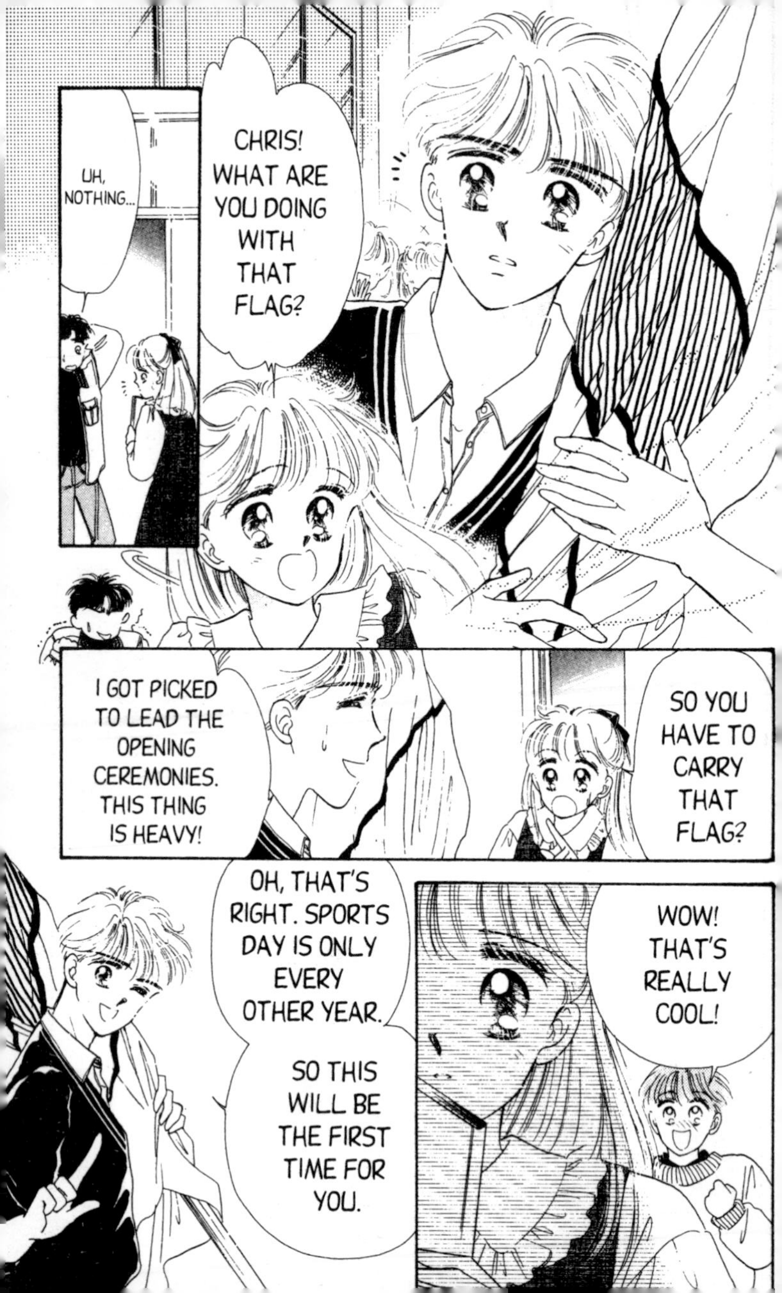
UH, NOTHING...
CHRIS! WHAT ARE YOU DOING WITH THAT FLAG?
I GOT PICKED TO LEAD THE OPENING CEREMONIES. THIS THING IS HEAVY!
SO YOU HAVE TO CARRY THAT FLAG?
OH, THAT'S RIGHT. SPORTS DAY IS ONLY EVERY OTHER YEAR.
SO THIS WILL BE THE FIRST TIME FOR YOU.
WOW! THAT'S REALLY COOL!

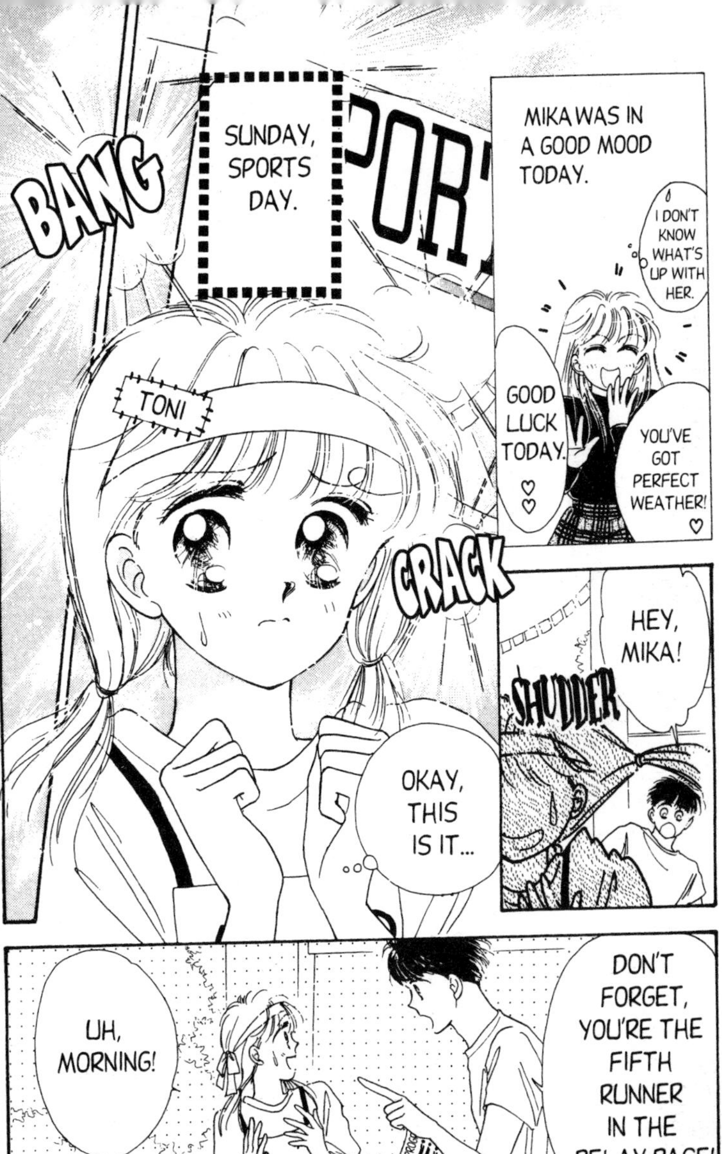
BANG
SUNDAY, SPORTS DAY.
TONI
CRACK
OKAY, THIS IS IT...
MIKA WAS IN A GOOD MOOD TODAY.
GOOD LUCK TODAY. ♡ ♡
I DON'T KNOW WHAT'S UP WITH HER.
YOU'VE GOT PERFECT WEATHER! ♡
SHUDDER
HEY, MIKA!
UH, MORNING!
DON'T FORGET, YOU'RE THE FIFTH RUNNER IN THE RELAY RACE!

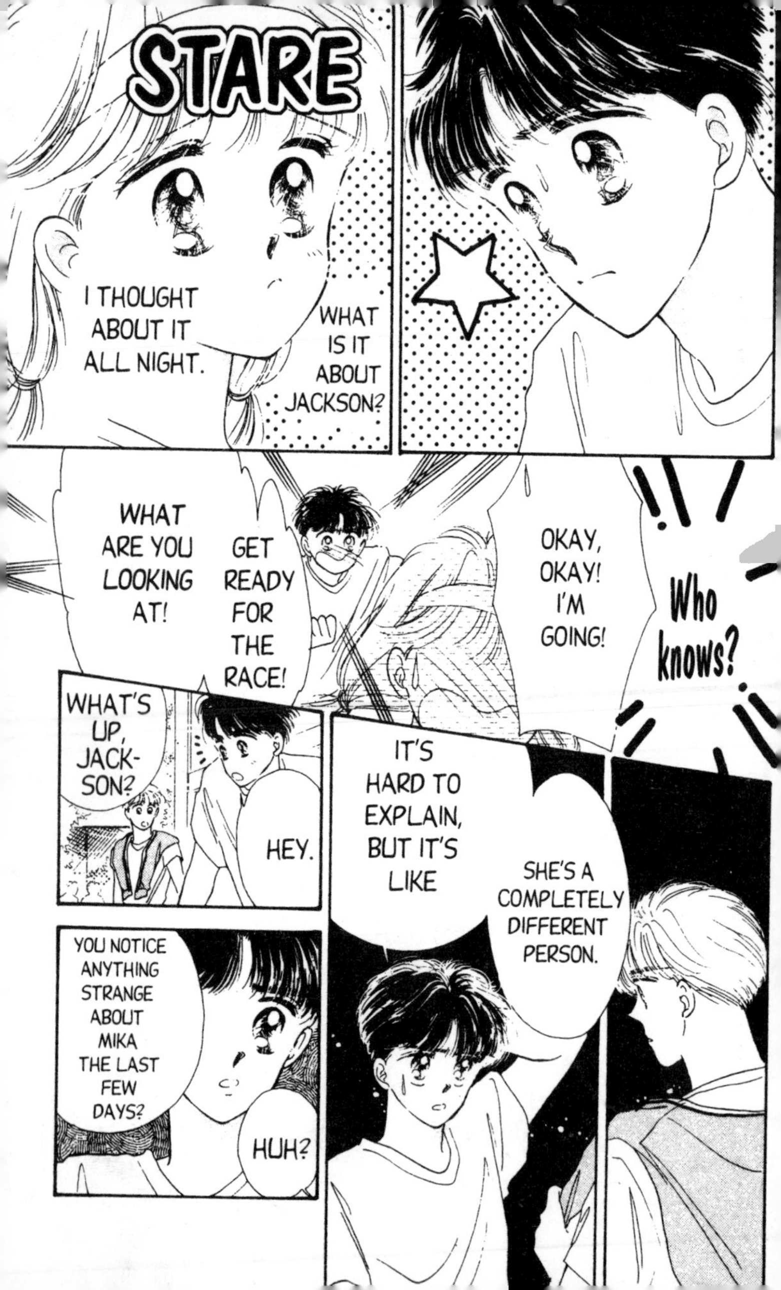
STARE
I THOUGHT ABOUT IT ALL NIGHT.
WHAT IS IT ABOUT JACKSON?
WHAT ARE YOU LOOKING AT!
GET READY FOR THE RACE!
OKAY, OKAY! I'M GOING!
Who knows?
WHAT'S UP, JACK-SON?
HEY.
YOU NOTICE ANYTHING STRANGE ABOUT MIKA THE LAST FEW DAYS?
HUH?
IT'S HARD TO EXPLAIN, BUT IT'S LIKE
SHE'S A COMPLETELY DIFFERENT PERSON.

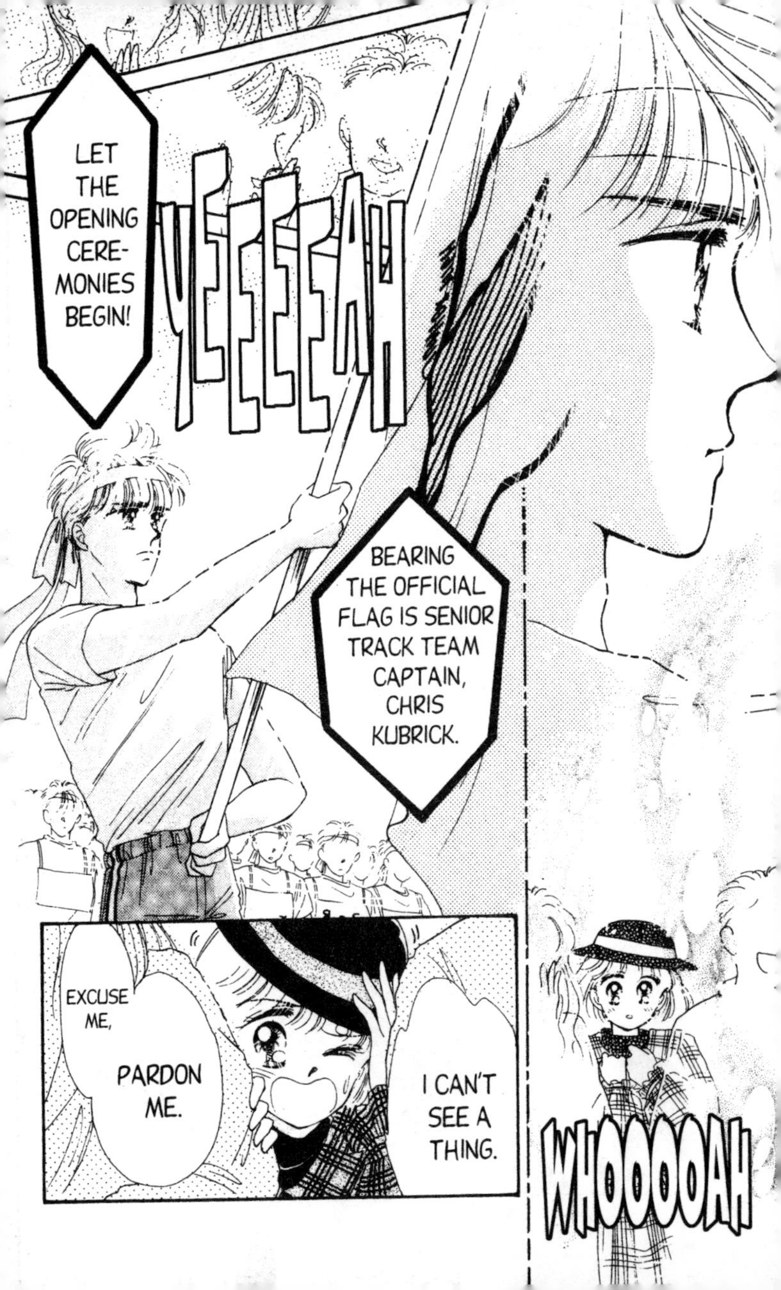
LET THE OPENING CERE-MONIES BEGIN!
YEEEEAH
BEARING THE OFFICIAL FLAG IS SENIOR TRACK TEAM CAPTAIN, CHRIS KUBRICK.
EXCUSE ME,
PARDON ME.
I CAN'T SEE A THING.
WHOOOOAH

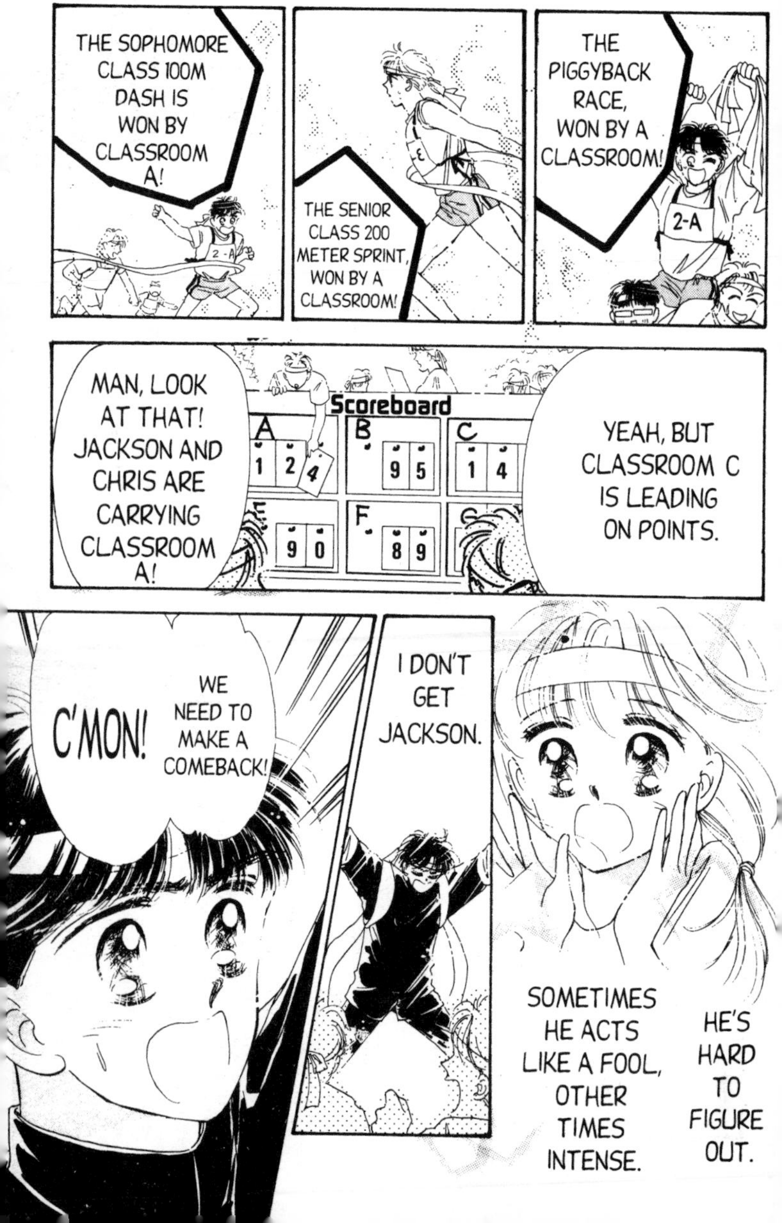
THE SOPHOMORE CLASS 100M DASH IS WON BY CLASSROOM A!
THE SENIOR CLASS 200 METER SPRINT, WON BY A CLASSROOM!
THE PIGGYBACK RACE, WON BY A CLASSROOM!
MAN, LOOK AT THAT! JACKSON AND CHRIS ARE CARRYING CLASSROOM A!
Scoreboard
YEAH, BUT CLASSROOM C IS LEADING ON POINTS.
C'MON!
WE NEED TO MAKE A COMEBACK!
I DON'T GET JACKSON.
SOMETIMES HE ACTS LIKE A FOOL, OTHER TIMES INTENSE.
HE'S HARD TO FIGURE OUT.

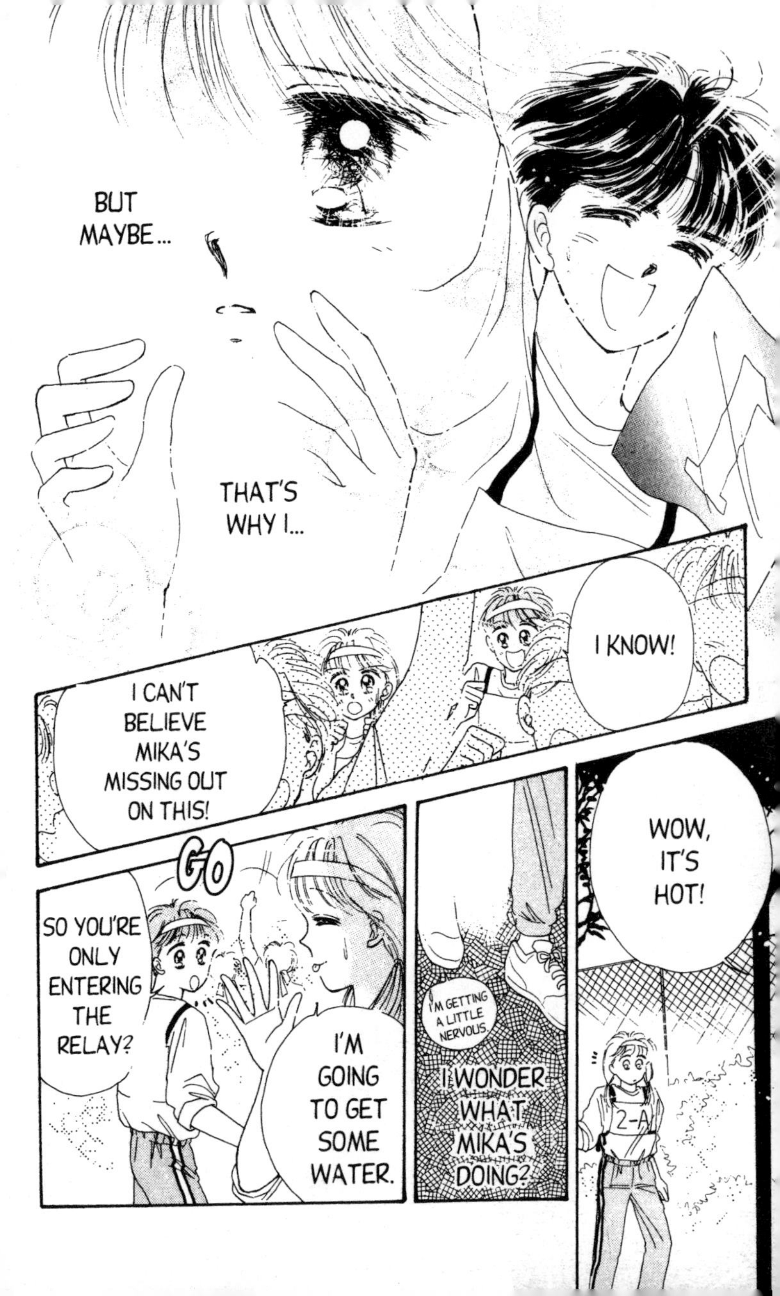
BUT MAYBE...
THAT'S WHY I...
I CAN'T BELIEVE MIKA'S MISSING OUT ON THIS!
I KNOW!
GO
SO YOU'RE ONLY ENTERING THE RELAY?
I'M GOING TO GET SOME WATER.
I'M GETTING A LITTLE NERVOUS.
I WONDER WHAT MIKA'S DOING?
WOW, IT'S HOT!
2-A

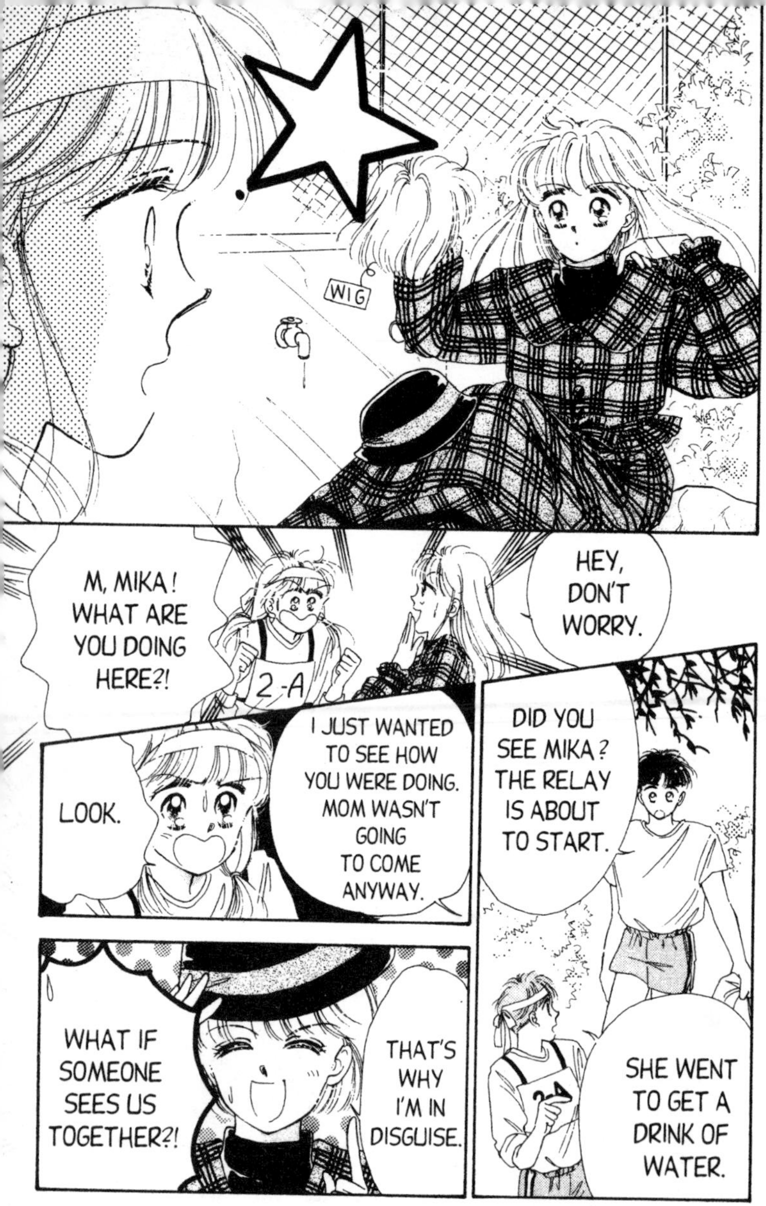
WIG
M, MIKA! WHAT ARE YOU DOING HERE?!
HEY, DON'T WORRY.
LOOK.
I JUST WANTED TO SEE HOW YOU WERE DOING. MOM WASN'T GOING TO COME ANYWAY.
WHAT IF SOMEONE SEES US TOGETHER?!
THAT'S WHY I'M IN DISGUISE.
DID YOU SEE MIKA? THE RELAY IS ABOUT TO START.
SHE WENT TO GET A DRINK OF WATER.

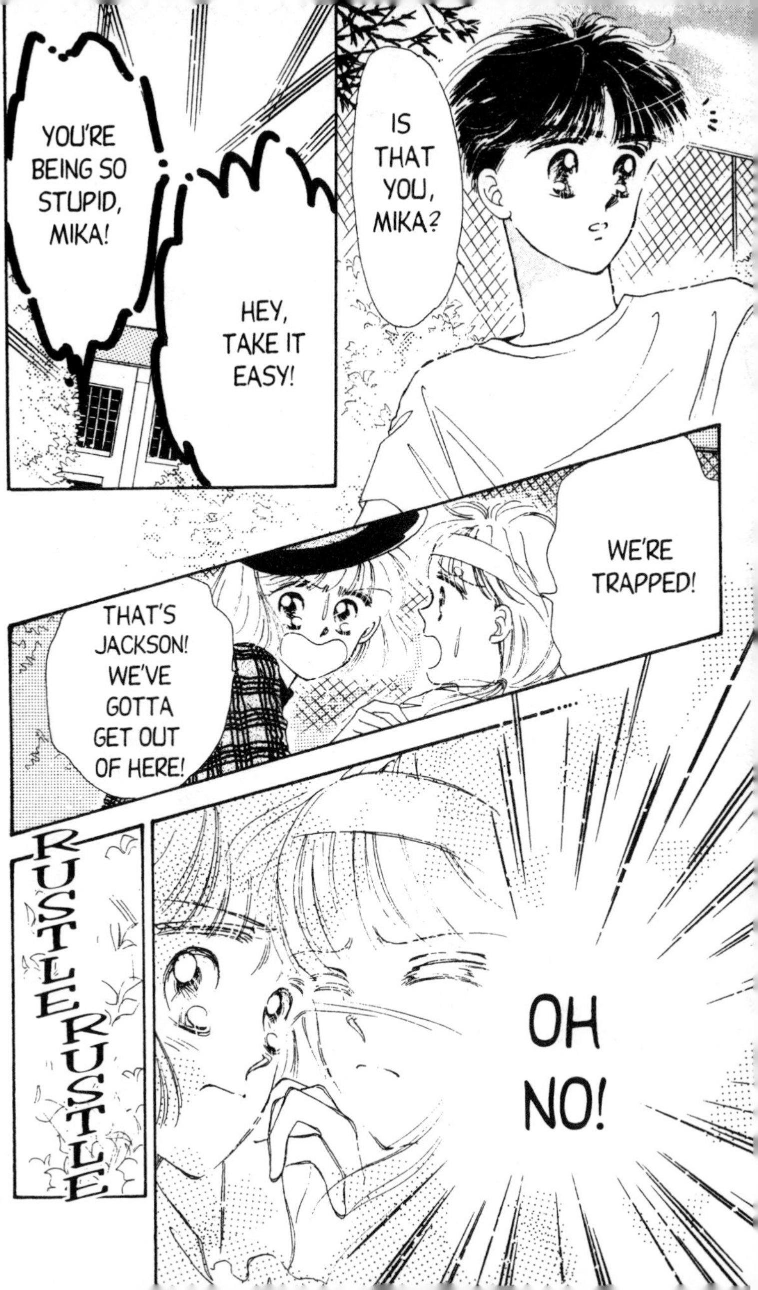
YOU'RE BEING SO STUPID, MIKA!
HEY, TAKE IT EASY!
IS THAT YOU, MIKA?
THAT'S JACKSON! WE'VE GOTTA GET OUT OF HERE!
WE'RE TRAPPED!
RUSTLE RUSTLE
OH NO!

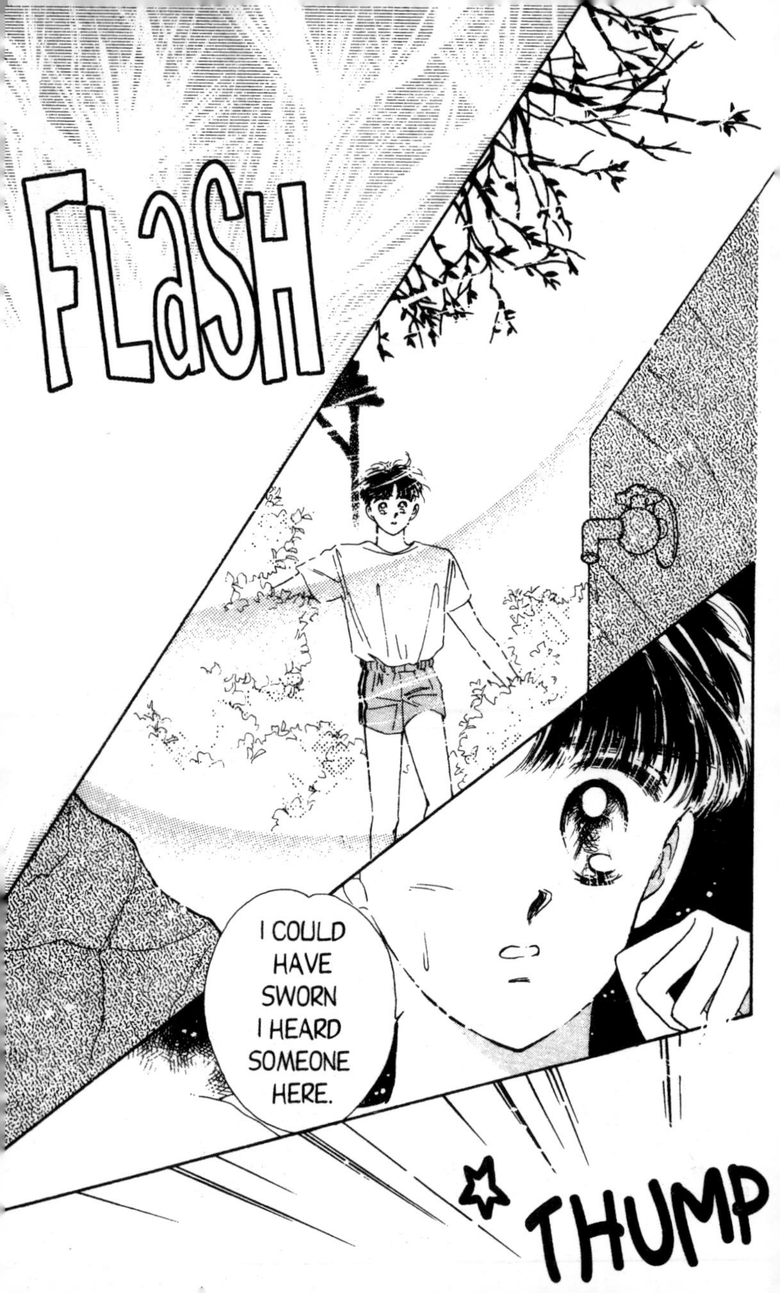
FLASH
I COULD HAVE SWORN I HEARD SOMEONE HERE.
THUMP

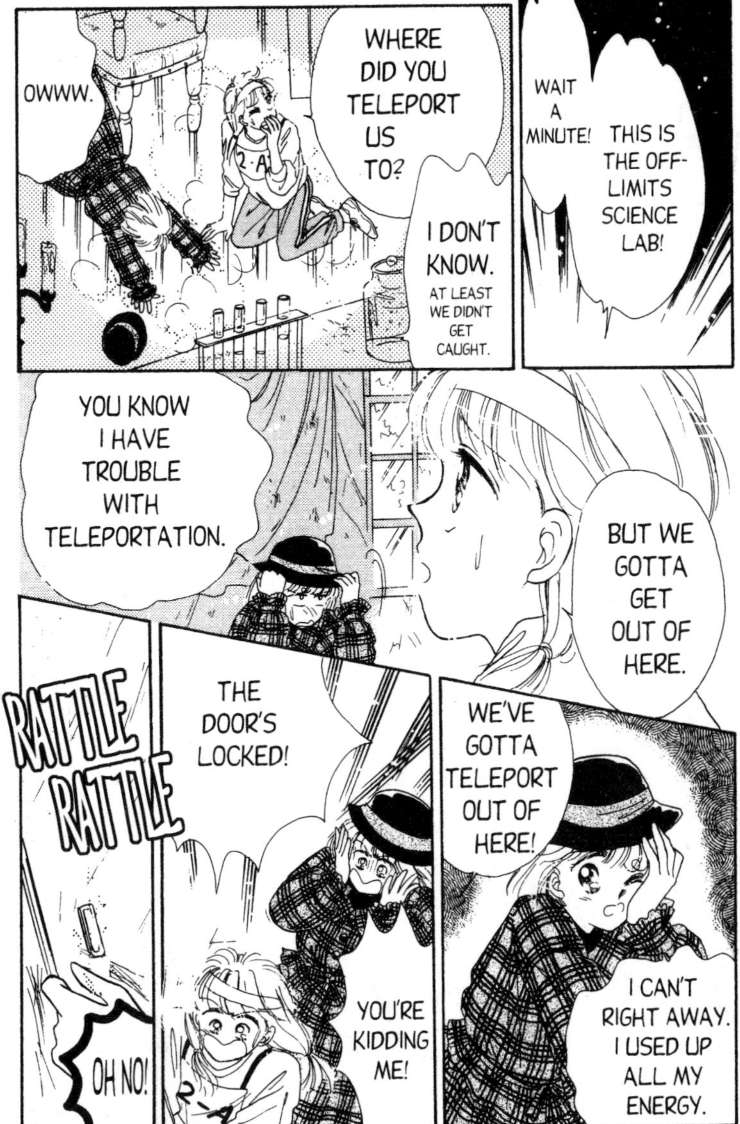
OWWW.
WHERE DID YOU TELEPORT US TO?
I DON'T KNOW. AT LEAST WE DIDN'T GET CAUGHT.
WAIT A MINUTE!
THIS IS THE OFF-LIMITS SCIENCE LAB!
YOU KNOW I HAVE TROUBLE WITH TELEPORTATION.
BUT WE GOTTA GET OUT OF HERE.
RATTLE RATTLE
OH NO!
THE DOOR'S LOCKED!
YOU'RE KIDDING ME!
WE'VE GOTTA TELEPORT OUT OF HERE!
I CAN'T RIGHT AWAY. I USED UP ALL MY ENERGY.

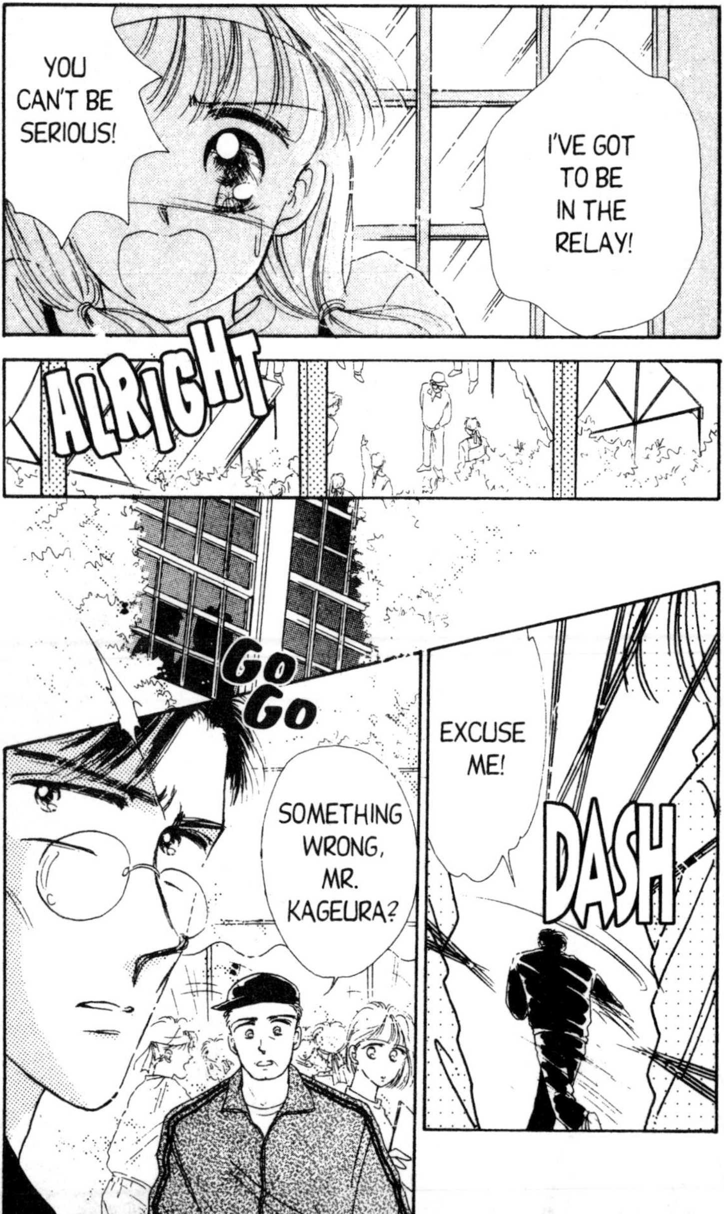
YOU CAN'T BE SERIOUS!
I'VE GOT TO BE IN THE RELAY!
ALRIGHT
GO GO
SOMETHING WRONG, MR. KAGEURA?
EXCUSE ME!
DASH

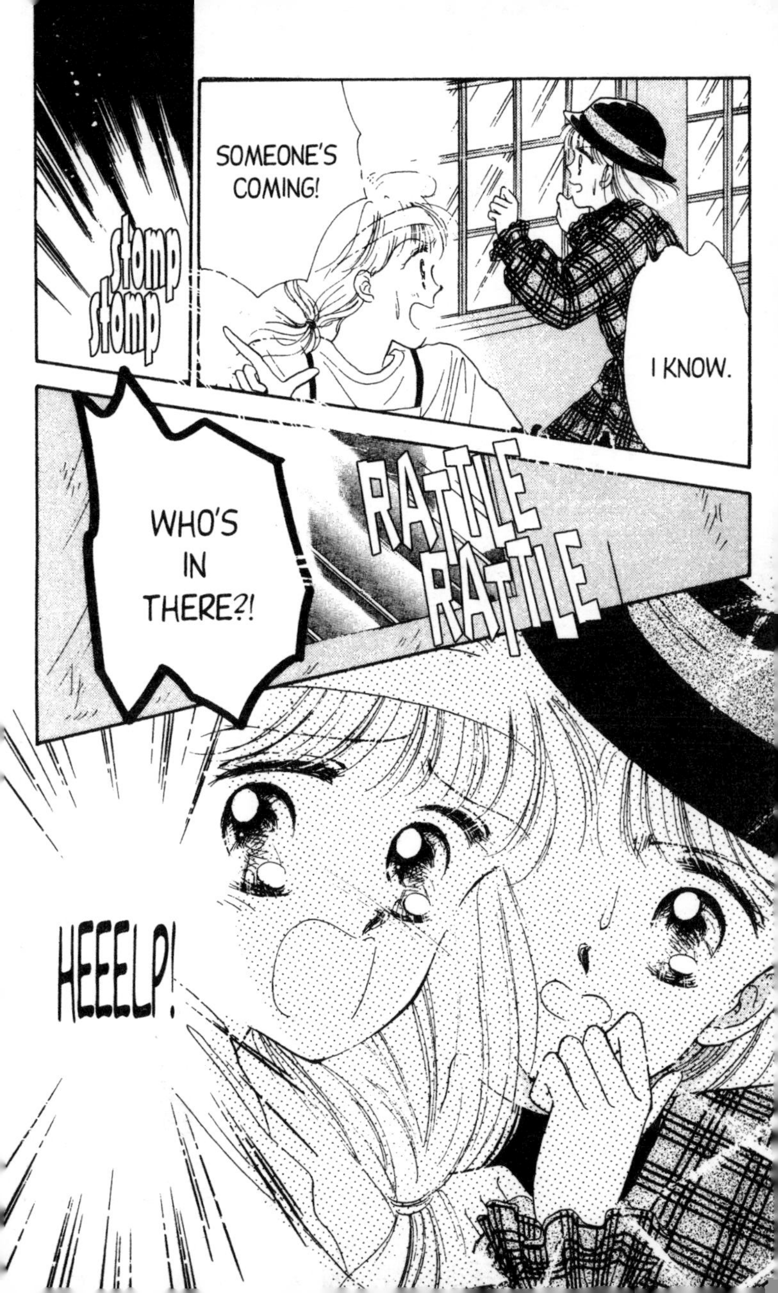
stomp stomp
SOMEONE'S COMING!
I KNOW.
WHO'S IN THERE?!
RATTLE RATTLE
HEEELP!

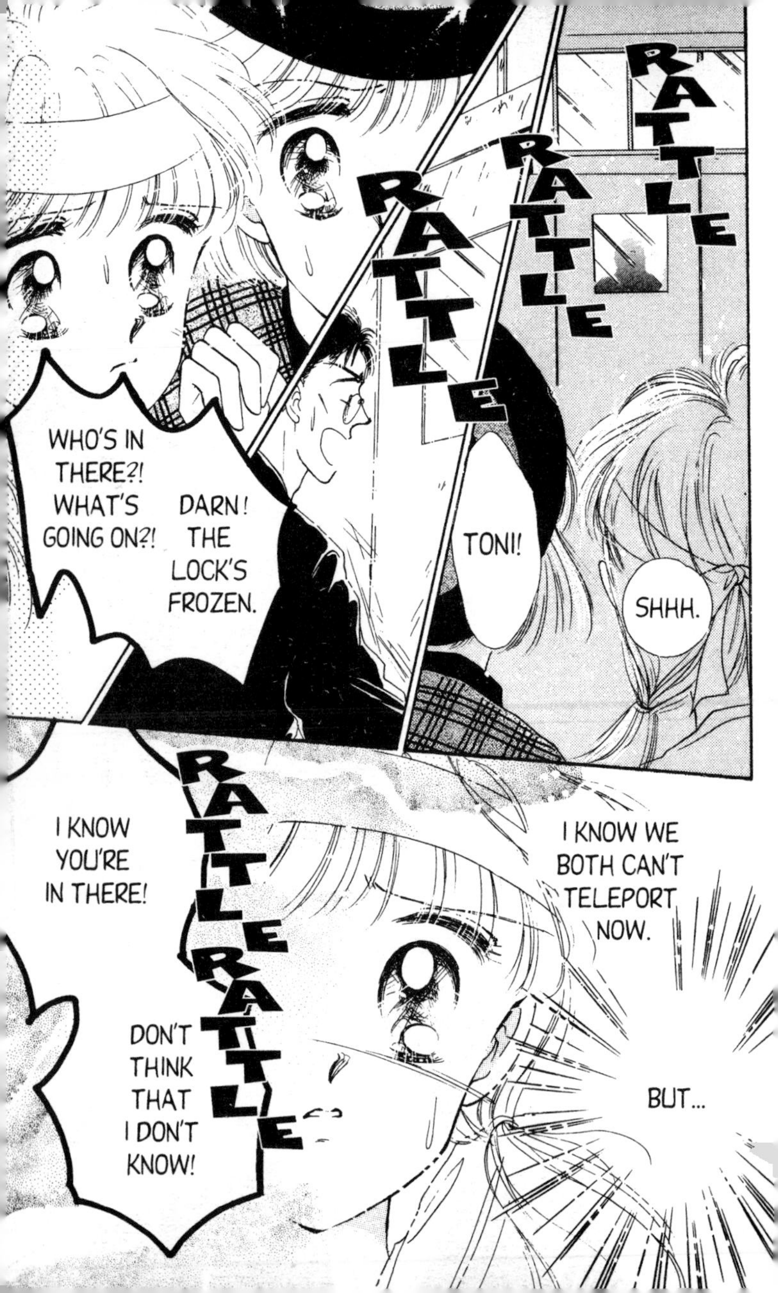
WHO'S IN THERE?! WHAT'S GOING ON?!
DARN! THE LOCK'S FROZEN.
RATTLE
RATTLE
RATTLE
TONI!
SHHH.
I KNOW YOU'RE IN THERE!
RATTLE RATTLE
DON'T THINK THAT I DON'T KNOW!
I KNOW WE BOTH CAN'T TELEPORT NOW.
BUT...

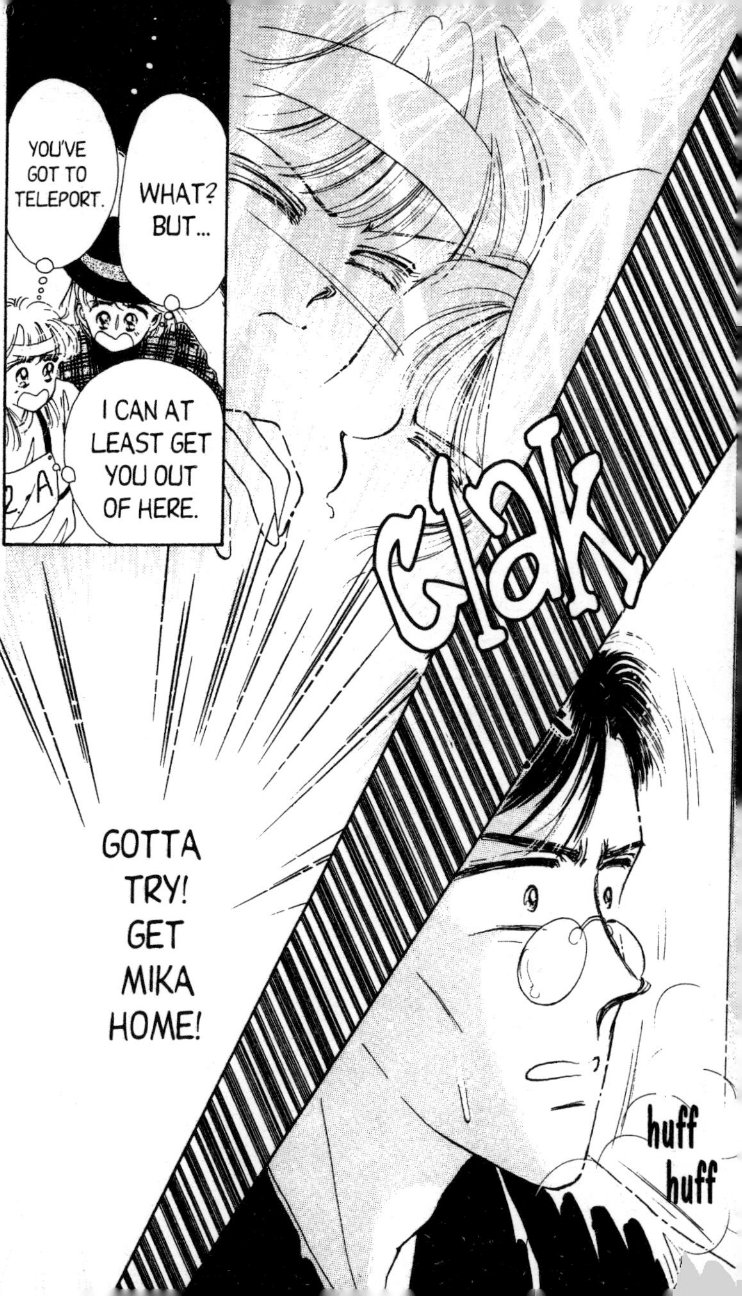
YOU'VE GOT TO TELEPORT.
WHAT? BUT...
I CAN AT LEAST GET YOU OUT OF HERE.
GOTTA TRY! GET MIKA HOME!
CLAK
huff huff

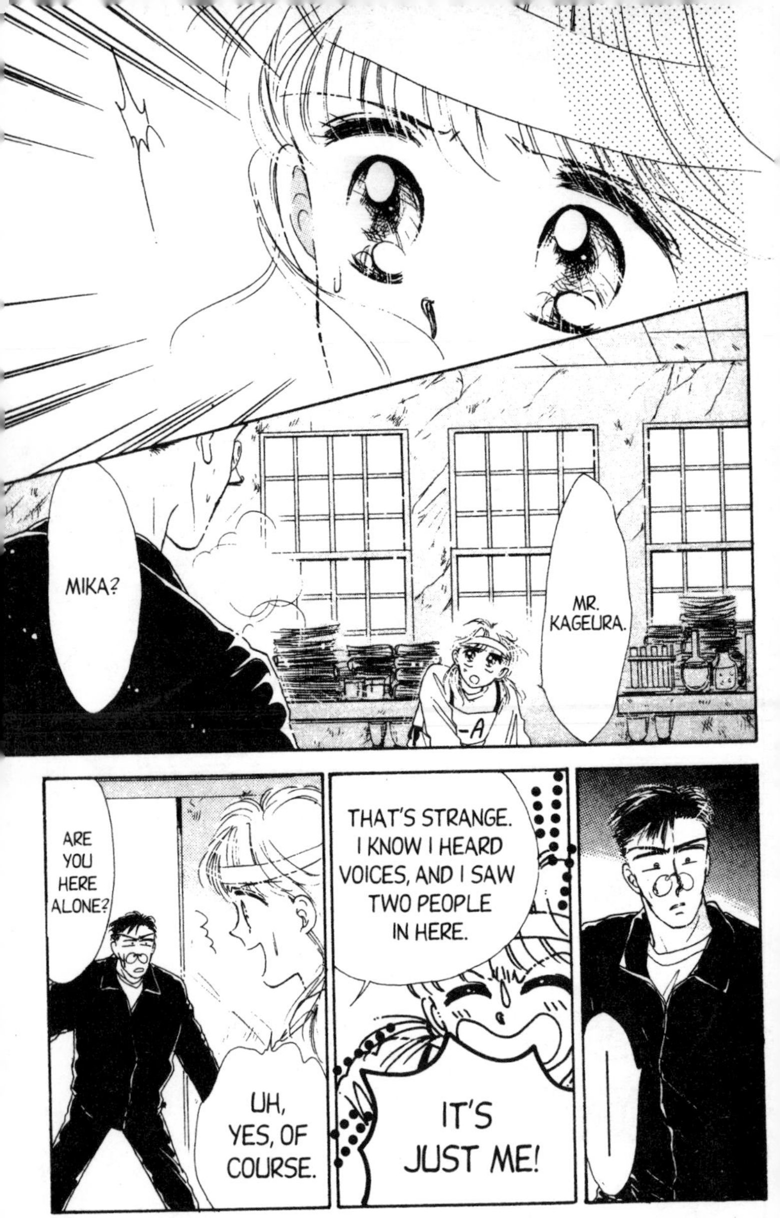
MIKA?
MR. KAGEURA.
ARE YOU HERE ALONE?
UH, YES, OF COURSE.
THAT'S STRANGE. I KNOW I HEARD VOICES, AND I SAW TWO PEOPLE IN HERE.
IT'S JUST ME!

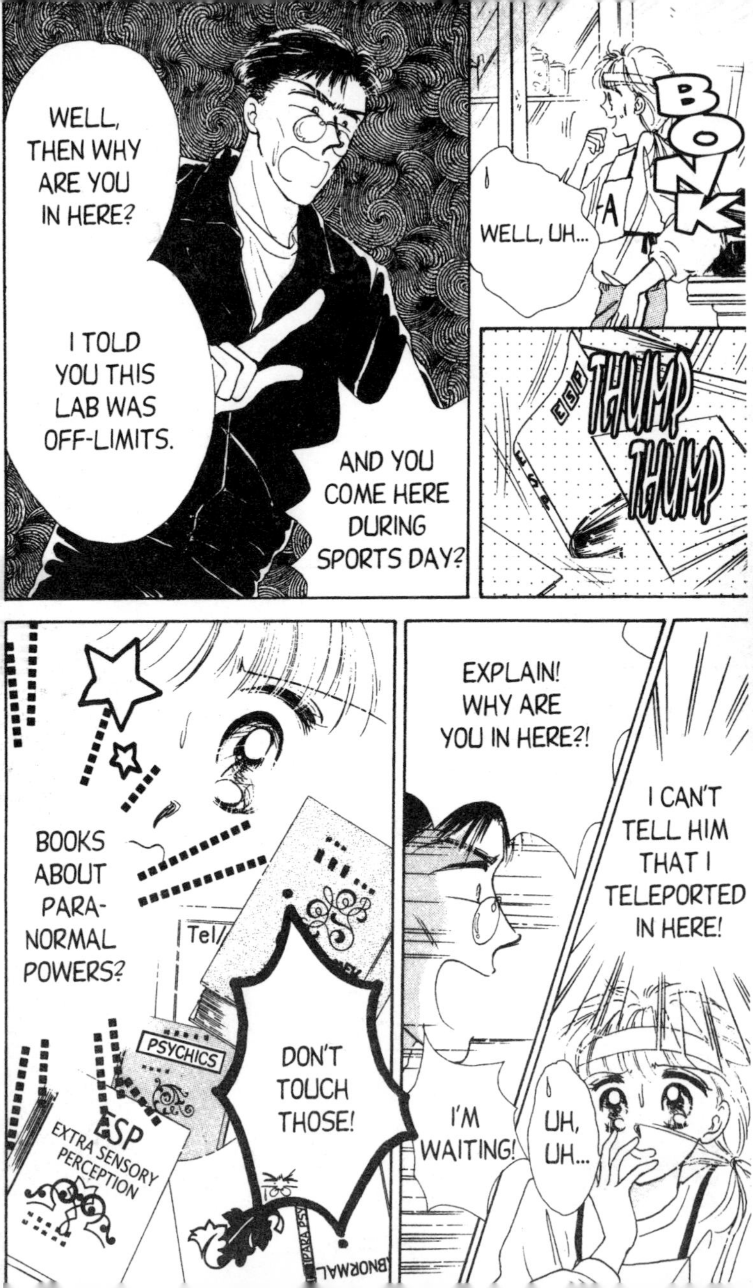

WELL, THEN WHY ARE YOU IN HERE?
I TOLD YOU THIS LAB WAS OFF-LIMITS.
AND YOU COME HERE DURING SPORTS DAY?
BONK
A
WELL, UH...
ESP
THUMP
THUMP
BOOKS ABOUT PARA-NORMAL POWERS?
Tel
PSYCHICS
ESP
EXTRA SENSORY PERCEPTION
DON'T TOUCH THOSE!
EXPLAIN! WHY ARE YOU IN HERE?!
I CAN'T TELL HIM THAT I TELEPORTED IN HERE!
I'M WAITING!
UH, UH...

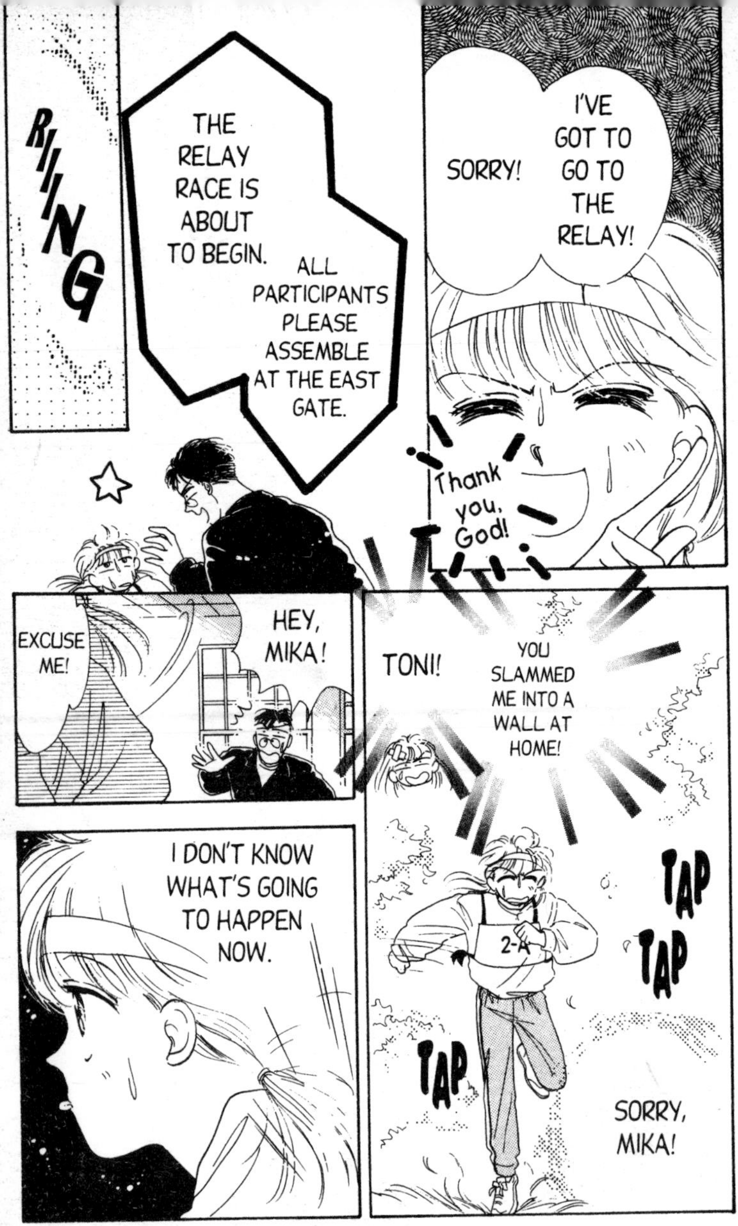
RIIING
THE RELAY RACE IS ABOUT TO BEGIN.
ALL PARTICIPANTS PLEASE ASSEMBLE AT THE EAST GATE.
SORRY!
I'VE GOT TO GO TO THE RELAY!
Thank you, God!
EXCUSE ME!
HEY, MIKA!
I DON'T KNOW WHAT'S GOING TO HAPPEN NOW.
TONI!
YOU SLAMMED ME INTO A WALL AT HOME!
TAP
TAP
TAP
SORRY, MIKA!

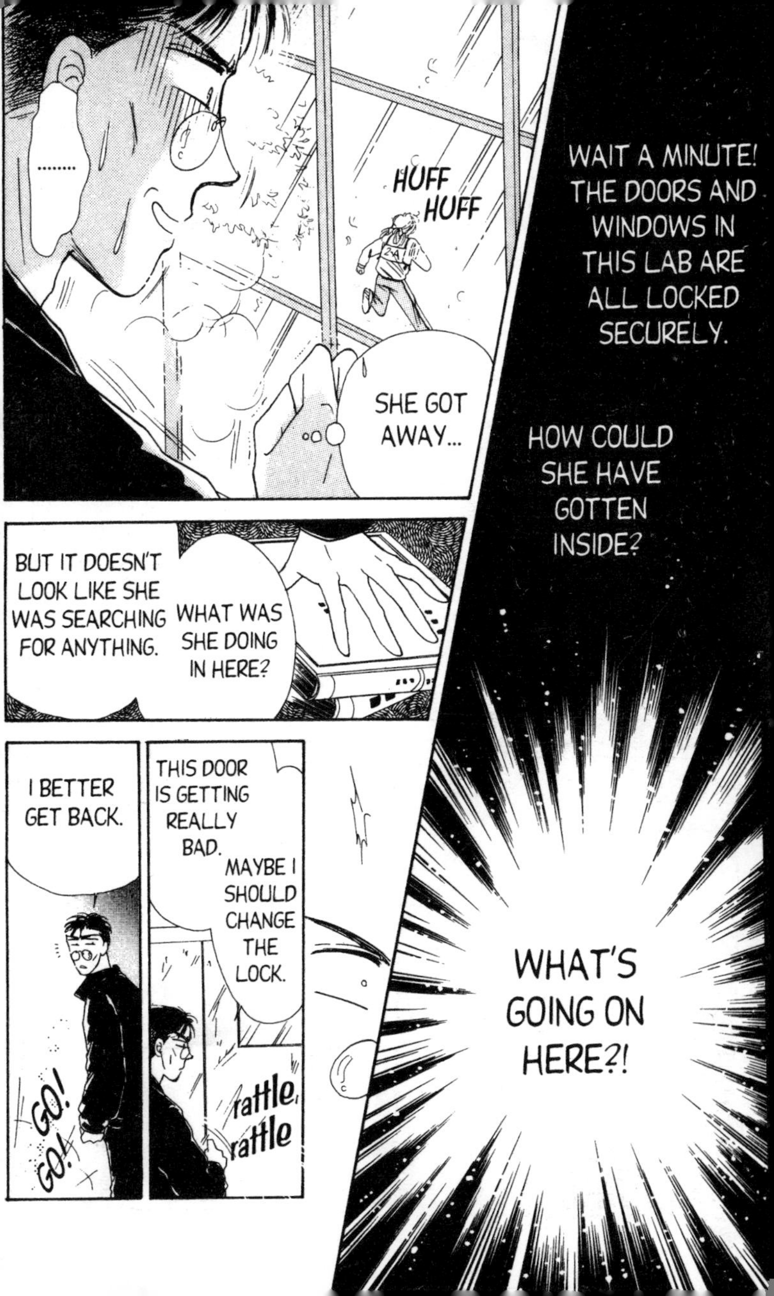

....
HUFF HUFF
SHE GOT AWAY...
BUT IT DOESN'T LOOK LIKE SHE WAS SEARCHING FOR ANYTHING.
WHAT WAS SHE DOING IN HERE?
I BETTER GET BACK.
GO! GO!
THIS DOOR IS GETTING REALLY BAD.
MAYBE I SHOULD CHANGE THE LOCK.
rattle, rattle
WAIT A MINUTE! THE DOORS AND WINDOWS IN THIS LAB ARE ALL LOCKED SECURELY.
HOW COULD SHE HAVE GOTTEN INSIDE?
WHAT'S GOING ON HERE?!

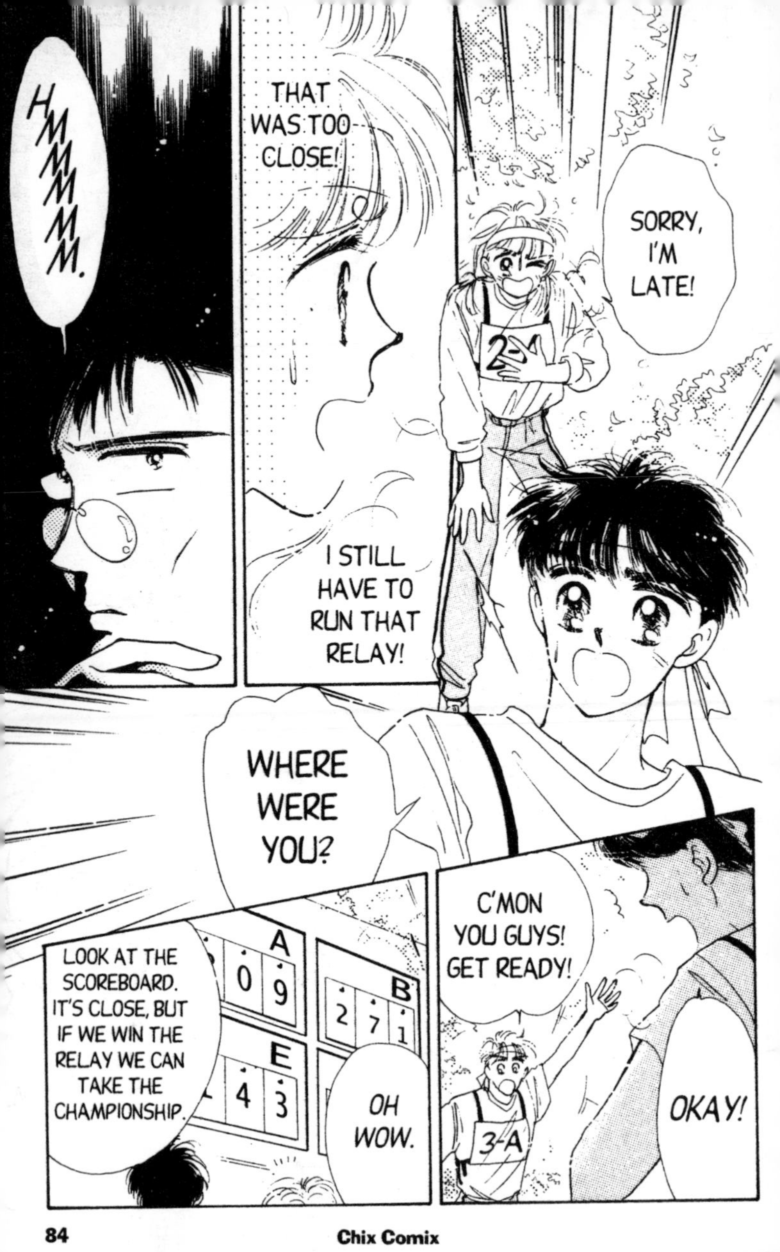
HMMMMM.
THAT WAS TOO CLOSE!
I STILL HAVE TO RUN THAT RELAY!
SORRY, I'M LATE!
WHERE WERE YOU?
LOOK AT THE SCOREBOARD. IT'S CLOSE, BUT IF WE WIN THE RELAY WE CAN TAKE THE CHAMPIONSHIP.
OH WOW.
C'MON YOU GUYS! GET READY!
OKAY!

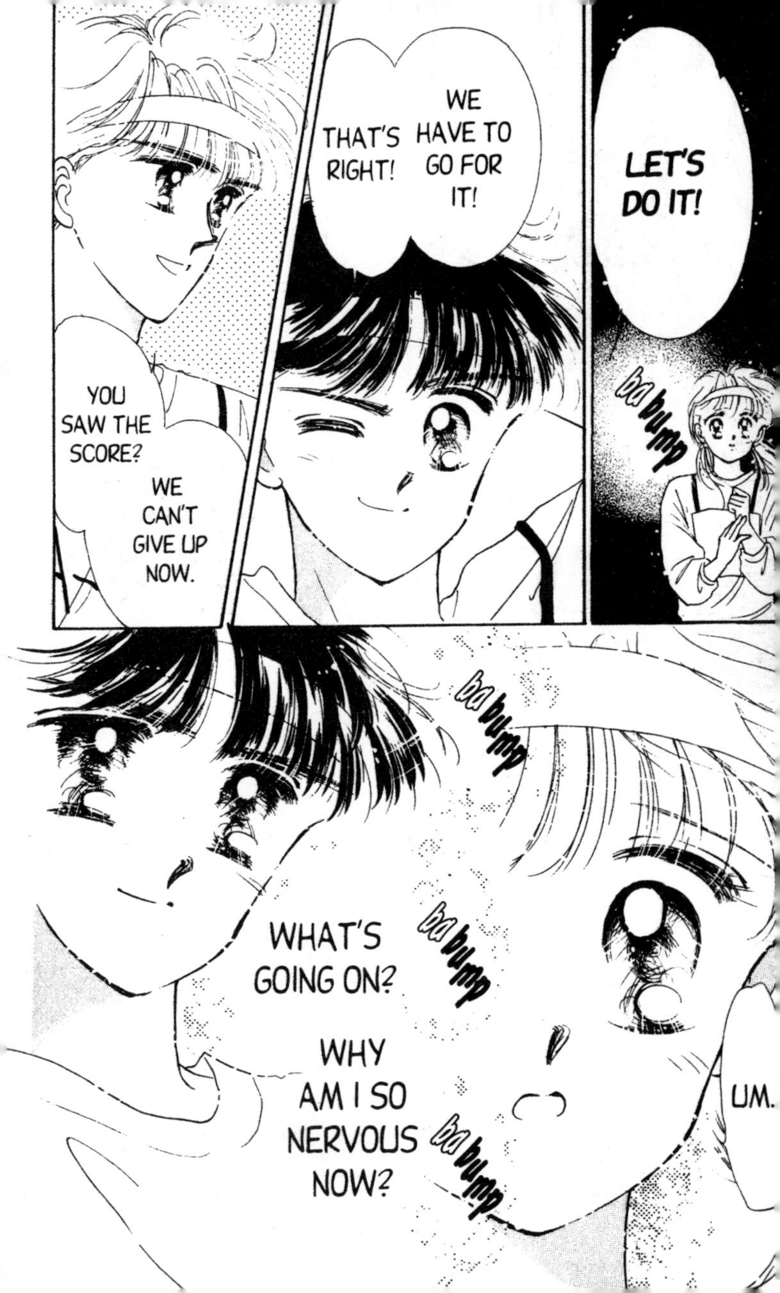
YOU SAW THE SCORE?
WE CAN'T GIVE UP NOW.
THAT'S RIGHT!
WE HAVE TO GO FOR IT!
LET'S DO IT!
ba bump
ba bump
WHAT'S GOING ON?
ba bump
WHY AM I SO NERVOUS NOW?
ba bump
UM.

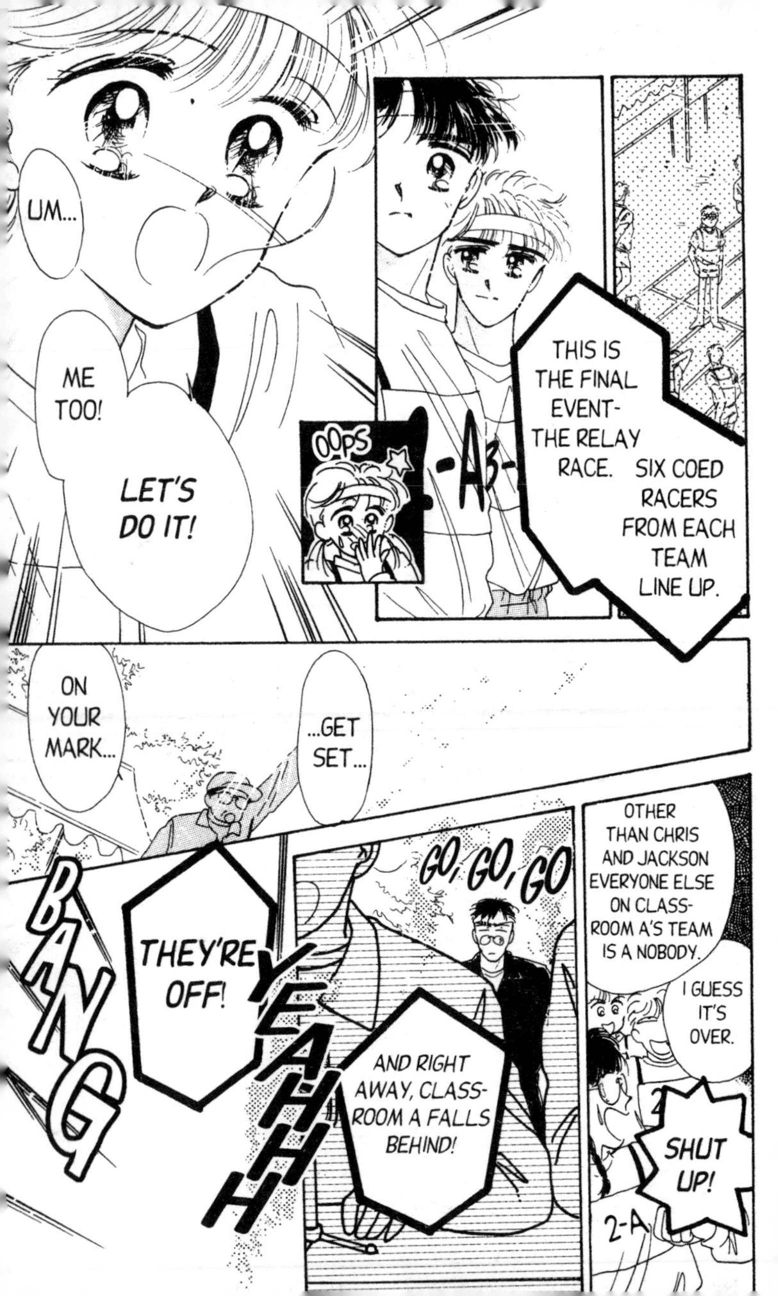
UM...
ME TOO!
LET'S DO IT!
OOPS
-A3-
THIS IS THE FINAL EVENT- THE RELAY RACE.
SIX COED RACERS FROM EACH TEAM LINE UP.
ON YOUR MARK...
...GET SET...
BANG
THEY'RE OFF!
YEAHHHH
GO, GO, GO
AND RIGHT AWAY, CLASSROOM A FALLS BEHIND!
OTHER THAN CHRIS AND JACKSON EVERYONE ELSE ON CLASSROOM A'S TEAM IS A NOBODY.
I GUESS IT'S OVER.
SHUT UP!
2-A

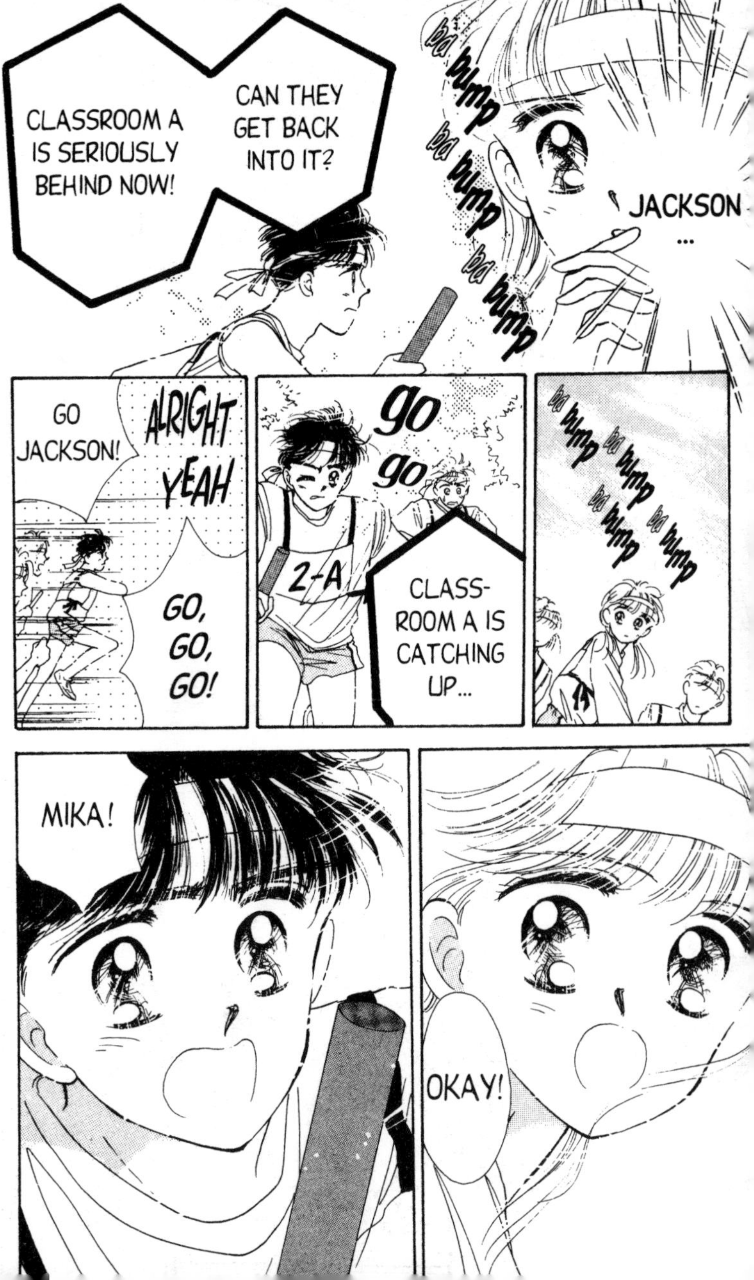
CLASSROOM A IS SERIOUSLY BEHIND NOW!
CAN THEY GET BACK INTO IT?
ba bump ba bump ba bump
JACKSON ...
GO JACKSON!
ALRIGHT YEAH
GO, GO, GO!
go go
2-A
CLASSROOM A IS CATCHING UP...
ba bump ba bump ba bump ba bump
MIKA!
OKAY!

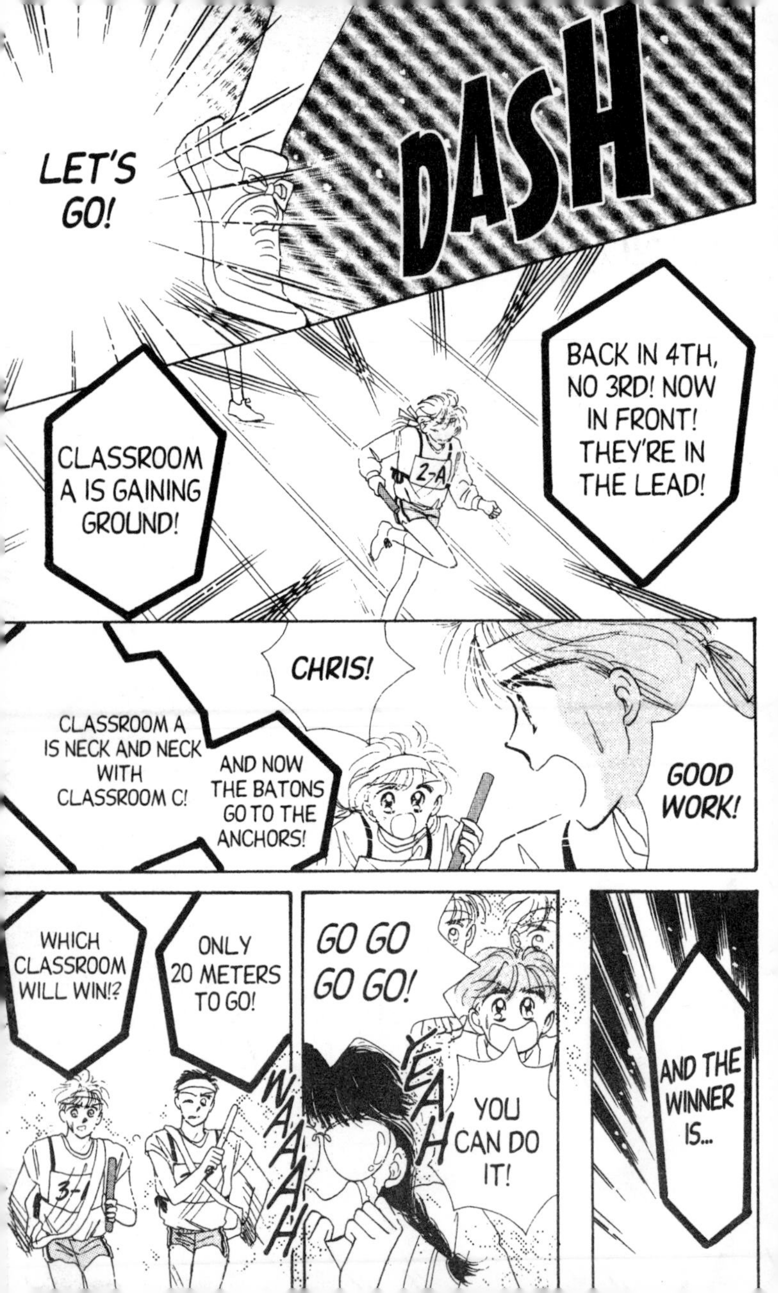
LET'S GO!
DASH
CLASSROOM A IS GAINING GROUND!
BACK IN 4TH, NO 3RD! NOW IN FRONT! THEY'RE IN THE LEAD!
2-A
CLASSROOM A IS NECK AND NECK WITH CLASSROOM C!
AND NOW THE BATONS GO TO THE ANCHORS!
CHRIS!
GOOD WORK!
WHICH CLASSROOM WILL WIN!?
ONLY 20 METERS TO GO!
GO GO GO GO!
WAAAAH
YEAH
YOU CAN DO IT!
AND THE WINNER IS...

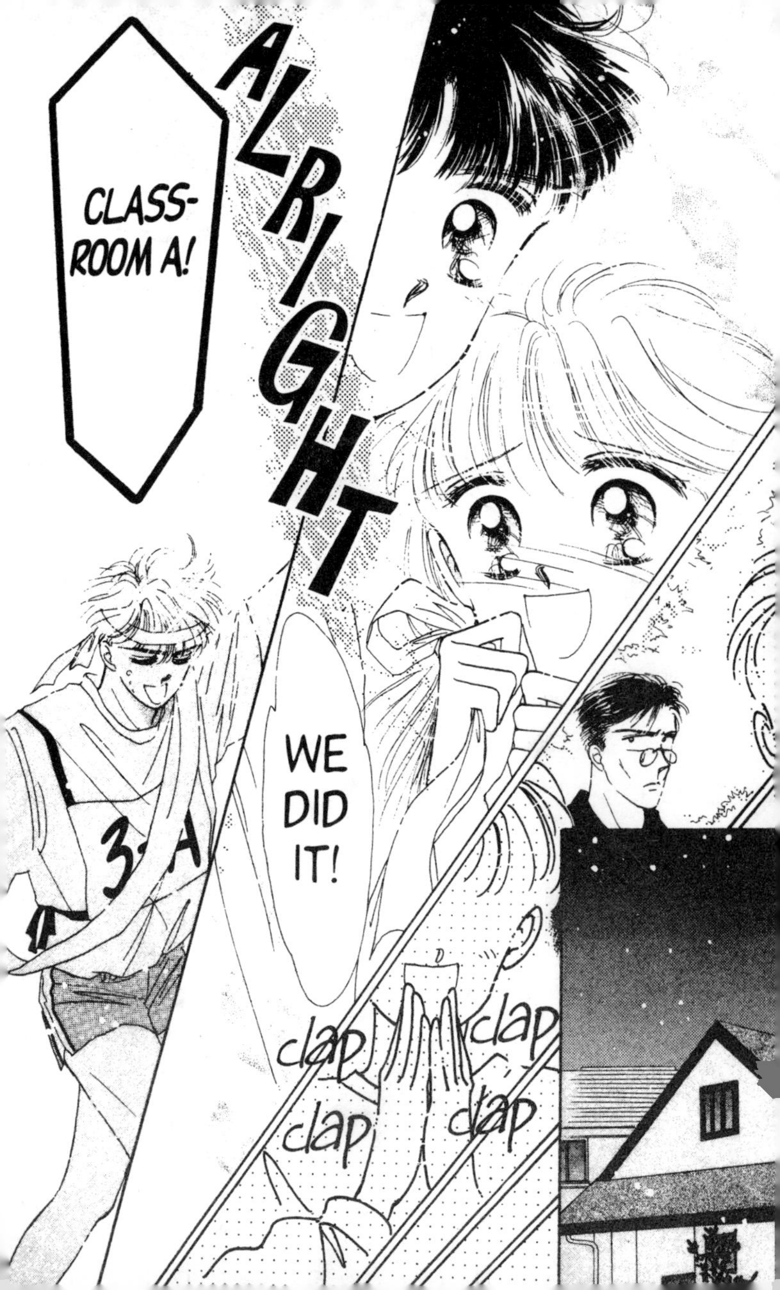
CLASS-ROOM A!
ALRIGHT
WE DID IT!
clap clap
clap clap

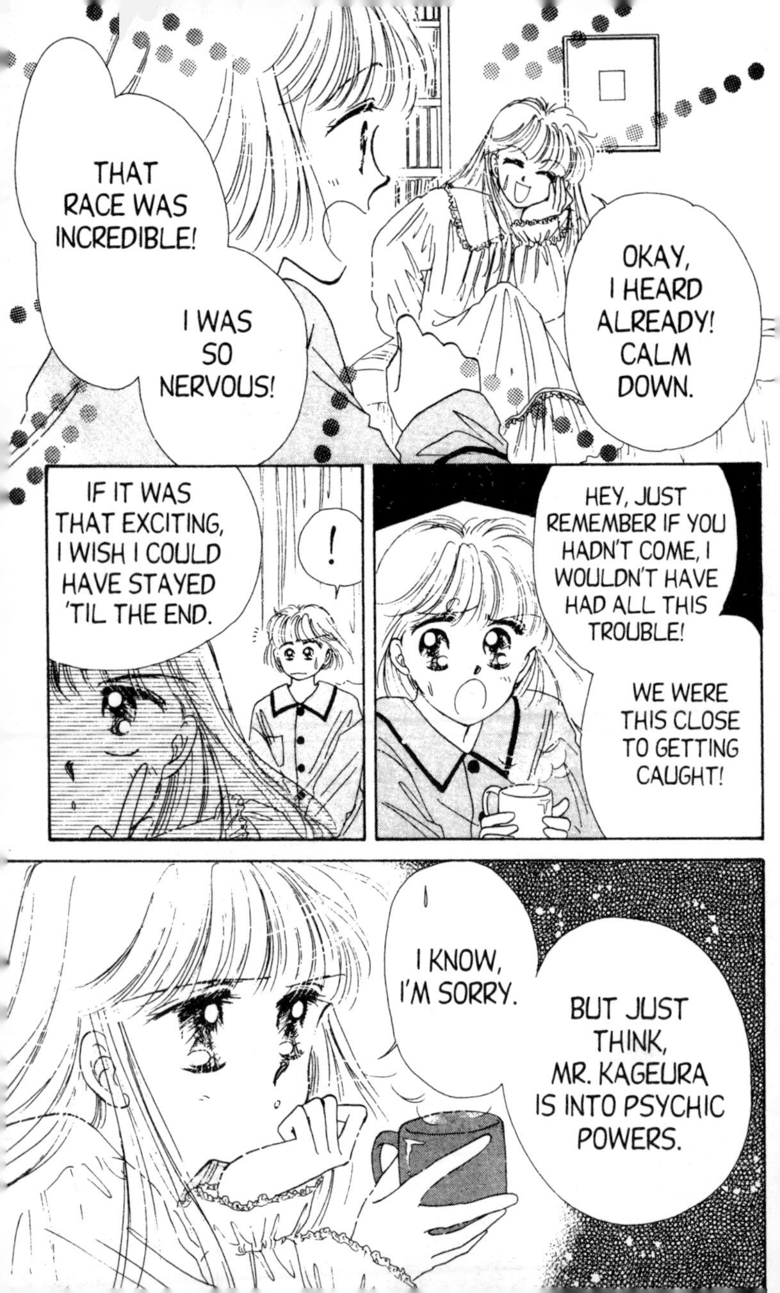
THAT RACE WAS INCREDIBLE!
I WAS SO NERVOUS!
OKAY, I HEARD ALREADY! CALM DOWN.
IF IT WAS THAT EXCITING, I WISH I COULD HAVE STAYED 'TIL THE END.
!
HEY, JUST REMEMBER IF YOU HADN'T COME, I WOULDN'T HAVE HAD ALL THIS TROUBLE!
WE WERE THIS CLOSE TO GETTING CAUGHT!
I KNOW, I'M SORRY.
BUT JUST THINK, MR. KAGEURA IS INTO PSYCHIC POWERS.

ANYWAY, OUR LITTLE GAME IS OVER.

THERE'S NO CHANCE OF GETTING CAUGHT ANYMORE.

I GUESS IT IS OVER.

NOW THAT SPORTS DAY IS FINISHED.

UM...

YEAH.

SO...

GAME OVER.

GOOD NIGHT, TONI.

THANKS FOR EVERYTHING.

BUT...

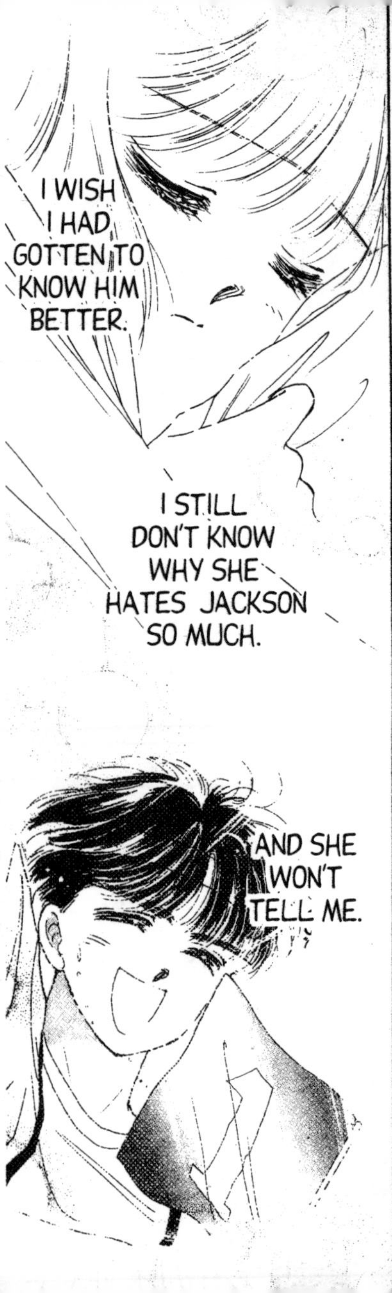
I WISH I HAD GOTTEN TO KNOW HIM BETTER.
I STILL DON'T KNOW WHY SHE HATES JACKSON SO MUCH.
AND SHE WON'T TELL ME.

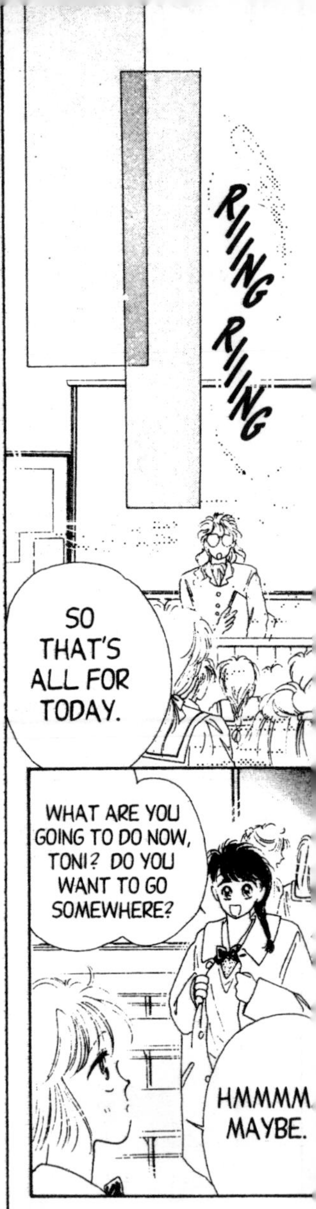
RIIING RIIING
SO THAT'S ALL FOR TODAY.
WHAT ARE YOU GOING TO DO NOW, TONI? DO YOU WANT TO GO SOMEWHERE?
HMMMM MAYBE.

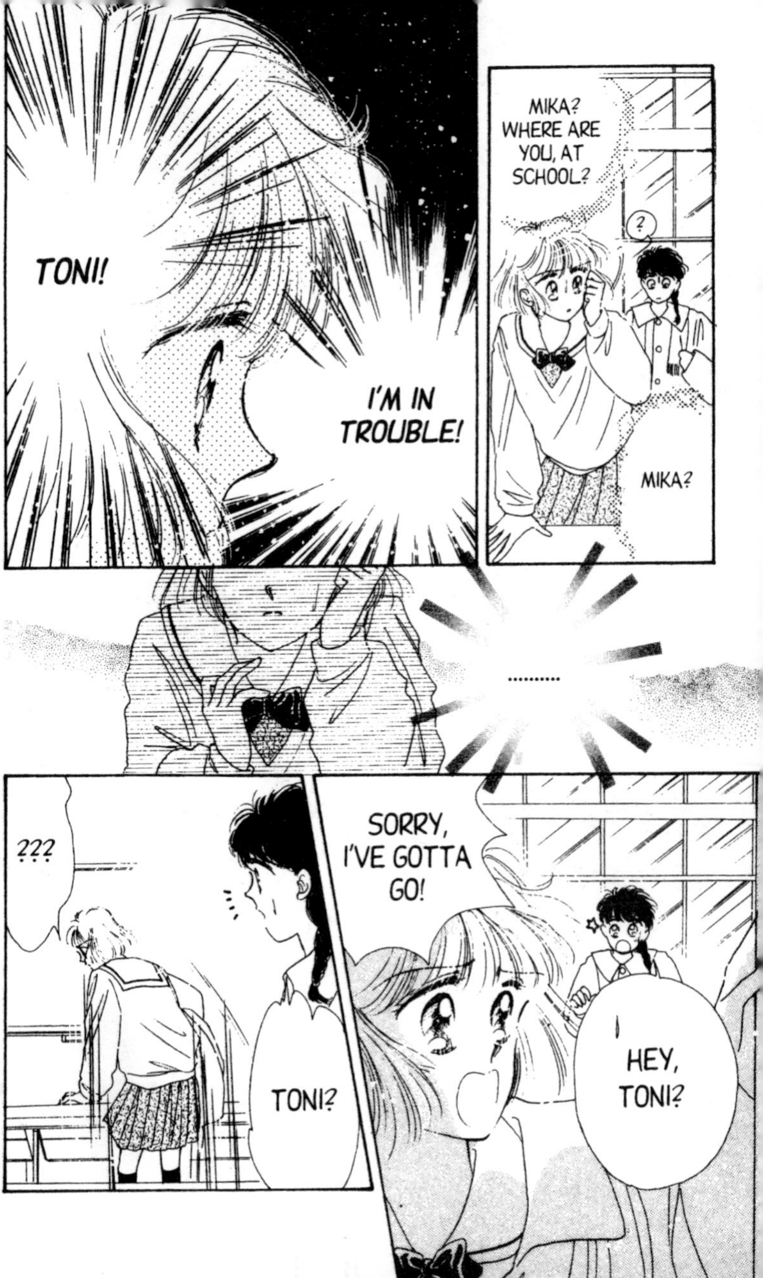
TONI!
I'M IN TROUBLE!
MIKA? WHERE ARE YOU, AT SCHOOL?
?
MIKA?
....
???
TONI?
SORRY, I'VE GOTTA GO!
HEY, TONI?

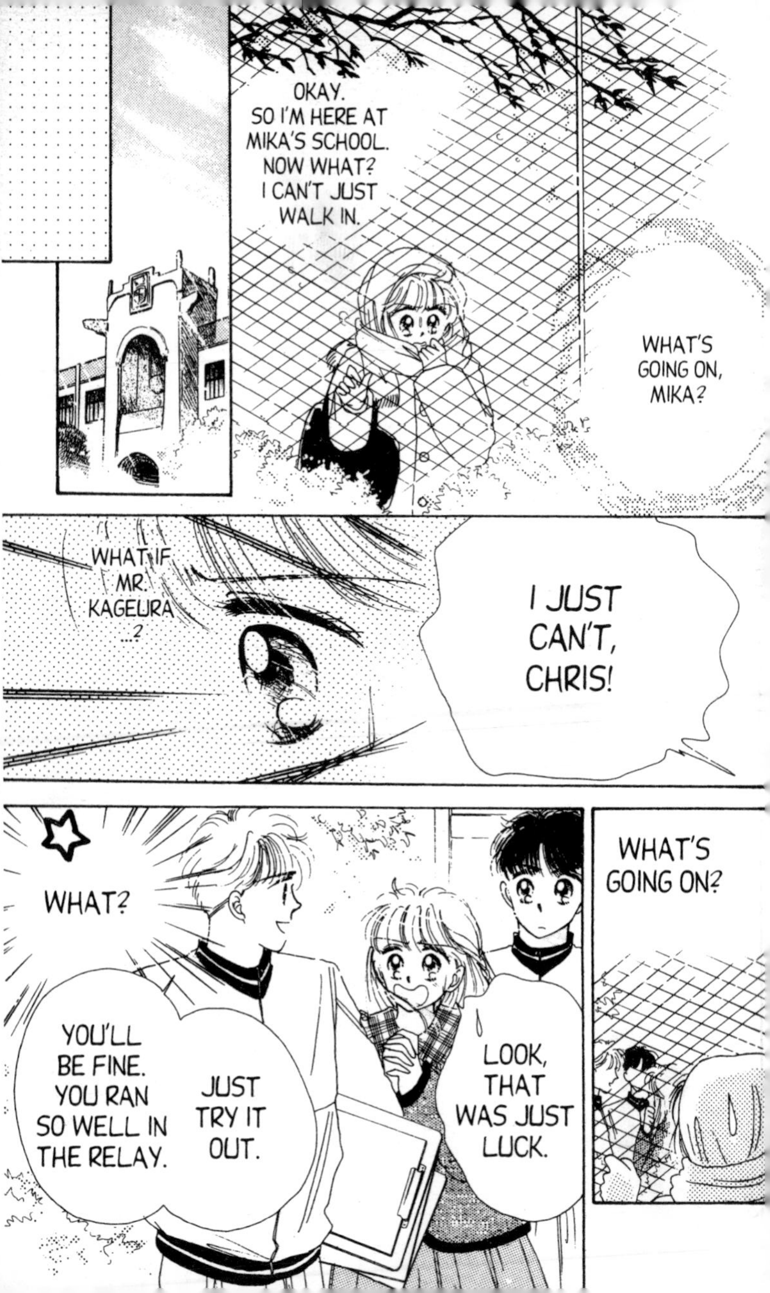
OKAY. SO I'M HERE AT MIKA'S SCHOOL. NOW WHAT? I CAN'T JUST WALK IN.
WHAT'S GOING ON, MIKA?
WHAT IF MR. KAGEURA ...?
I JUST CAN'T, CHRIS!
WHAT?
YOU'LL BE FINE. YOU RAN SO WELL IN THE RELAY.
JUST TRY IT OUT.
LOOK, THAT WAS JUST LUCK.
WHAT'S GOING ON?

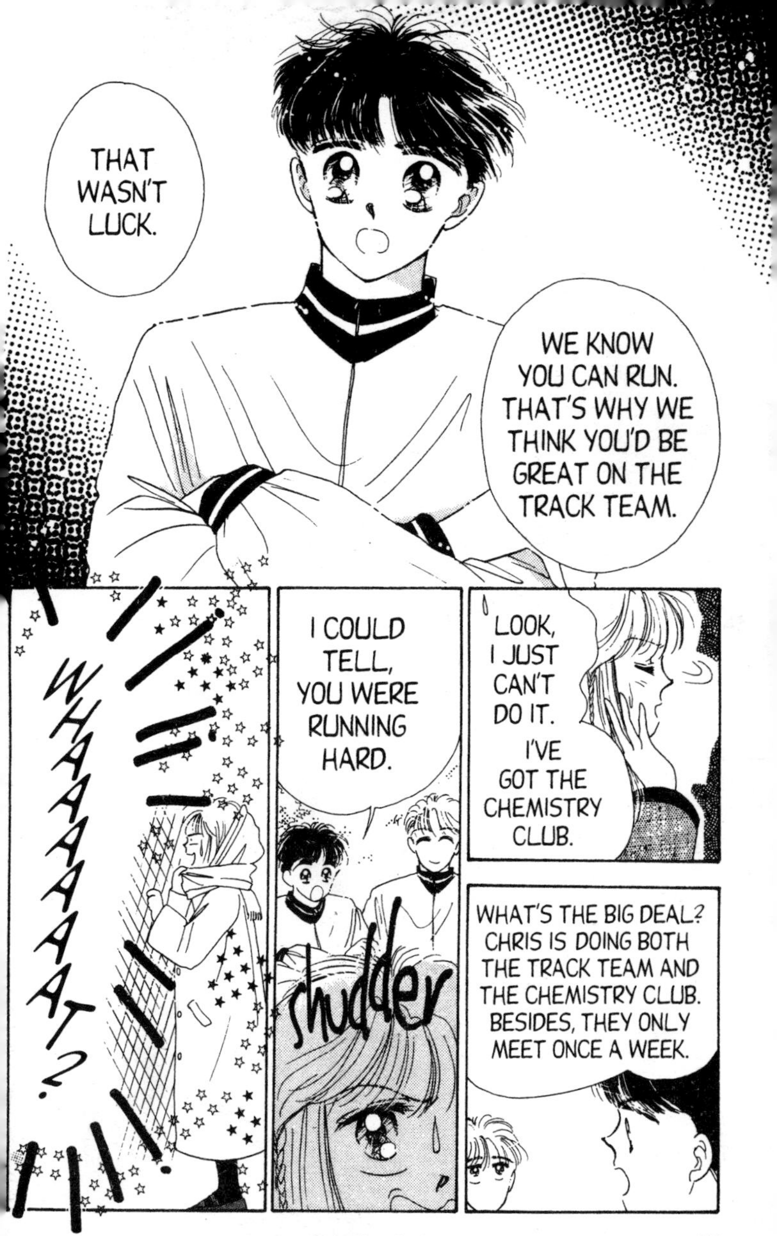
THAT WASN'T LUCK.
WE KNOW YOU CAN RUN. THAT'S WHY WE THINK YOU'D BE GREAT ON THE TRACK TEAM.
WHAAAAAAAT?
I COULD TELL, YOU WERE RUNNING HARD.
shudder
LOOK, I JUST CAN'T DO IT.
I'VE GOT THE CHEMISTRY CLUB.
WHAT'S THE BIG DEAL? CHRIS IS DOING BOTH THE TRACK TEAM AND THE CHEMISTRY CLUB. BESIDES, THEY ONLY MEET ONCE A WEEK.

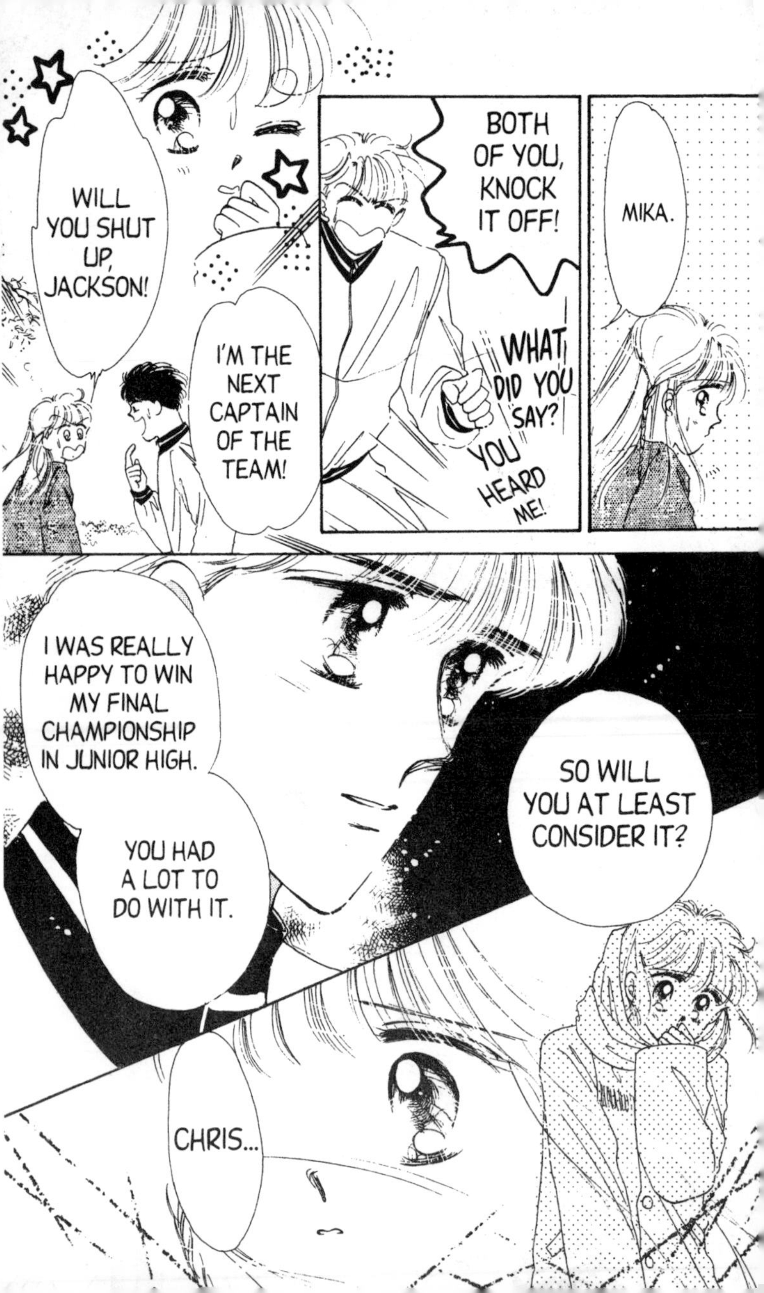
WILL YOU SHUT UP, JACKSON!
I'M THE NEXT CAPTAIN OF THE TEAM!
BOTH OF YOU, KNOCK IT OFF!
WHAT DID YOU SAY?
YOU HEARD ME!
MIKA.
I WAS REALLY HAPPY TO WIN MY FINAL CHAMPIONSHIP IN JUNIOR HIGH.
YOU HAD A LOT TO DO WITH IT.
SO WILL YOU AT LEAST CONSIDER IT?
CHRIS...

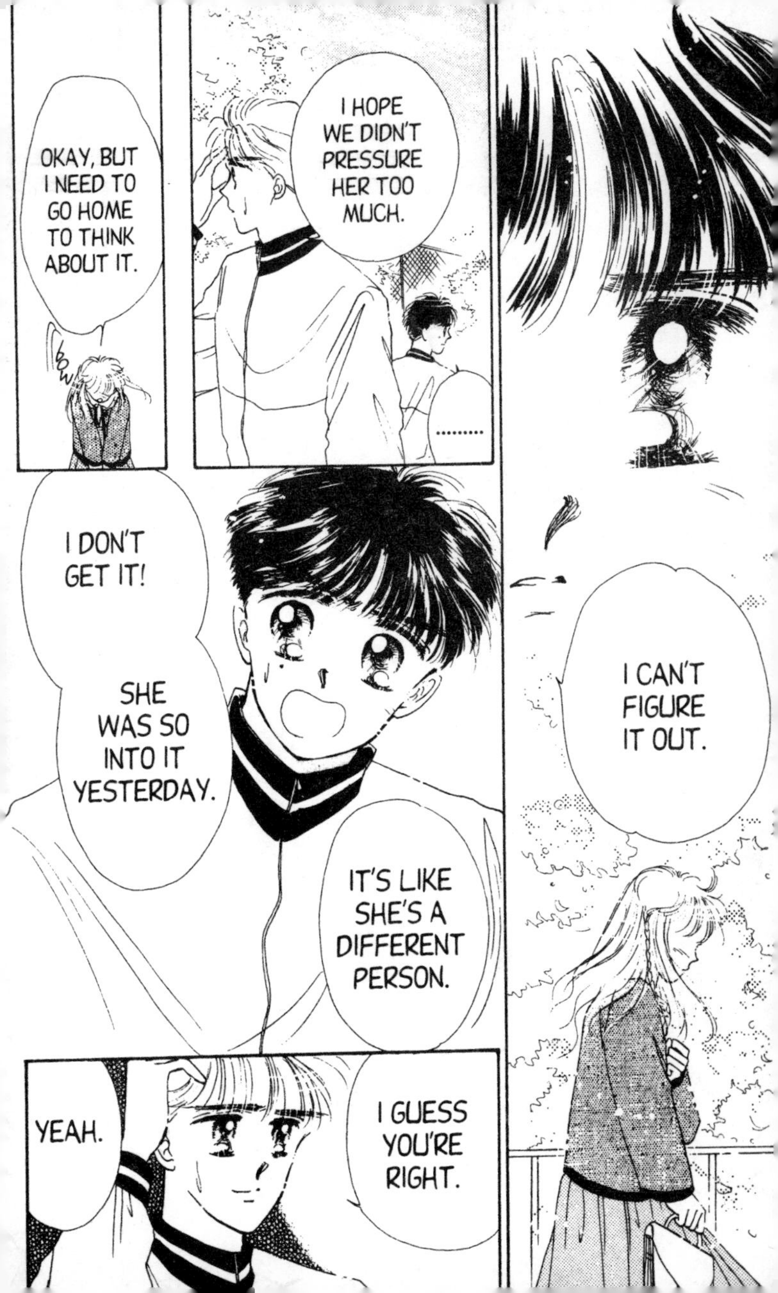

OKAY, BUT I NEED TO GO HOME TO THINK ABOUT IT.
BOW
I HOPE WE DIDN'T PRESSURE HER TOO MUCH.
....
I DON'T GET IT!
SHE WAS SO INTO IT YESTERDAY.
IT'S LIKE SHE'S A DIFFERENT PERSON.
YEAH.
I GUESS YOU'RE RIGHT.
I CAN'T FIGURE IT OUT.

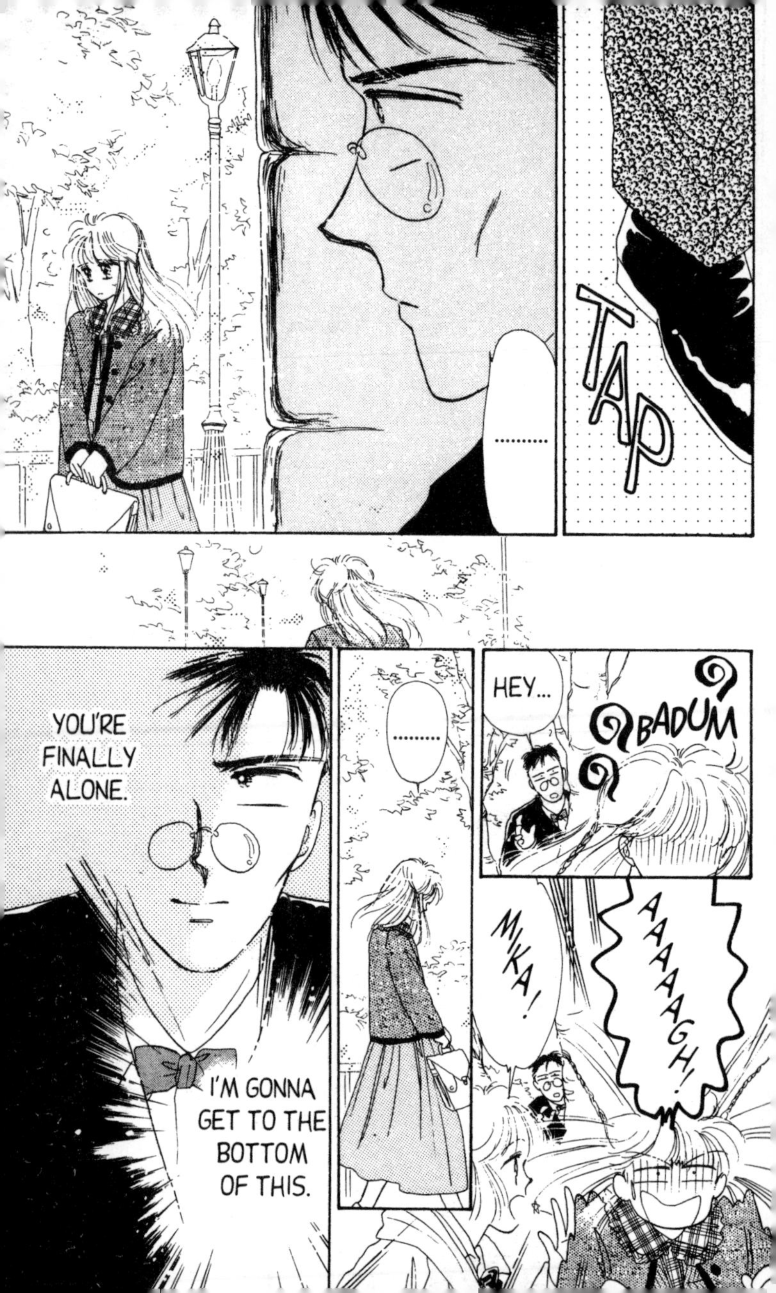
TAP
....
HEY...
BADUM
AAAAAGH!
MIKA!
....
YOU'RE FINALLY ALONE.
I'M GONNA GET TO THE BOTTOM OF THIS.

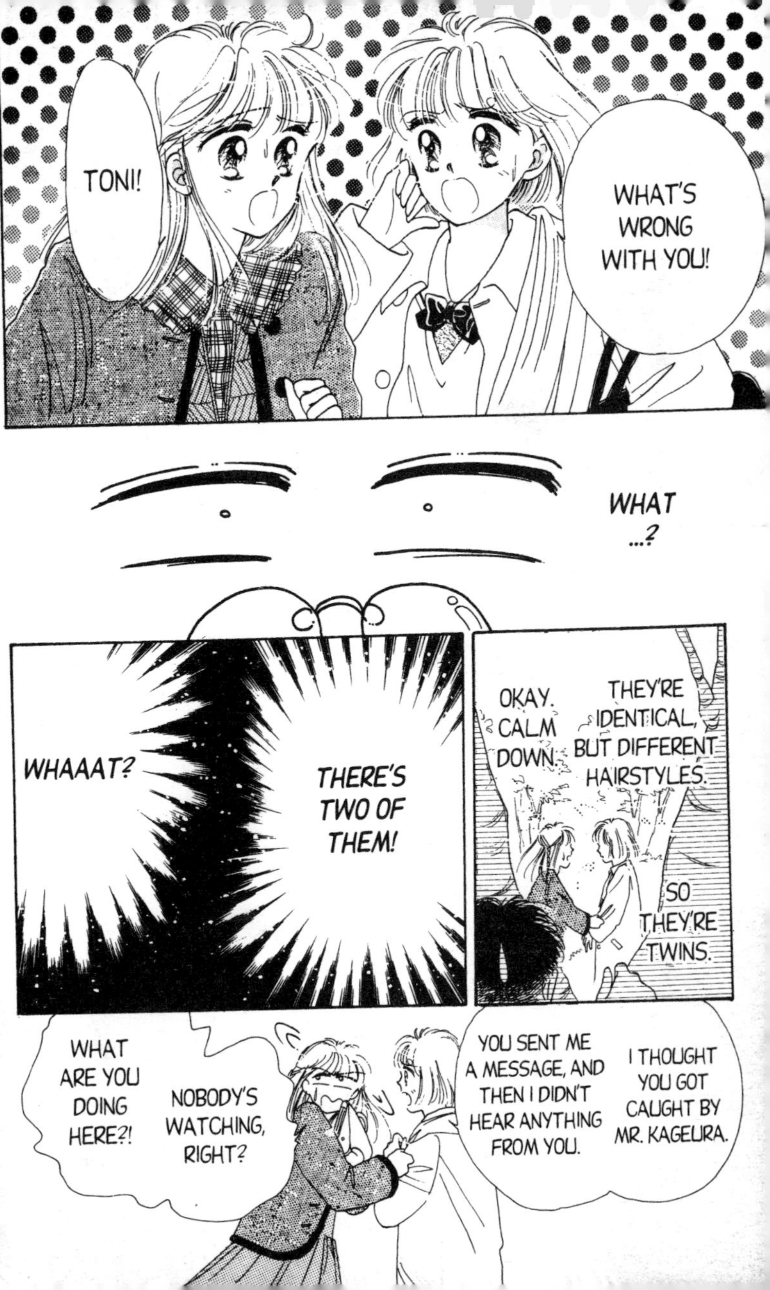
TONI!
WHAT'S WRONG WITH YOU!
WHAT ...?
WHAAAT?
THERE'S TWO OF THEM!
OKAY. CALM DOWN.
THEY'RE IDENTICAL, BUT DIFFERENT HAIRSTYLES.
SO THEY'RE TWINS.
WHAT ARE YOU DOING HERE?!
NOBODY'S WATCHING, RIGHT?
YOU SENT ME A MESSAGE, AND THEN I DIDN'T HEAR ANYTHING FROM YOU.
I THOUGHT YOU GOT CAUGHT BY MR. KAGEURA.

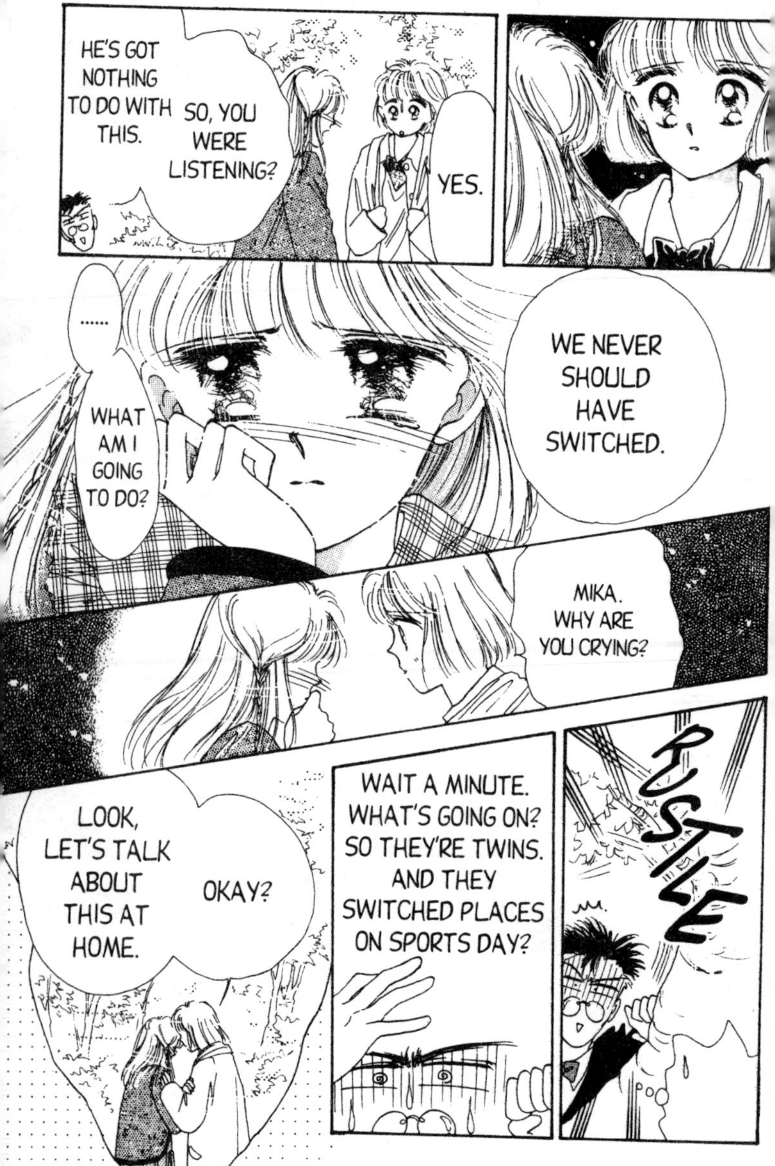
HE'S GOT NOTHING TO DO WITH THIS.
SO, YOU WERE LISTENING?
YES.
......
WHAT AM I GOING TO DO?
WE NEVER SHOULD HAVE SWITCHED.
MIKA. WHY ARE YOU CRYING?
LOOK, LET'S TALK ABOUT THIS AT HOME.
OKAY?
WAIT A MINUTE. WHAT'S GOING ON? SO THEY'RE TWINS. AND THEY SWITCHED PLACES ON SPORTS DAY?
RUSTLE

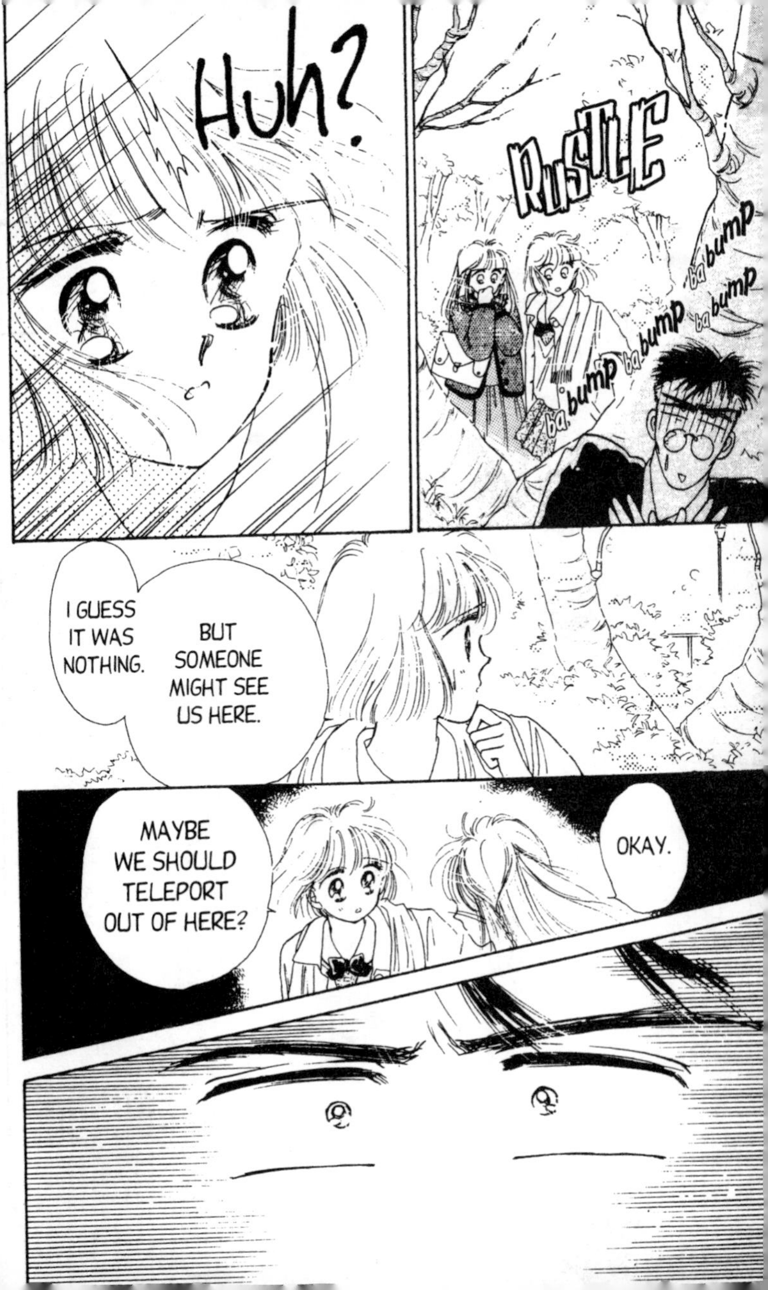
Huh?
RUSTLE
ba bump ba bump ba bump ba bump ba bump
I GUESS IT WAS NOTHING.
BUT SOMEONE MIGHT SEE US HERE.
MAYBE WE SHOULD TELEPORT OUT OF HERE?
OKAY.

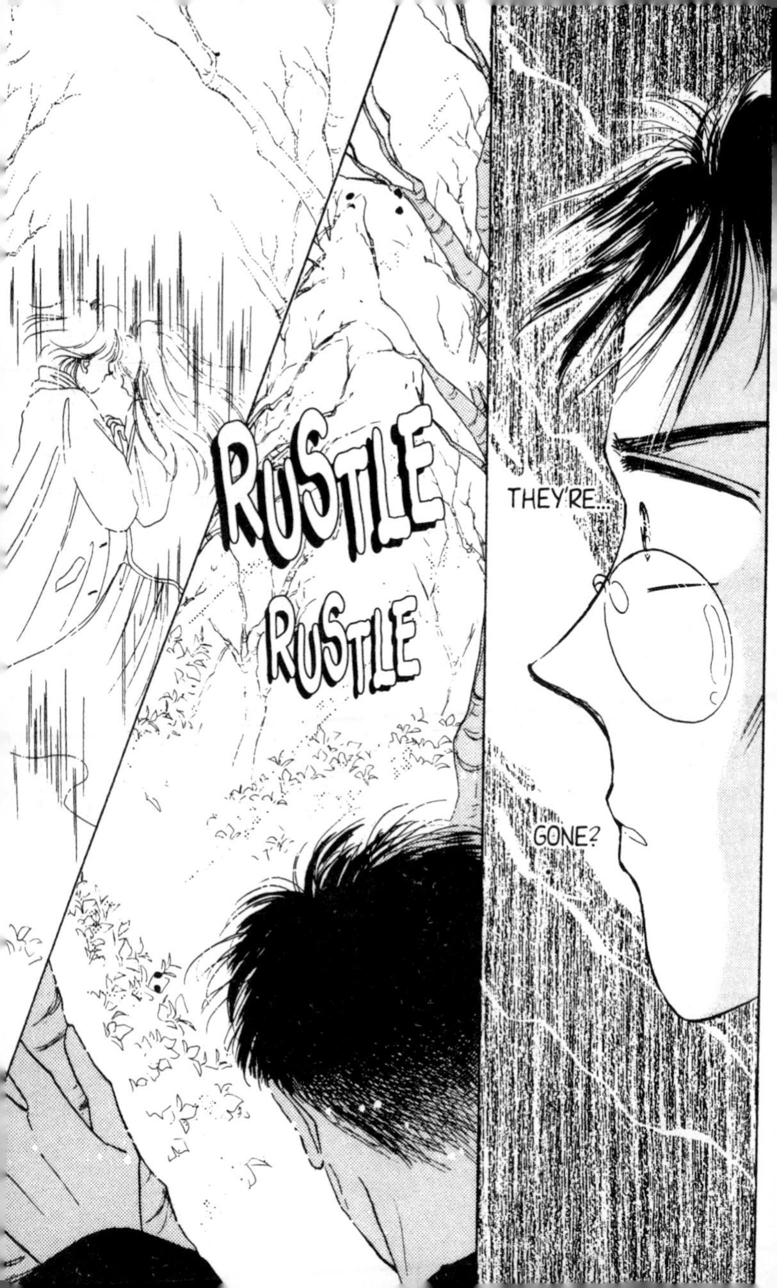
RUSTLE
RUSTLE
THEY'RE...
GONE?

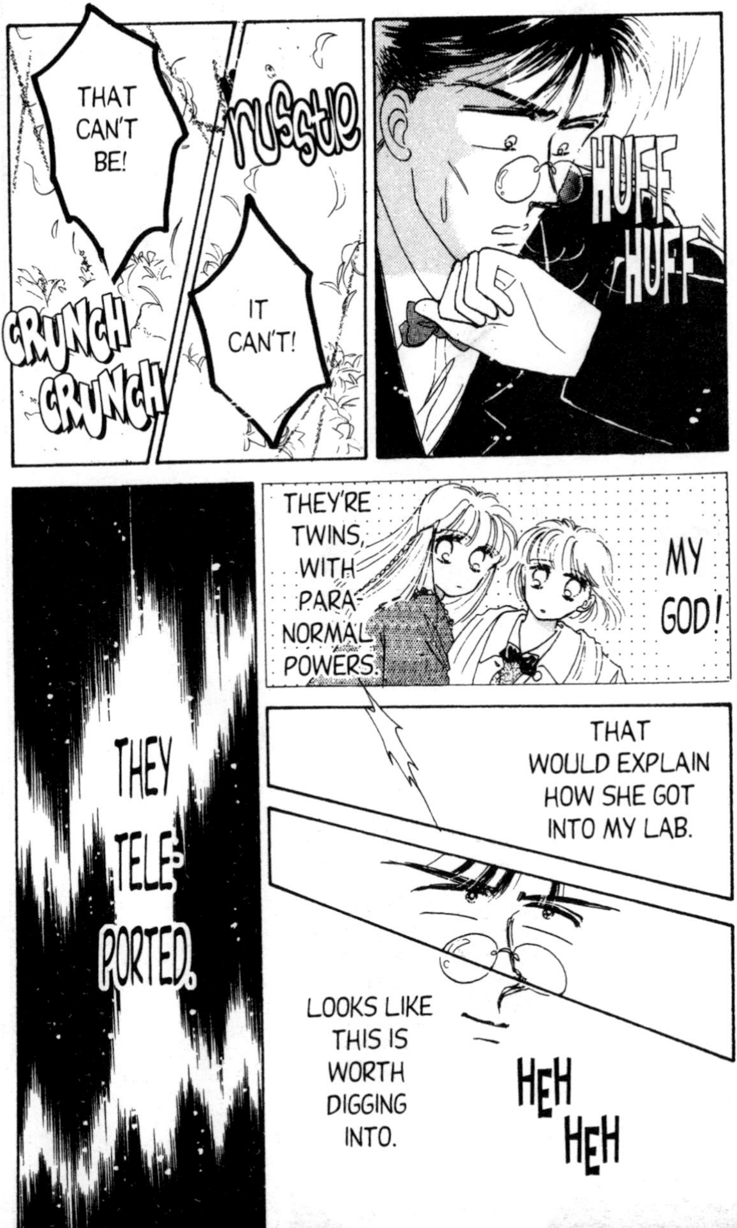
THAT CAN'T BE!
CRUNCH CRUNCH
rustle
IT CAN'T!
HUFF HUFF
THEY TELE-PORTED.
THEY'RE TWINS, WITH PARANORMAL POWERS.
MY GOD!
THAT WOULD EXPLAIN HOW SHE GOT INTO MY LAB.
LOOKS LIKE THIS IS WORTH DIGGING INTO.
HEH HEH

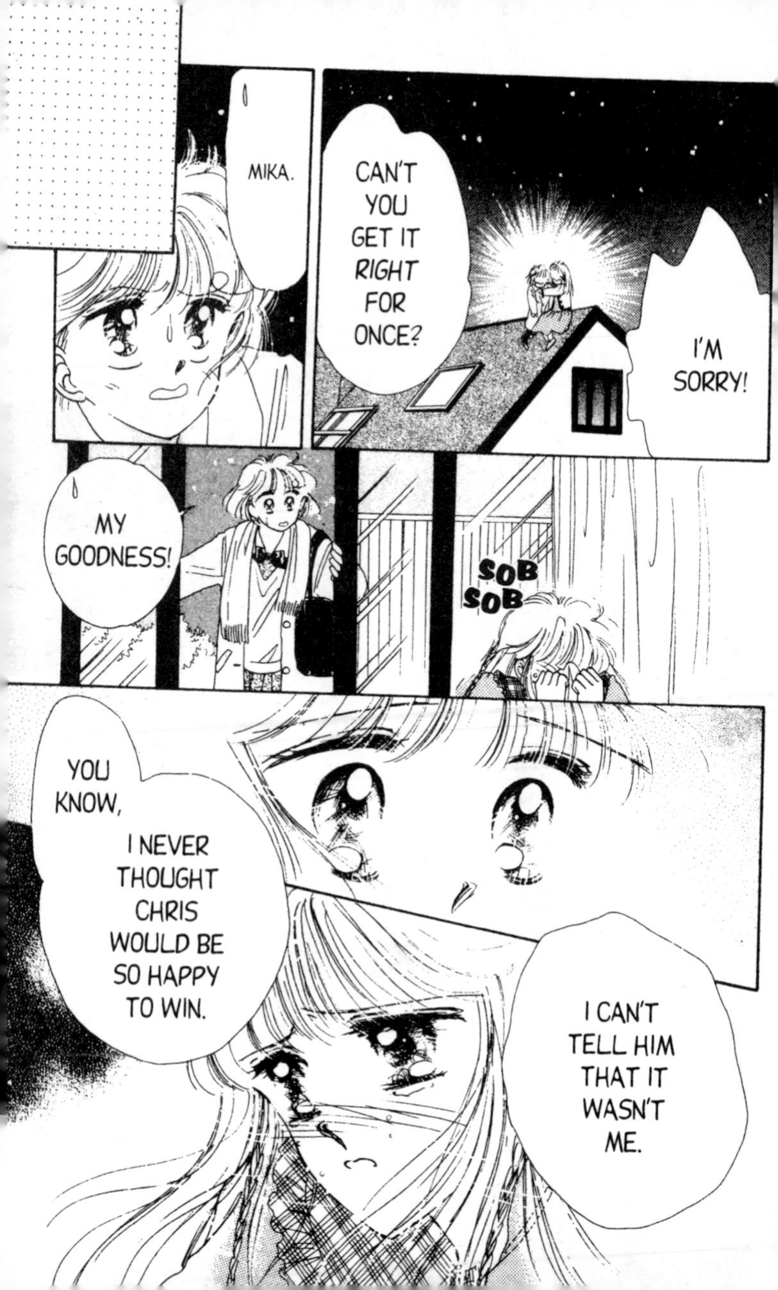
MIKA.
CAN'T YOU GET IT RIGHT FOR ONCE?
I'M SORRY!
MY GOODNESS!
SOB SOB
YOU KNOW,
I NEVER THOUGHT CHRIS WOULD BE SO HAPPY TO WIN.
I CAN'T TELL HIM THAT IT WASN'T ME.

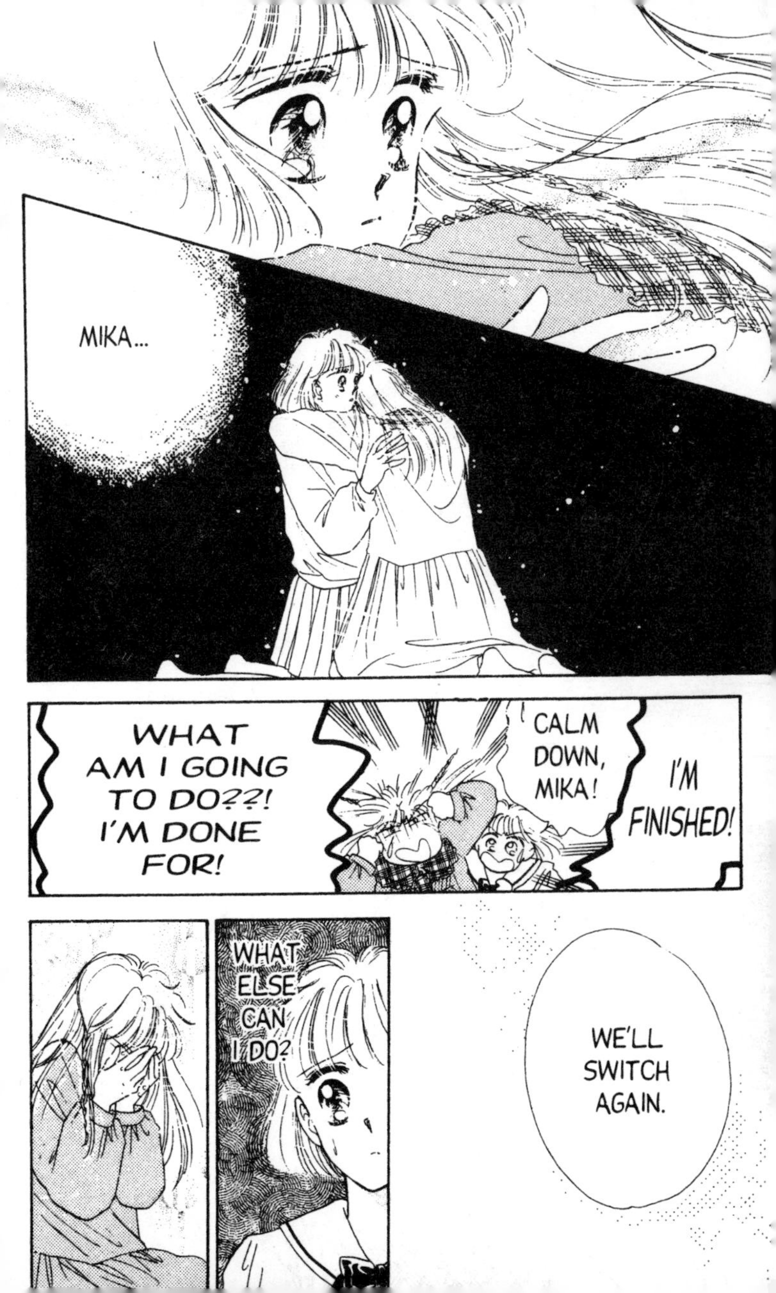
MIKA...
WHAT AM I GOING TO DO??! I'M DONE FOR!
CALM DOWN, MIKA!
I'M FINISHED!
WHAT ELSE CAN I DO?
WE'LL SWITCH AGAIN.

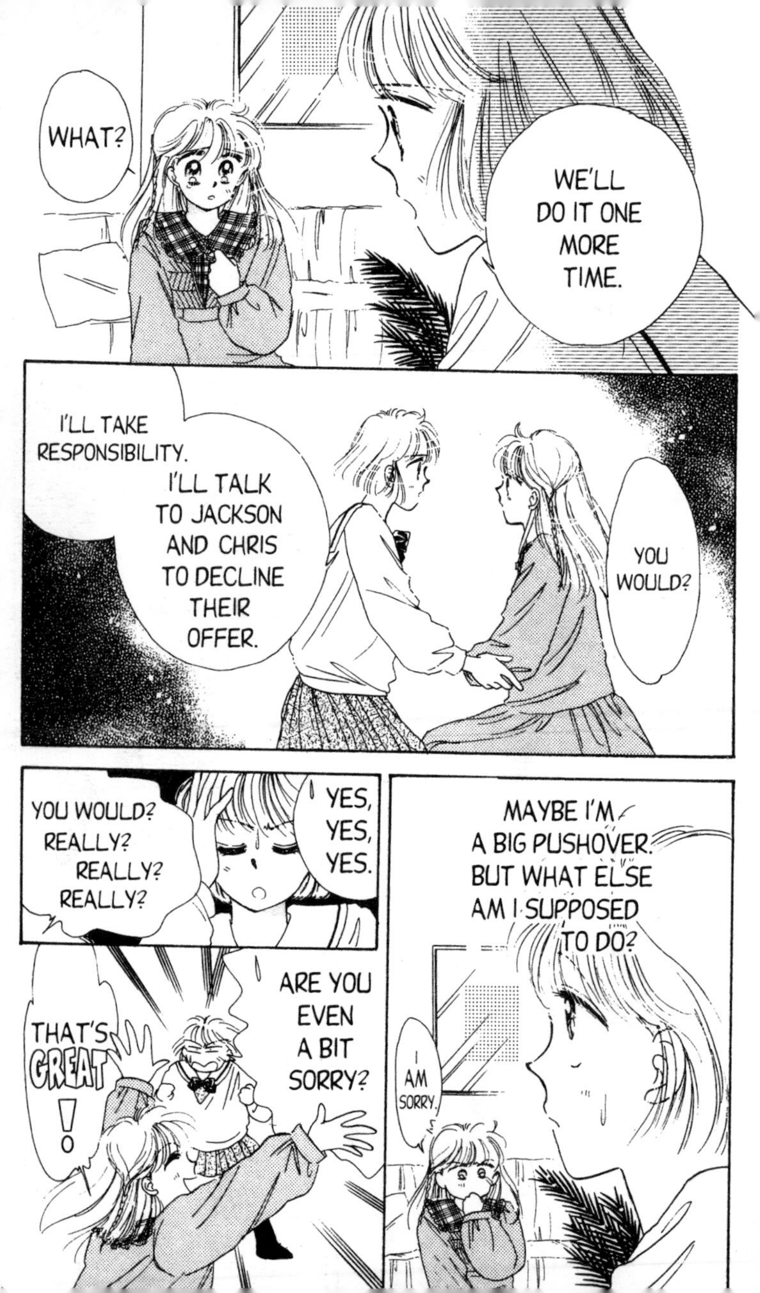
WHAT?
WE'LL DO IT ONE MORE TIME.
I'LL TAKE RESPONSIBILITY. I'LL TALK TO JACKSON AND CHRIS TO DECLINE THEIR OFFER.
YOU WOULD?
YOU WOULD? REALLY? REALLY? REALLY?
YES, YES, YES.
MAYBE I'M A BIG PUSHOVER. BUT WHAT ELSE AM I SUPPOSED TO DO?
THAT'S GREAT!
ARE YOU EVEN A BIT SORRY?
I AM SORRY.

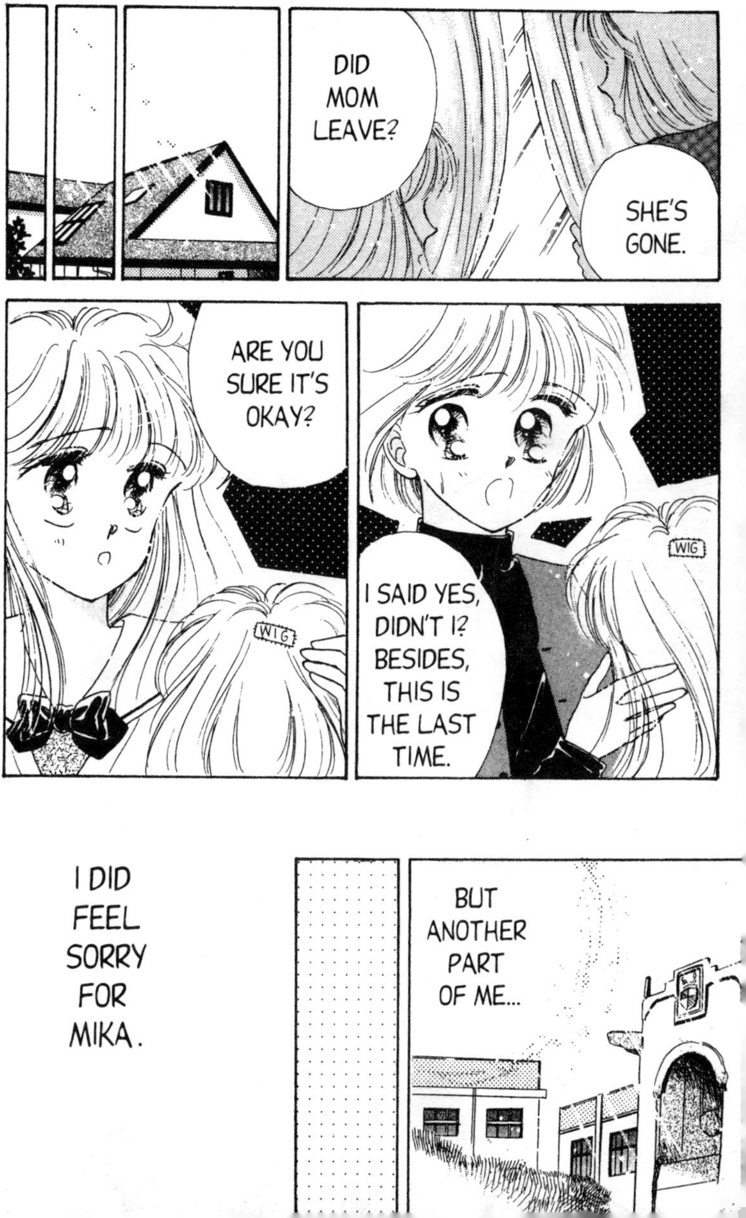
DID MOM LEAVE?
SHE'S GONE.
ARE YOU SURE IT'S OKAY?
WIG
I SAID YES, DIDN'T I? BESIDES, THIS IS THE LAST TIME.
WIG
I DID FEEL SORRY FOR MIKA.
BUT ANOTHER PART OF ME...

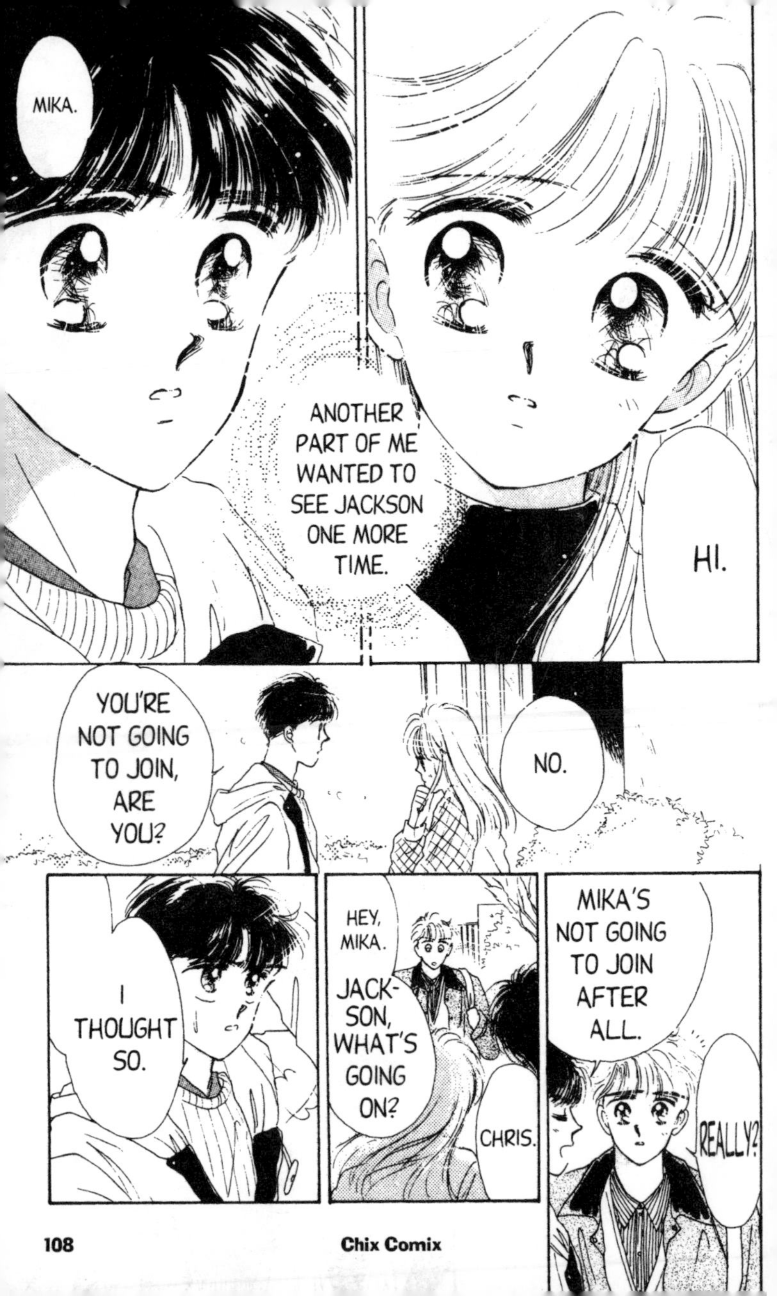
MIKA.
ANOTHER PART OF ME WANTED TO SEE JACKSON ONE MORE TIME.
HI.
YOU'RE NOT GOING TO JOIN, ARE YOU?
NO.
I THOUGHT SO.
HEY, MIKA.
JACKSON, WHAT'S GOING ON?
CHRIS.
MIKA'S NOT GOING TO JOIN AFTER ALL.
REALLY?

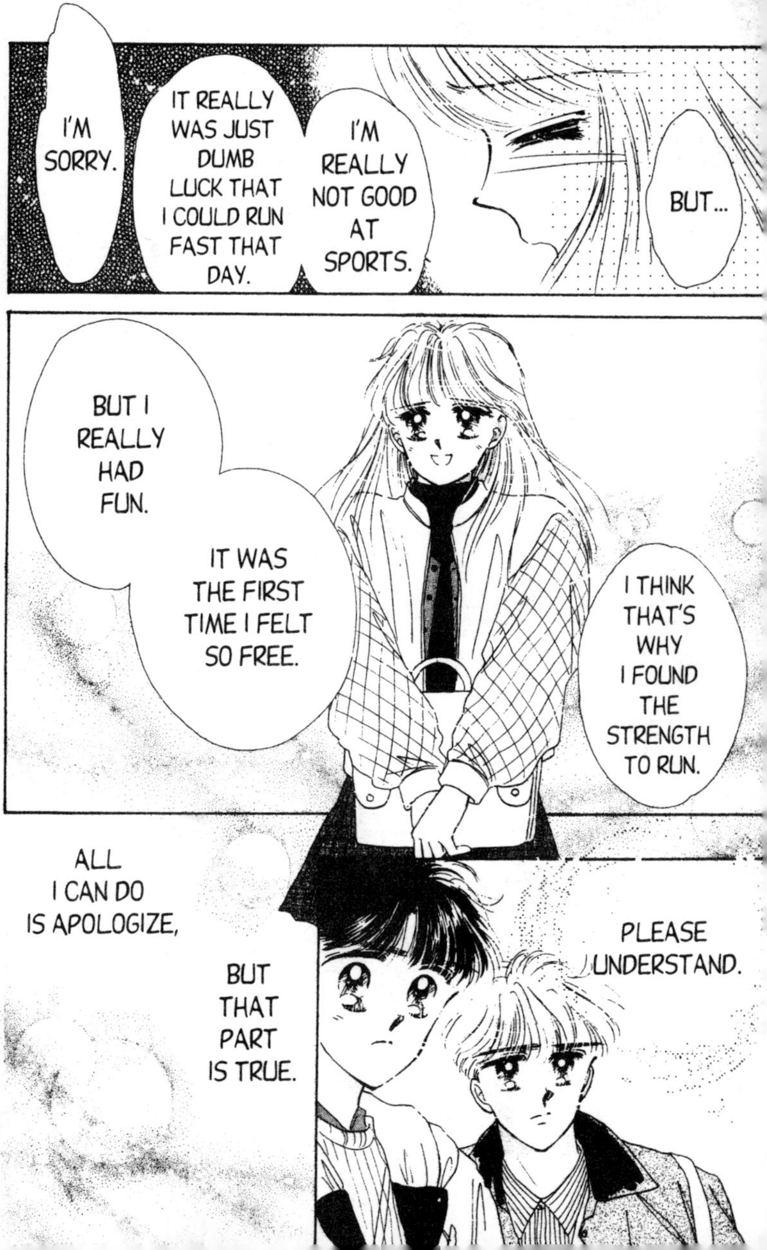
I'M SORRY.
IT REALLY WAS JUST DUMB LUCK THAT I COULD RUN FAST THAT DAY.
I'M REALLY NOT GOOD AT SPORTS.
BUT...
BUT I REALLY HAD FUN.
IT WAS THE FIRST TIME I FELT SO FREE.
I THINK THAT'S WHY I FOUND THE STRENGTH TO RUN.
ALL I CAN DO IS APOLOGIZE,
BUT THAT PART IS TRUE.
PLEASE UNDERSTAND.

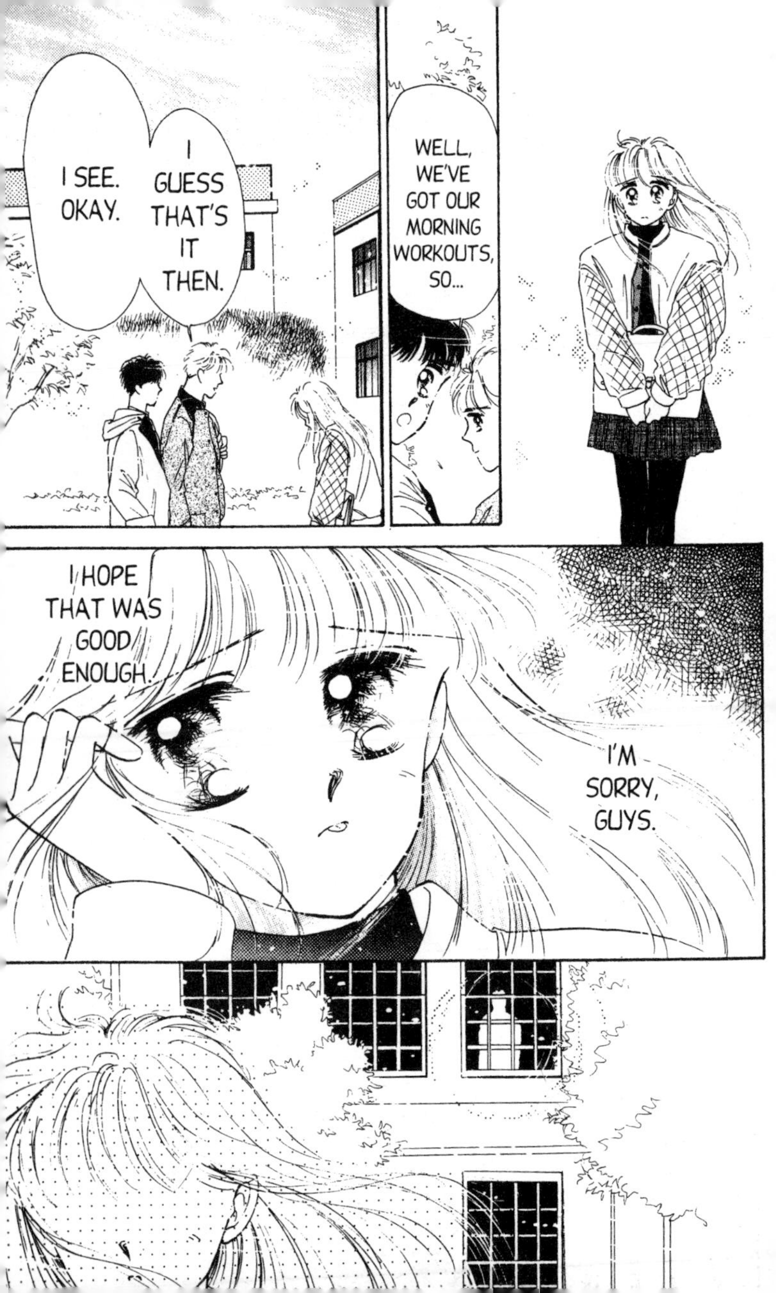
I SEE. OKAY.
I GUESS THAT'S IT THEN.
WELL, WE'VE GOT OUR MORNING WORKOUTS, SO...
I HOPE THAT WAS GOOD ENOUGH.
I'M SORRY, GUYS.

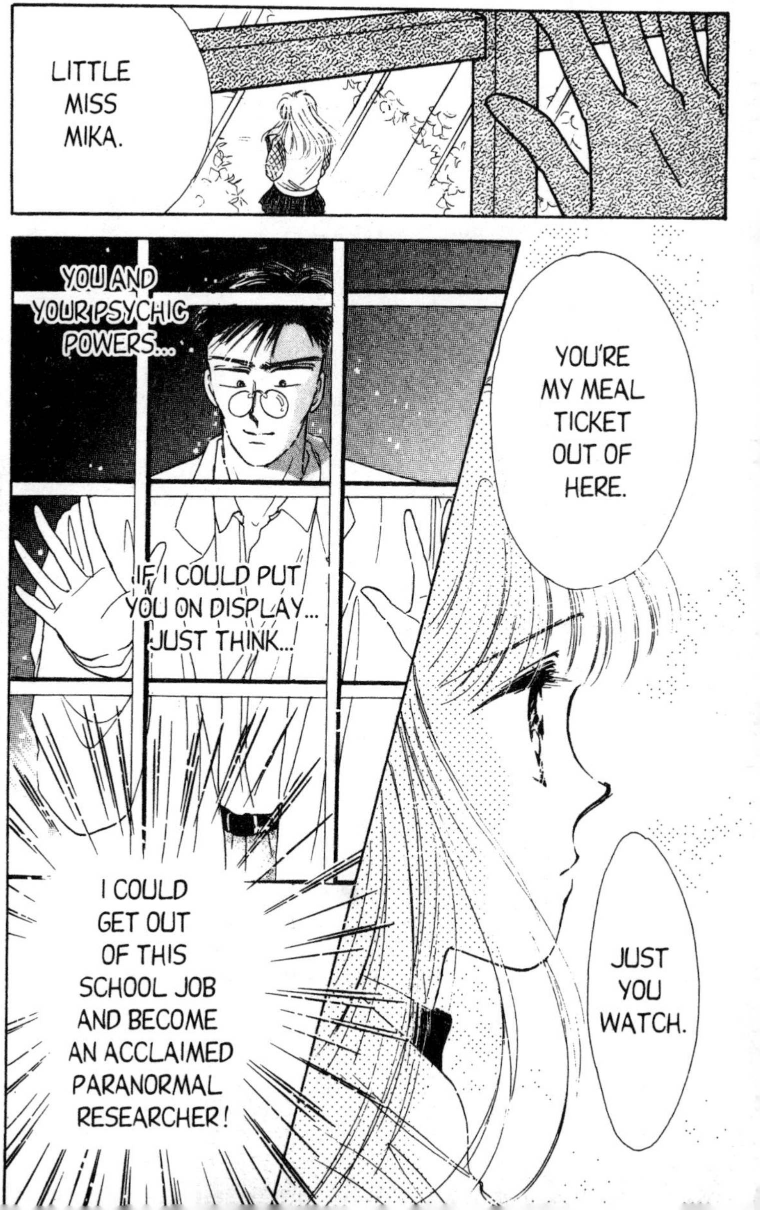
LITTLE MISS MIKA.
YOU AND YOUR PSYCHIC POWERS...
IF I COULD PUT YOU ON DISPLAY... JUST THINK...
YOU'RE MY MEAL TICKET OUT OF HERE.
I COULD GET OUT OF THIS SCHOOL JOB AND BECOME AN ACCLAIMED PARANORMAL RESEARCHER!
JUST YOU WATCH.

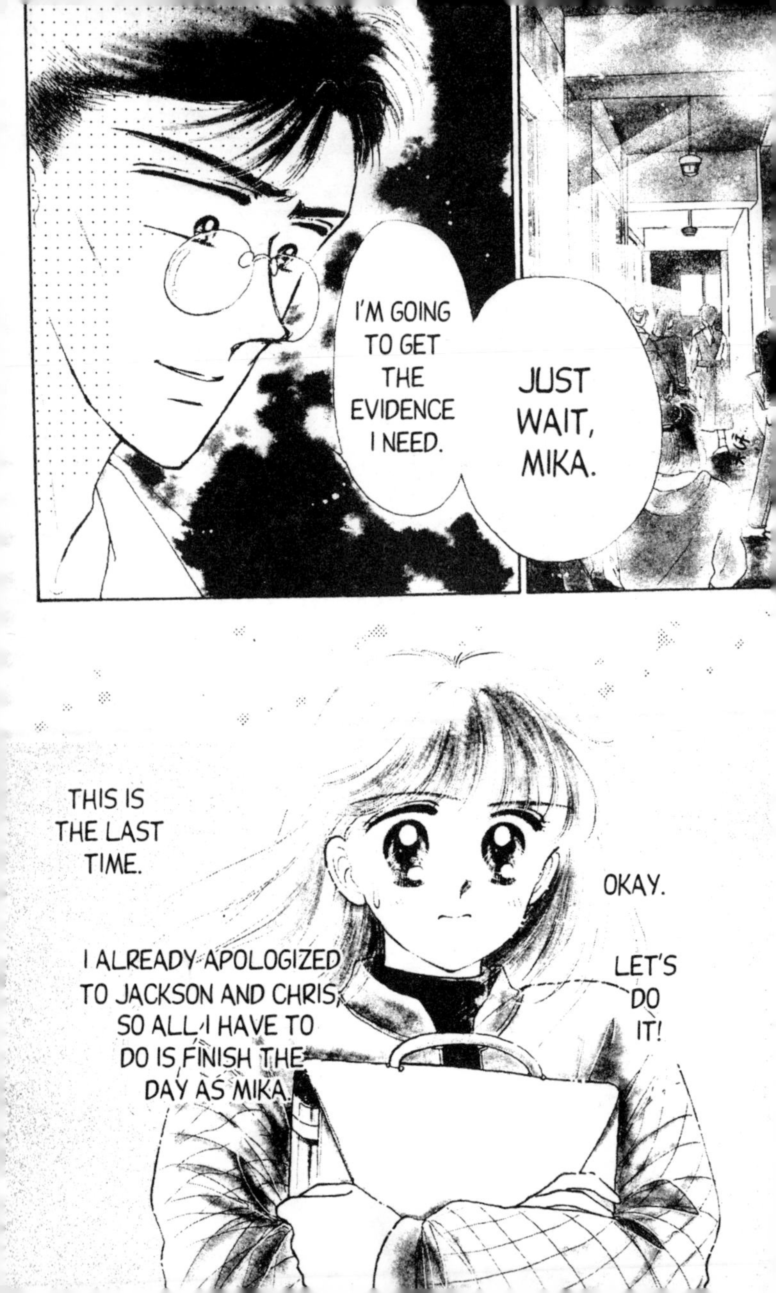
I'M GOING TO GET THE EVIDENCE I NEED.
JUST WAIT, MIKA.
THIS IS THE LAST TIME.
I ALREADY APOLOGIZED TO JACKSON AND CHRIS, SO ALL I HAVE TO DO IS FINISH THE DAY AS MIKA.
OKAY.
LET'S DO IT!

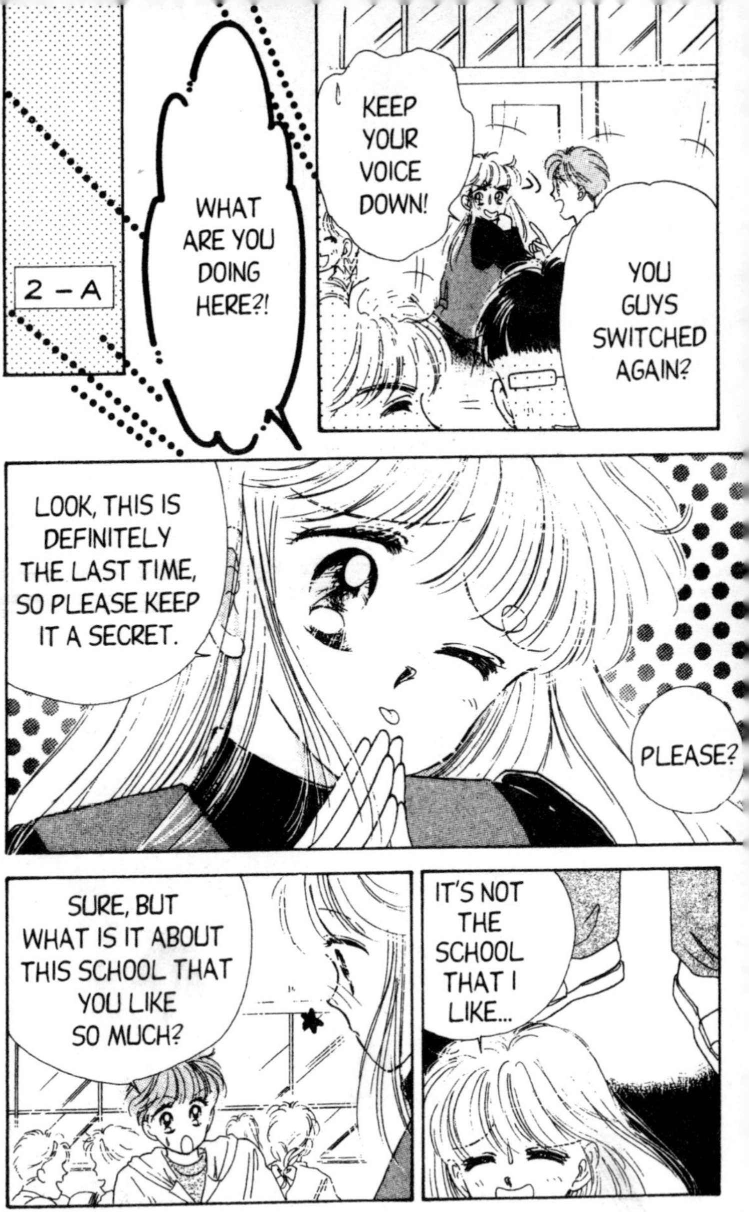
2 – A
WHAT ARE YOU DOING HERE?!
KEEP YOUR VOICE DOWN!
YOU GUYS SWITCHED AGAIN?
LOOK, THIS IS DEFINITELY THE LAST TIME, SO PLEASE KEEP IT A SECRET.
PLEASE?
SURE, BUT WHAT IS IT ABOUT THIS SCHOOL THAT YOU LIKE SO MUCH?
IT'S NOT THE SCHOOL THAT I LIKE...

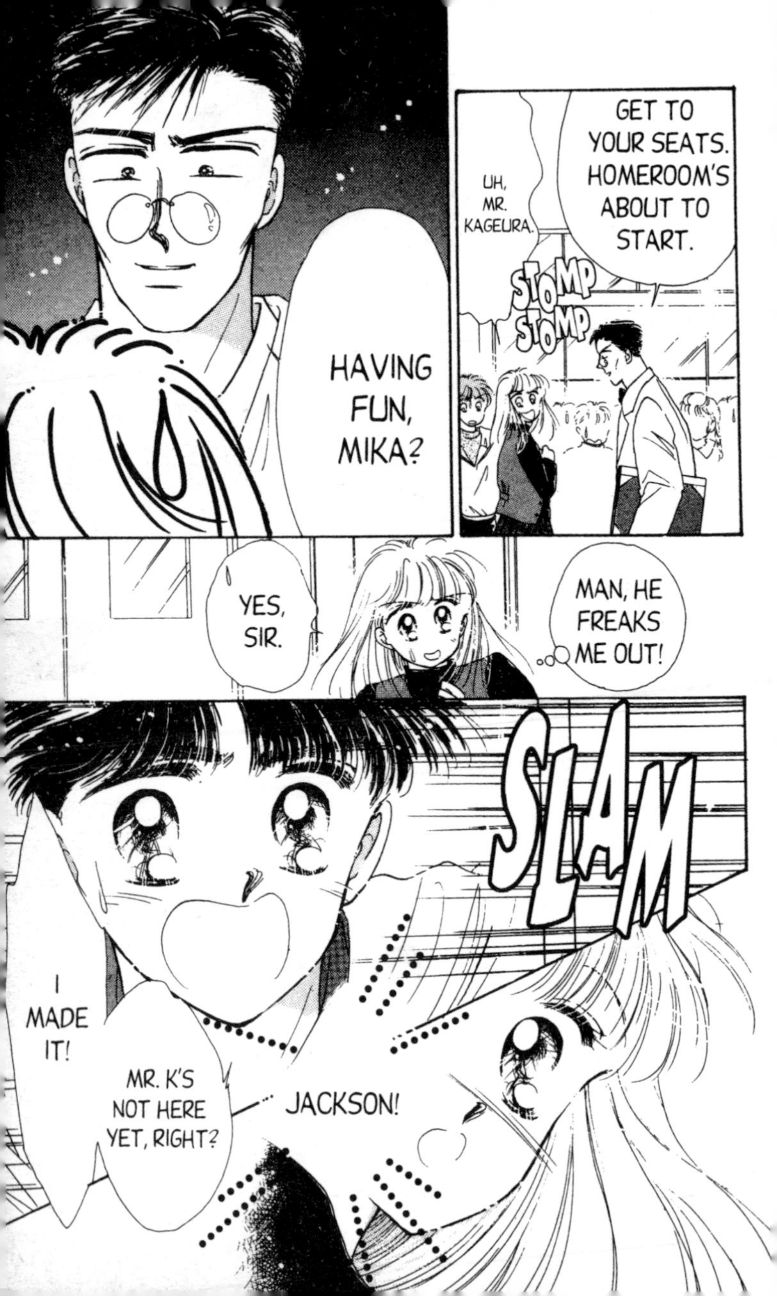
HAVING FUN, MIKA?
UH, MR. KAGEURA.
GET TO YOUR SEATS. HOMEROOM'S ABOUT TO START.
STOMP STOMP
YES, SIR.
MAN, HE FREAKS ME OUT!
SLAM
I MADE IT!
MR. K'S NOT HERE YET, RIGHT?
JACKSON!

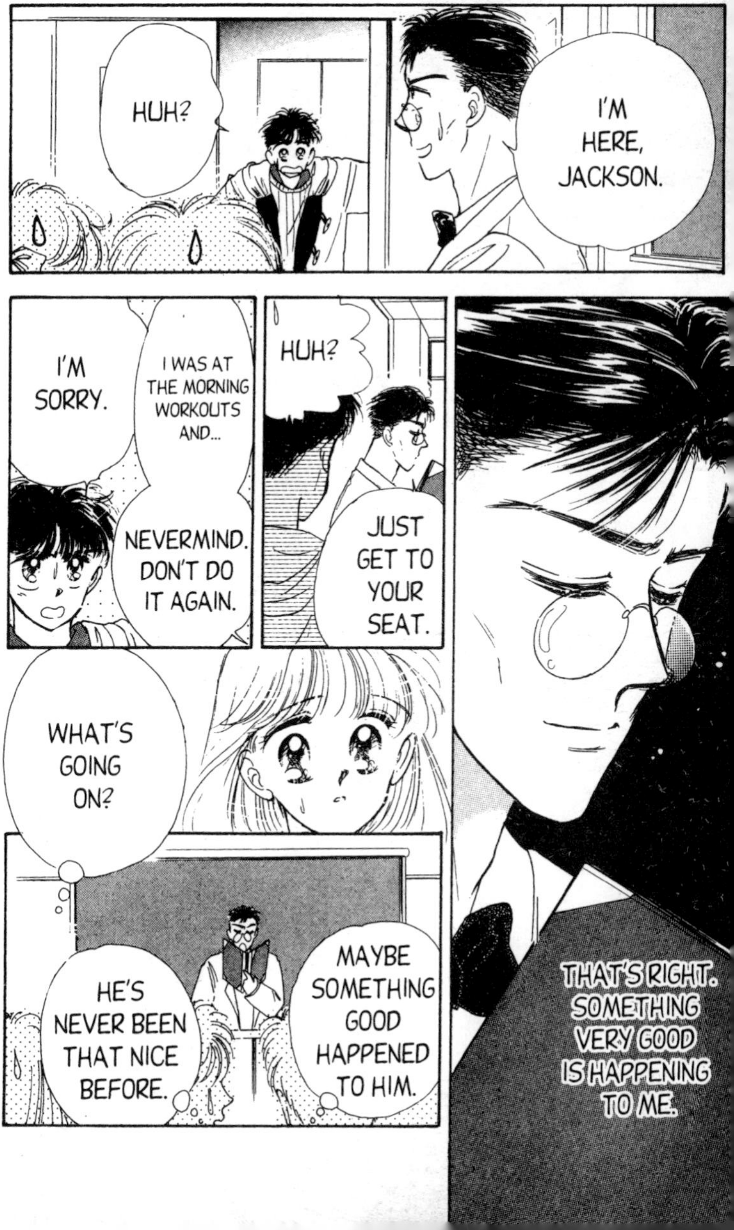
HUH?
I'M HERE, JACKSON.
I'M SORRY.
I WAS AT THE MORNING WORKOUTS AND...
NEVERMIND. DON'T DO IT AGAIN.
HUH?
JUST GET TO YOUR SEAT.
WHAT'S GOING ON?
HE'S NEVER BEEN THAT NICE BEFORE.
MAYBE SOMETHING GOOD HAPPENED TO HIM.
THAT'S RIGHT. SOMETHING VERY GOOD IS HAPPENING TO ME.

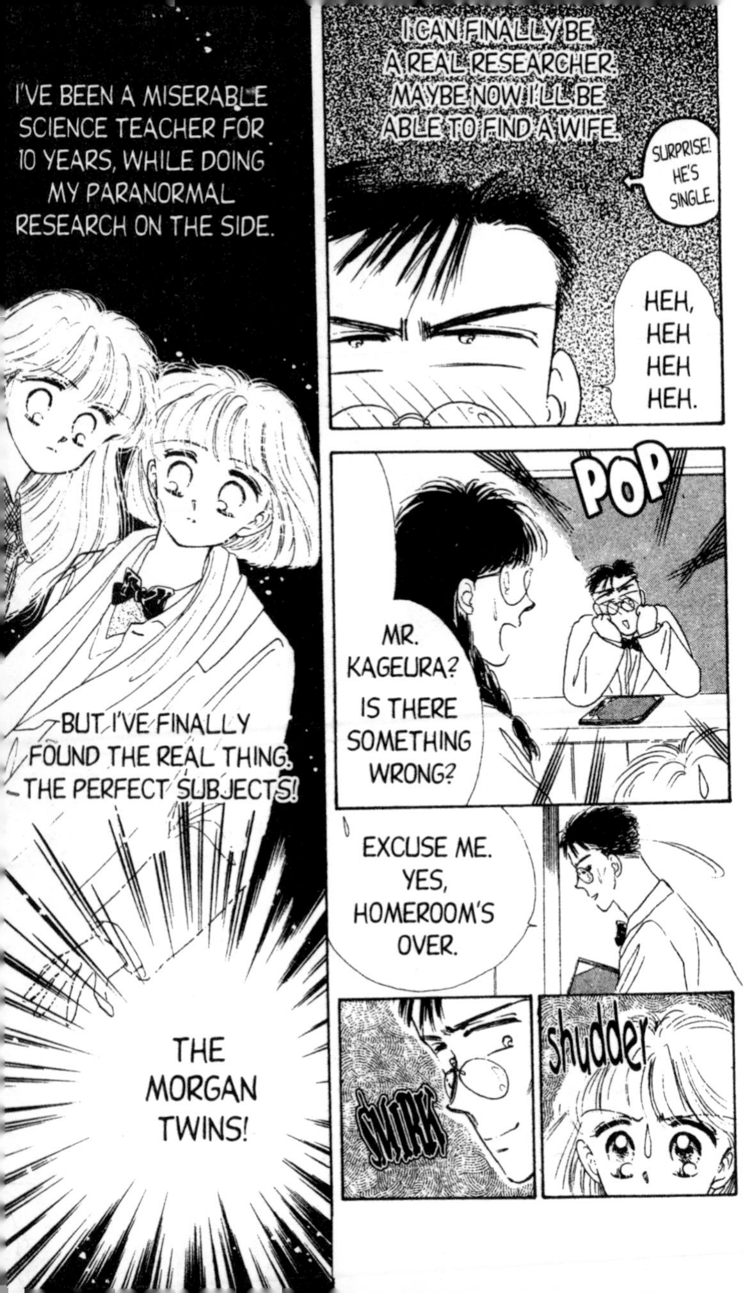
I'VE BEEN A MISERABLE SCIENCE TEACHER FOR 10 YEARS, WHILE DOING MY PARANORMAL RESEARCH ON THE SIDE.
BUT I'VE FINALLY FOUND THE REAL THING. THE PERFECT SUBJECTS!
THE MORGAN TWINS!
I CAN FINALLY BE A REAL RESEARCHER. MAYBE NOW I'LL BE ABLE TO FIND A WIFE.
SURPRISE! HE'S SINGLE.
HEH, HEH HEH HEH.
POP
MR. KAGEURA?
IS THERE SOMETHING WRONG?
EXCUSE ME. YES, HOMEROOM'S OVER.
SMIRK
shudder

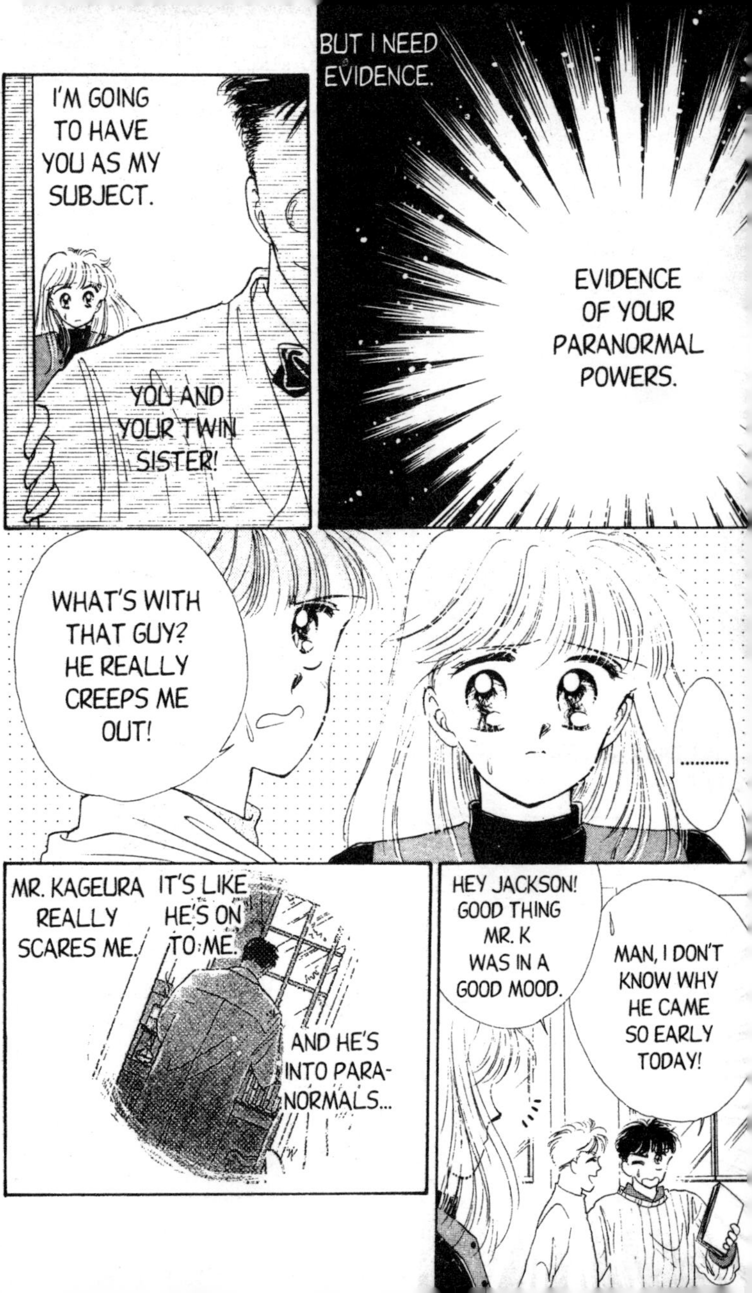
I'M GOING TO HAVE YOU AS MY SUBJECT.
YOU AND YOUR TWIN SISTER!
BUT I NEED EVIDENCE.
EVIDENCE OF YOUR PARANORMAL POWERS.
WHAT'S WITH THAT GUY? HE REALLY CREEPS ME OUT!
....
MR. KAGEURA REALLY SCARES ME.
IT'S LIKE HE'S ON TO ME.
AND HE'S INTO PARA-NORMALS...
HEY JACKSON! GOOD THING MR. K WAS IN A GOOD MOOD.
MAN, I DON'T KNOW WHY HE CAME SO EARLY TODAY!

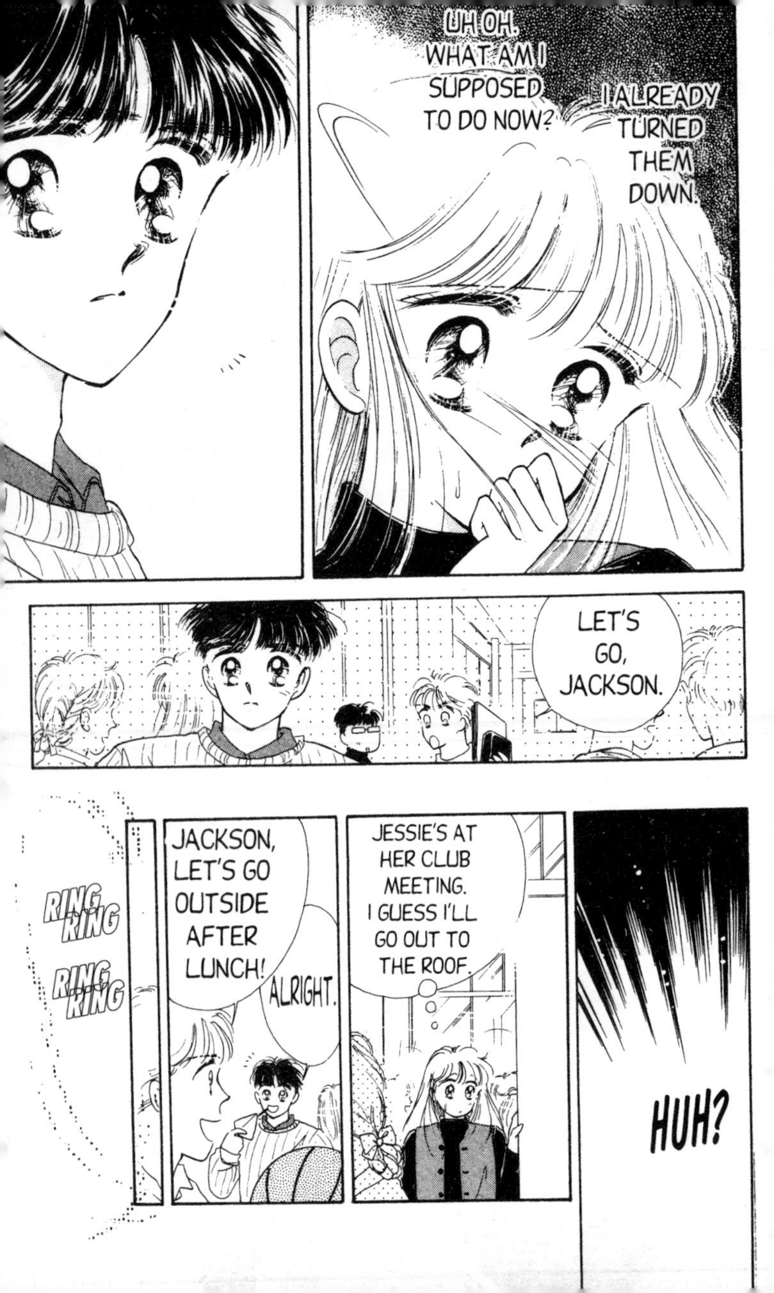
UH OH. WHAT AM I SUPPOSED TO DO NOW?
I ALREADY TURNED THEM DOWN.
LET'S GO, JACKSON.
RING RING
RING RING
JACKSON, LET'S GO OUTSIDE AFTER LUNCH!
ALRIGHT.
JESSIE'S AT HER CLUB MEETING. I GUESS I'LL GO OUT TO THE ROOF.
HUH?

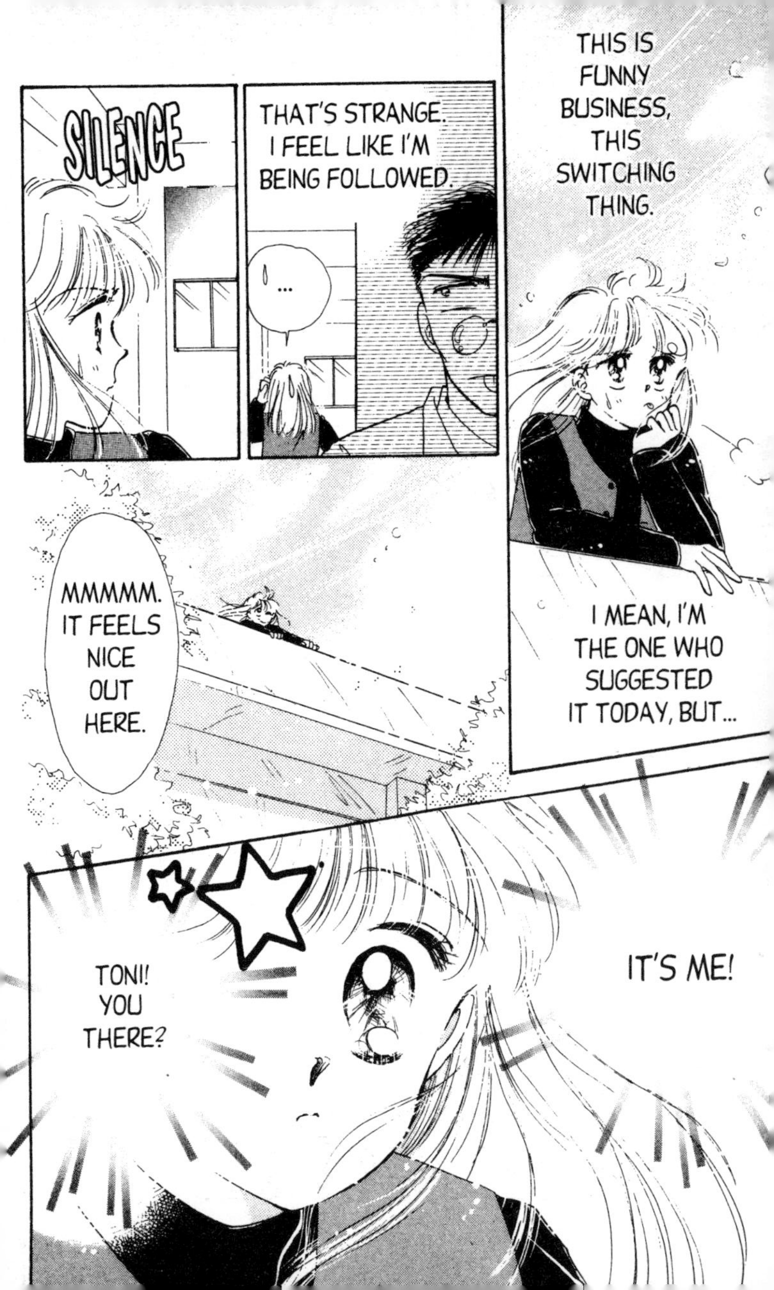
SILENCE
THAT'S STRANGE. I FEEL LIKE I'M BEING FOLLOWED.
...
THIS IS FUNNY BUSINESS, THIS SWITCHING THING.
MMMMM. IT FEELS NICE OUT HERE.
I MEAN, I'M THE ONE WHO SUGGESTED IT TODAY, BUT...
TONI! YOU THERE?
IT'S ME!

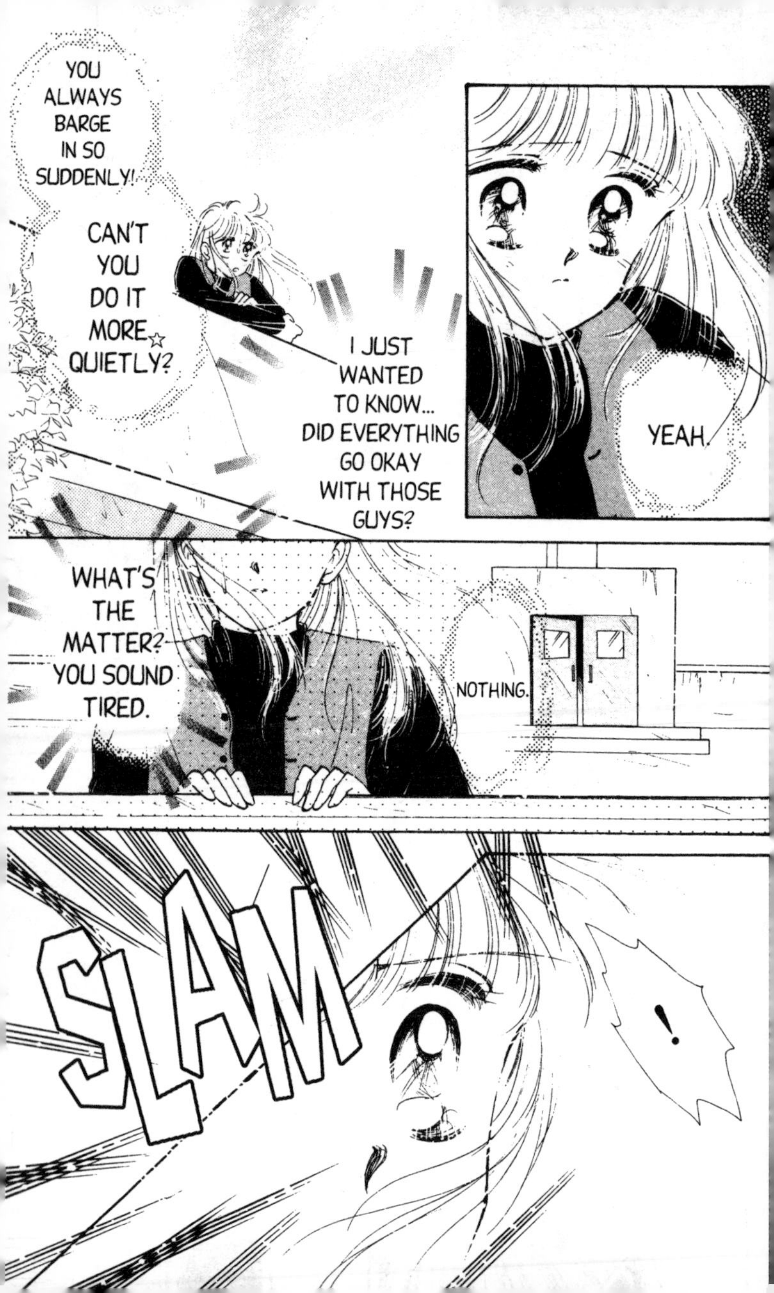
YOU ALWAYS BARGE IN SO SUDDENLY!
CAN'T YOU DO IT MORE☆ QUIETLY?
I JUST WANTED TO KNOW... DID EVERYTHING GO OKAY WITH THOSE GUYS?
YEAH.
WHAT'S THE MATTER? YOU SOUND TIRED.
NOTHING.
SLAM
!

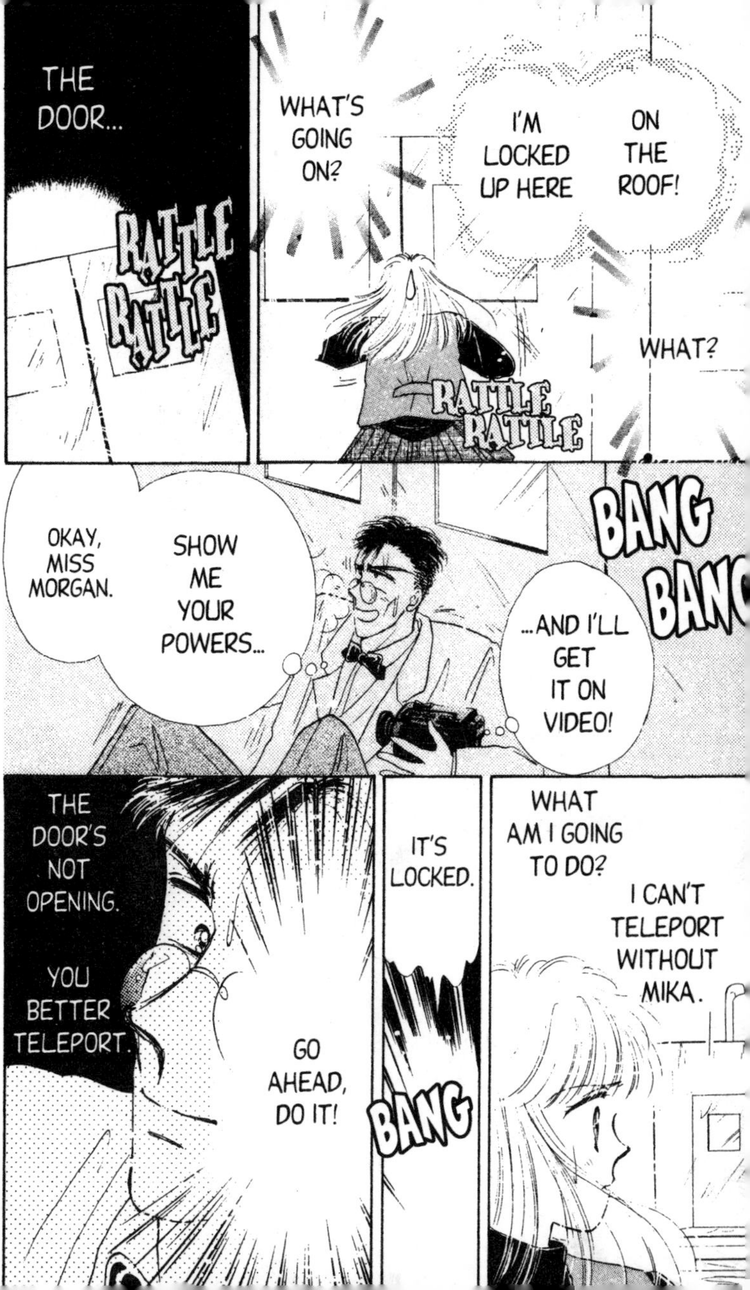
THE DOOR...
RATTLE RATTLE
WHAT'S GOING ON?
I'M LOCKED UP HERE
ON THE ROOF!
RATTLE RATTLE
WHAT?
OKAY, MISS MORGAN.
SHOW ME YOUR POWERS...
...AND I'LL GET IT ON VIDEO!
BANG
BANG
THE DOOR'S NOT OPENING.
YOU BETTER TELEPORT.
GO AHEAD, DO IT!
IT'S LOCKED.
BANG
WHAT AM I GOING TO DO?
I CAN'T TELEPORT WITHOUT MIKA.

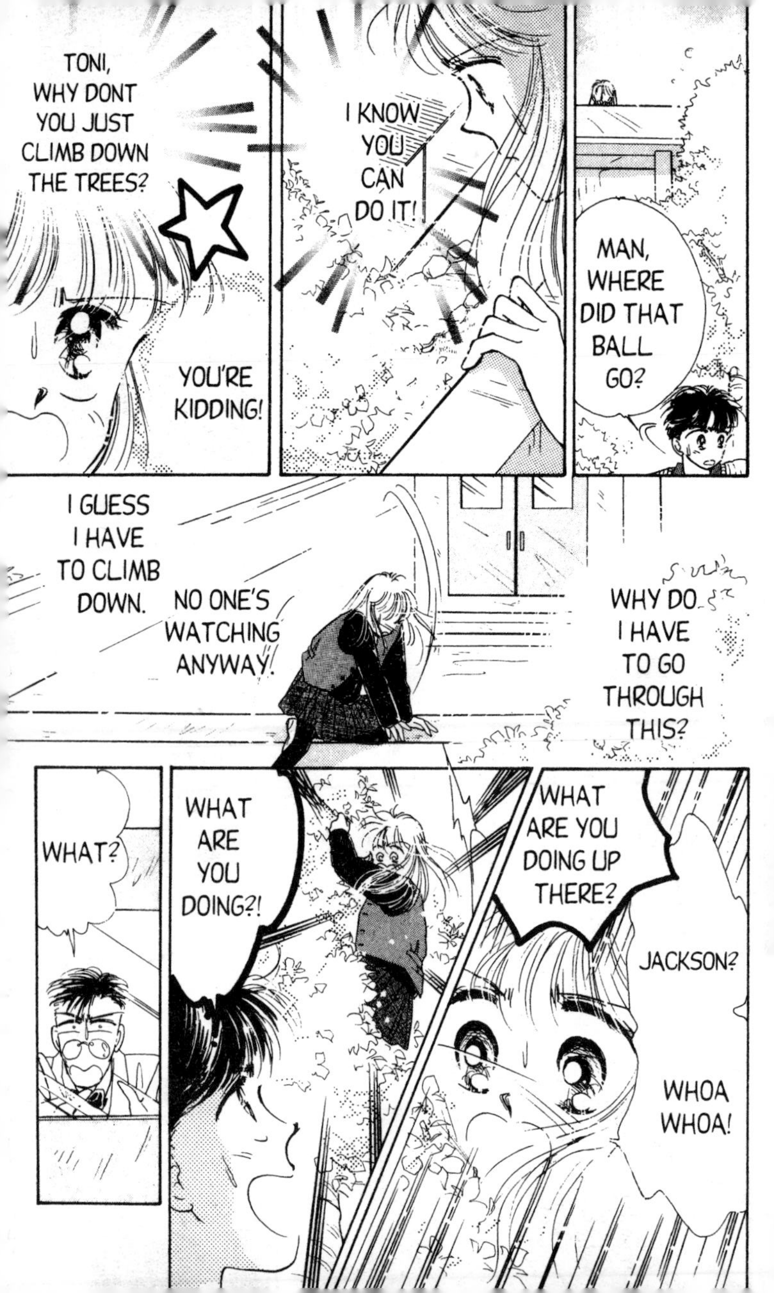
TONI, WHY DONT YOU JUST CLIMB DOWN THE TREES?
YOU'RE KIDDING!
I KNOW YOU CAN DO IT!
MAN, WHERE DID THAT BALL GO?
I GUESS I HAVE TO CLIMB DOWN.
NO ONE'S WATCHING ANYWAY.
WHY DO I HAVE TO GO THROUGH THIS?
WHAT?
WHAT ARE YOU DOING?!
WHAT ARE YOU DOING UP THERE?
JACKSON?
WHOA WHOA!

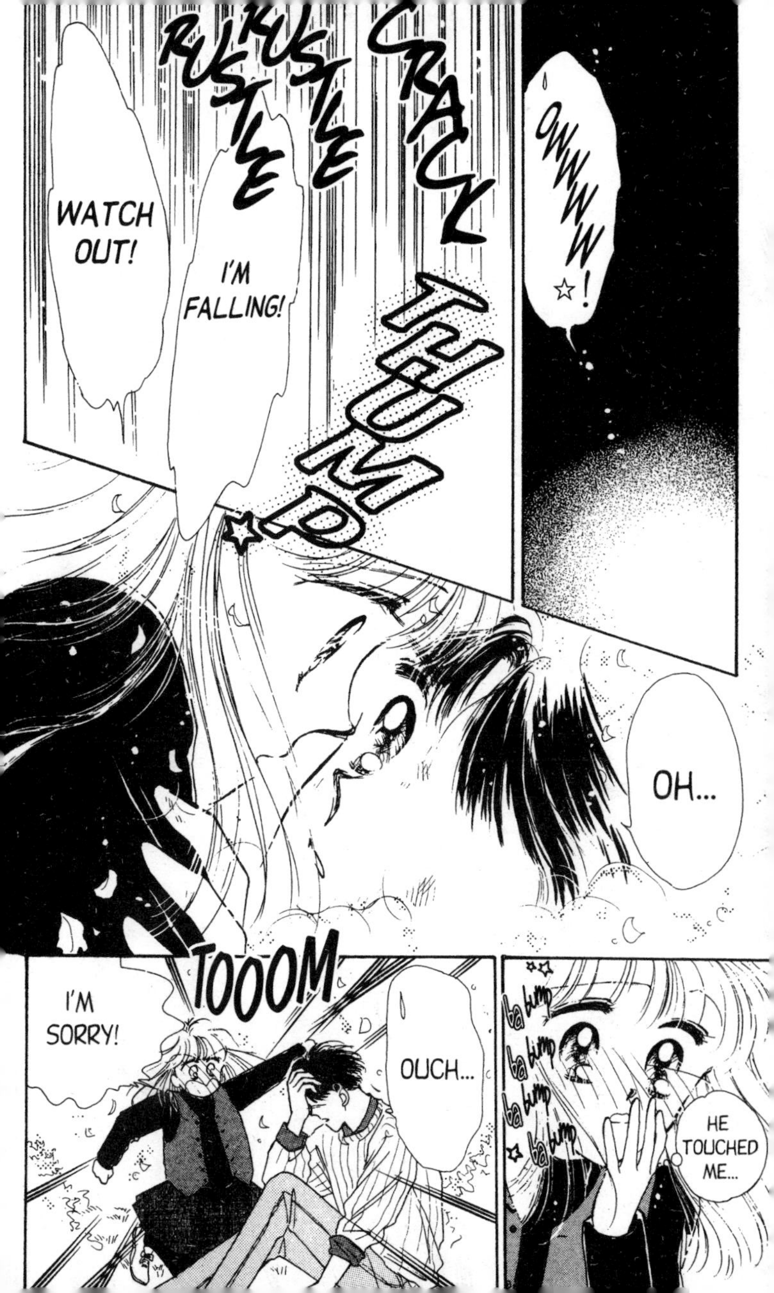
WATCH OUT!
RUSTLE
RUSTLE
I'M FALLING!
CRACK
OWWWW! ☆
THUMP
OH...
I'M SORRY!
TOOOM
OUCH...
ba bump ba bump ba bump ba bump
HE TOUCHED ME...

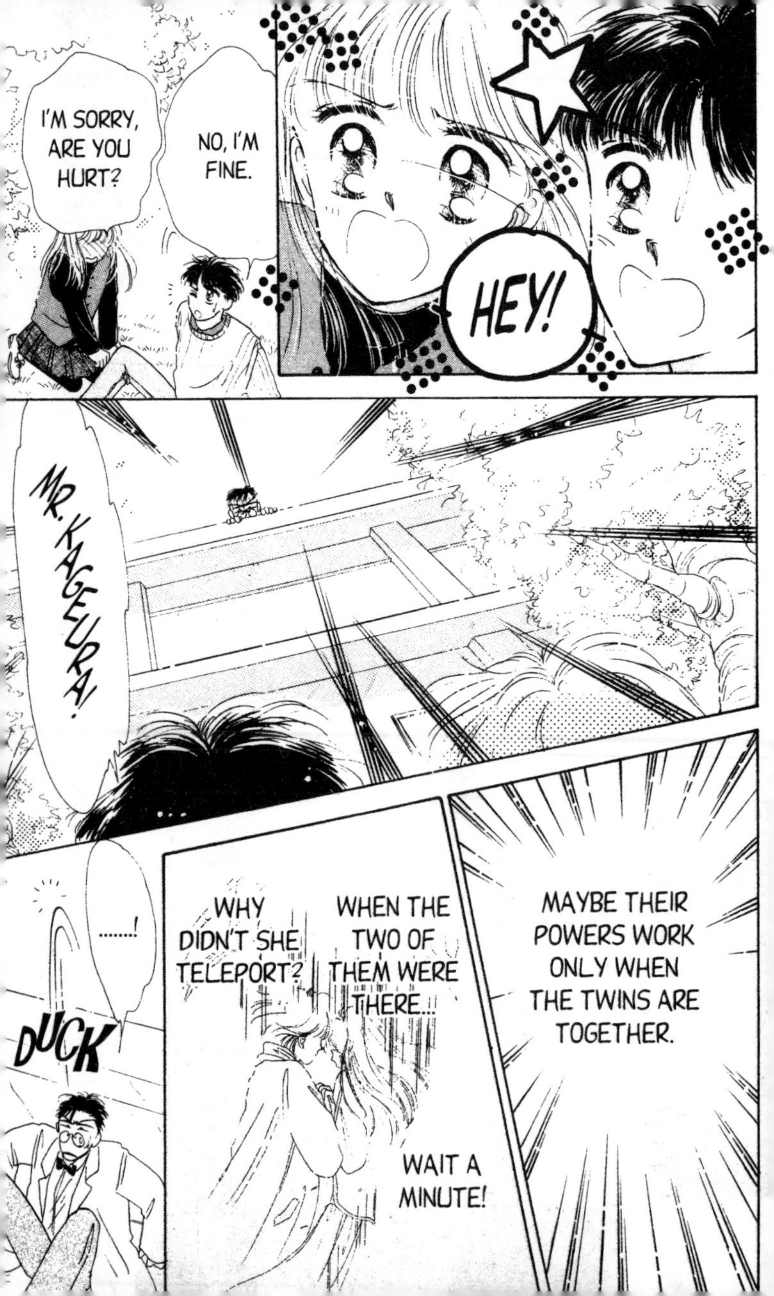

I'M SORRY, ARE YOU HURT?
NO, I'M FINE.
HEY!
MR. KAGEURA!
.......!
DUCK
WHY DIDN'T SHE TELEPORT?
WHEN THE TWO OF THEM WERE THERE...
WAIT A MINUTE!
MAYBE THEIR POWERS WORK ONLY WHEN THE TWINS ARE TOGETHER.

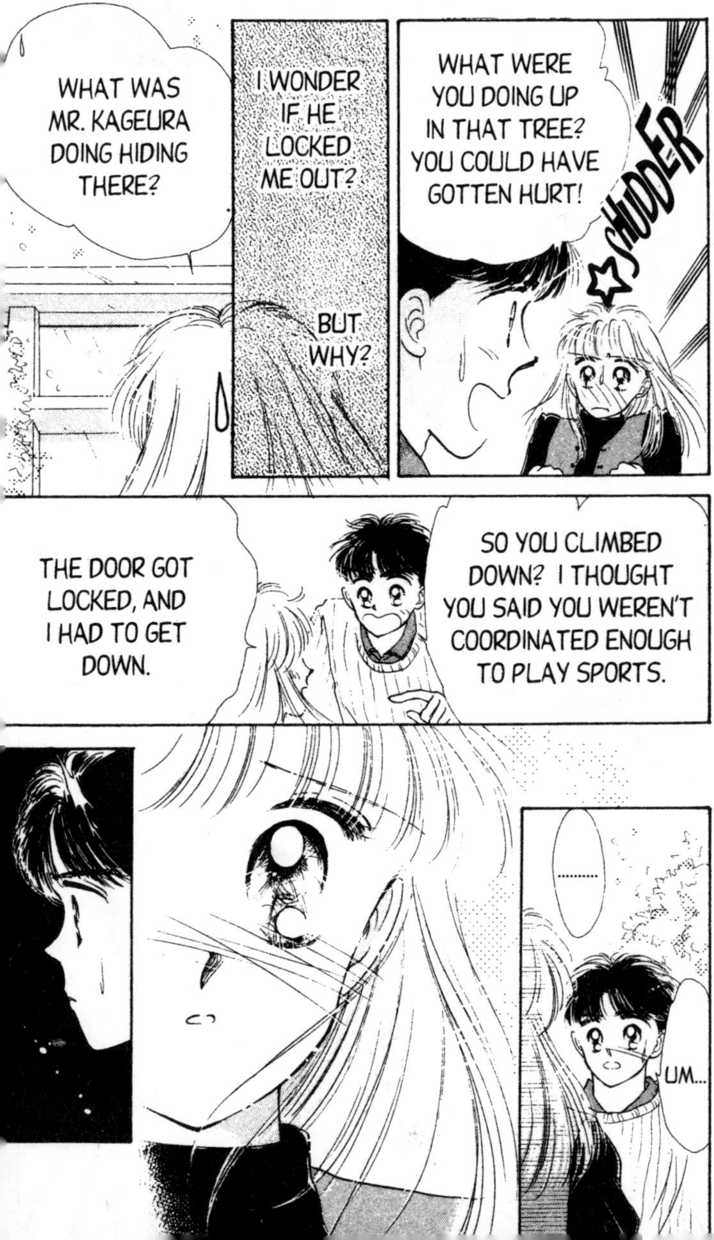
WHAT WAS MR. KAGEURA DOING HIDING THERE?
I WONDER IF HE LOCKED ME OUT?
BUT WHY?
WHAT WERE YOU DOING UP IN THAT TREE? YOU COULD HAVE GOTTEN HURT!
SHUDDER
THE DOOR GOT LOCKED, AND I HAD TO GET DOWN.
SO YOU CLIMBED DOWN? I THOUGHT YOU SAID YOU WEREN'T COORDINATED ENOUGH TO PLAY SPORTS.
....
UM...

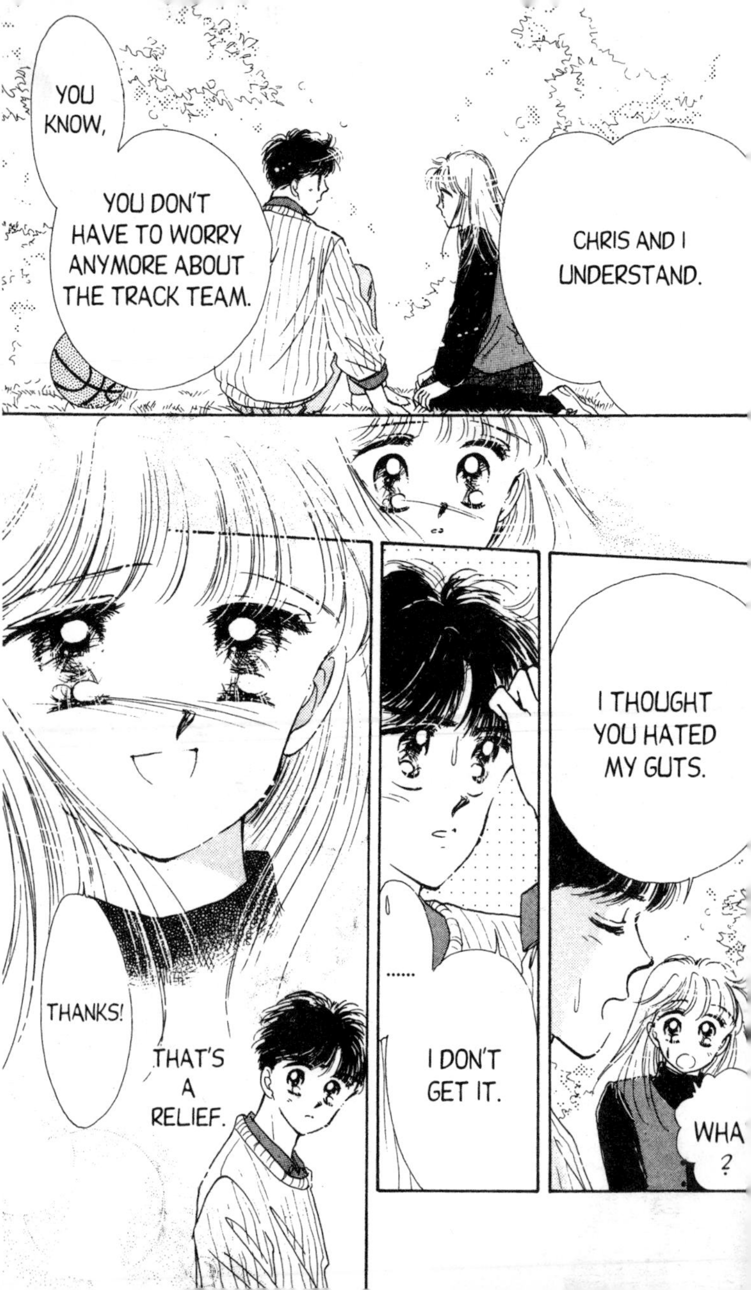
YOU KNOW,
YOU DON'T HAVE TO WORRY ANYMORE ABOUT THE TRACK TEAM.
CHRIS AND I UNDERSTAND.
THANKS!
THAT'S A RELIEF.
......
I DON'T GET IT.
I THOUGHT YOU HATED MY GUTS.
WHA ?

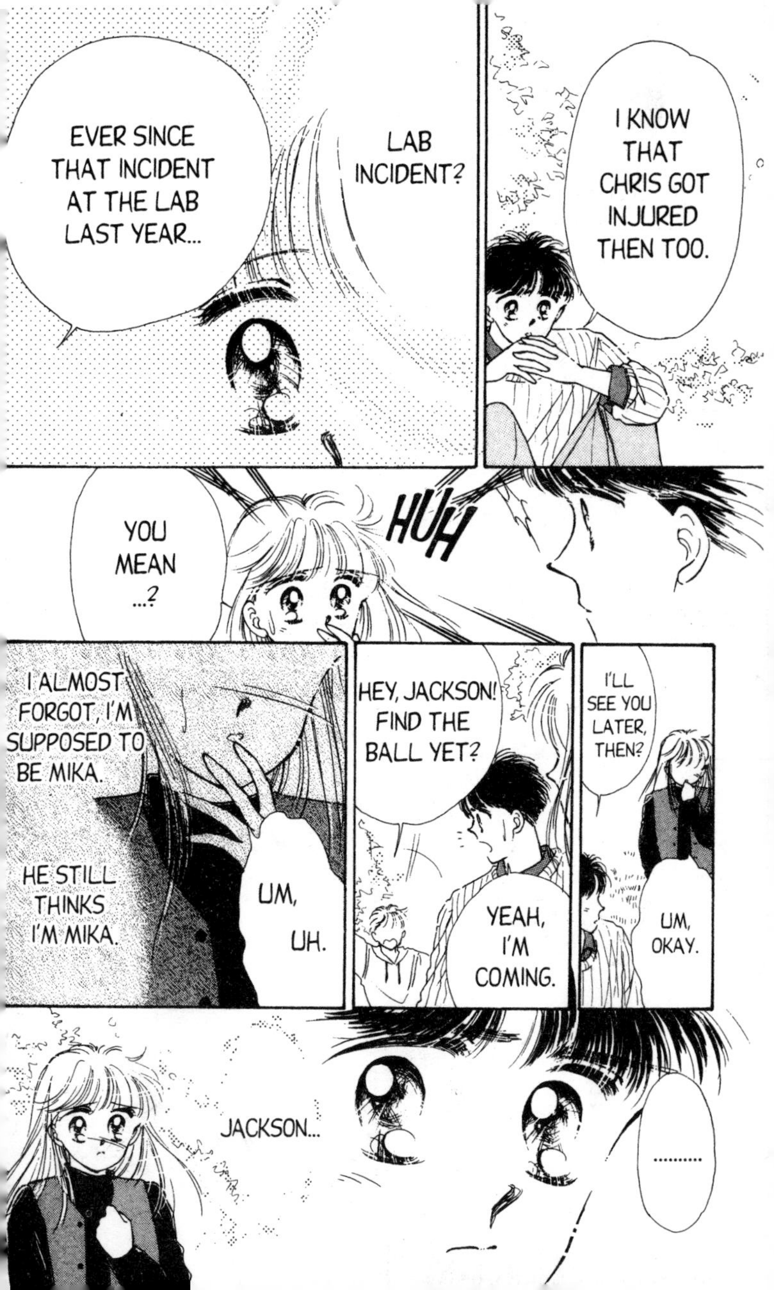
EVER SINCE THAT INCIDENT AT THE LAB LAST YEAR...
LAB INCIDENT?
I KNOW THAT CHRIS GOT INJURED THEN TOO.
YOU MEAN ...?
HUH
I ALMOST FORGOT, I'M SUPPOSED TO BE MIKA.
HE STILL THINKS I'M MIKA.
UM,
UH.
HEY, JACKSON! FIND THE BALL YET?
YEAH, I'M COMING.
I'LL SEE YOU LATER, THEN?
UM, OKAY.
JACKSON...
....

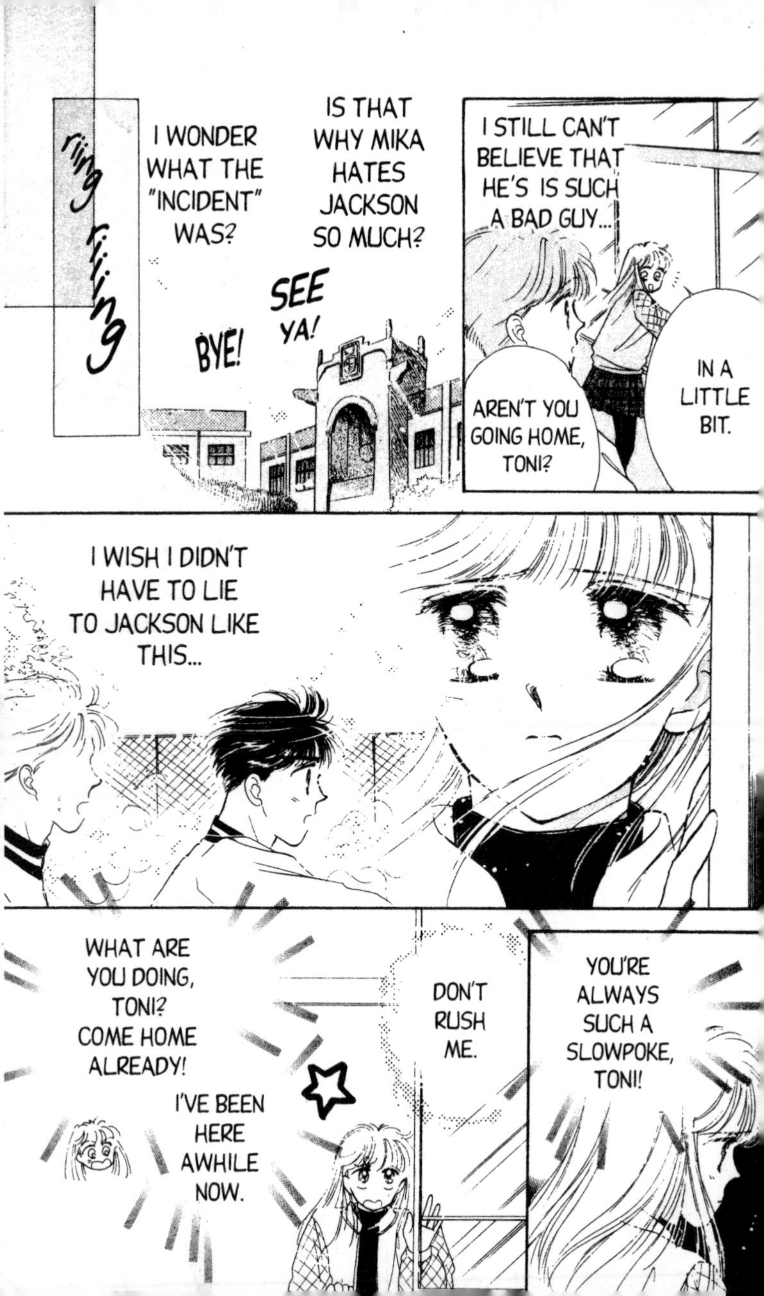
riing riiiing
I WONDER WHAT THE "INCIDENT" WAS?
IS THAT WHY MIKA HATES JACKSON SO MUCH?
SEE YA!
BYE!
I STILL CAN'T BELIEVE THAT HE'S IS SUCH A BAD GUY...
AREN'T YOU GOING HOME, TONI?
IN A LITTLE BIT.
I WISH I DIDN'T HAVE TO LIE TO JACKSON LIKE THIS...
WHAT ARE YOU DOING, TONI? COME HOME ALREADY!
I'VE BEEN HERE AWHILE NOW.
DON'T RUSH ME.
YOU'RE ALWAYS SUCH A SLOWPOKE, TONI!

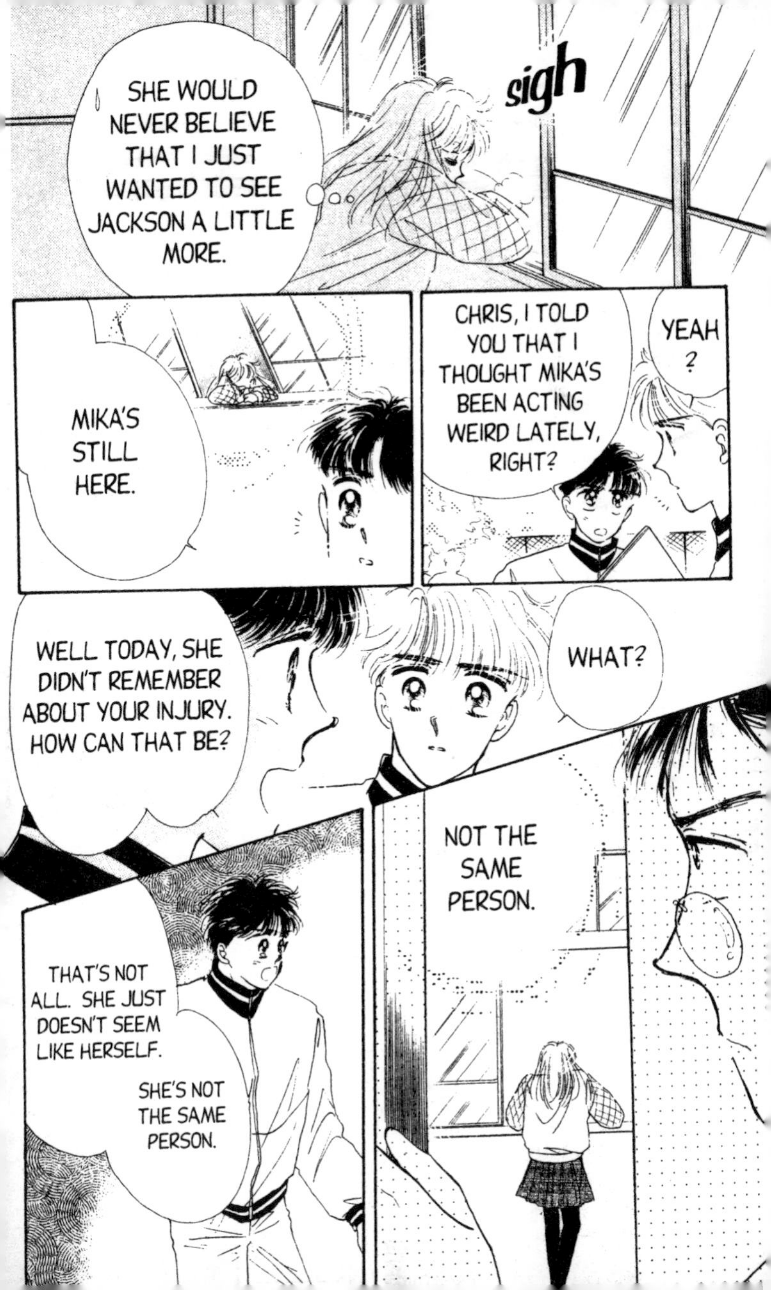
SHE WOULD NEVER BELIEVE THAT I JUST WANTED TO SEE JACKSON A LITTLE MORE.
sigh
MIKA'S STILL HERE.
CHRIS, I TOLD YOU THAT I THOUGHT MIKA'S BEEN ACTING WEIRD LATELY, RIGHT?
YEAH?
WELL TODAY, SHE DIDN'T REMEMBER ABOUT YOUR INJURY. HOW CAN THAT BE?
WHAT?
THAT'S NOT ALL. SHE JUST DOESN'T SEEM LIKE HERSELF.
SHE'S NOT THE SAME PERSON.
NOT THE SAME PERSON.

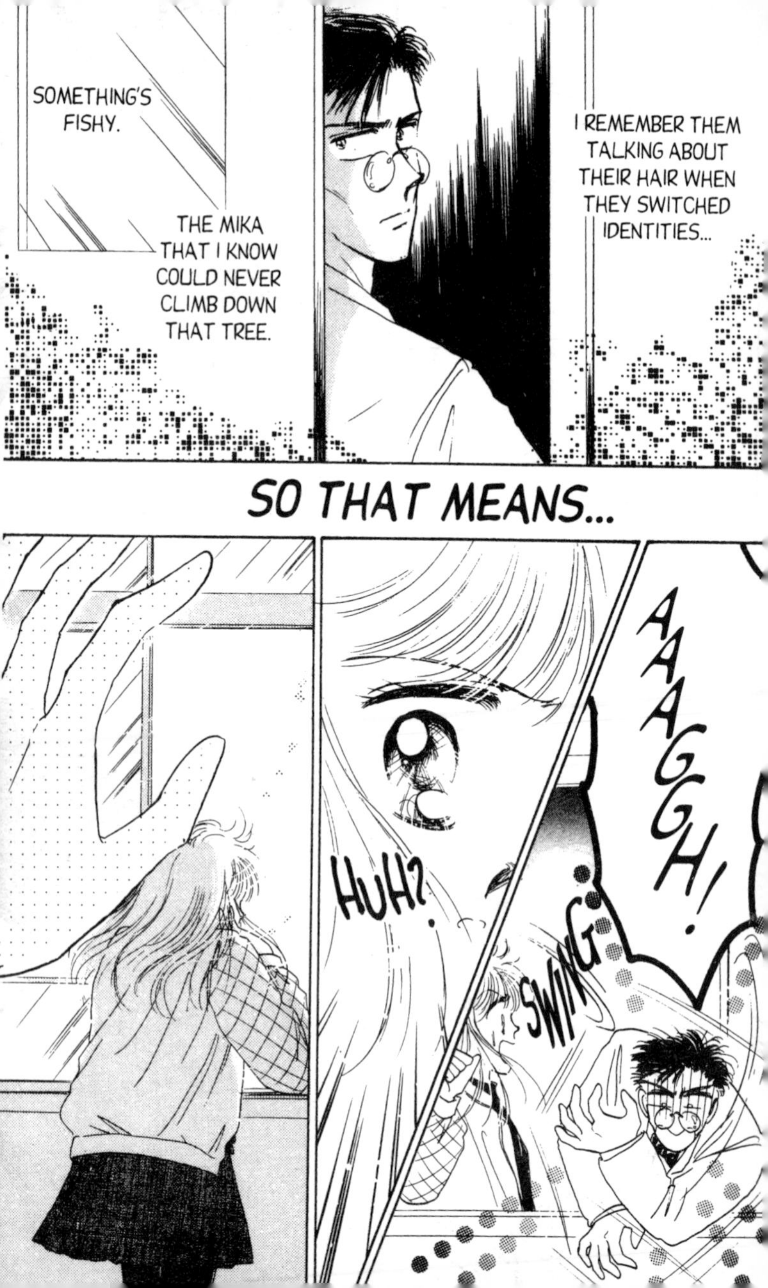
SOMETHING'S FISHY.
THE MIKA THAT I KNOW COULD NEVER CLIMB DOWN THAT TREE.
I REMEMBER THEM TALKING ABOUT THEIR HAIR WHEN THEY SWITCHED IDENTITIES...
SO THAT MEANS...
HUH?
AAAGGH!
SWING

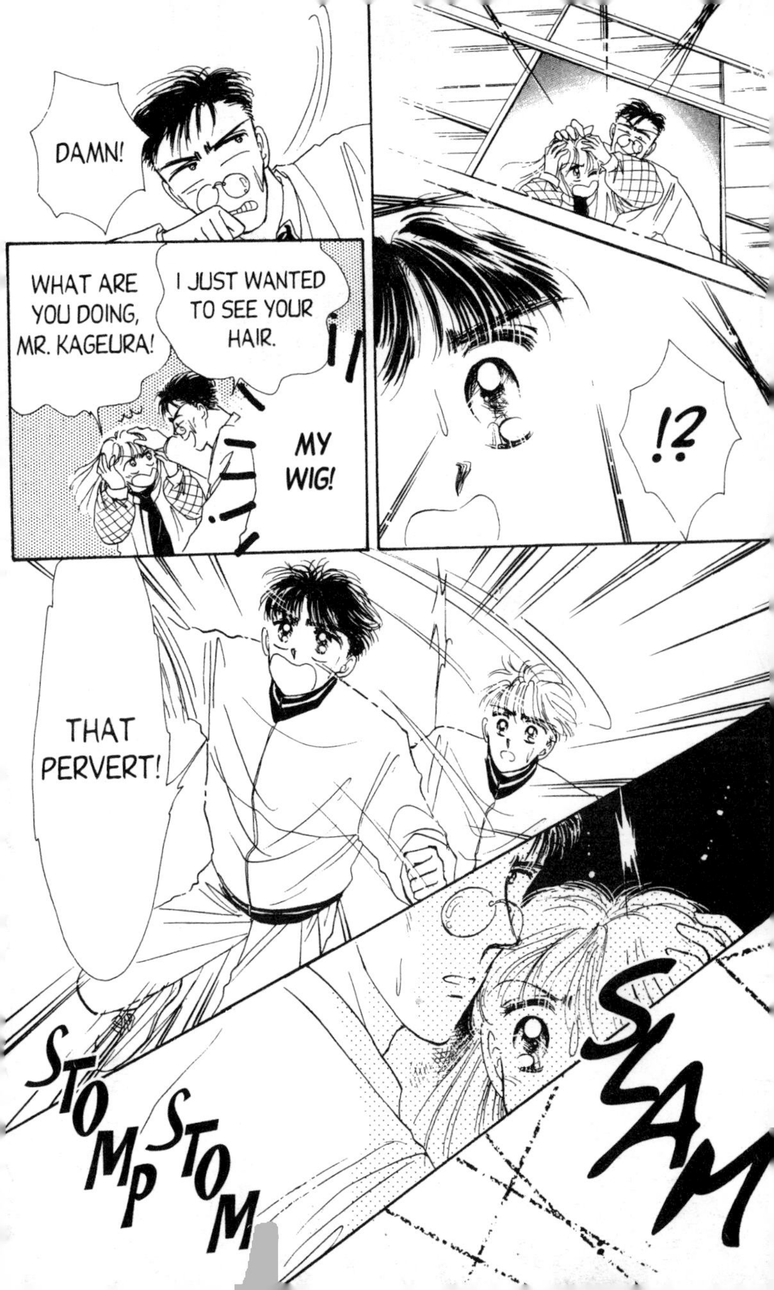
DAMN!
WHAT ARE YOU DOING, MR. KAGEURA!
I JUST WANTED TO SEE YOUR HAIR.
MY WIG!
!?
THAT PERVERT!
STOMP STOMP
SLAM

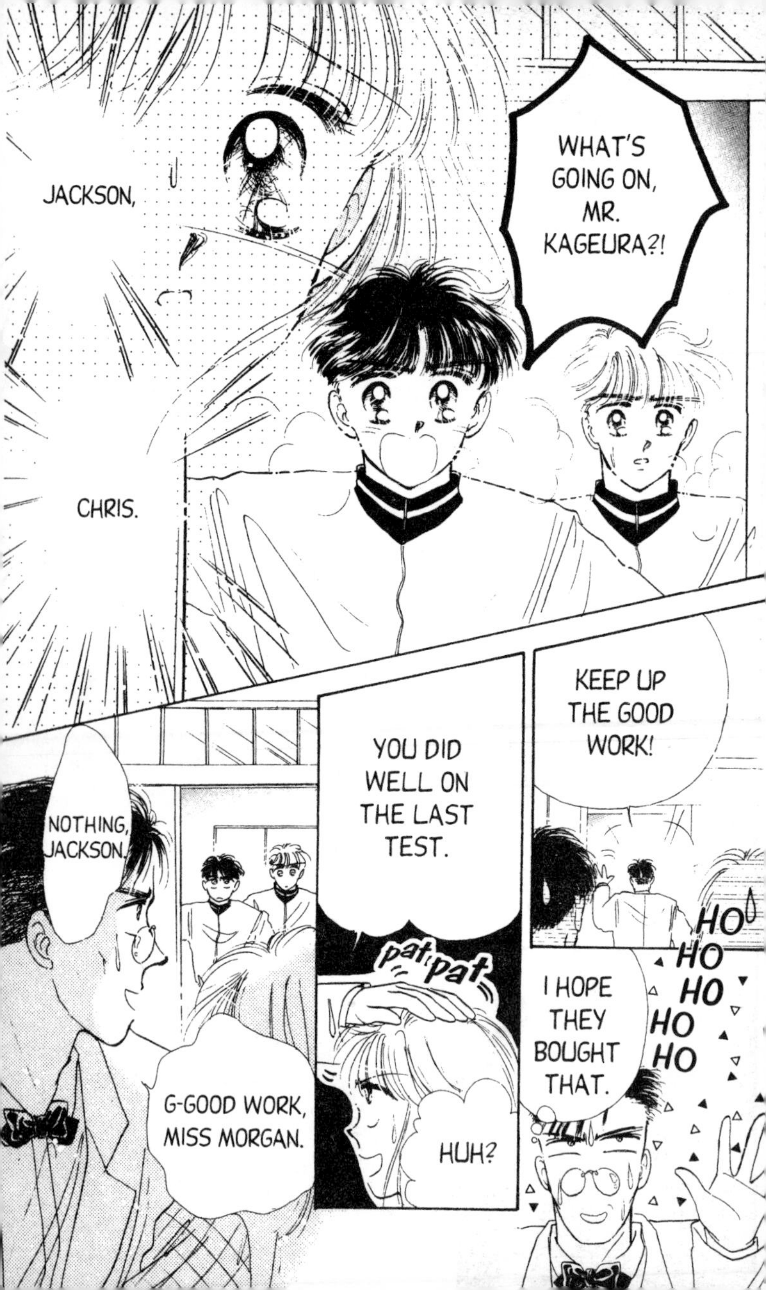
JACKSON,
CHRIS.
WHAT'S GOING ON, MR. KAGEURA?!
NOTHING, JACKSON.
G-GOOD WORK, MISS MORGAN.
YOU DID WELL ON THE LAST TEST.
pat pat
HUH?
KEEP UP THE GOOD WORK!
I HOPE THEY BOUGHT THAT.
HO HO HO HO HO

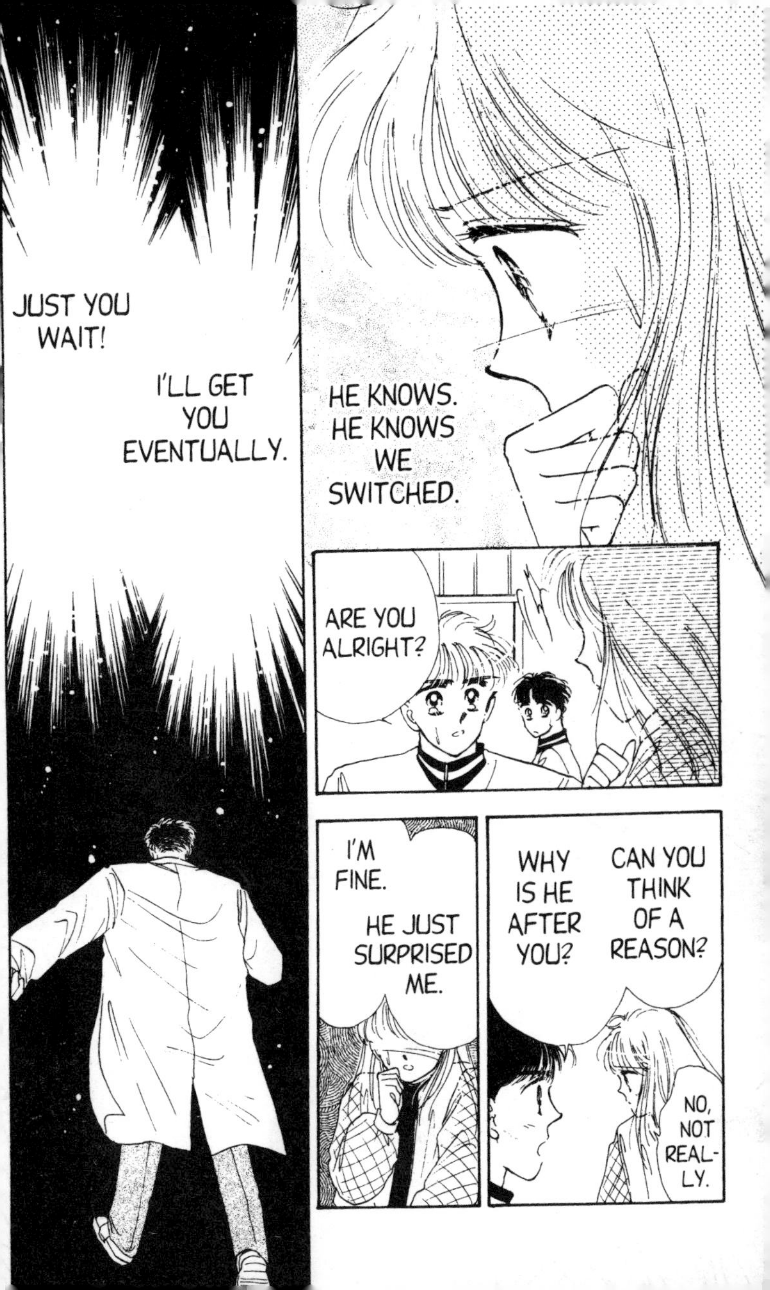
JUST YOU WAIT!
I'LL GET YOU EVENTUALLY.
HE KNOWS. HE KNOWS WE SWITCHED.
ARE YOU ALRIGHT?
I'M FINE.
HE JUST SURPRISED ME.
WHY IS HE AFTER YOU?
CAN YOU THINK OF A REASON?
NO, NOT REAL-LY.

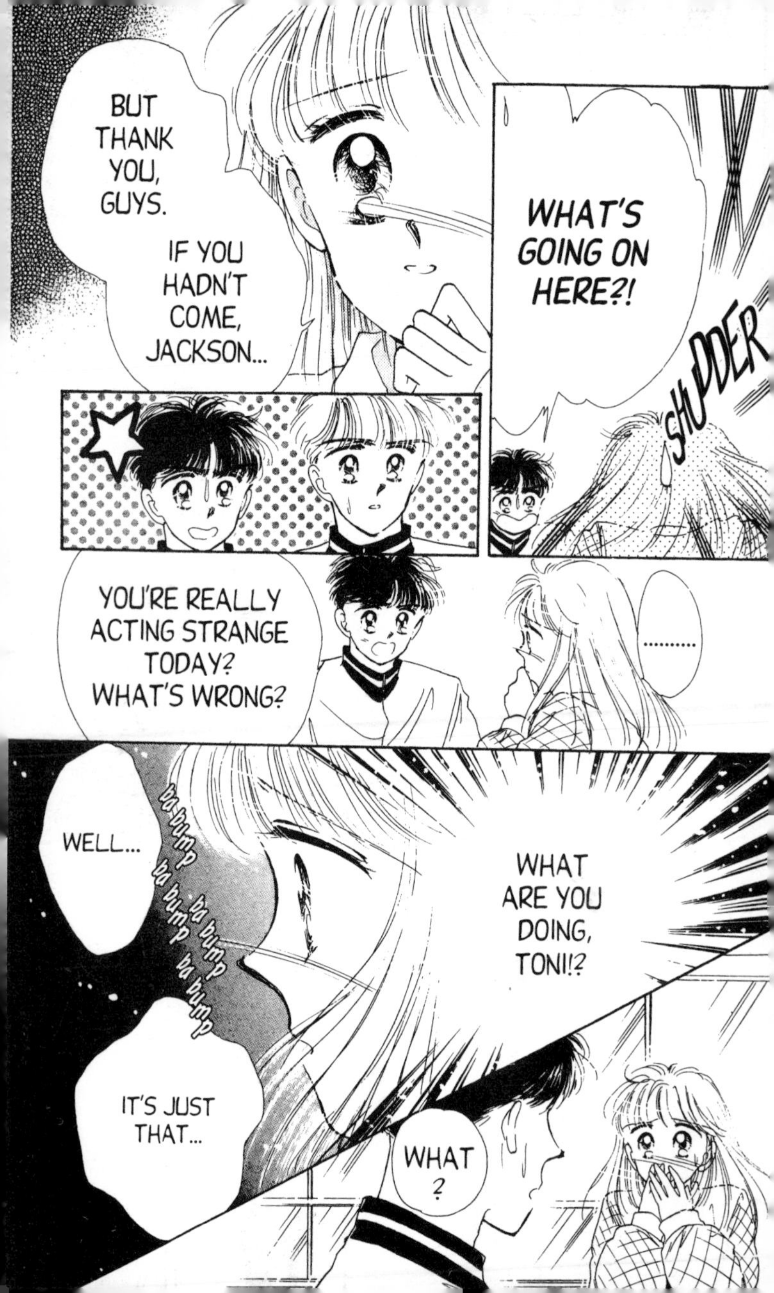
BUT THANK YOU, GUYS.
IF YOU HADN'T COME, JACKSON...
WHAT'S GOING ON HERE?!
SHUDDER
YOU'RE REALLY ACTING STRANGE TODAY? WHAT'S WRONG?
....
WELL...
ba bump ba bump ba bump ba bump ba bump
IT'S JUST THAT...
WHAT ARE YOU DOING, TONI!?
WHAT?

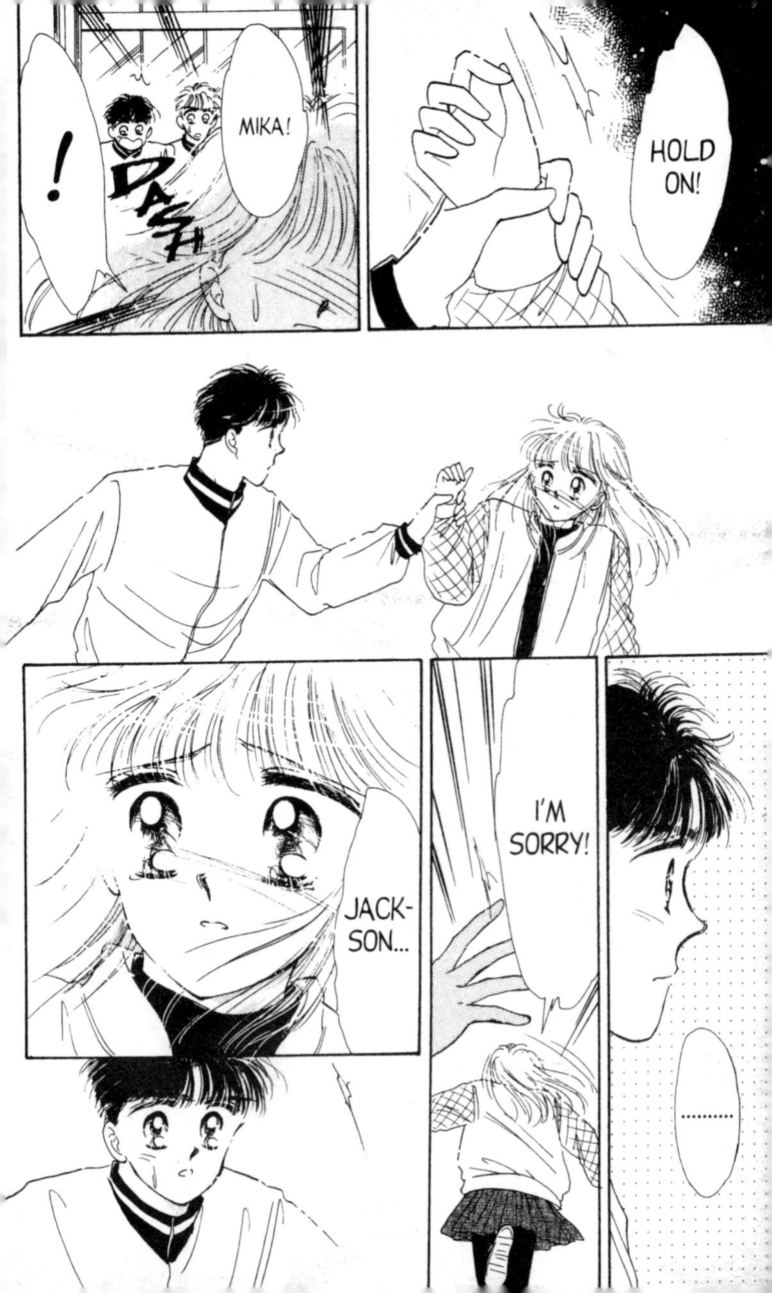
!
DASH
MIKA!
HOLD ON!
JACK-SON...
I'M SORRY!
....

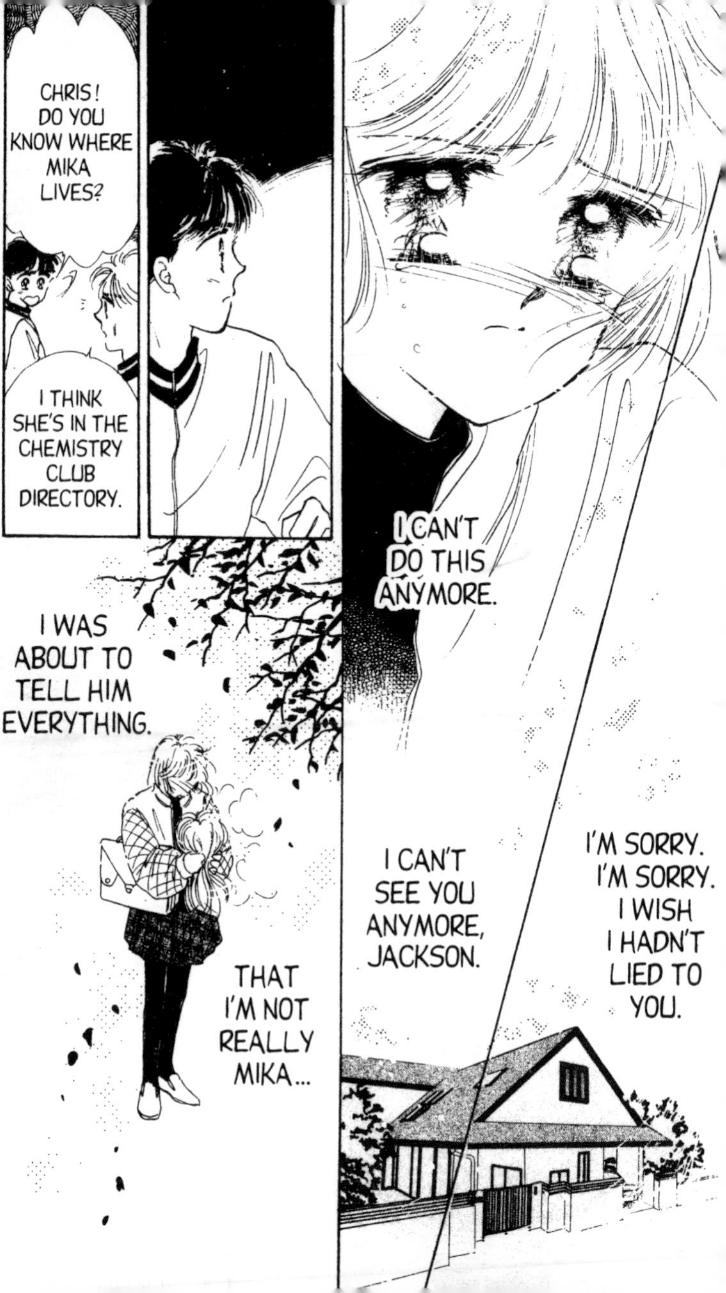
CHRIS! DO YOU KNOW WHERE MIKA LIVES?
I THINK SHE'S IN THE CHEMISTRY CLUB DIRECTORY.
I CAN'T DO THIS ANYMORE.
I WAS ABOUT TO TELL HIM EVERYTHING.
THAT I'M NOT REALLY MIKA...
I CAN'T SEE YOU ANYMORE, JACKSON.
I'M SORRY. I'M SORRY. I WISH I HADN'T LIED TO YOU.

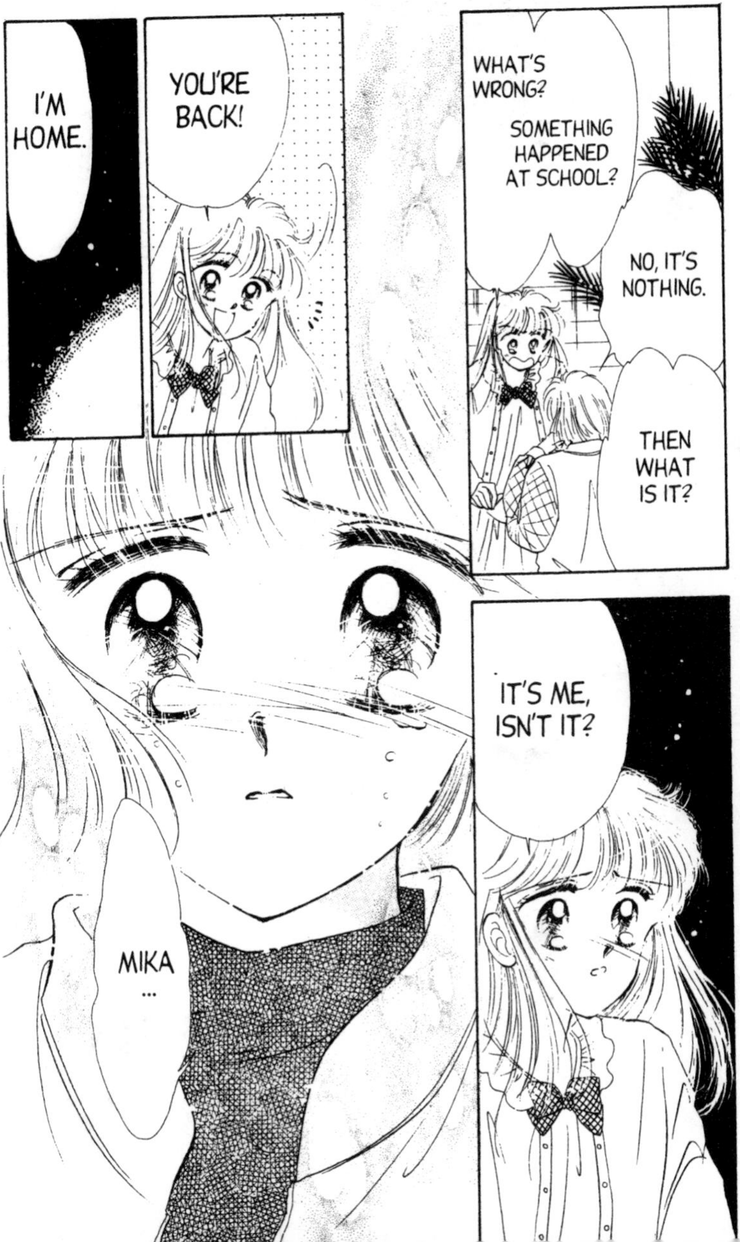
I'M HOME.
YOU'RE BACK!
WHAT'S WRONG?
SOMETHING HAPPENED AT SCHOOL?
NO, IT'S NOTHING.
THEN WHAT IS IT?
MIKA ...
IT'S ME, ISN'T IT?

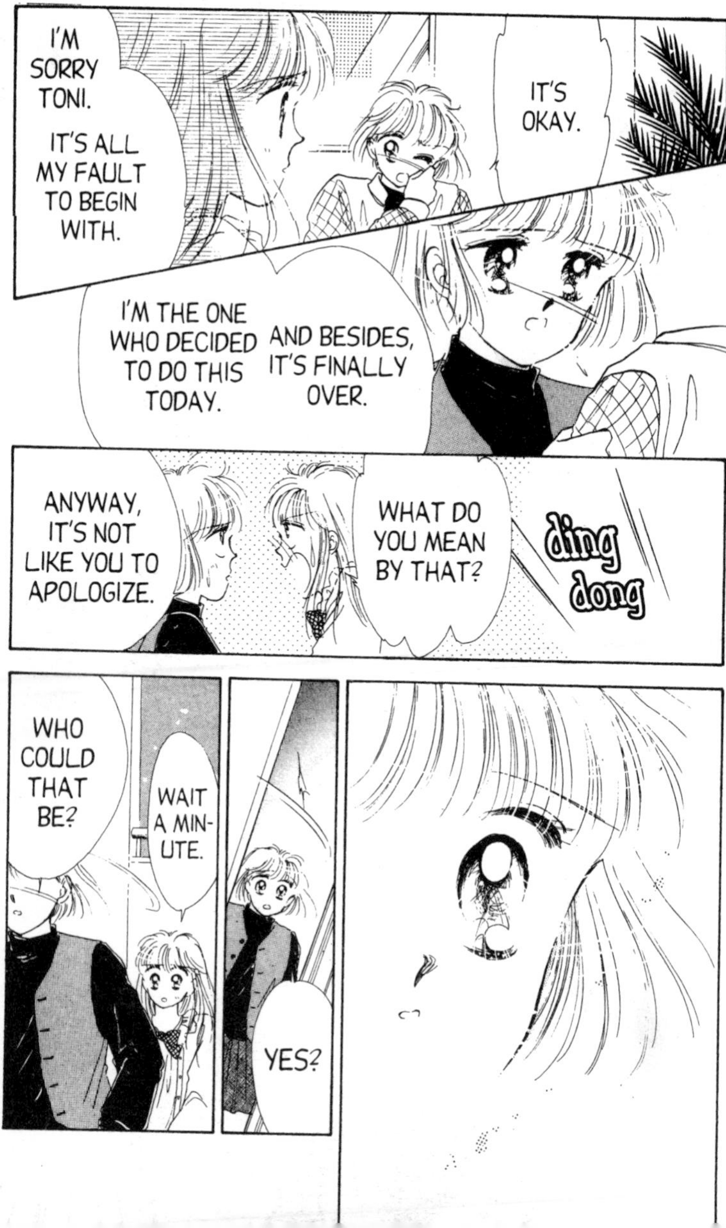
I'M SORRY TONI.
IT'S ALL MY FAULT TO BEGIN WITH.
IT'S OKAY.
I'M THE ONE WHO DECIDED TO DO THIS TODAY.
AND BESIDES, IT'S FINALLY OVER.
ANYWAY, IT'S NOT LIKE YOU TO APOLOGIZE.
WHAT DO YOU MEAN BY THAT?
ding dong
WHO COULD THAT BE?
WAIT A MIN-UTE.
YES?

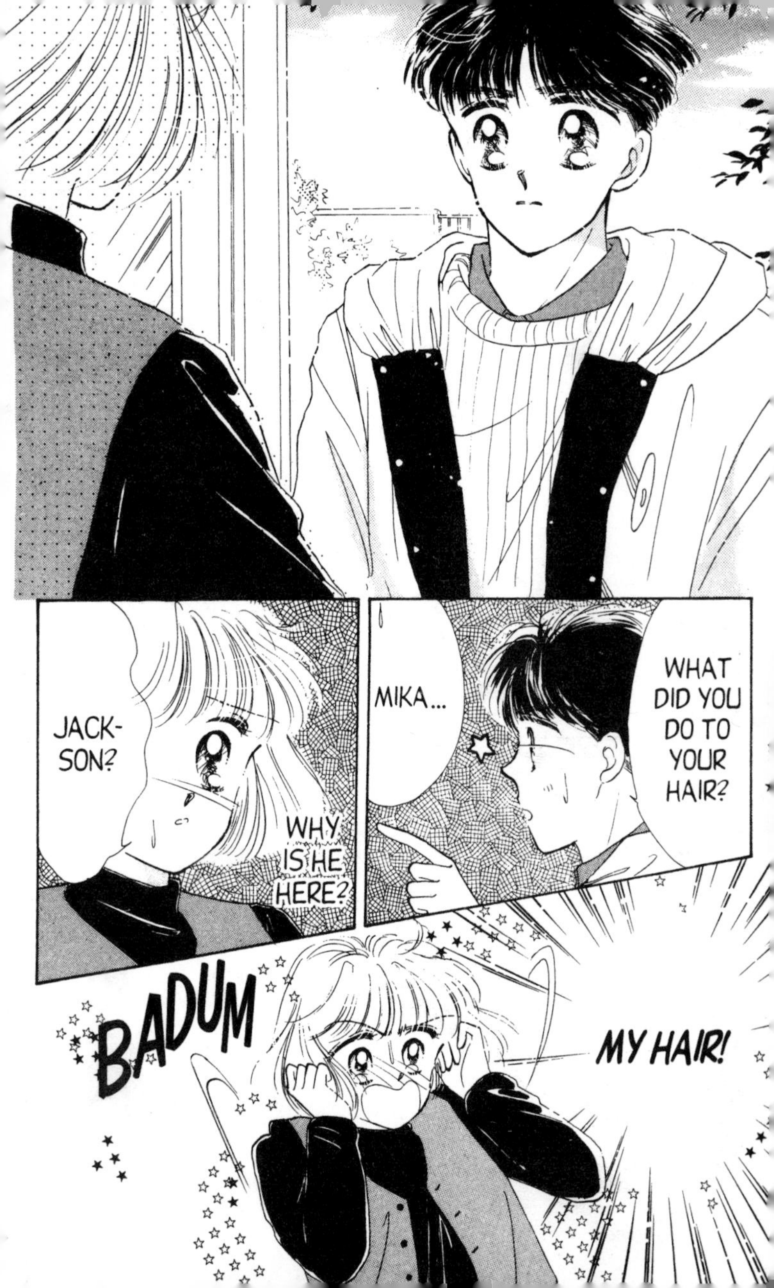
MIKA...
WHAT DID YOU DO TO YOUR HAIR?
JACK-SON?
WHY IS HE HERE?
MY HAIR!
BADUM

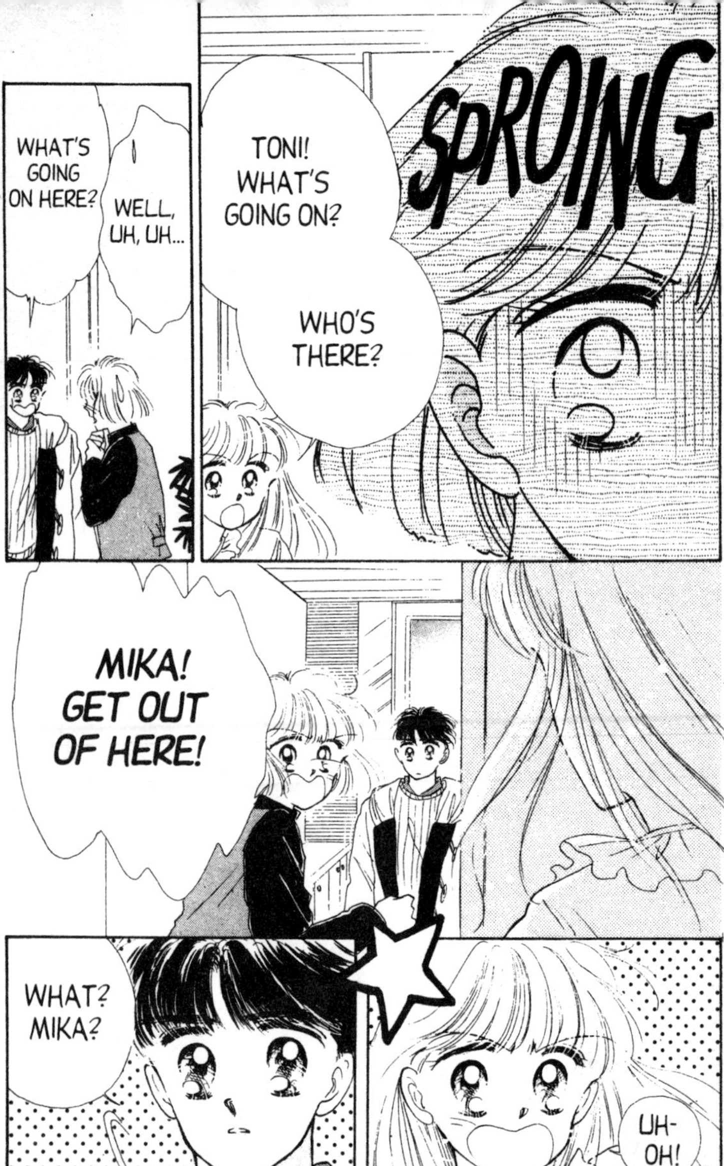
WHAT'S GOING ON HERE?
I WELL, UH, UH...
TONI! WHAT'S GOING ON?
WHO'S THERE?
SPROING
MIKA! GET OUT OF HERE!
WHAT? MIKA?
UH-OH!

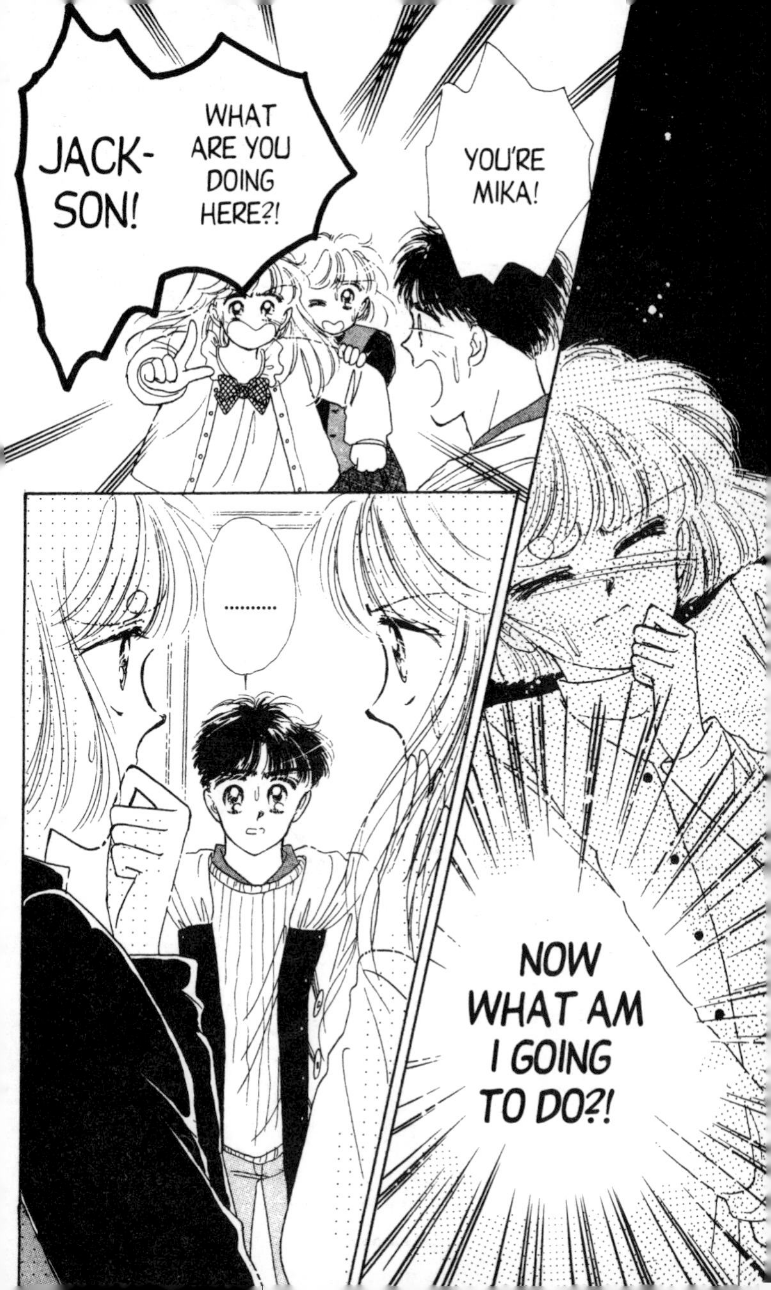
JACK-SON!
WHAT ARE YOU DOING HERE?!
YOU'RE MIKA!
....
NOW WHAT AM I GOING TO DO?!

BONUS PAGE 1

Hello! This is Nami Akimoto, author of "Miracle Girls." How did you like Book 1? I'd love to hear what you thought, so please send me those letters!

Whenever I'm down, or stuck on something, your letters really cheer me up, and I'm ready to work again! Thank you everyone! Since I'm so busy it's not easy to write back, though. But I'll be sure to make Book 2 just as exciting and fun. Thanks for your support! We'll see you again! Oh, and don't forget the bonus story!

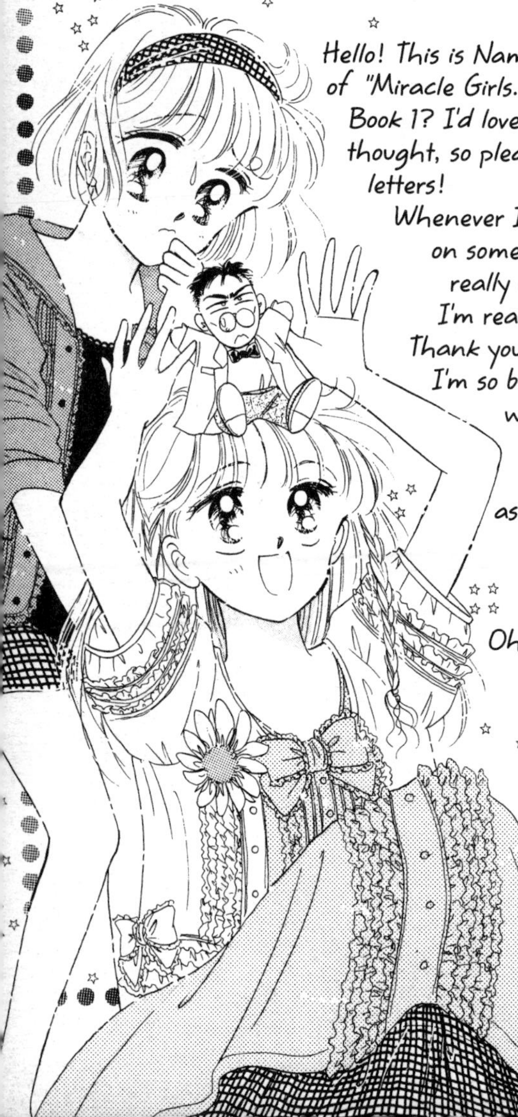

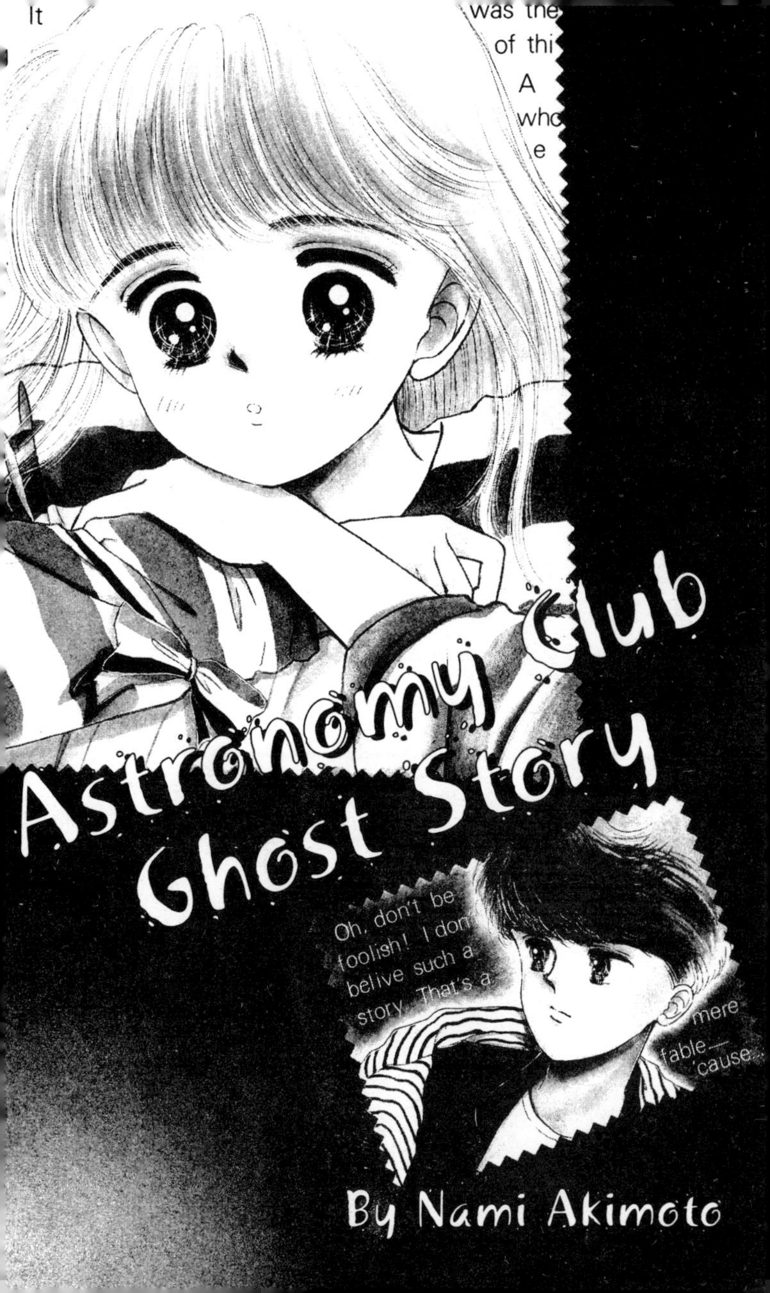
Astronomy Club Ghost Story
Oh, don't be foolish! I don't belive such a story. That's a mere fable—'cause...
By Nami Akimoto

BONUS PAGE 2

This story actually served as the inspiration for "Miracle Girls," so it is very dear to me. I was inspired by a university one of my friends attended. It was housed in a very beautiful, classically designed building. The creepy science hall actually came from my old school. I was never good at science, so it was a chamber of horrors for me! By the way, while creating this story I was beset by a number of "accidents." One time I lost my wallet. Another time, on my way to deliver the manuscript, I tripped and scattered the pages all over the train station.
I must have been cursed!
Hee hee!

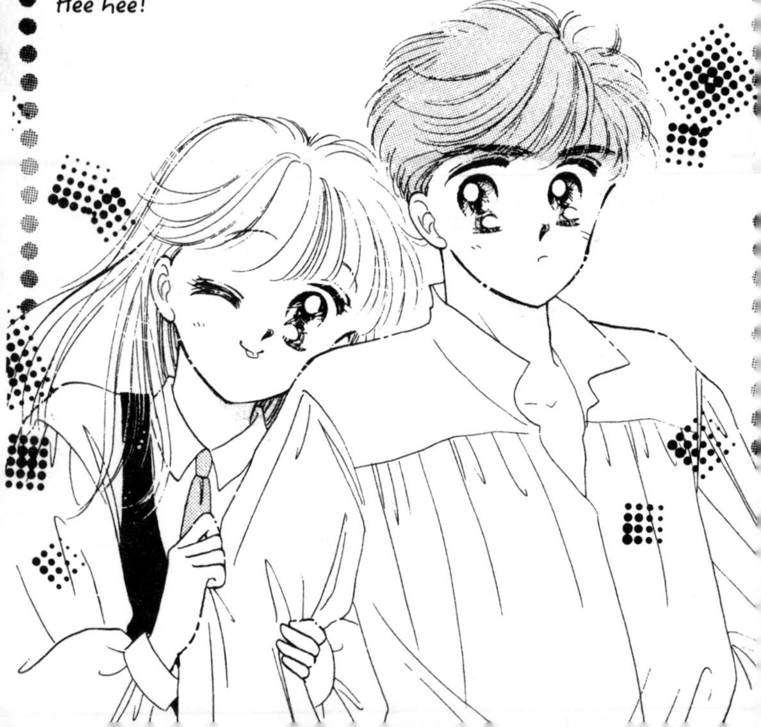

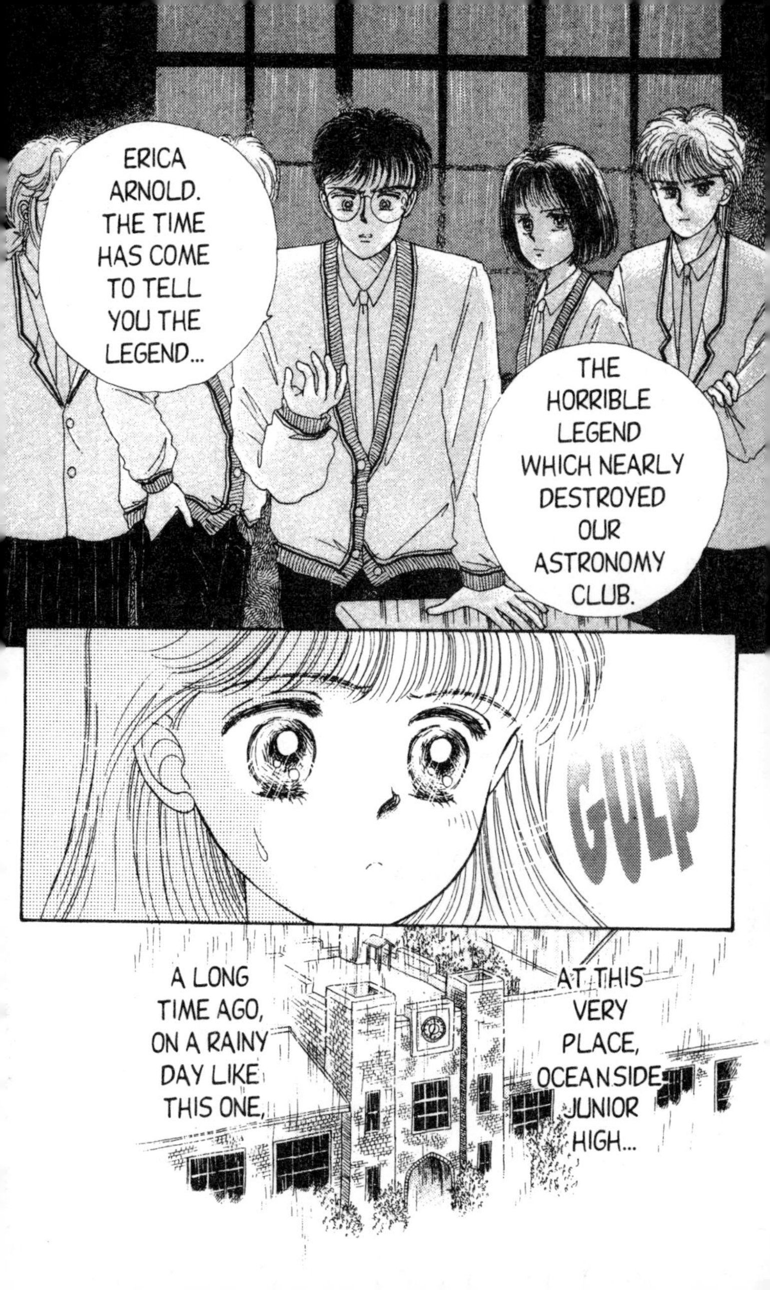
ERICA ARNOLD. THE TIME HAS COME TO TELL YOU THE LEGEND...
THE HORRIBLE LEGEND WHICH NEARLY DESTROYED OUR ASTRONOMY CLUB.
GULP
A LONG TIME AGO, ON A RAINY DAY LIKE THIS ONE,
AT THIS VERY PLACE, OCEANSIDE JUNIOR HIGH...

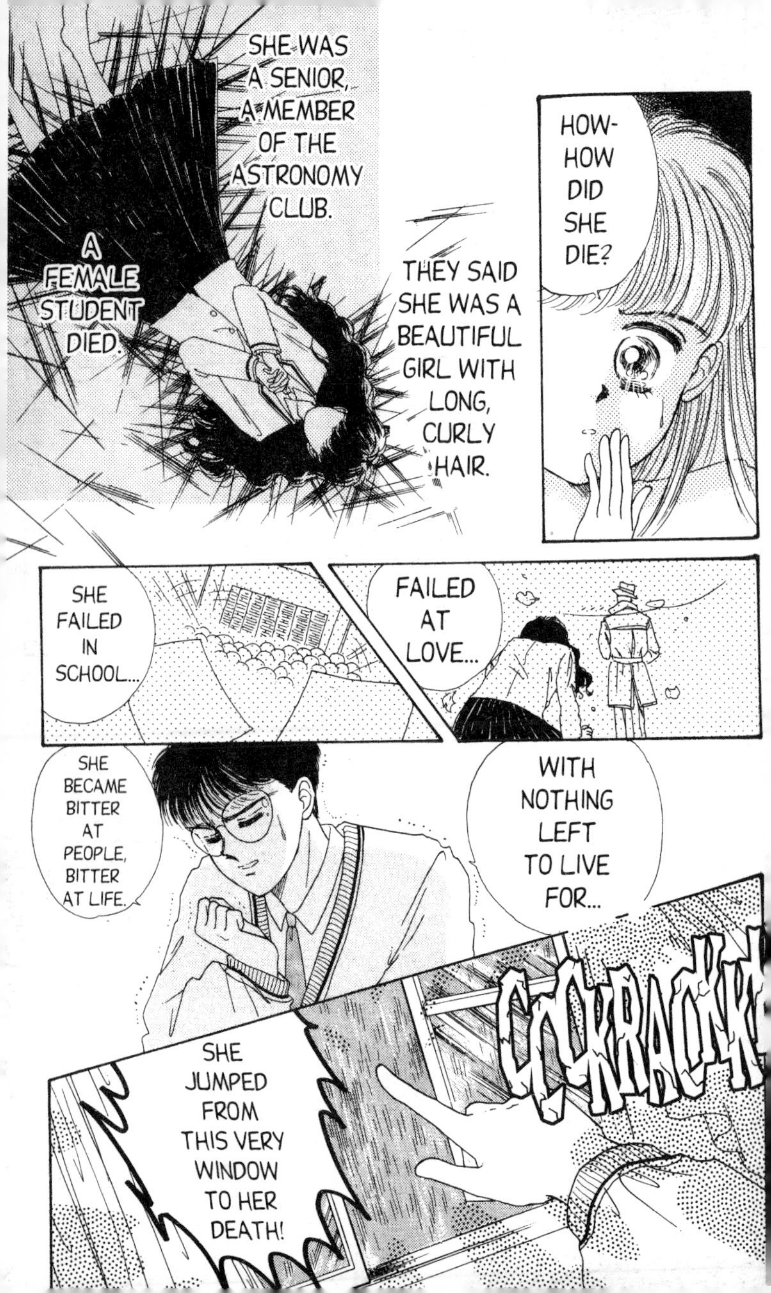
A FEMALE STUDENT DIED.
SHE WAS A SENIOR, A MEMBER OF THE ASTRONOMY CLUB.
THEY SAID SHE WAS A BEAUTIFUL GIRL WITH LONG, CURLY HAIR.
HOW-HOW DID SHE DIE?
SHE FAILED IN SCHOOL...
FAILED AT LOVE...
SHE BECAME BITTER AT PEOPLE, BITTER AT LIFE.
WITH NOTHING LEFT TO LIVE FOR...
SHE JUMPED FROM THIS VERY WINDOW TO HER DEATH!

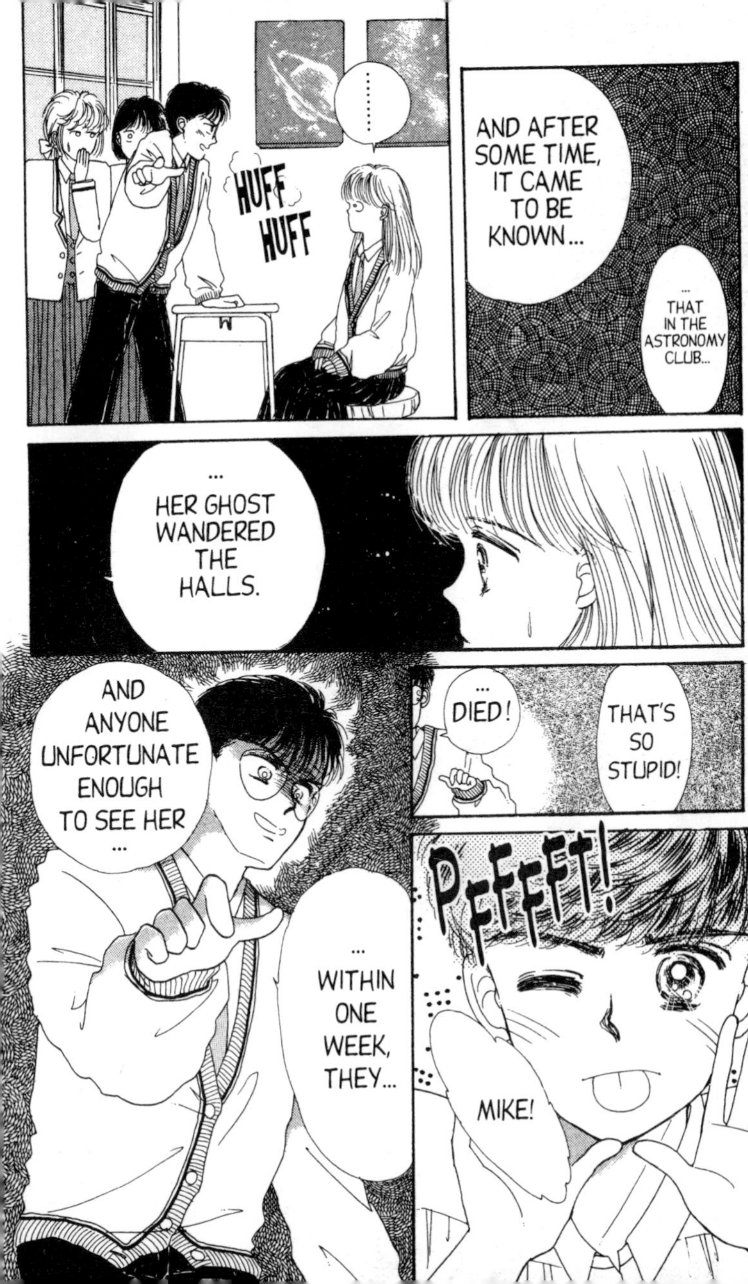

HUFF HUFF
....
AND AFTER SOME TIME, IT CAME TO BE KNOWN...
... THAT IN THE ASTRONOMY CLUB...
... HER GHOST WANDERED THE HALLS.
AND ANYONE UNFORTUNATE ENOUGH TO SEE HER ...
... WITHIN ONE WEEK, THEY...
... DIED!
THAT'S SO STUPID!
PFFFFT!
MIKE!

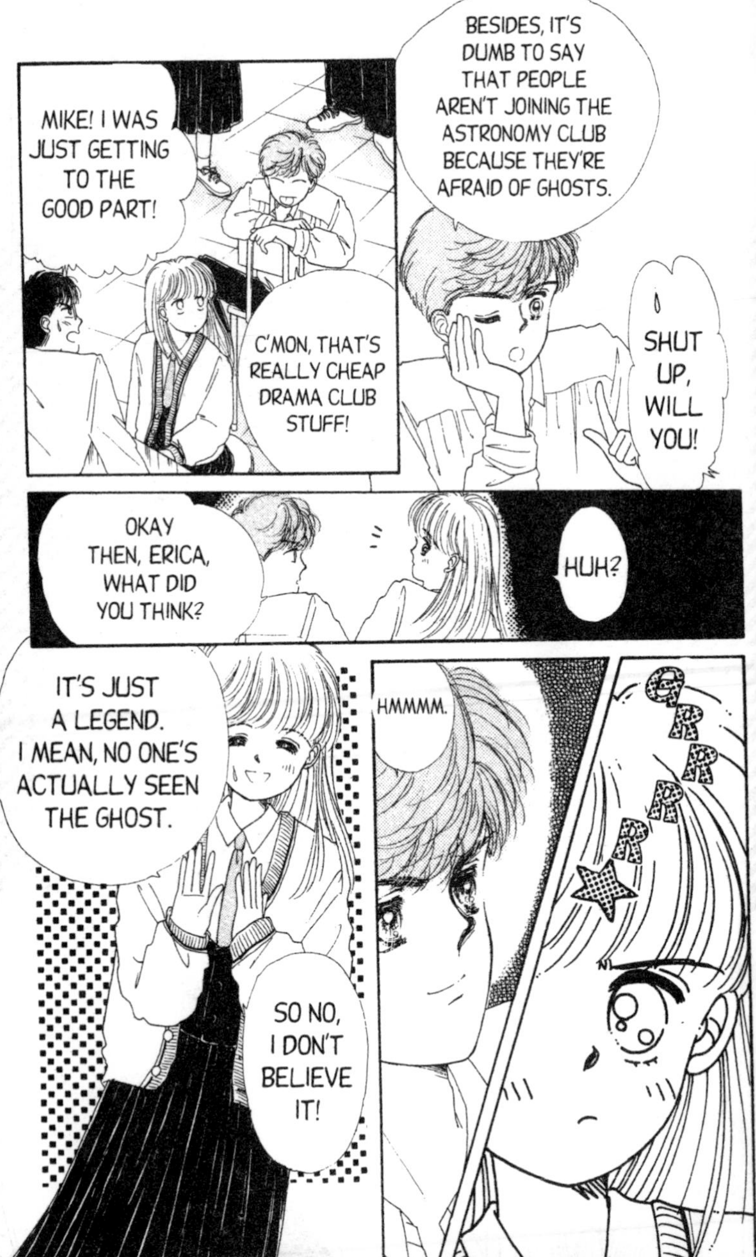
MIKE! I WAS JUST GETTING TO THE GOOD PART!
C'MON, THAT'S REALLY CHEAP DRAMA CLUB STUFF!
BESIDES, IT'S DUMB TO SAY THAT PEOPLE AREN'T JOINING THE ASTRONOMY CLUB BECAUSE THEY'RE AFRAID OF GHOSTS.
SHUT UP, WILL YOU!
OKAY THEN, ERICA, WHAT DID YOU THINK?
HUH?
IT'S JUST A LEGEND. I MEAN, NO ONE'S ACTUALLY SEEN THE GHOST.
SO NO, I DON'T BELIEVE IT!
HMMMM.
GRRRR

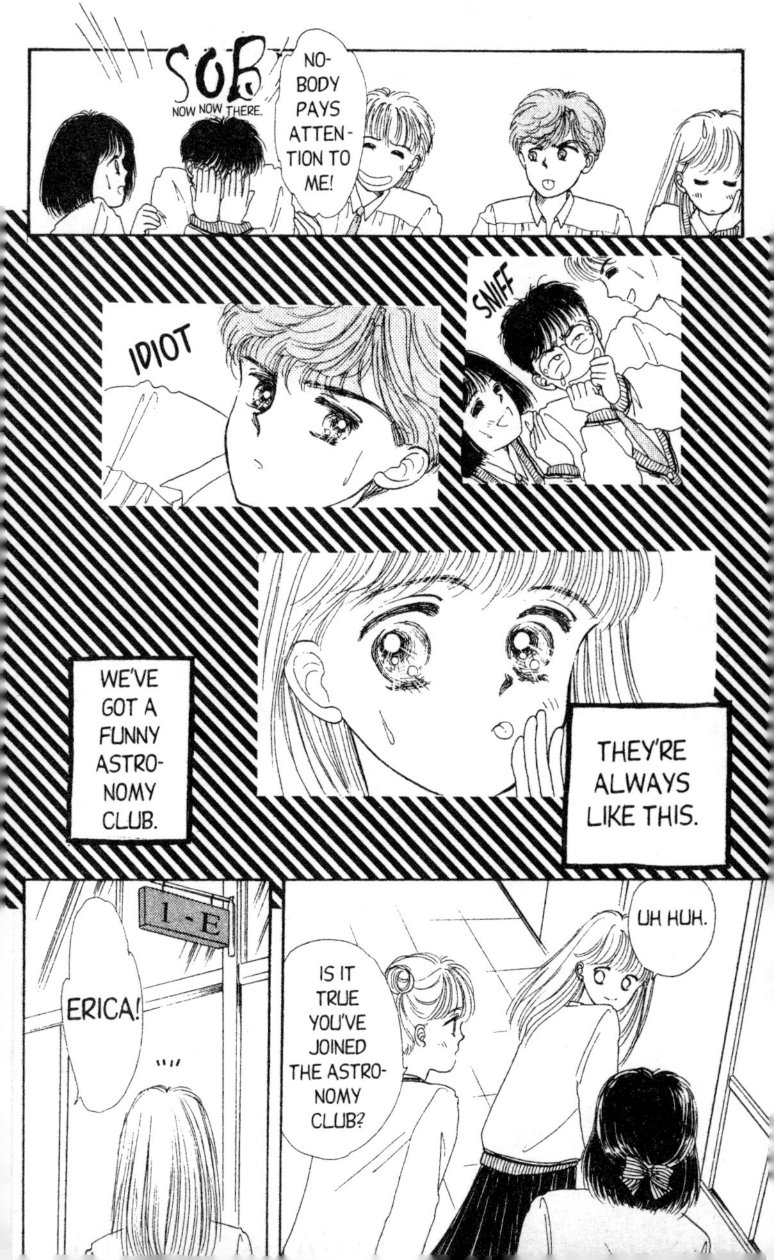
SOB
NOW NOW THERE.
NO-BODY PAYS ATTEN-TION TO ME!
IDIOT
SNIFF
WE'VE GOT A FUNNY ASTRO-NOMY CLUB.
THEY'RE ALWAYS LIKE THIS.
1-E
ERICA!
...
IS IT TRUE YOU'VE JOINED THE ASTRO-NOMY CLUB?
UH HUH.

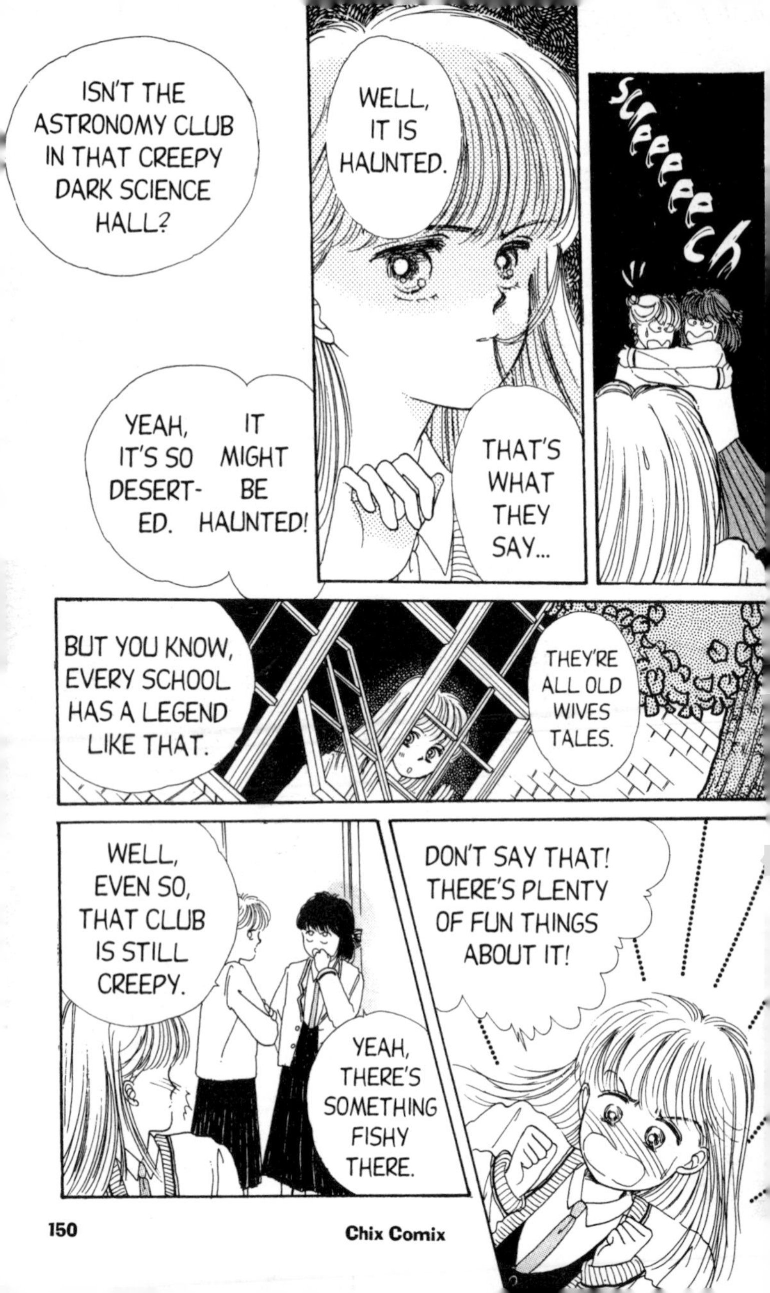
ISN'T THE ASTRONOMY CLUB IN THAT CREEPY DARK SCIENCE HALL?
WELL, IT IS HAUNTED.
YEAH, IT'S SO DESERT-ED.
IT MIGHT BE HAUNTED!
THAT'S WHAT THEY SAY...
BUT YOU KNOW, EVERY SCHOOL HAS A LEGEND LIKE THAT.
THEY'RE ALL OLD WIVES TALES.
WELL, EVEN SO, THAT CLUB IS STILL CREEPY.
YEAH, THERE'S SOMETHING FISHY THERE.
DON'T SAY THAT! THERE'S PLENTY OF FUN THINGS ABOUT IT!

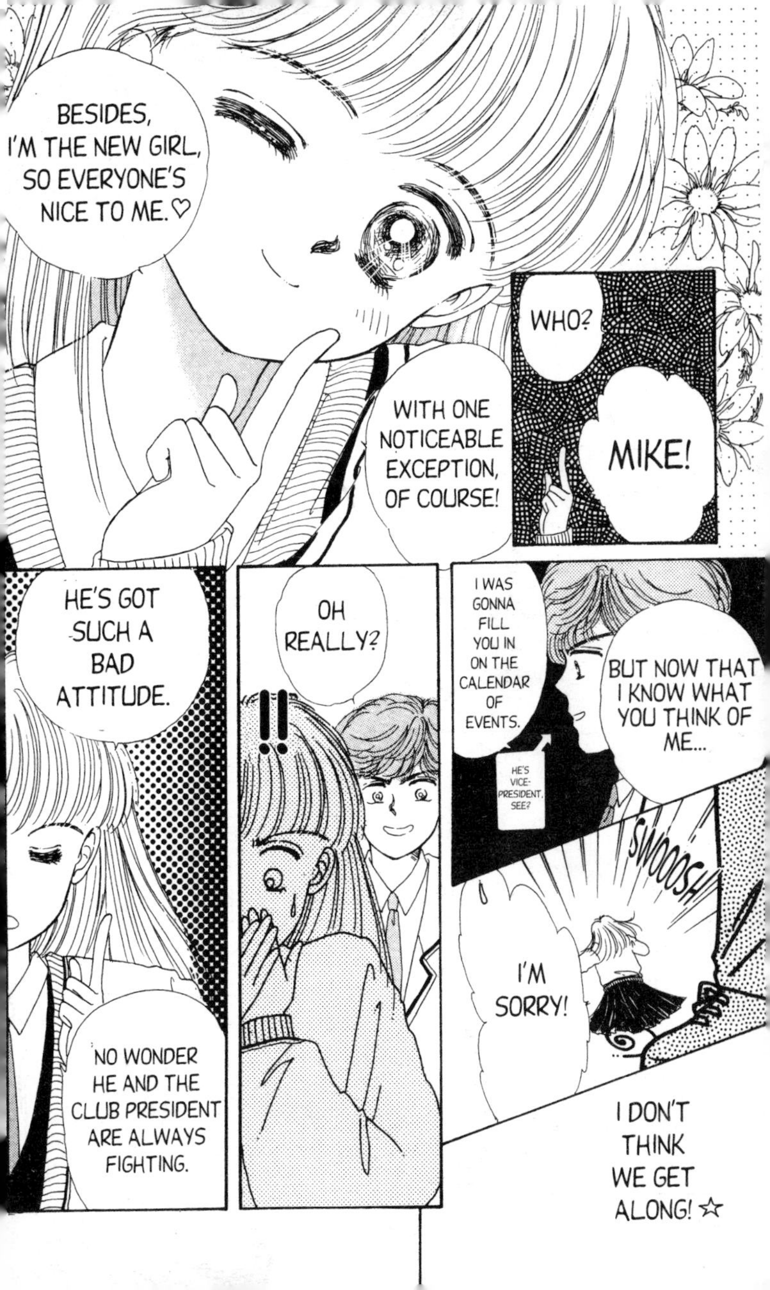
BESIDES, I'M THE NEW GIRL, SO EVERYONE'S NICE TO ME. ♡
WITH ONE NOTICEABLE EXCEPTION, OF COURSE!
WHO?
MIKE!
HE'S GOT SUCH A BAD ATTITUDE.
NO WONDER HE AND THE CLUB PRESIDENT ARE ALWAYS FIGHTING.
OH REALLY?
!!
I WAS GONNA FILL YOU IN ON THE CALENDAR OF EVENTS.
HE'S VICE-PRESIDENT, SEE?
BUT NOW THAT I KNOW WHAT YOU THINK OF ME...
SWOOOSH
I'M SORRY!
I DON'T THINK WE GET ALONG! ☆

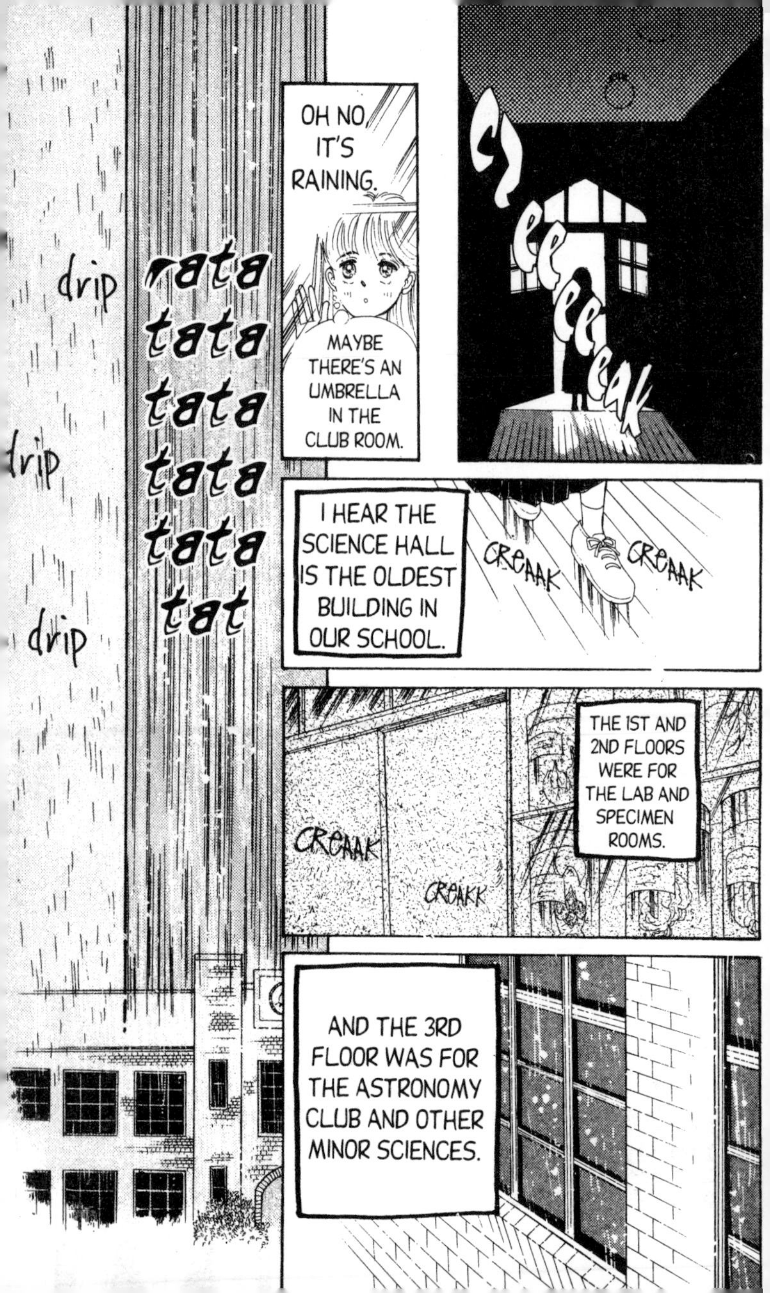
drip
tata
tata
tata
tata
tata
tat
drip
drip
OH NO, IT'S RAINING.
MAYBE THERE'S AN UMBRELLA IN THE CLUB ROOM.
creeeeeak
I HEAR THE SCIENCE HALL IS THE OLDEST BUILDING IN OUR SCHOOL.
CREAAK
CREAAK
CREAAK
THE 1ST AND 2ND FLOORS WERE FOR THE LAB AND SPECIMEN ROOMS.
CREAKK
AND THE 3RD FLOOR WAS FOR THE ASTRONOMY CLUB AND OTHER MINOR SCIENCES.

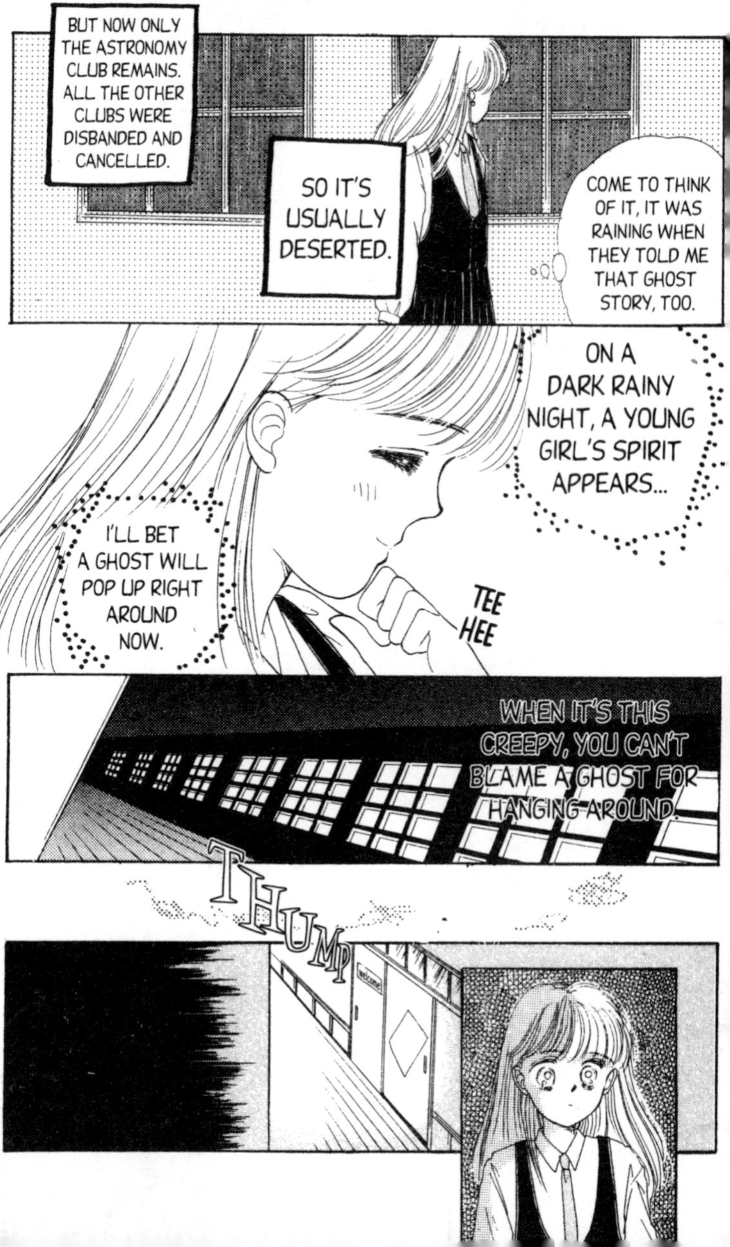
BUT NOW ONLY THE ASTRONOMY CLUB REMAINS. ALL THE OTHER CLUBS WERE DISBANDED AND CANCELLED.
SO IT'S USUALLY DESERTED.
COME TO THINK OF IT, IT WAS RAINING WHEN THEY TOLD ME THAT GHOST STORY, TOO.
I'LL BET A GHOST WILL POP UP RIGHT AROUND NOW.
ON A DARK RAINY NIGHT, A YOUNG GIRL'S SPIRIT APPEARS...
TEE HEE
WHEN IT'S THIS CREEPY, YOU CAN'T BLAME A GHOST FOR HANGING AROUND.
THUMP
welcome

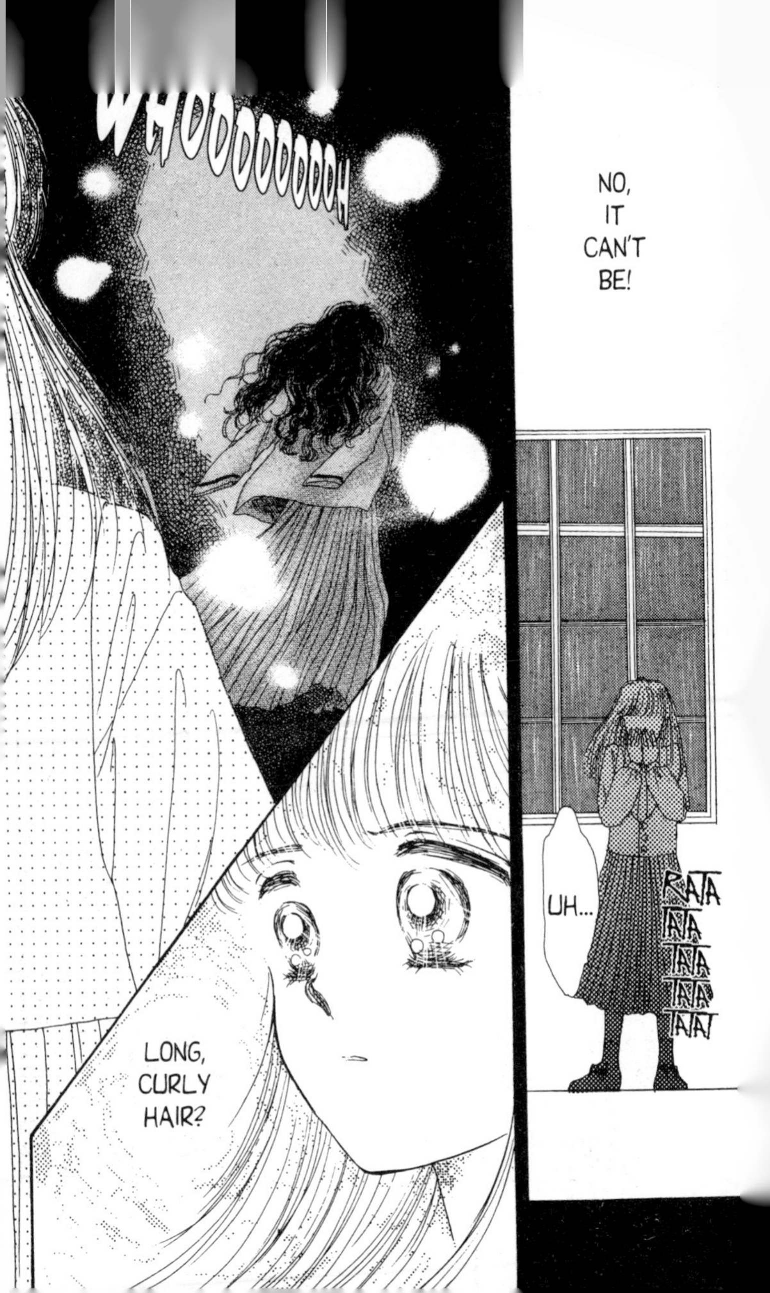
WHOOOOOOOOOH
LONG, CURLY HAIR?
NO, IT CAN'T BE!
UH...
RATATATATATATATATAT

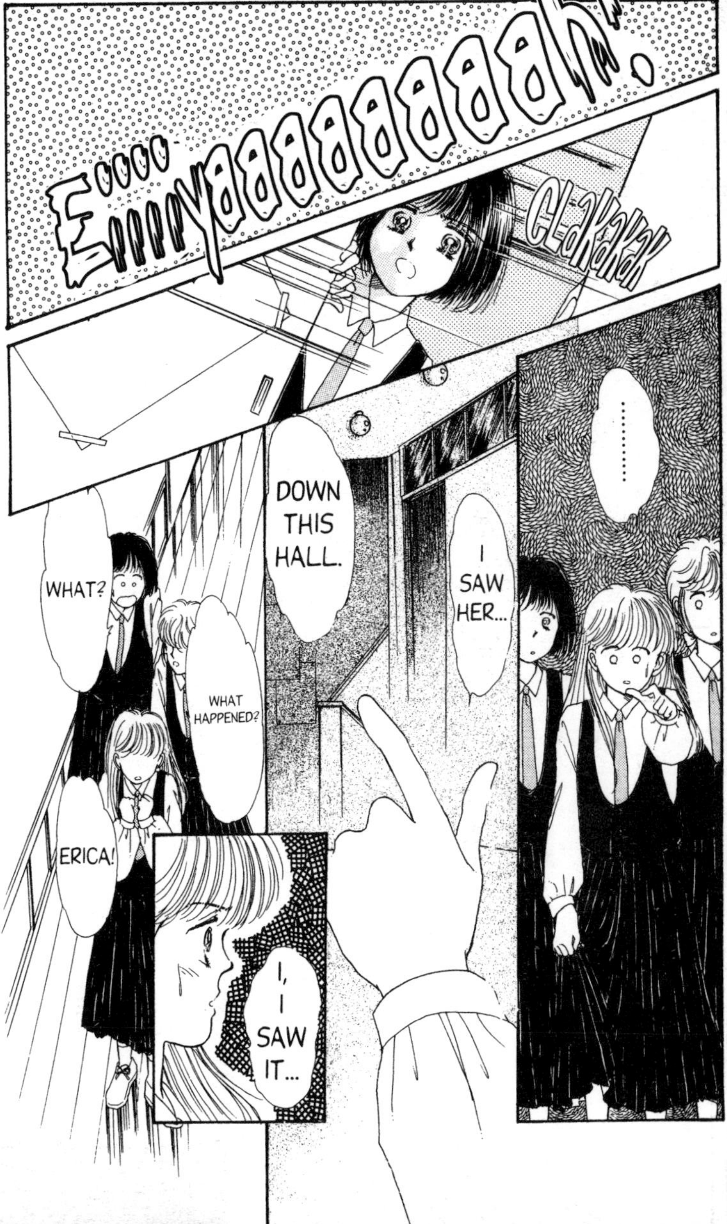

Eeeeeyaaaaaaaaah!
CLAKAKAK
WHAT?
WHAT HAPPENED?
ERICA!
DOWN THIS HALL.
I SAW HER...
I, I SAW IT...
......

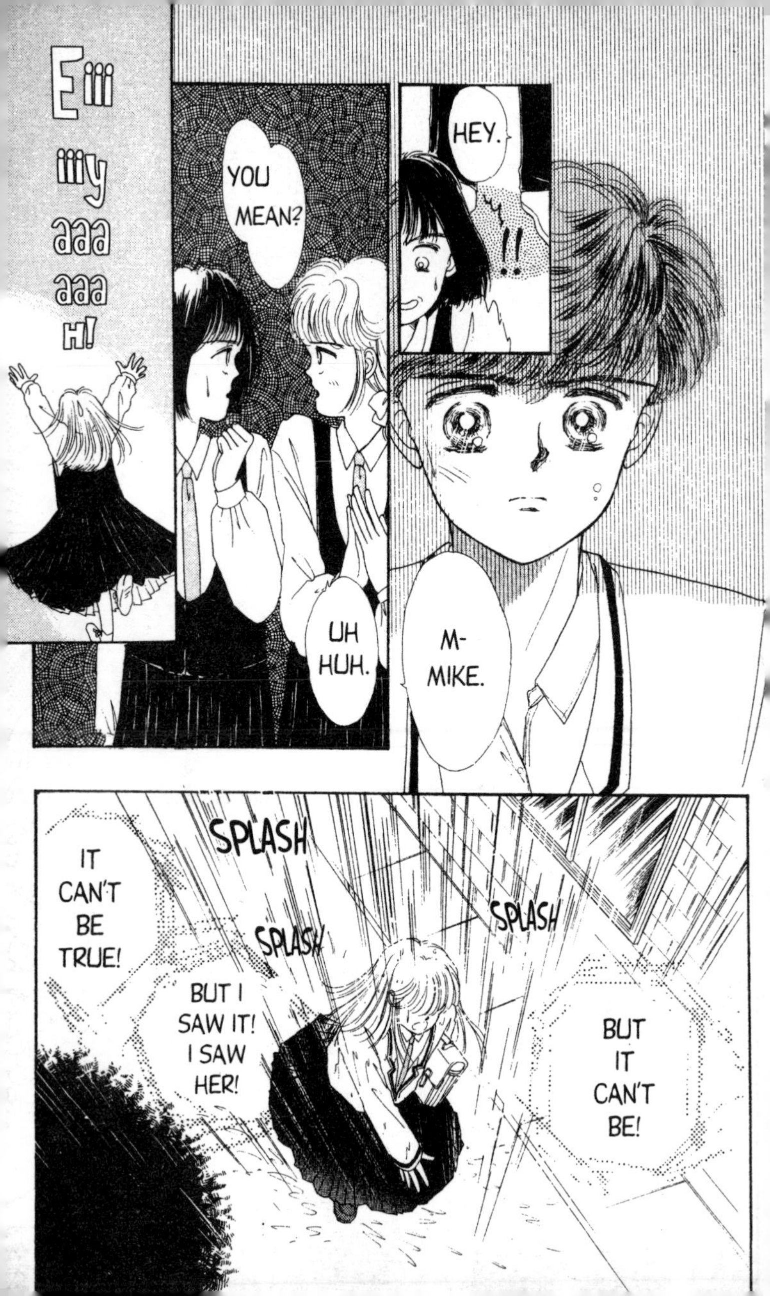
Eiiiiiiy aaaaaah!
YOU MEAN?
UH HUH.
HEY.
!!
M-MIKE.
IT CAN'T BE TRUE!
SPLASH
SPLASH
BUT I SAW IT! I SAW HER!
SPLASH
BUT IT CAN'T BE!

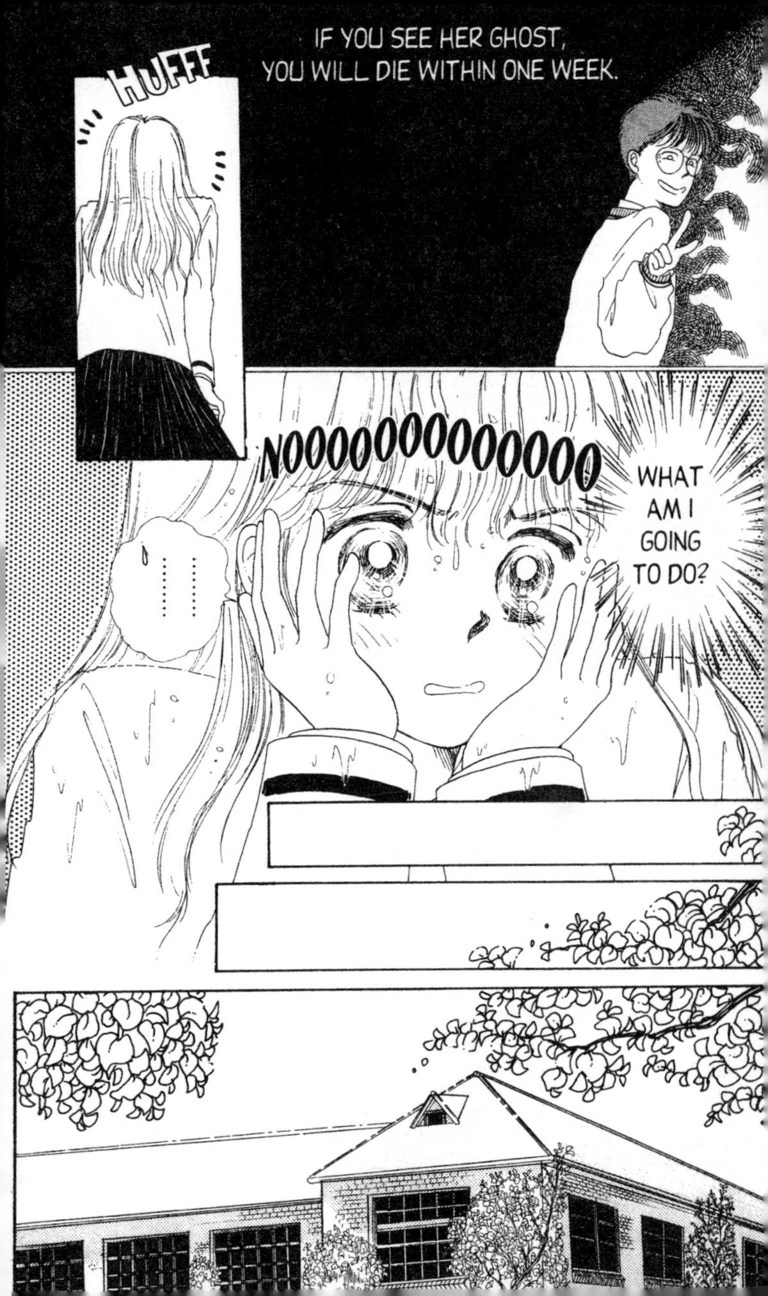
HUFFF
IF YOU SEE HER GHOST, YOU WILL DIE WITHIN ONE WEEK.
NOOOOOOOOOOOOOO
WHAT AM I GOING TO DO?
......
......

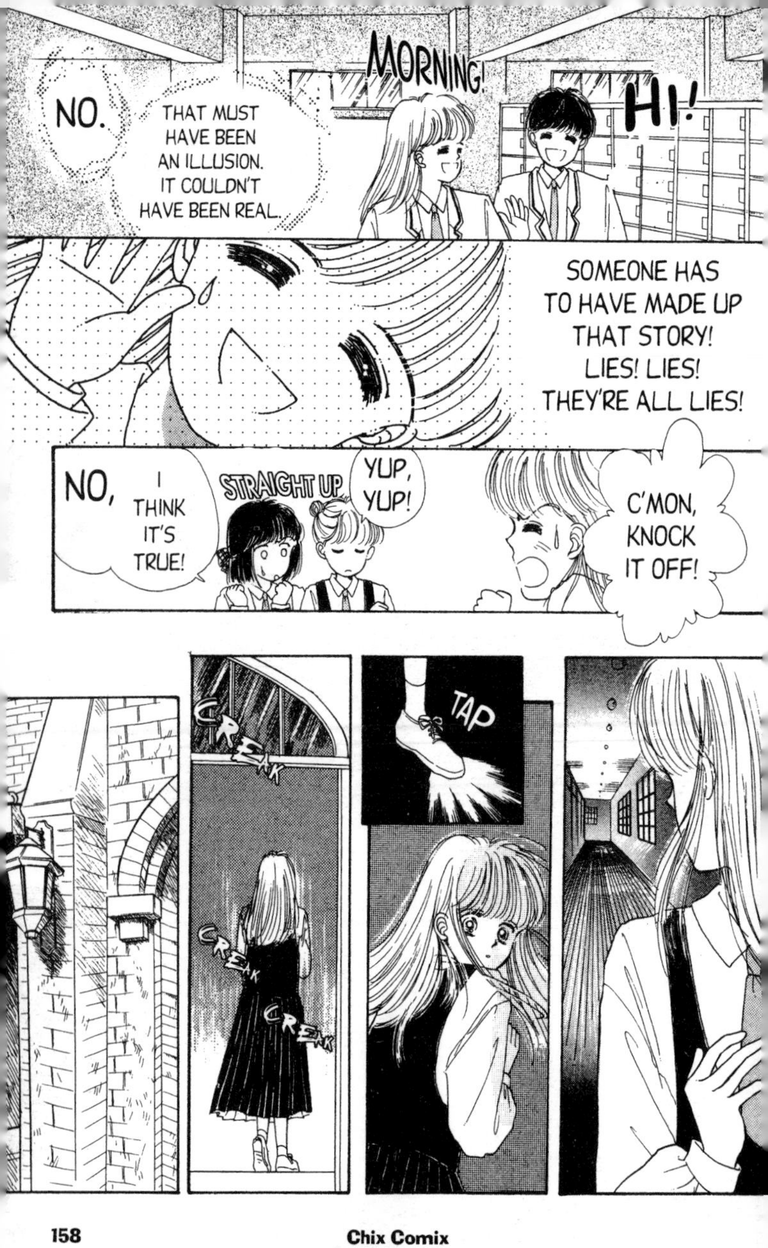
NO.
THAT MUST HAVE BEEN AN ILLUSION. IT COULDN'T HAVE BEEN REAL.
MORNING!
HI!
SOMEONE HAS TO HAVE MADE UP THAT STORY! LIES! LIES! THEY'RE ALL LIES!
NO, I THINK IT'S TRUE!
STRAIGHT UP
YUP, YUP!
C'MON, KNOCK IT OFF!
CREAK
CREAK
CREAK
TAP

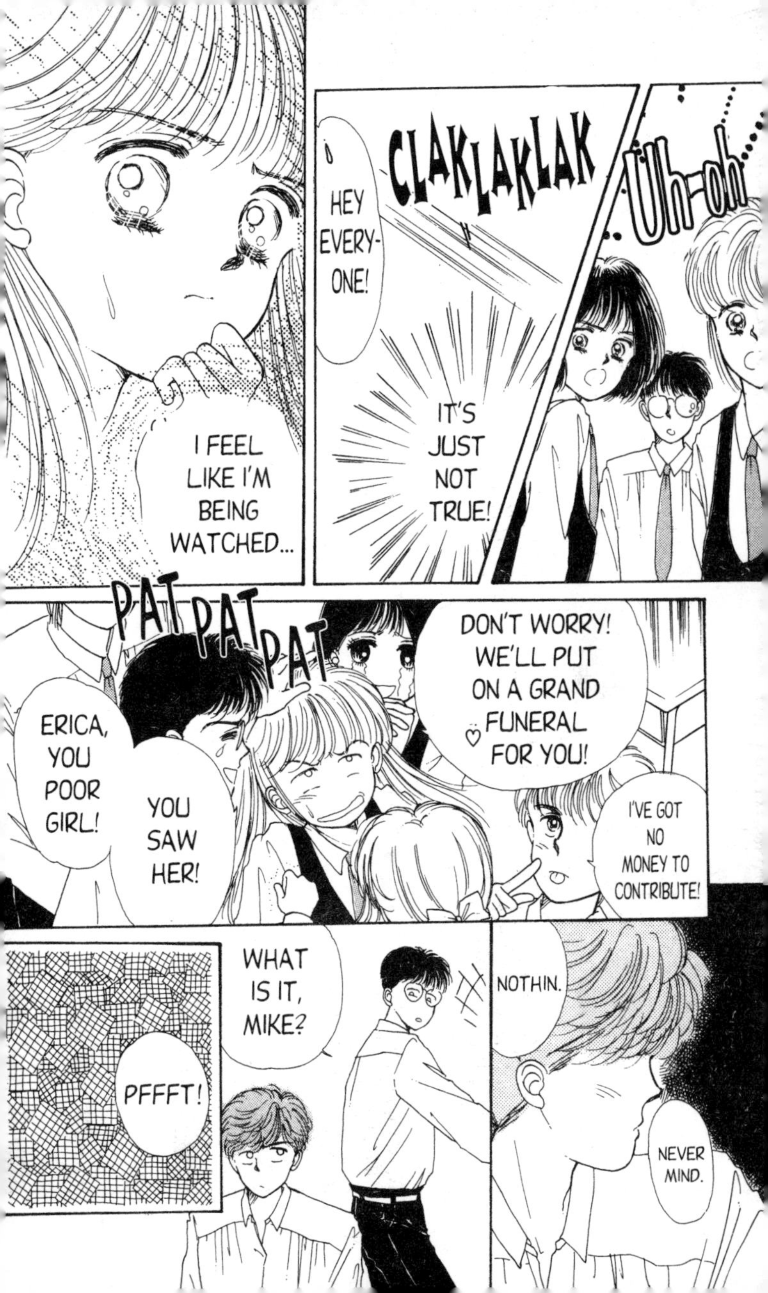
I FEEL LIKE I'M BEING WATCHED...
HEY EVERY-ONE!
CLAKLAKLAK
IT'S JUST NOT TRUE!
Uh-oh
PAT PAT PAT
ERICA, YOU POOR GIRL!
YOU SAW HER!
DON'T WORRY! WE'LL PUT ON A GRAND FUNERAL FOR YOU!
I'VE GOT NO MONEY TO CONTRIBUTE!
PFFFT!
WHAT IS IT, MIKE?
NOTHIN.
NEVER MIND.

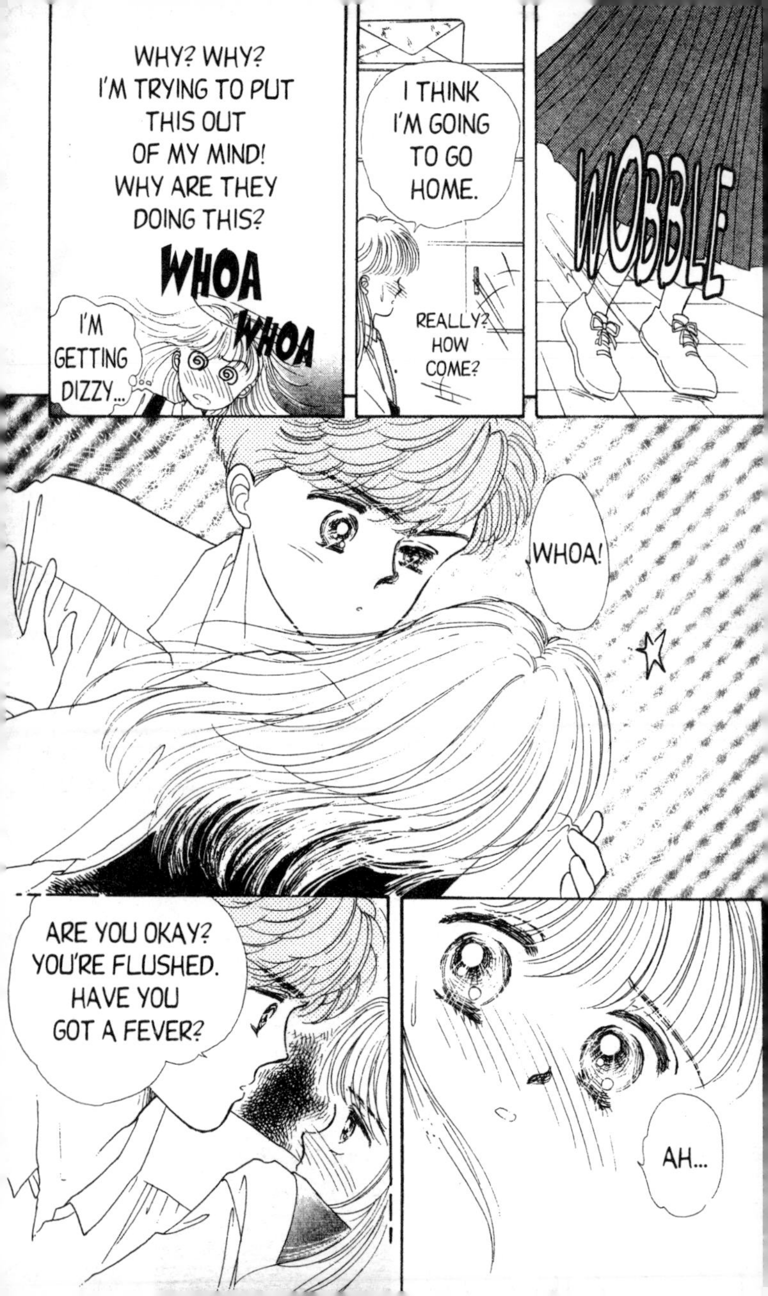
WHY? WHY? I'M TRYING TO PUT THIS OUT OF MY MIND! WHY ARE THEY DOING THIS?
WHOA
WHOA
I'M GETTING DIZZY...
I THINK I'M GOING TO GO HOME.
REALLY? HOW COME?
WOBBLE
WHOA!
ARE YOU OKAY? YOU'RE FLUSHED. HAVE YOU GOT A FEVER?
AH...

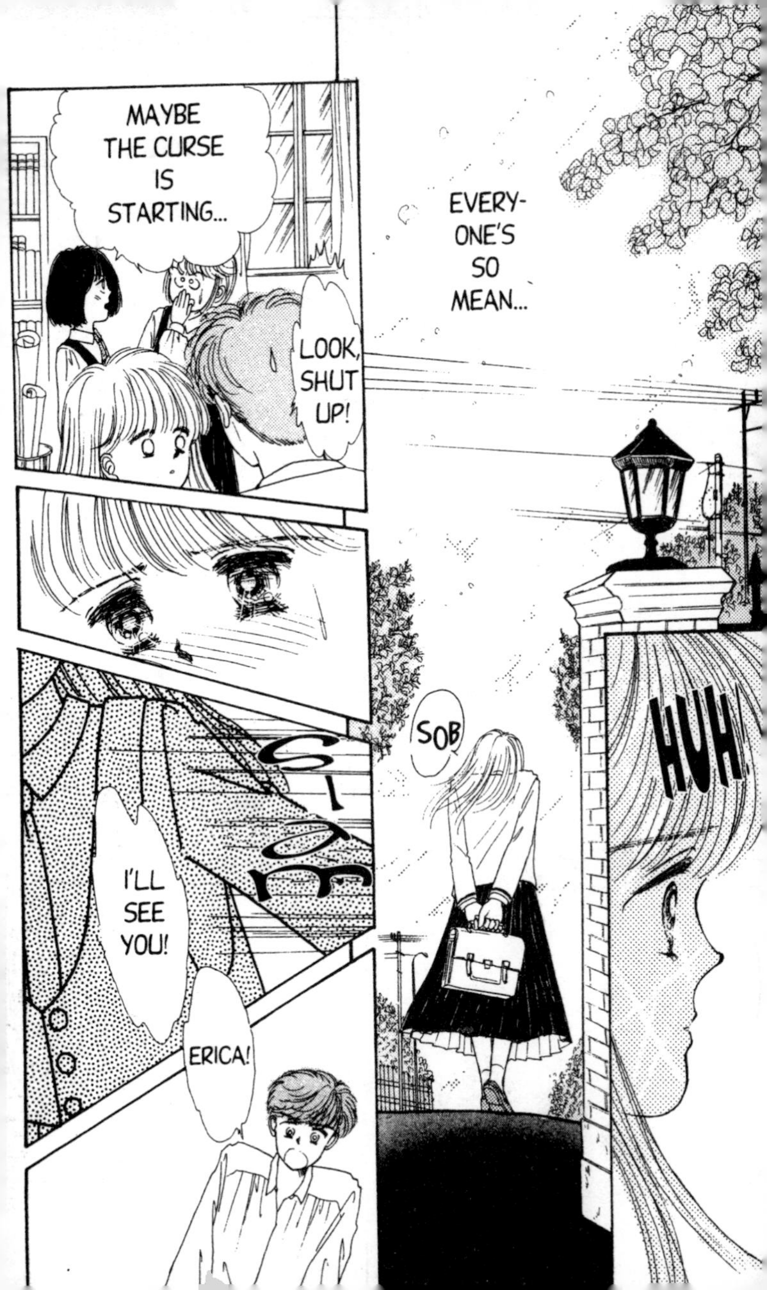
MAYBE THE CURSE IS STARTING...
LOOK, SHUT UP!
I'LL SEE YOU!
ERICA!
EVERY-ONE'S SO MEAN...
SOB
HUH!

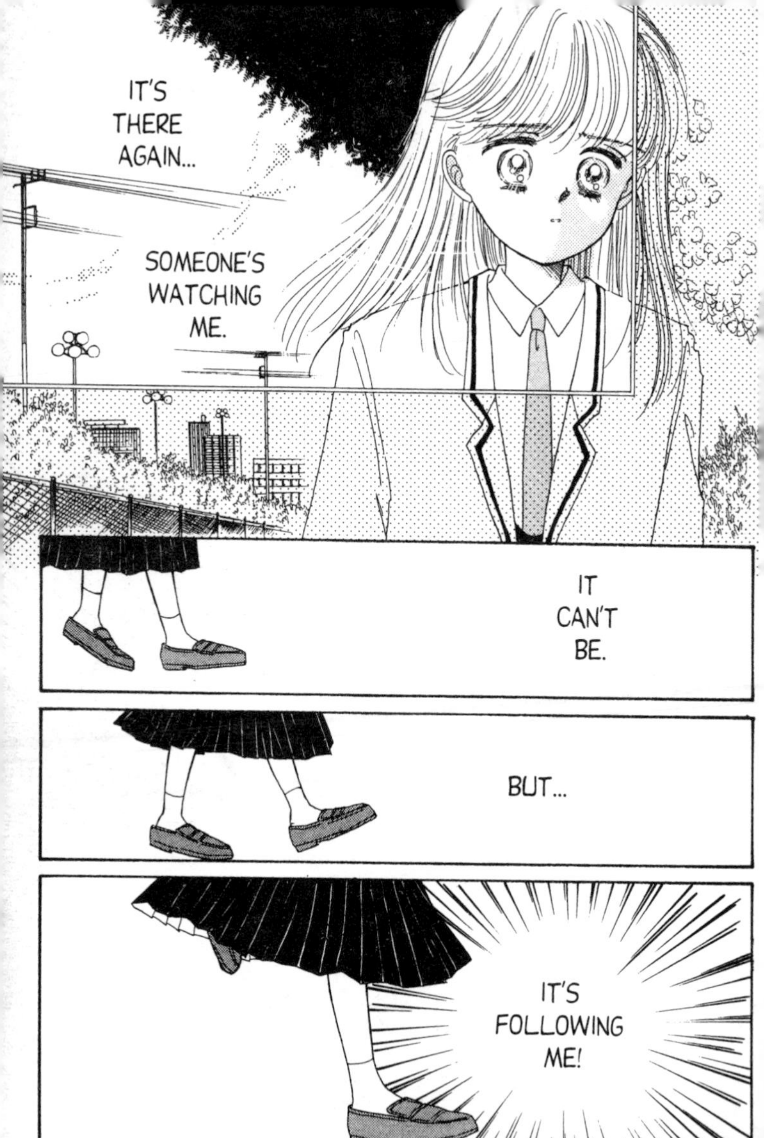
IT'S THERE AGAIN...
SOMEONE'S WATCHING ME.
IT CAN'T BE.
BUT...
IT'S FOLLOWING ME!

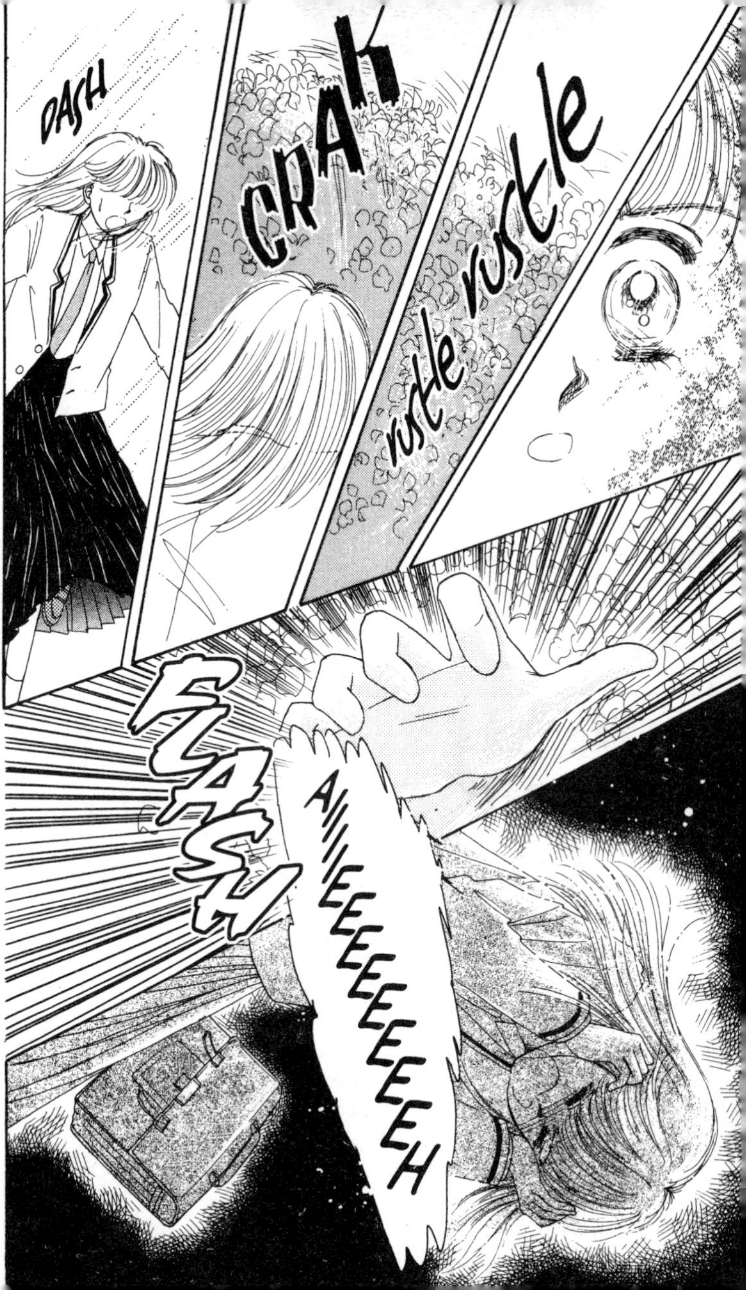

DASH
CRAK
rustle rustle
FLASH
AIIIEEEEEEEEH

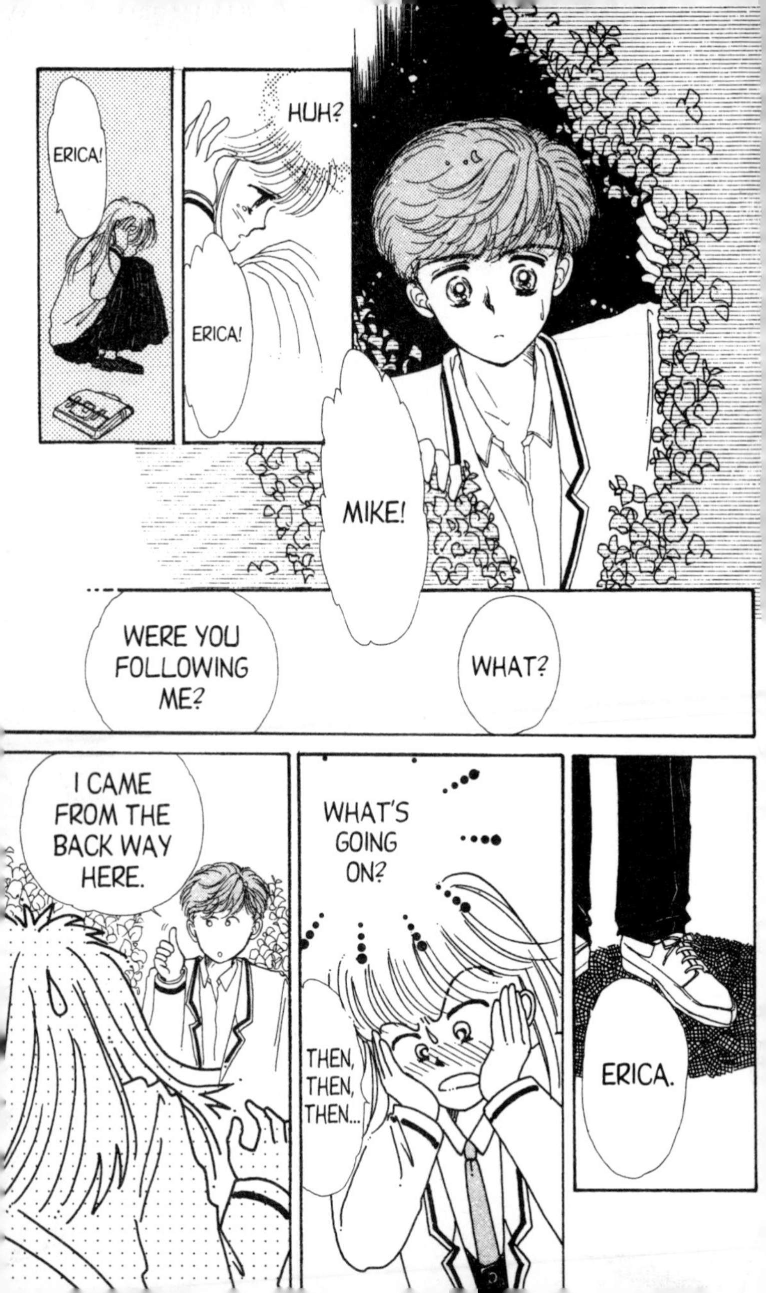
ERICA!
HUH?
ERICA!
MIKE!
WERE YOU FOLLOWING ME?
WHAT?
I CAME FROM THE BACK WAY HERE.
WHAT'S GOING ON?
THEN, THEN, THEN...
ERICA.

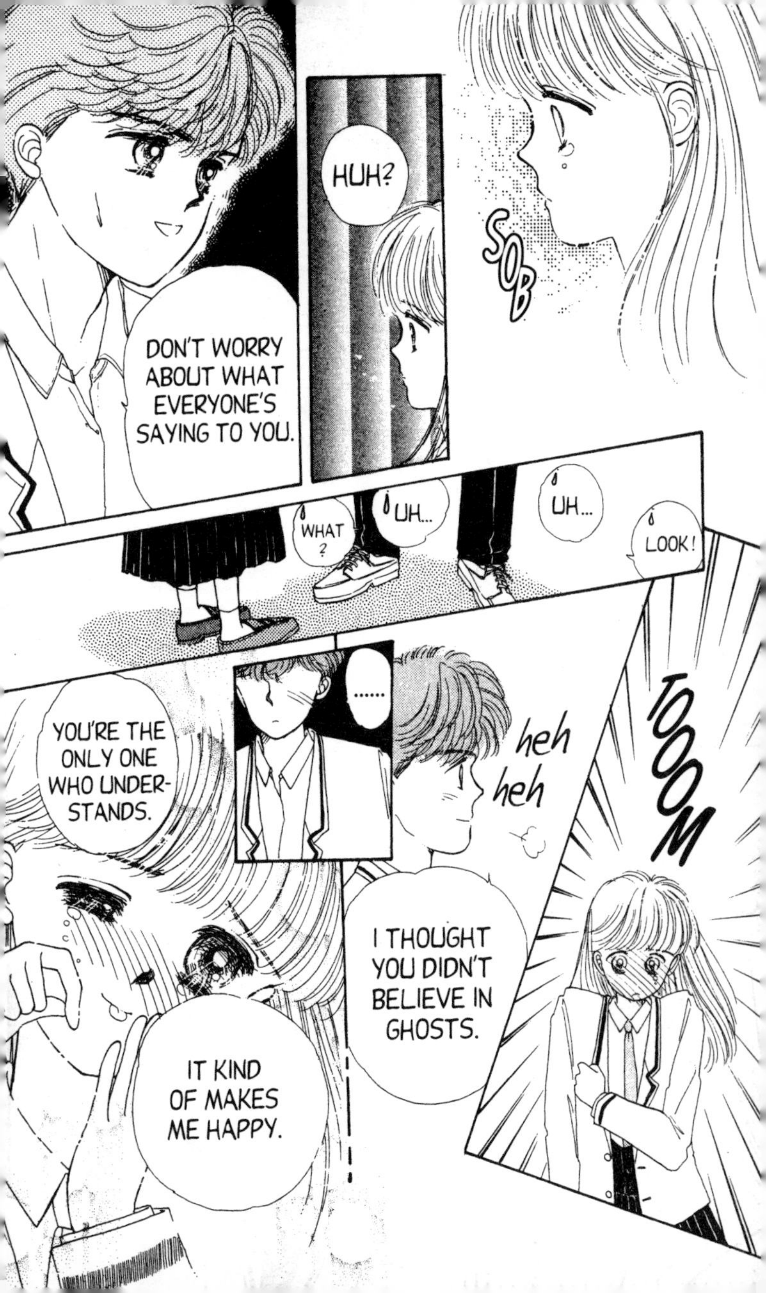
DON'T WORRY ABOUT WHAT EVERYONE'S SAYING TO YOU.
HUH?
SOB
WHAT ?
UH...
UH...
LOOK!
YOU'RE THE ONLY ONE WHO UNDER-STANDS.
IT KIND OF MAKES ME HAPPY.
......
heh heh
I THOUGHT YOU DIDN'T BELIEVE IN GHOSTS.
TOOOOM

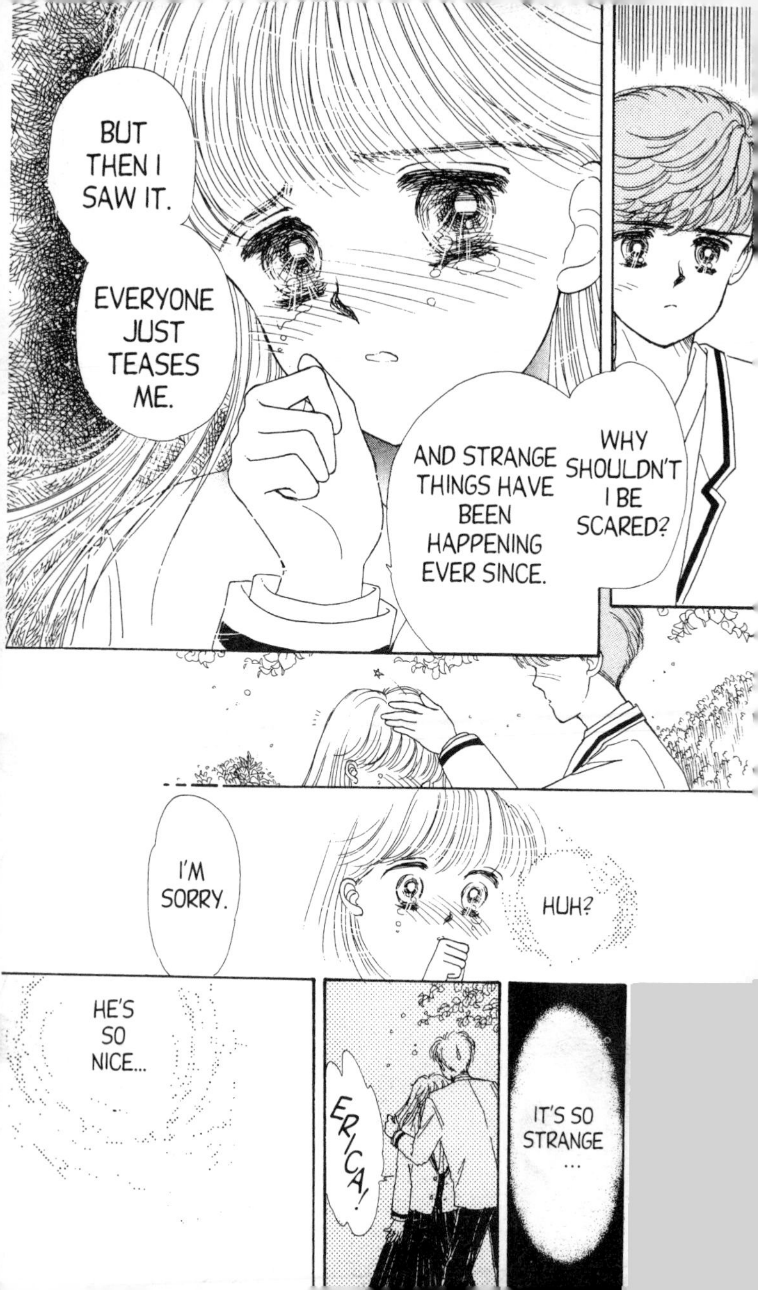
BUT THEN I SAW IT.
EVERYONE JUST TEASES ME.
AND STRANGE THINGS HAVE BEEN HAPPENING EVER SINCE.
WHY SHOULDN'T I BE SCARED?
I'M SORRY.
HUH?
HE'S SO NICE...
ERICA!
IT'S SO STRANGE ...

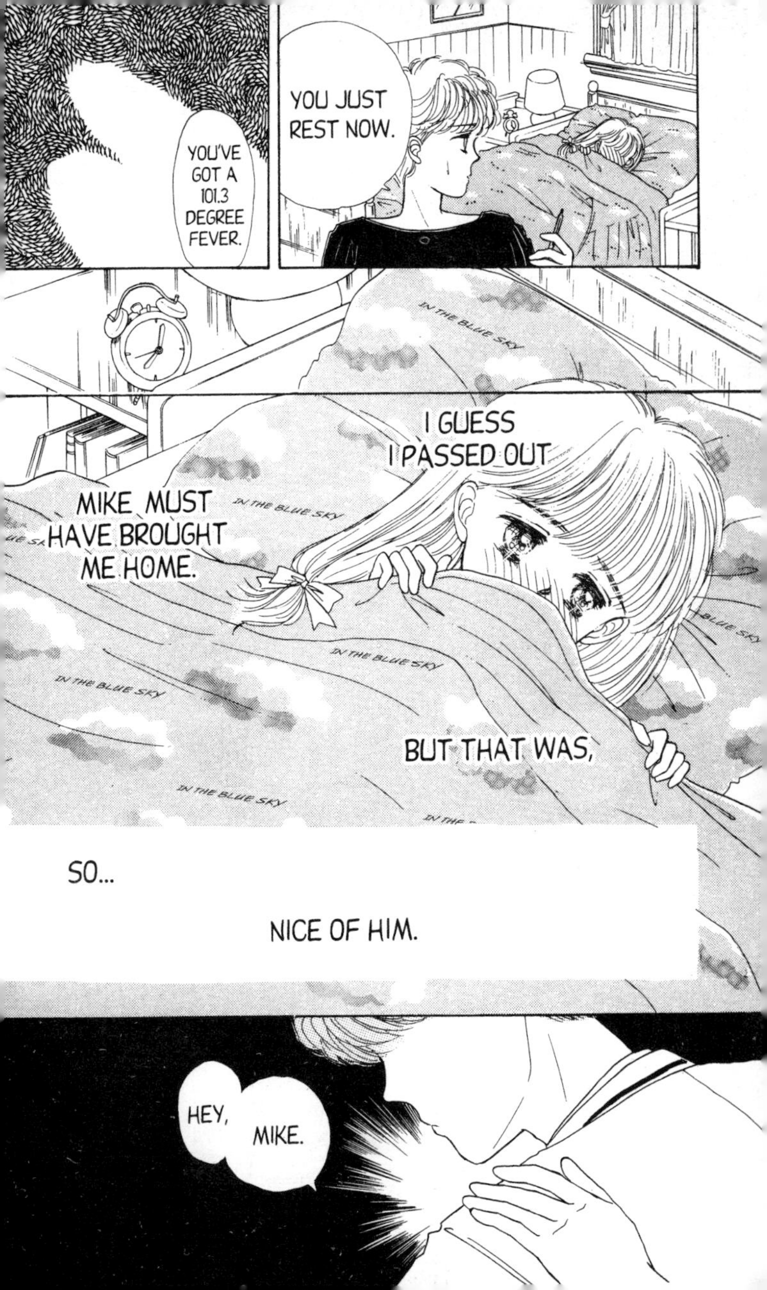
YOU'VE GOT A 101.3 DEGREE FEVER.
YOU JUST REST NOW.
IN THE BLUE SKY
I GUESS I PASSED OUT
MIKE MUST HAVE BROUGHT ME HOME.
BUT THAT WAS,
SO...
NICE OF HIM.
HEY, MIKE.

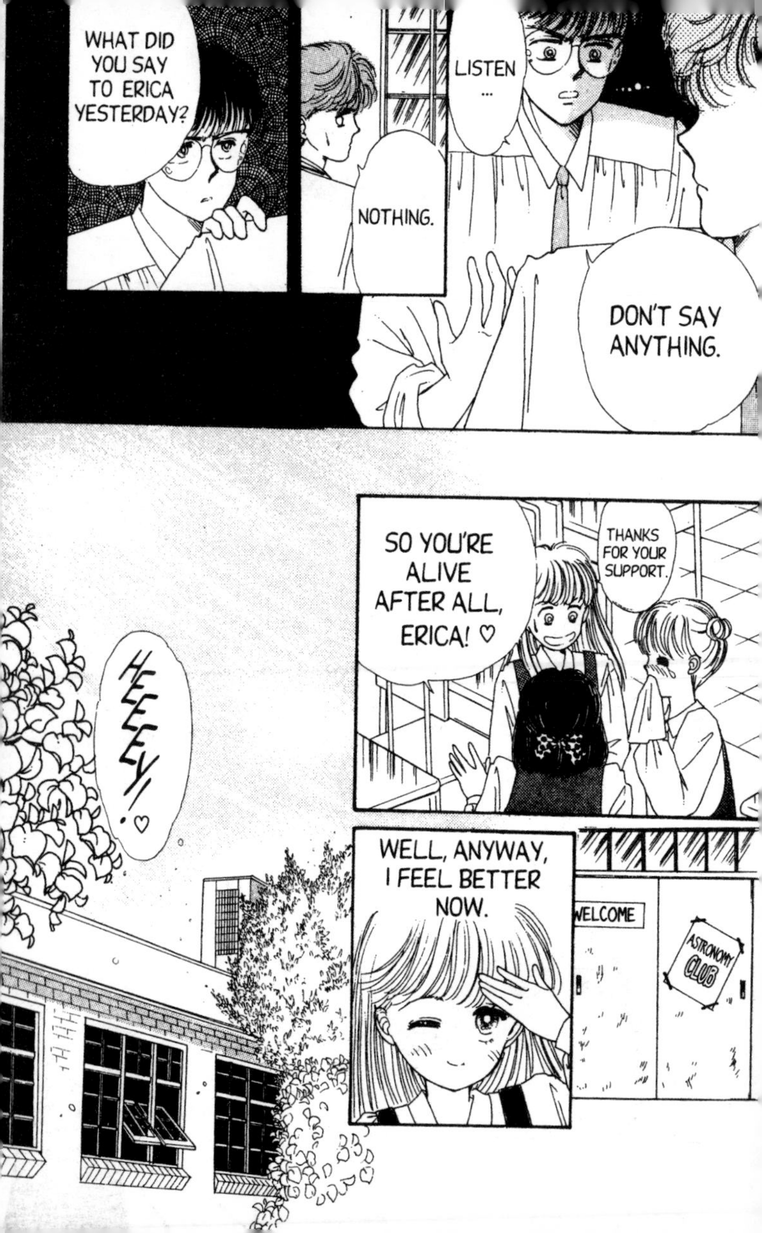
WHAT DID YOU SAY TO ERICA YESTERDAY?
NOTHING.
LISTEN ...
DON'T SAY ANYTHING.
HEEEEY! ♡
SO YOU'RE ALIVE AFTER ALL, ERICA! ♡
THANKS FOR YOUR SUPPORT.
WELL, ANYWAY, I FEEL BETTER NOW.
WELCOME
ASTRONOMY CLUB

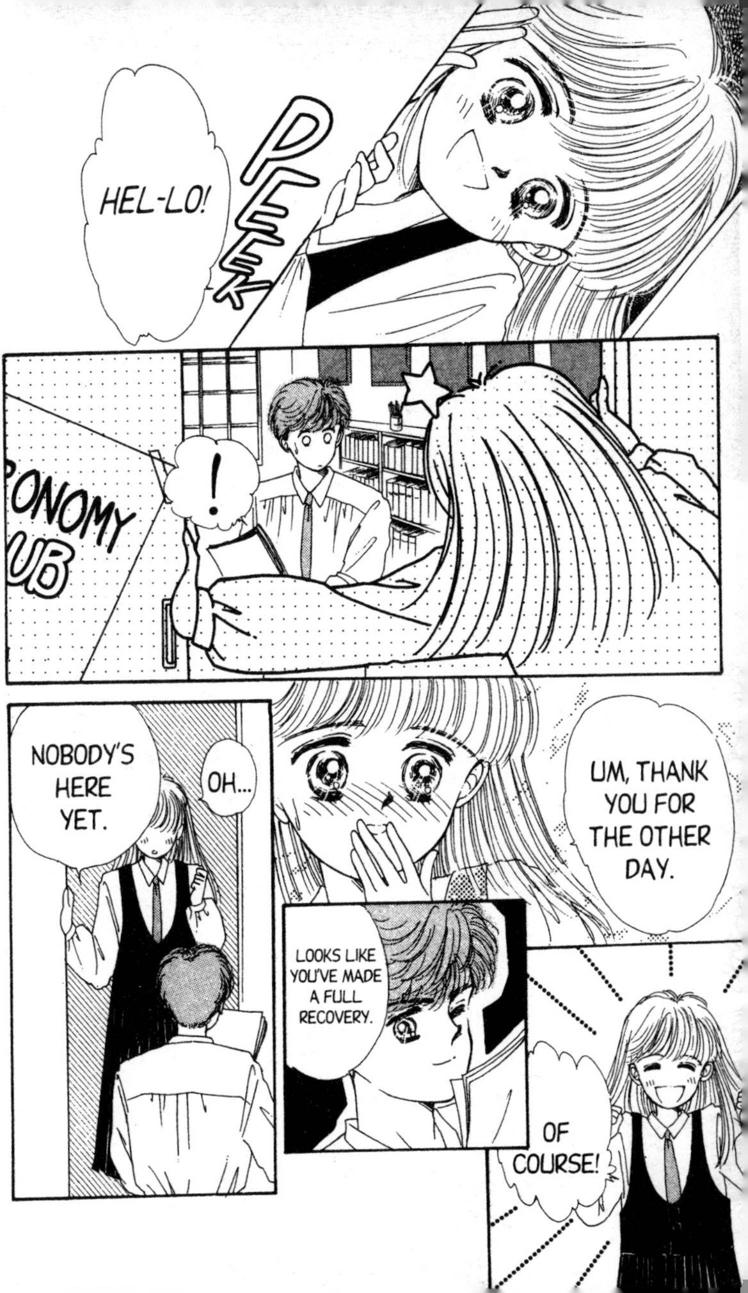
HEL-LO!
PEEK
!
ONOMY
UB
NOBODY'S HERE YET.
OH...
UM, THANK YOU FOR THE OTHER DAY.
LOOKS LIKE YOU'VE MADE A FULL RECOVERY.
OF COURSE!

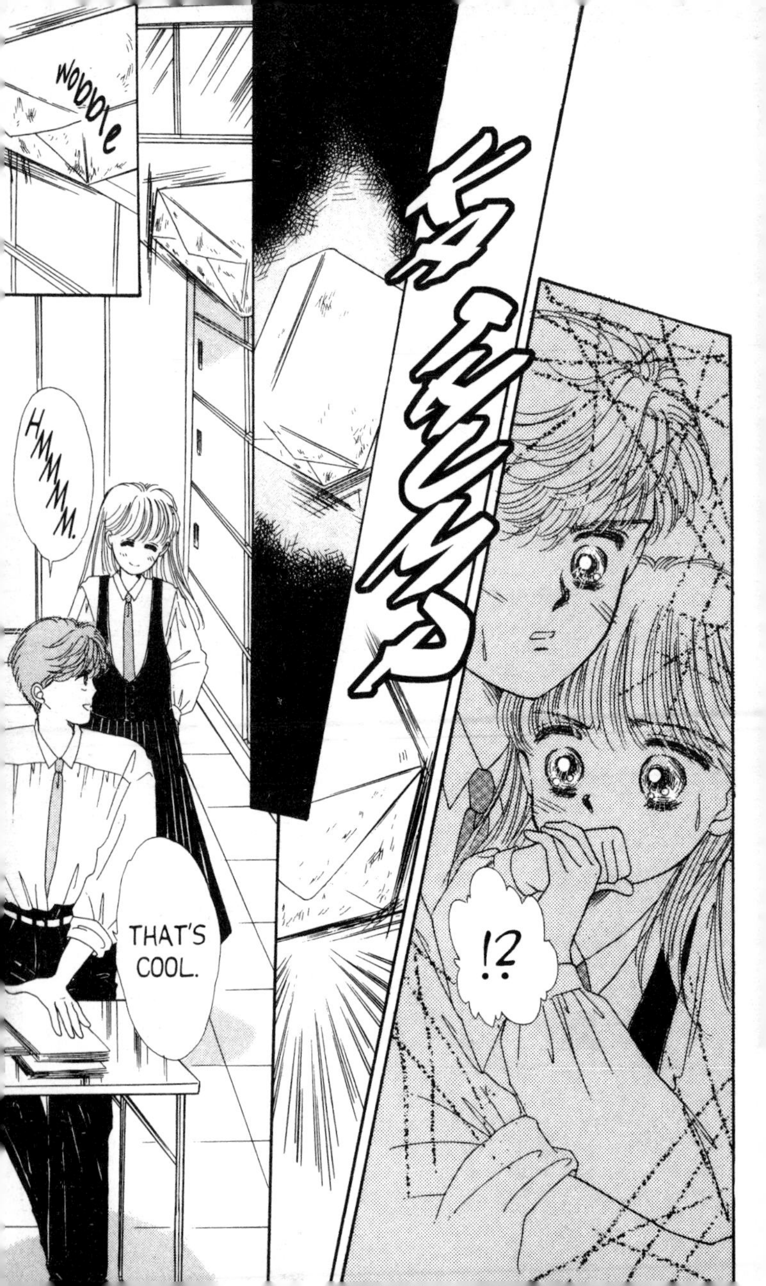
WOBBLE
HMMMM.
THAT'S COOL.
KA-THUMP
!?

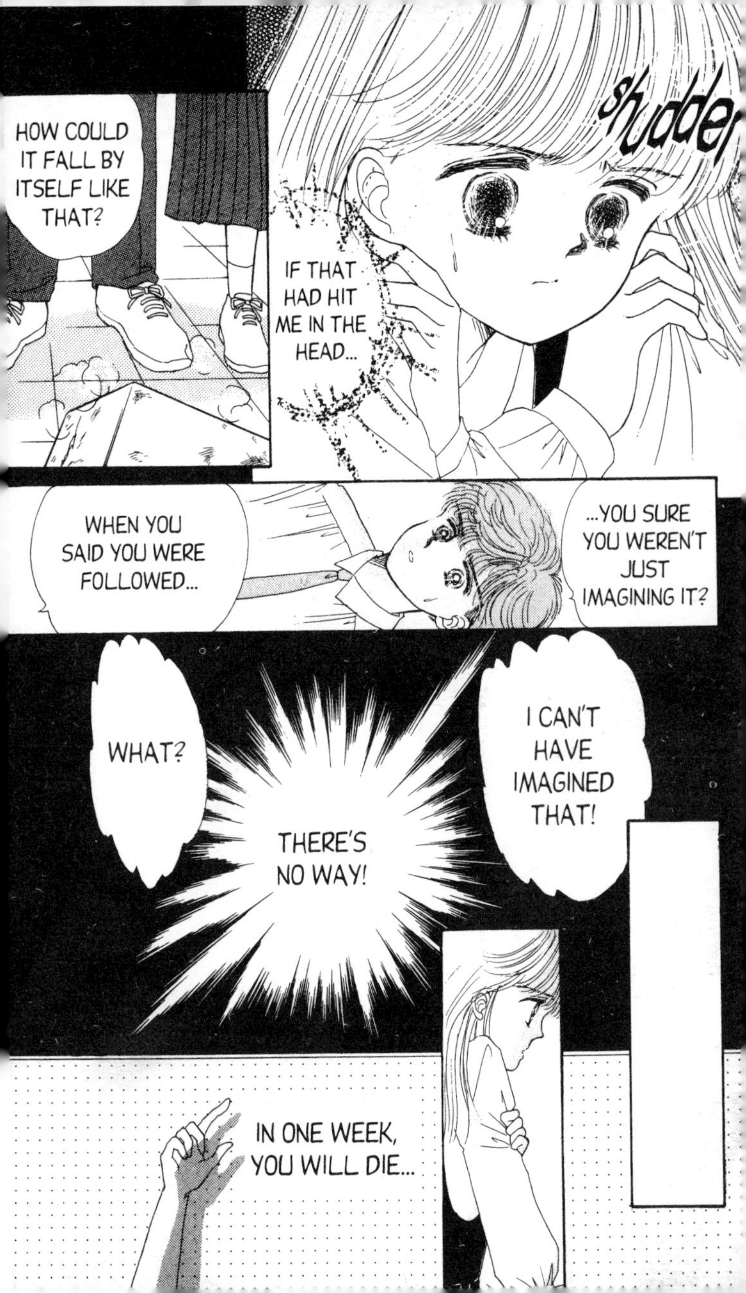
HOW COULD IT FALL BY ITSELF LIKE THAT?
IF THAT HAD HIT ME IN THE HEAD...
shudder
WHEN YOU SAID YOU WERE FOLLOWED...
...YOU SURE YOU WEREN'T JUST IMAGINING IT?
WHAT?
THERE'S NO WAY!
I CAN'T HAVE IMAGINED THAT!
IN ONE WEEK, YOU WILL DIE...

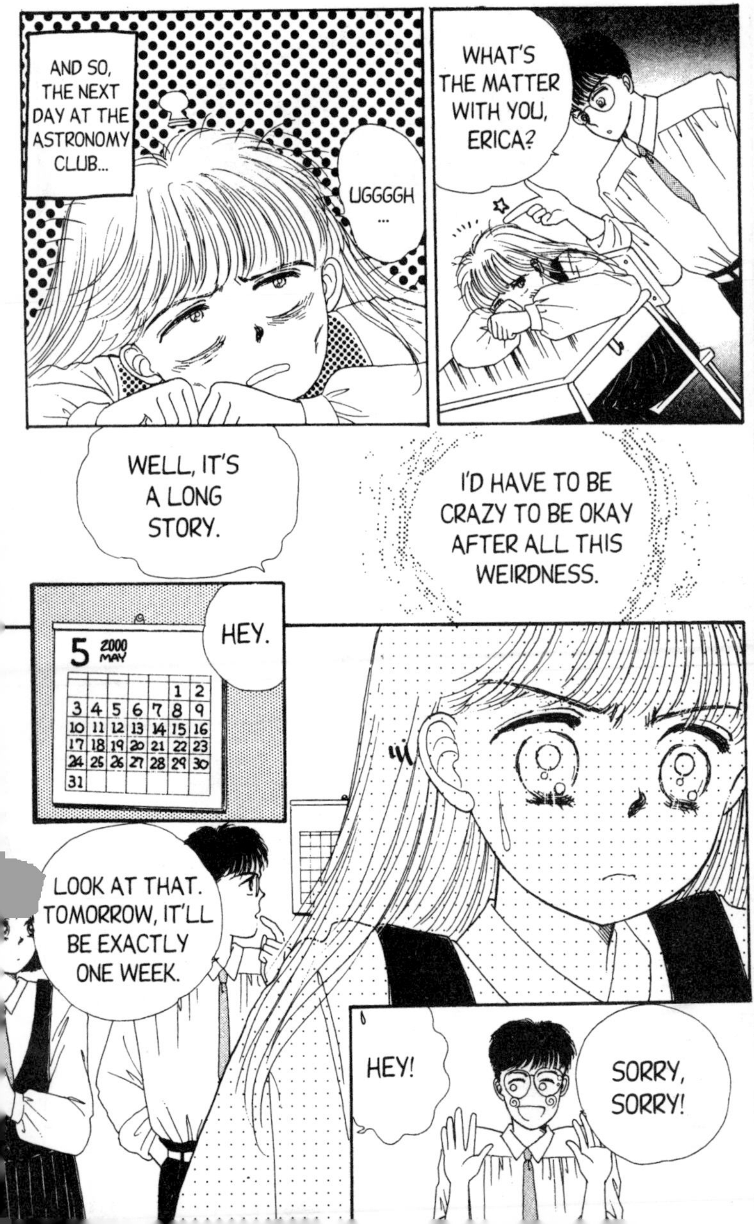
AND SO, THE NEXT DAY AT THE ASTRONOMY CLUB...
UGGGGH ...
WHAT'S THE MATTER WITH YOU, ERICA?
WELL, IT'S A LONG STORY.
I'D HAVE TO BE CRAZY TO BE OKAY AFTER ALL THIS WEIRDNESS.
5 2000 MAY
HEY.
LOOK AT THAT. TOMORROW, IT'LL BE EXACTLY ONE WEEK.
HEY!
SORRY, SORRY!

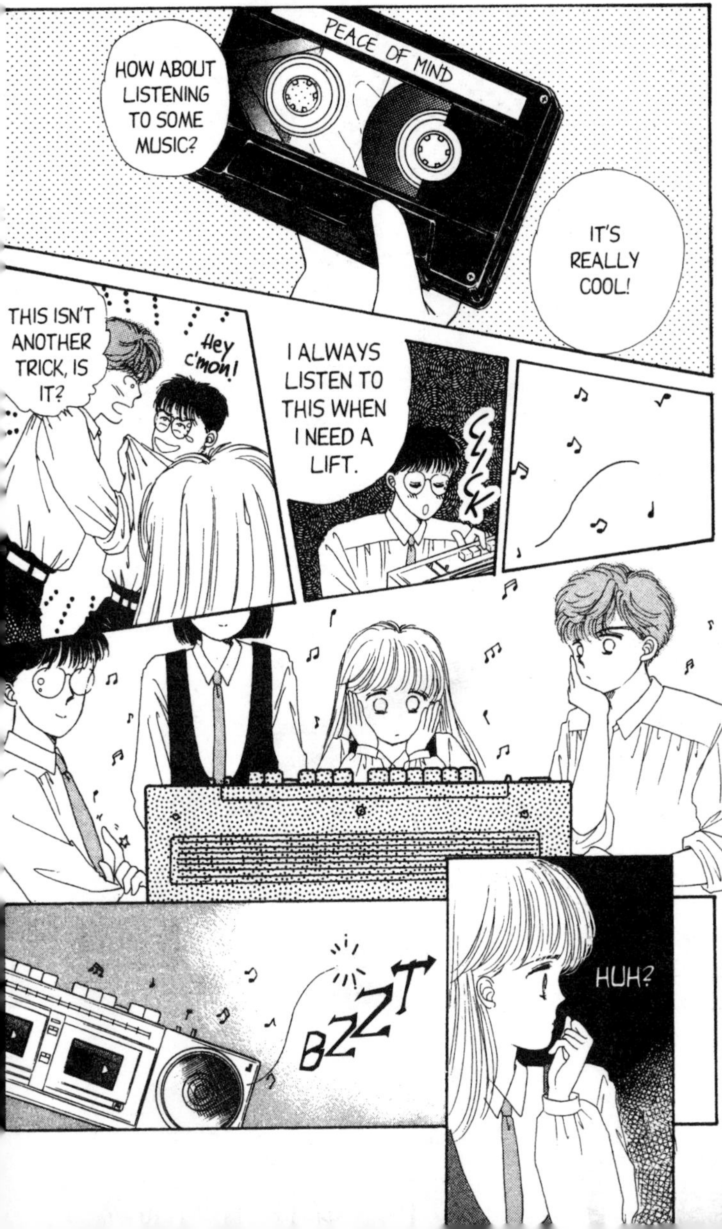
HOW ABOUT LISTENING TO SOME MUSIC?
PEACE OF MIND
IT'S REALLY COOL!
THIS ISN'T ANOTHER TRICK, IS IT?
Hey c'mon!
I ALWAYS LISTEN TO THIS WHEN I NEED A LIFT.
CLICK
BZZZT
HUH?

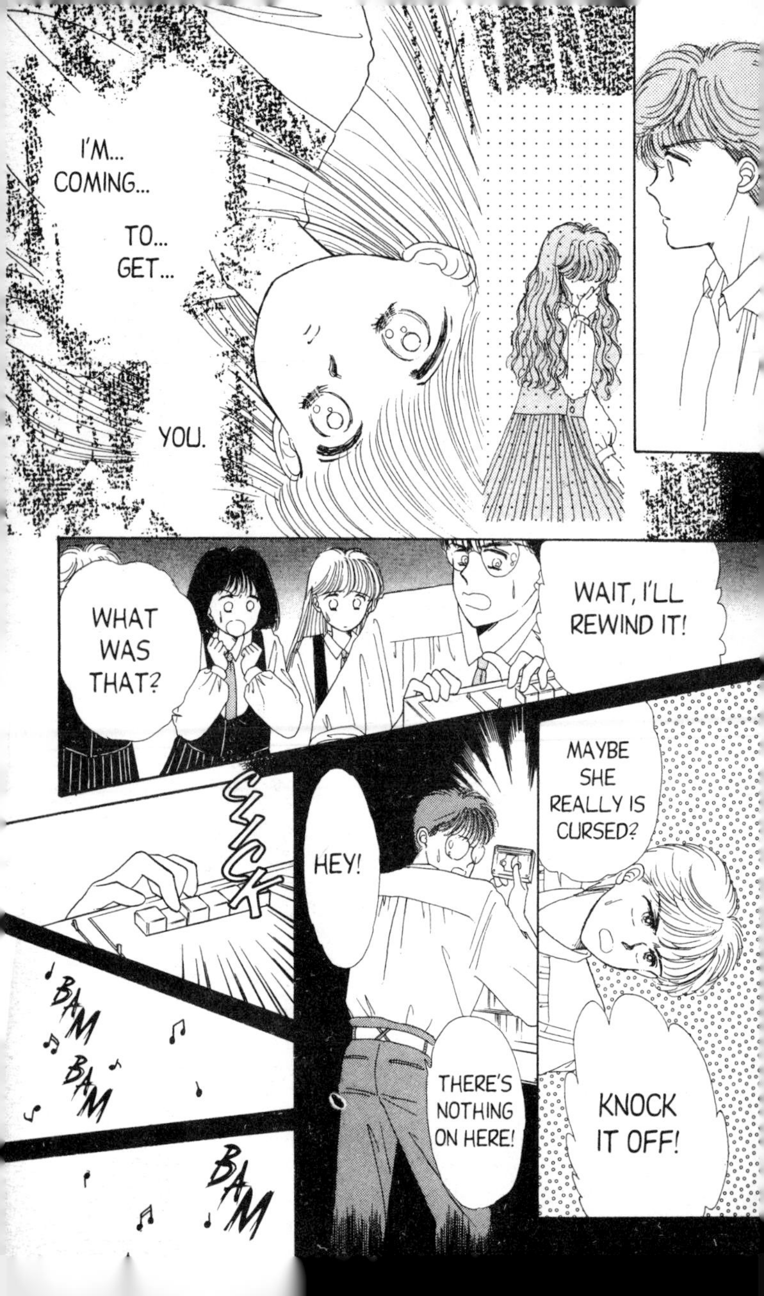
I'M... COMING...
TO... GET...
YOU.
WHAT WAS THAT?
WAIT, I'LL REWIND IT!
CLICK
BAM BAM
BAM
HEY!
THERE'S NOTHING ON HERE!
MAYBE SHE REALLY IS CURSED?
KNOCK IT OFF!

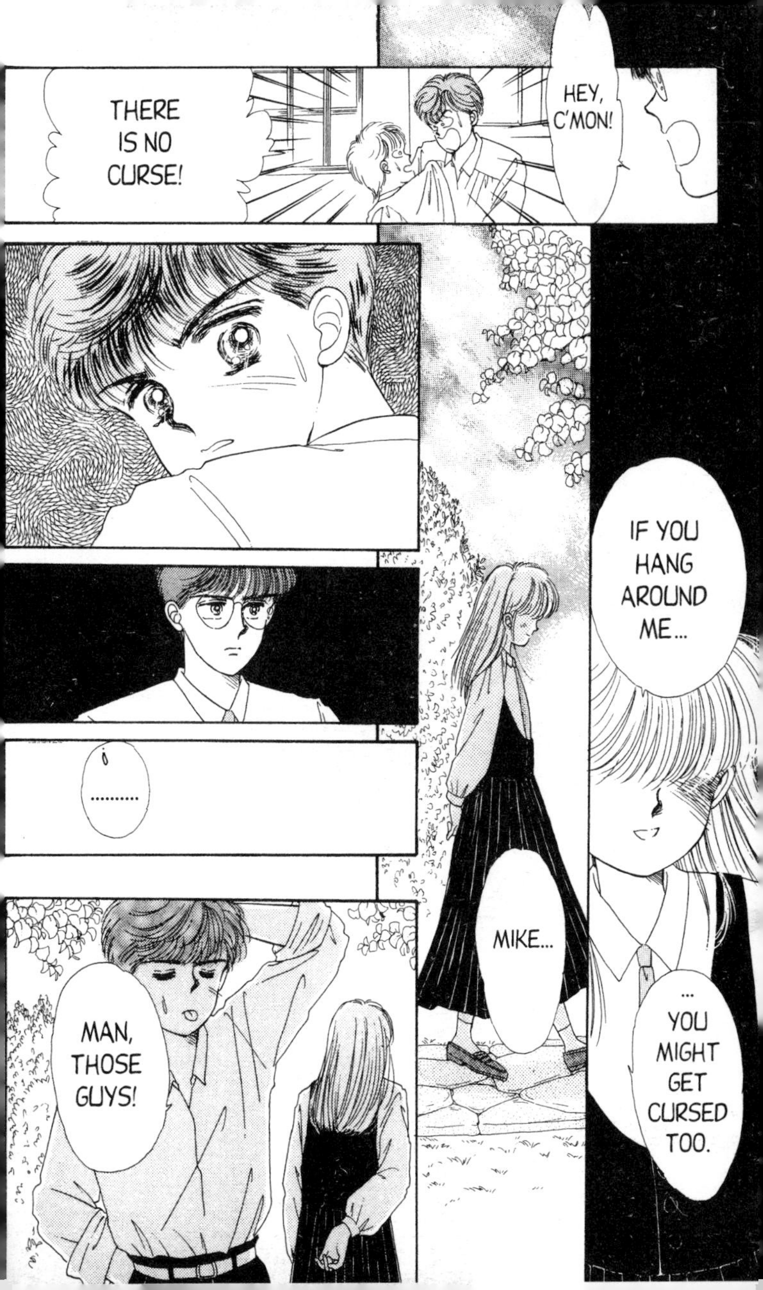
THERE IS NO CURSE!
HEY, C'MON!
....
MAN, THOSE GUYS!
MIKE...
IF YOU HANG AROUND ME...
... YOU MIGHT GET CURSED TOO.

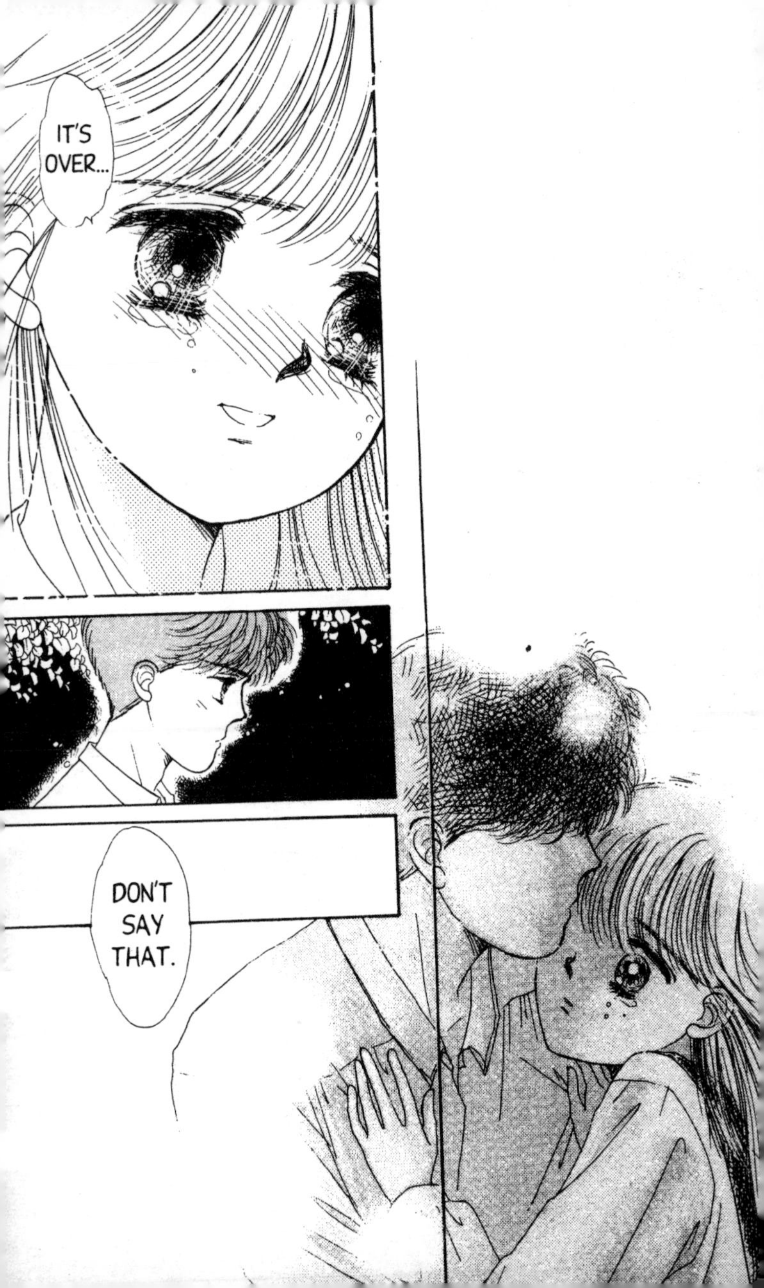
IT'S OVER...
DON'T SAY THAT.

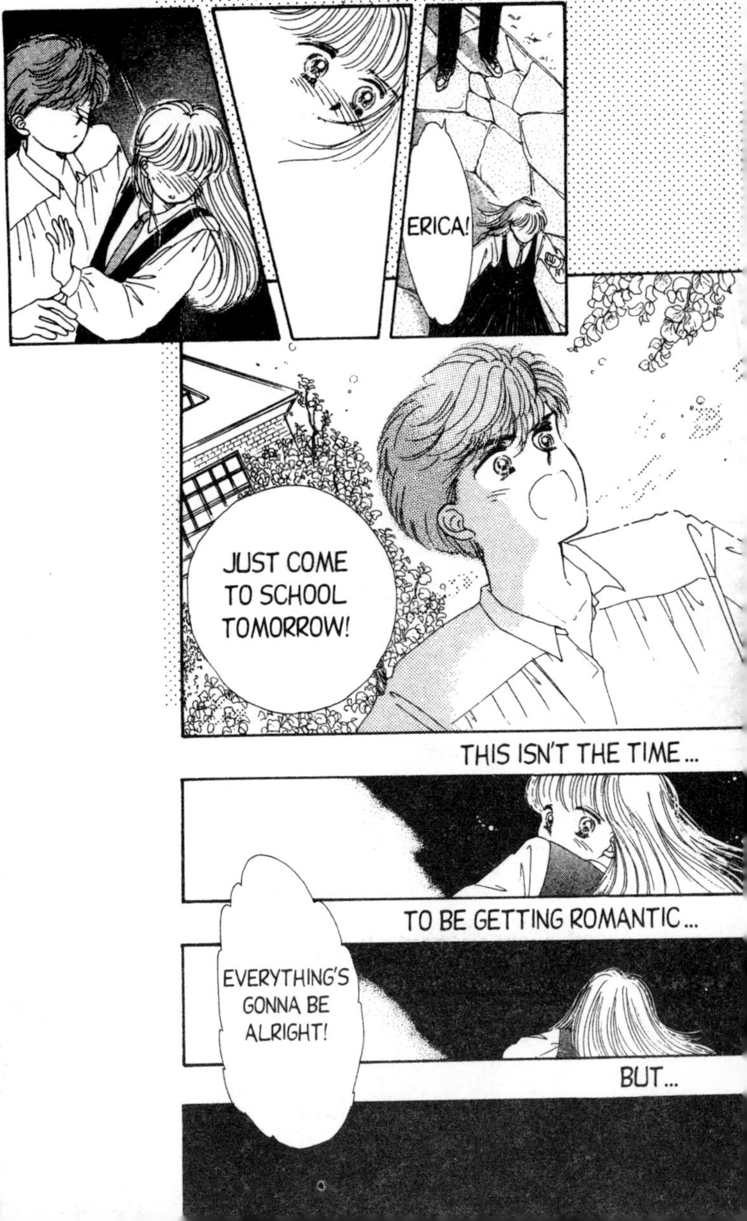
ERICA!
JUST COME TO SCHOOL TOMORROW!
THIS ISN'T THE TIME...
TO BE GETTING ROMANTIC...
EVERYTHING'S GONNA BE ALRIGHT!
BUT...

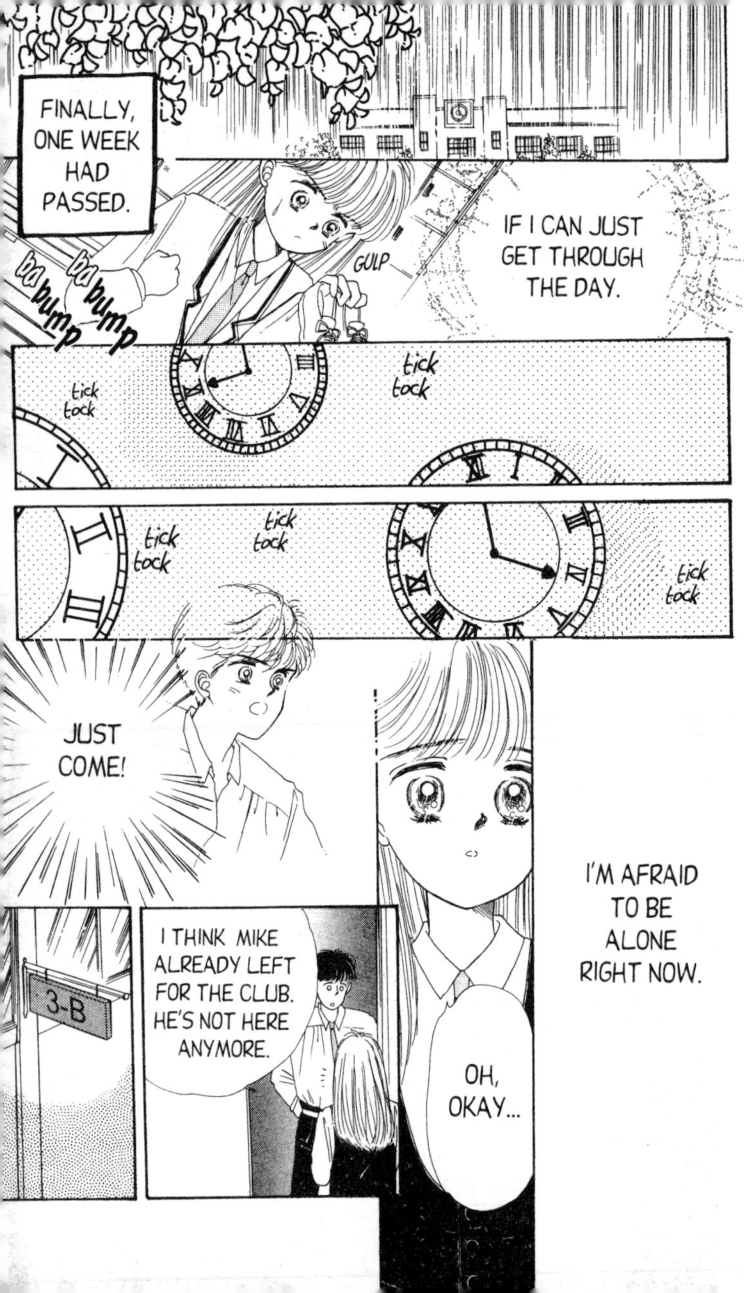
FINALLY, ONE WEEK HAD PASSED.
ba bump
ba bump
GULP
IF I CAN JUST GET THROUGH THE DAY.
tick tock
tick tock
tick tock
tick tock
tick tock
JUST COME!
I'M AFRAID TO BE ALONE RIGHT NOW.
3-B
I THINK MIKE ALREADY LEFT FOR THE CLUB. HE'S NOT HERE ANYMORE.
OH, OKAY...

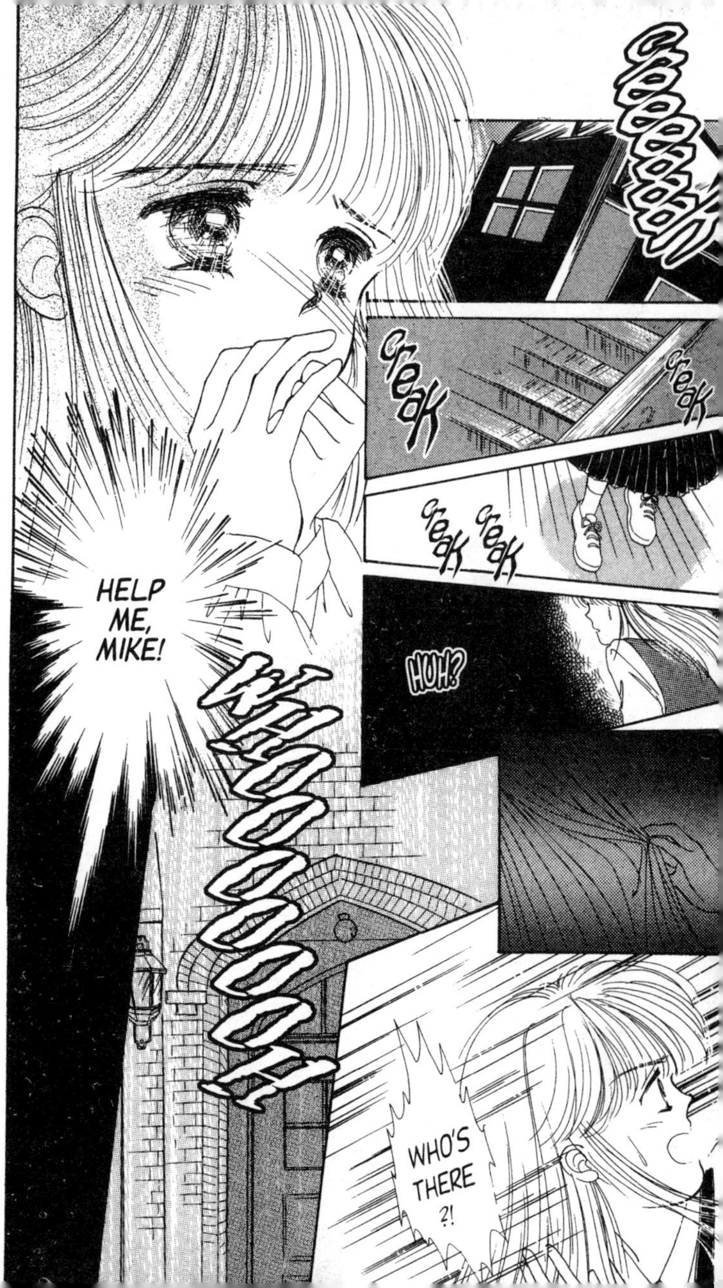
HELP ME, MIKE!
WHOOOOOOM
creeeeeak
creak
creak
creak
creak
HUH?
WHO'S THERE ?!

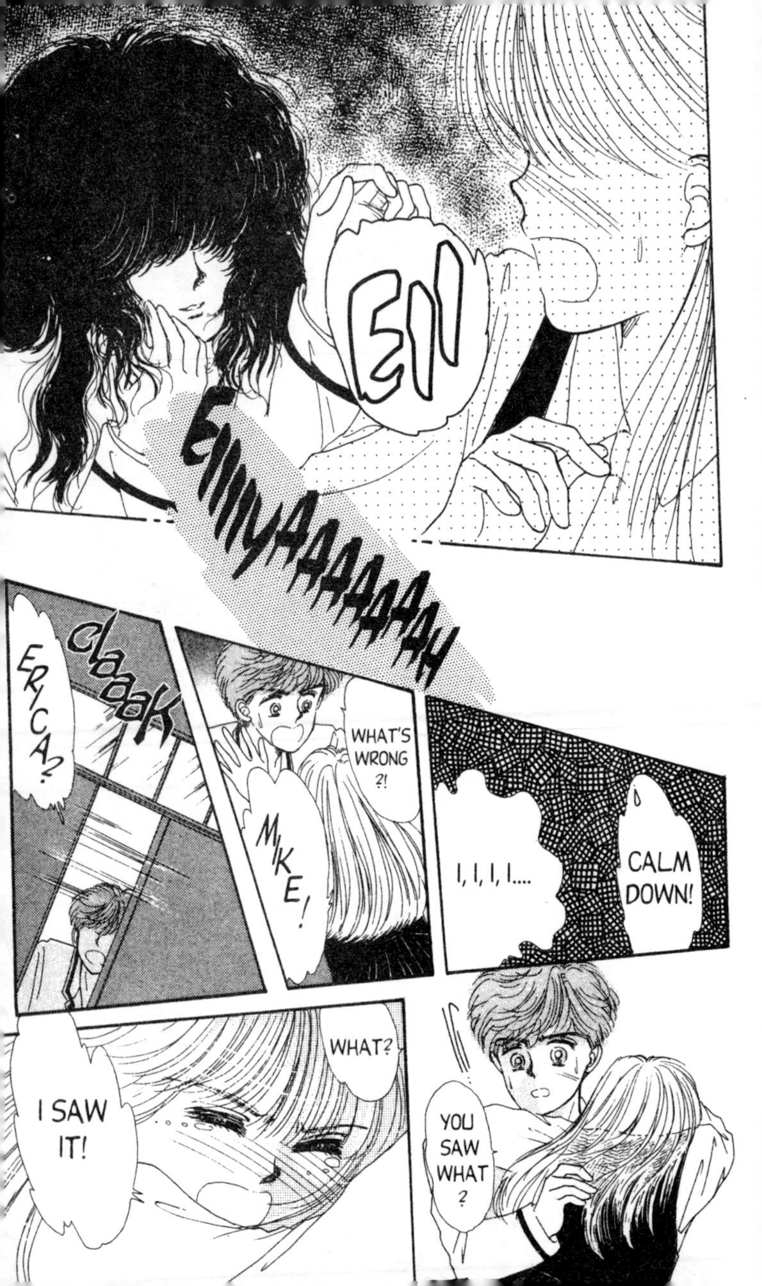

EII
EIIIYAAAAAAAAH
ERICA?
CLAAAAK
WHAT'S WRONG?!
MIKE!
I, I, I, I....
CALM DOWN!
I SAW IT!
WHAT?
YOU SAW WHAT?

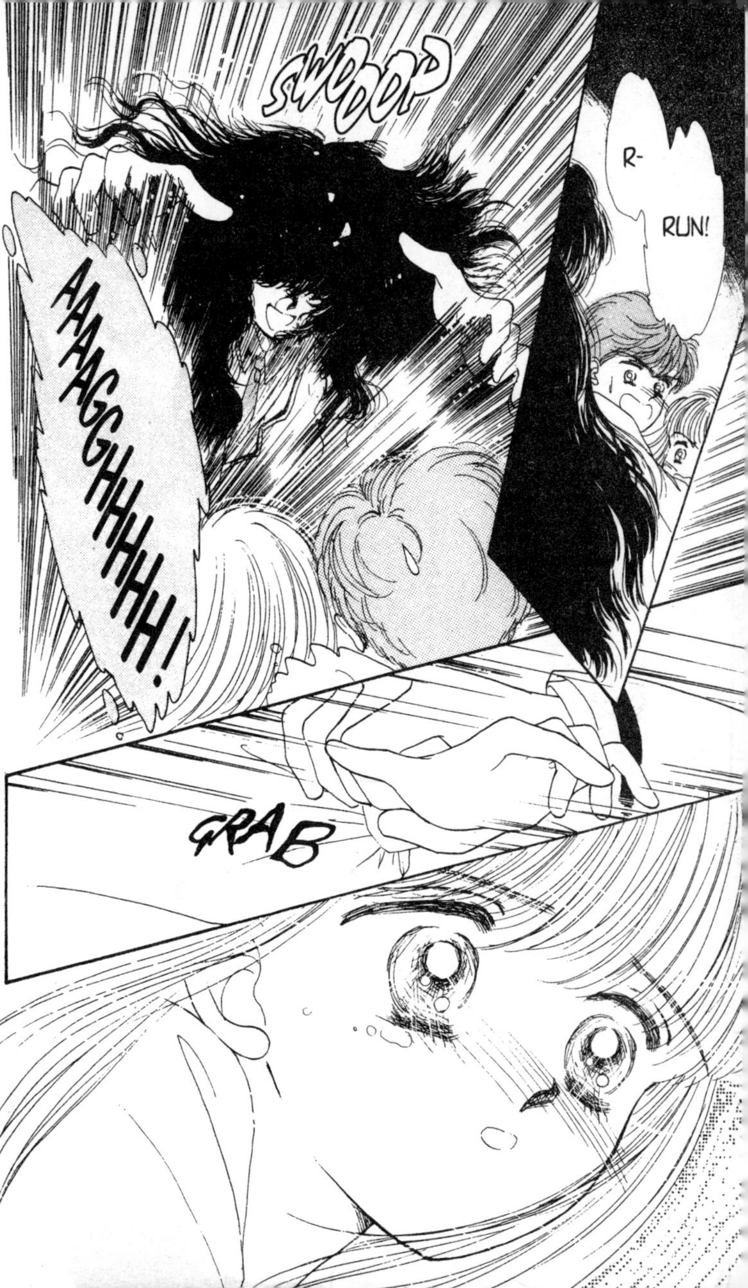
SWOOOP
AAAAGHHHHHH!
R-
RUN!
GRAB

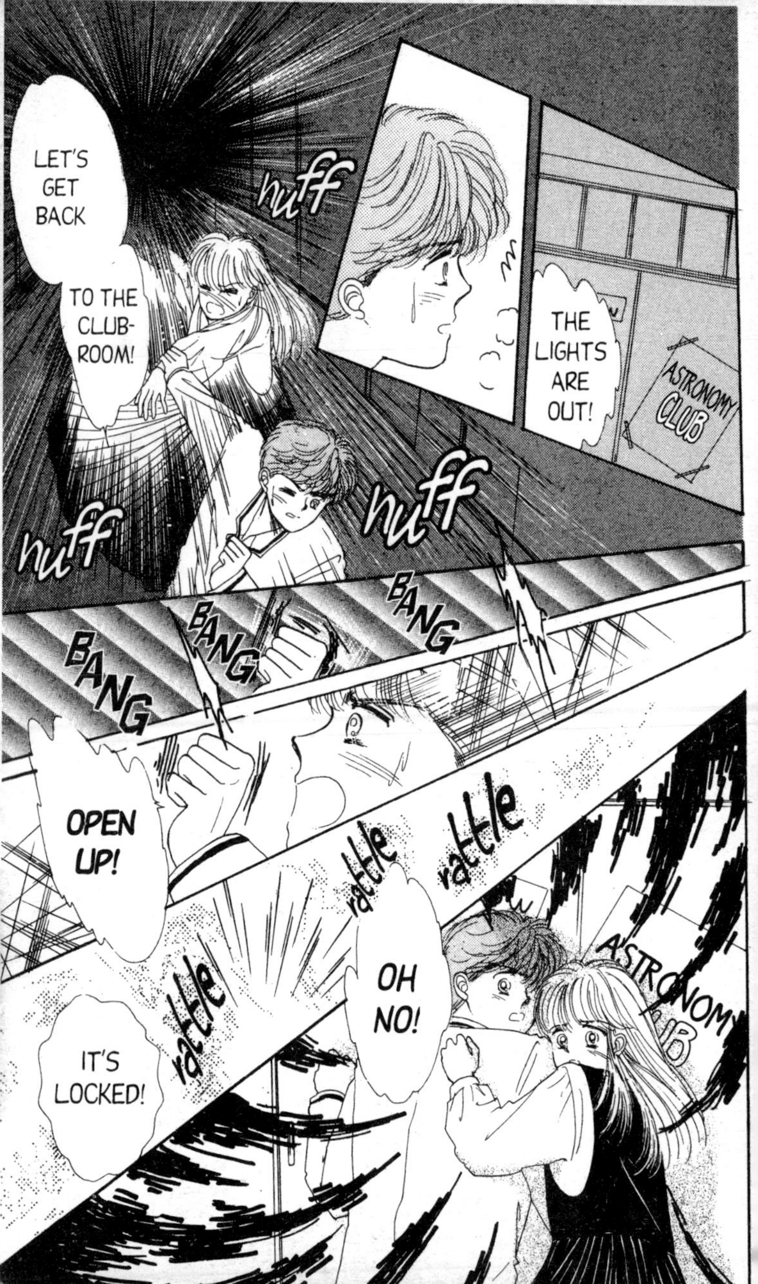
LET'S GET BACK
TO THE CLUB-ROOM!
huff
huff
huff
THE LIGHTS ARE OUT!
ASTRONOMY CLUB
BANG
BANG
BANG
OPEN UP!
rattle
rattle
rattle
rattle
OH NO!
IT'S LOCKED!
ASTRONOMY

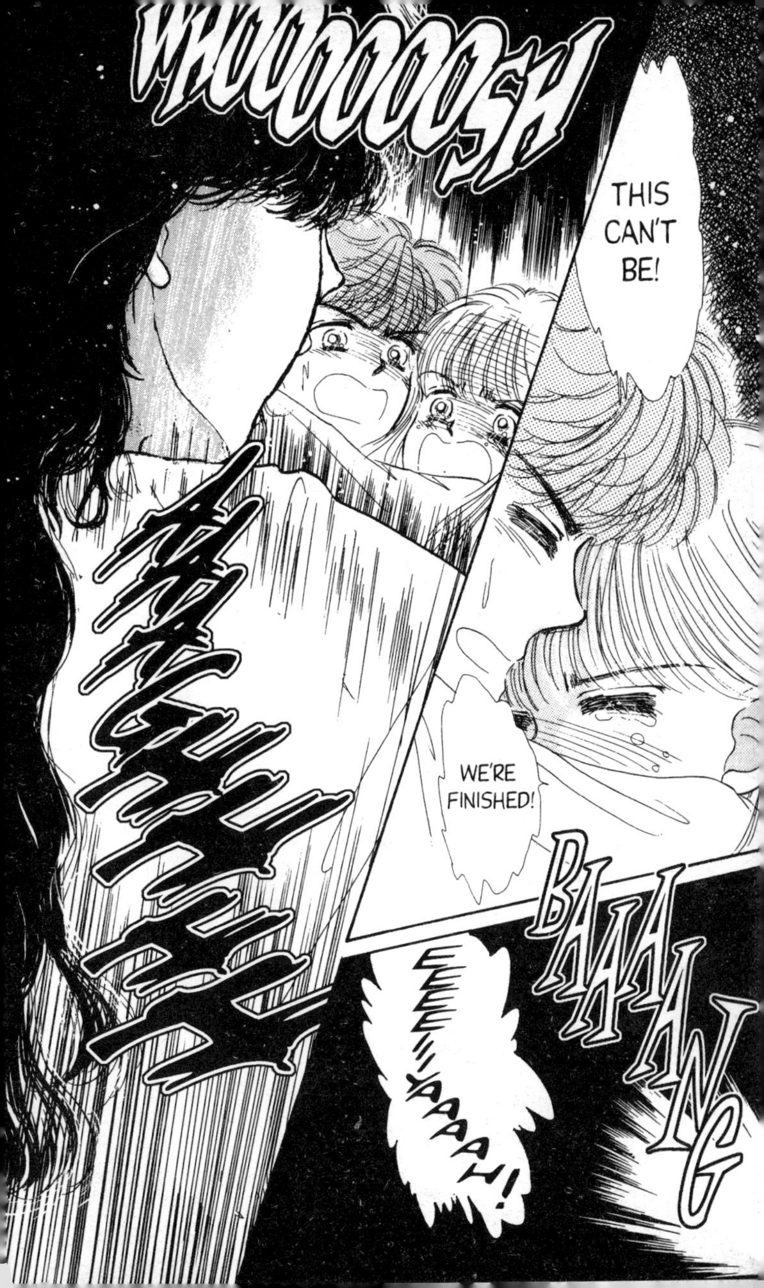

WHOOOOOSH
THIS CAN'T BE!
WE'RE FINISHED!
EEEEE!!!YAAAAH!
BAAAANG

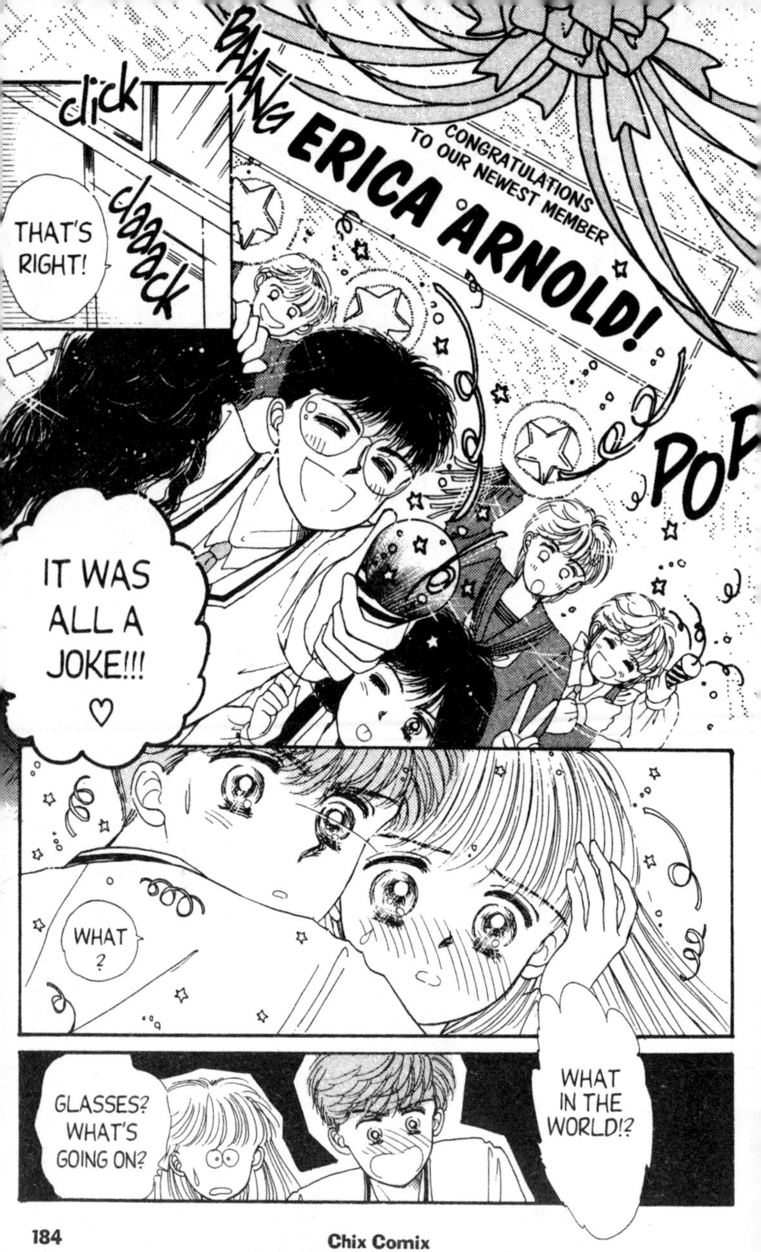
click
BAANG
CONGRATULATIONS TO OUR NEWEST MEMBER
ERICA ARNOLD!
THAT'S RIGHT!
claaack
POP
IT WAS ALL A JOKE!!! ♡
WHAT ?
WHAT IN THE WORLD!?
GLASSES? WHAT'S GOING ON?

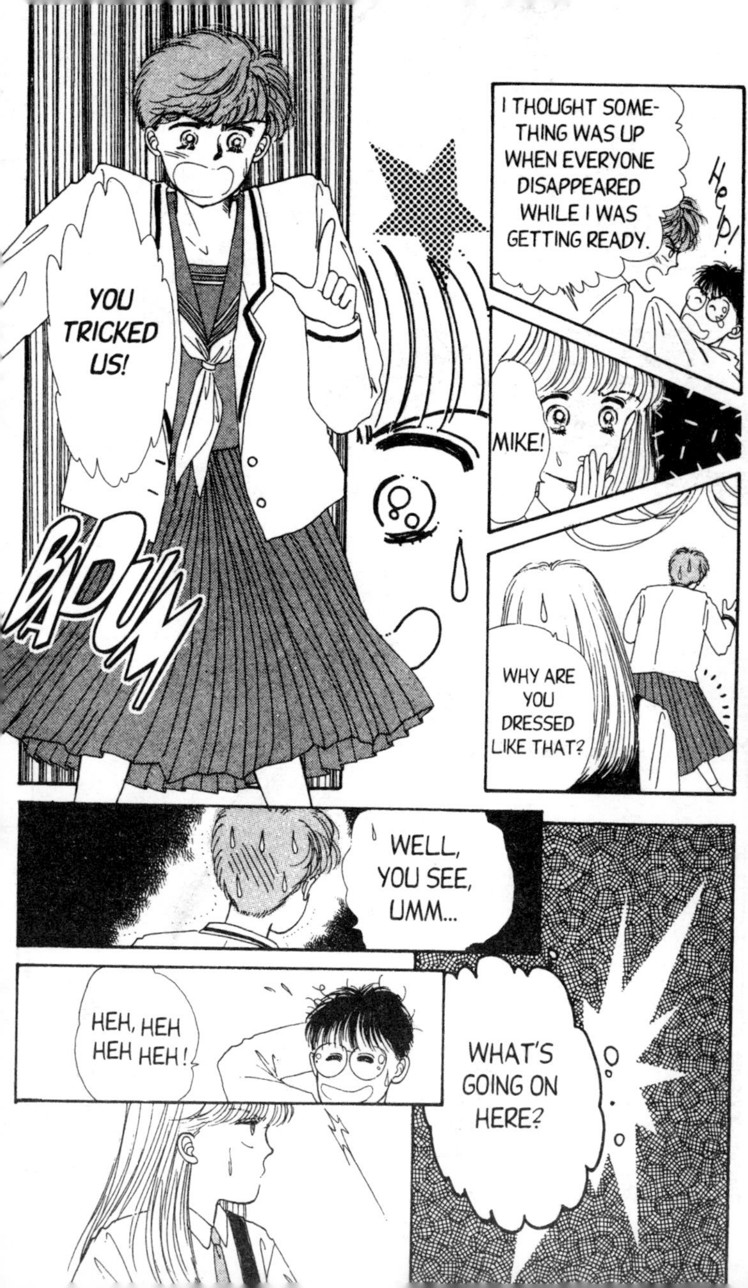
YOU TRICKED US!
BADUM
I THOUGHT SOMETHING WAS UP WHEN EVERYONE DISAPPEARED WHILE I WAS GETTING READY.
Help!
MIKE!
WHY ARE YOU DRESSED LIKE THAT?
WELL, YOU SEE, UMM...
HEH, HEH HEH HEH!
WHAT'S GOING ON HERE?

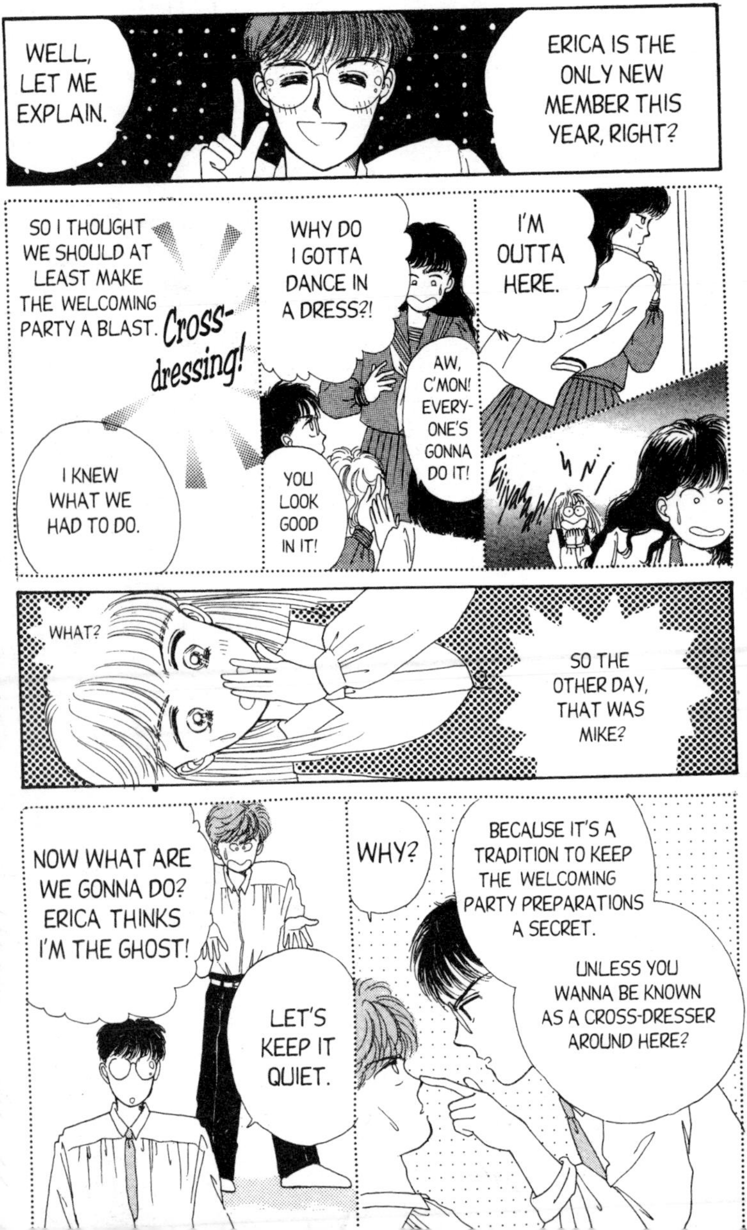
WELL, LET ME EXPLAIN.
ERICA IS THE ONLY NEW MEMBER THIS YEAR, RIGHT?
SO I THOUGHT WE SHOULD AT LEAST MAKE THE WELCOMING PARTY A BLAST.
Cross-dressing!
I KNEW WHAT WE HAD TO DO.
WHY DO I GOTTA DANCE IN A DRESS?!
AW, C'MON! EVERYONE'S GONNA DO IT!
YOU LOOK GOOD IN IT!
I'M OUTTA HERE.
WHAT?
SO THE OTHER DAY, THAT WAS MIKE?
NOW WHAT ARE WE GONNA DO? ERICA THINKS I'M THE GHOST!
LET'S KEEP IT QUIET.
WHY?
BECAUSE IT'S A TRADITION TO KEEP THE WELCOMING PARTY PREPARATIONS A SECRET.
UNLESS YOU WANNA BE KNOWN AS A CROSS-DRESSER AROUND HERE?

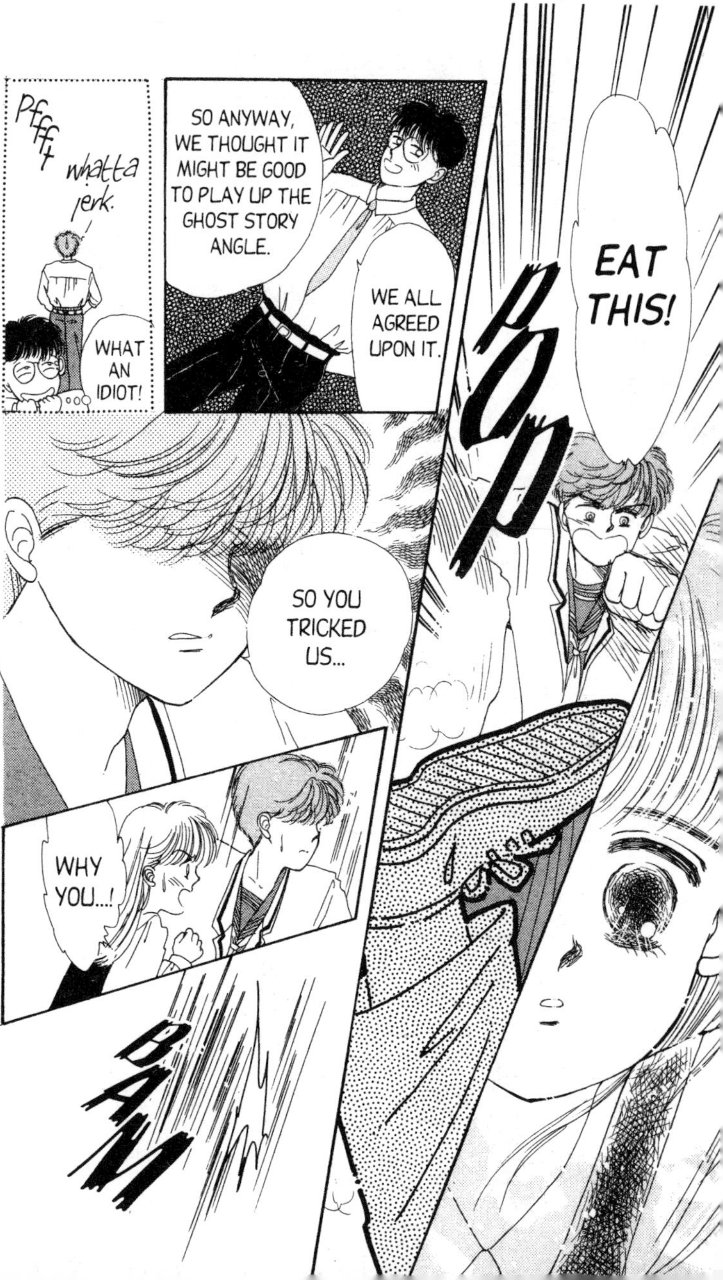
Pffft whatta jerk.
WHAT AN IDIOT!
SO ANYWAY, WE THOUGHT IT MIGHT BE GOOD TO PLAY UP THE GHOST STORY ANGLE.
WE ALL AGREED UPON IT.
SO YOU TRICKED US...
WHY YOU...!
BAM
EAT THIS!
BOP

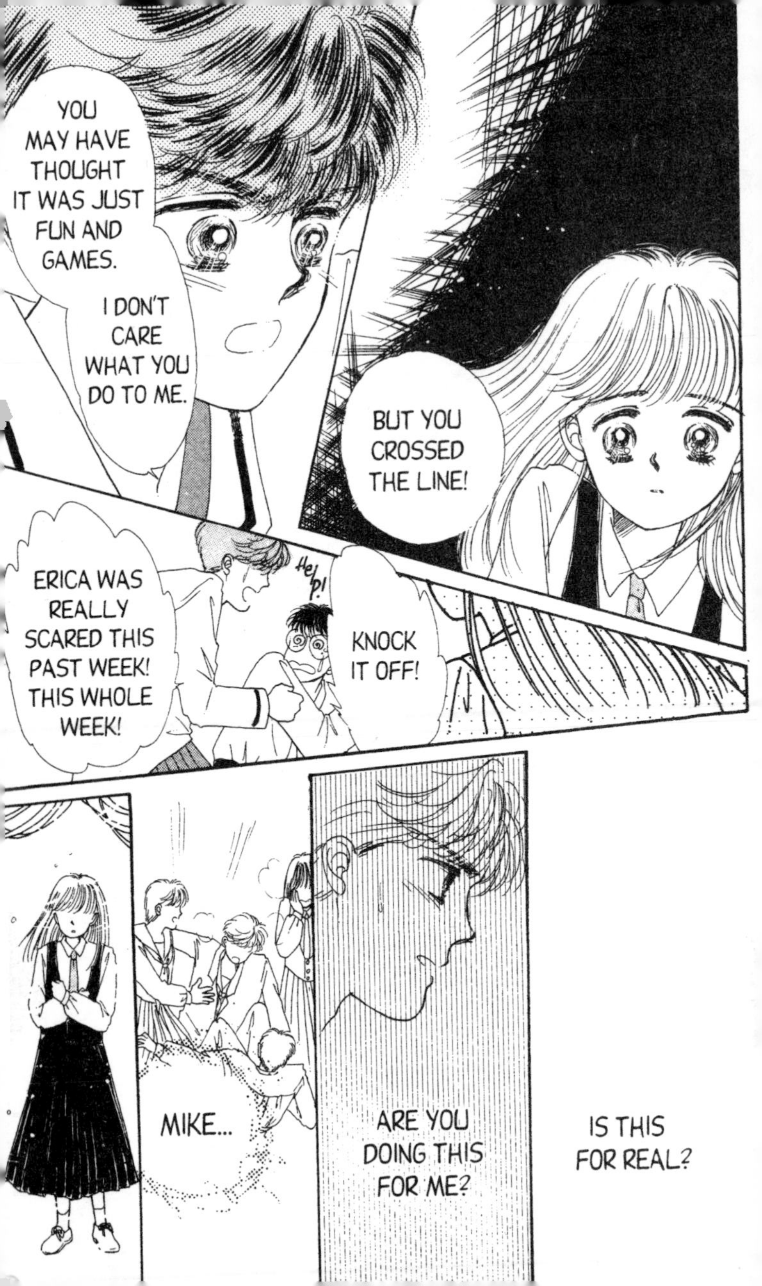
YOU MAY HAVE THOUGHT IT WAS JUST FUN AND GAMES.
I DON'T CARE WHAT YOU DO TO ME.
BUT YOU CROSSED THE LINE!
ERICA WAS REALLY SCARED THIS PAST WEEK! THIS WHOLE WEEK!
Help!
KNOCK IT OFF!
MIKE...
ARE YOU DOING THIS FOR ME?
IS THIS FOR REAL?

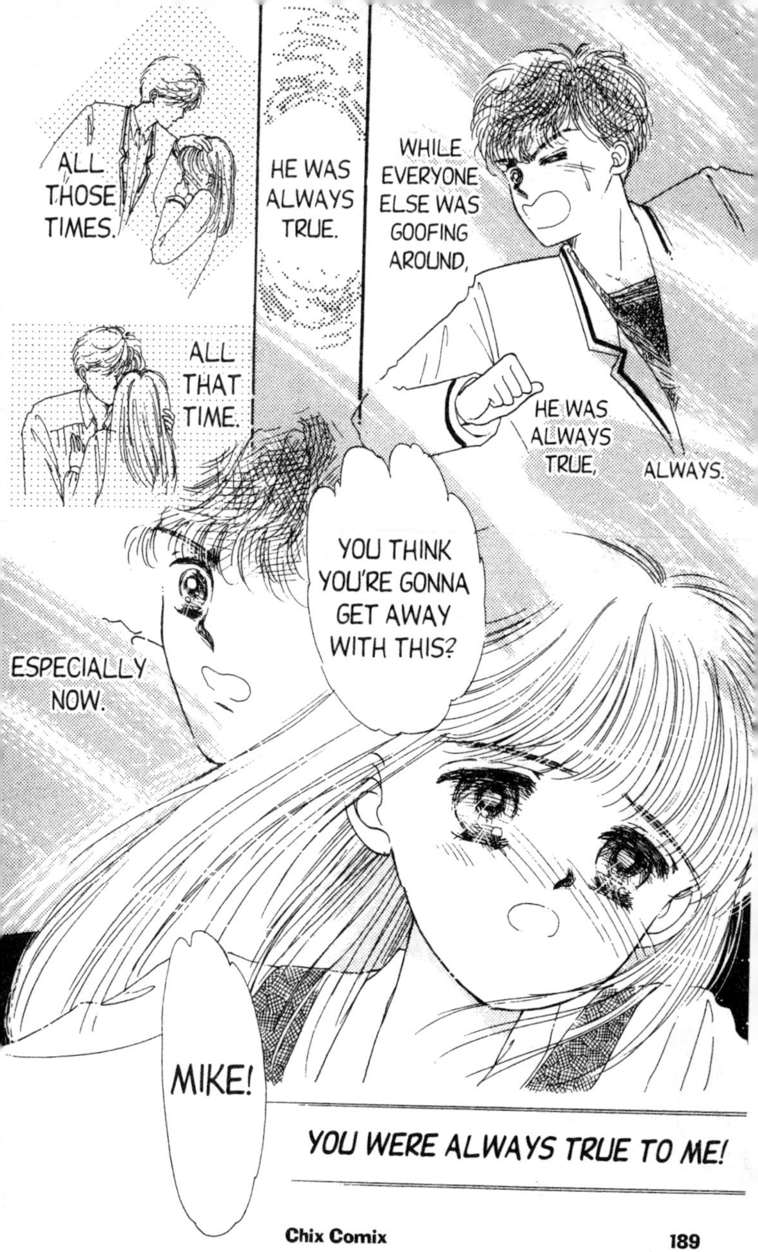
ALL THOSE TIMES.
ALL THAT TIME.
HE WAS ALWAYS TRUE.
WHILE EVERYONE ELSE WAS GOOFING AROUND,
HE WAS ALWAYS TRUE,
ALWAYS.
ESPECIALLY NOW.
YOU THINK YOU'RE GONNA GET AWAY WITH THIS?
MIKE!
YOU WERE ALWAYS TRUE TO ME!

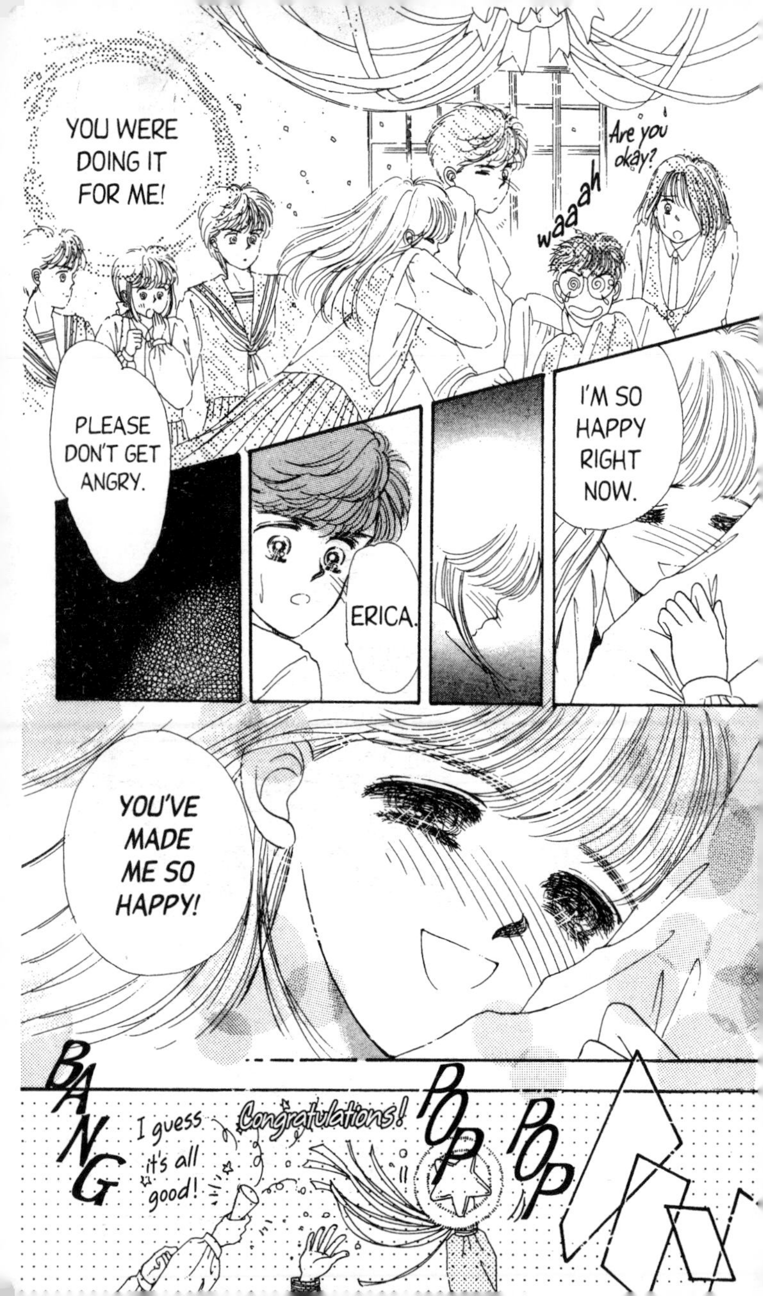
YOU WERE DOING IT FOR ME!
Are you okay?
waaah
PLEASE DON'T GET ANGRY.
ERICA.
I'M SO HAPPY RIGHT NOW.
YOU'VE MADE ME SO HAPPY!
BANG
I guess it's all good!
Congratulations!
POP
POP

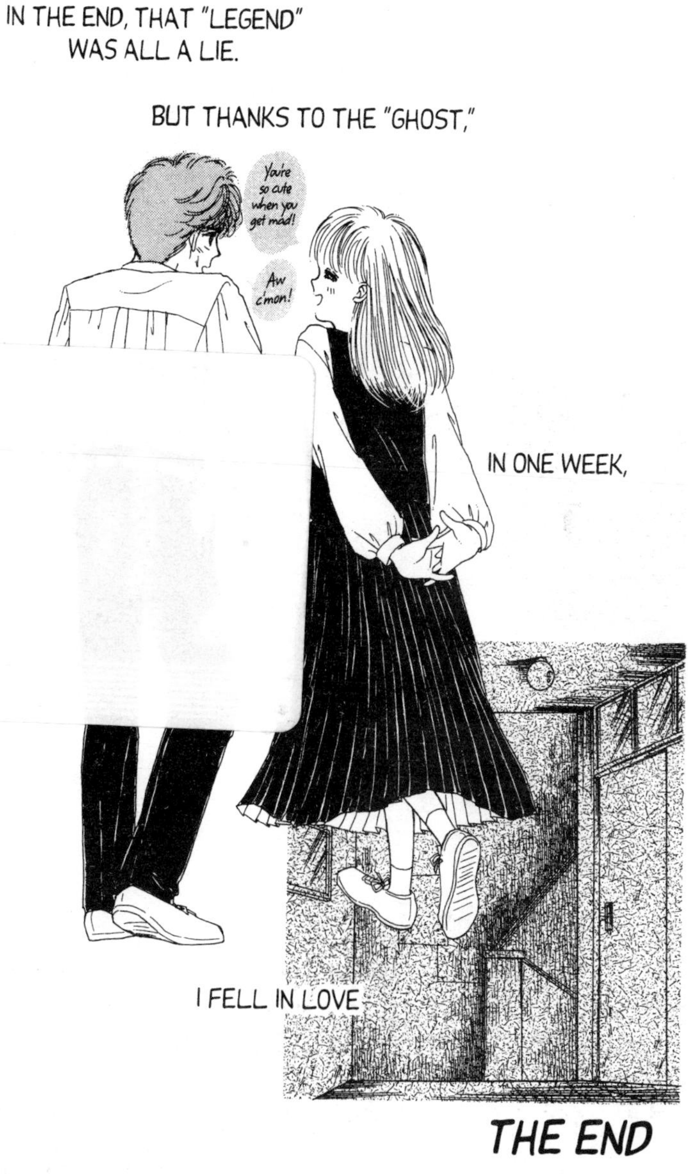
IN THE END, THAT "LEGEND" WAS ALL A LIE.
BUT THANKS TO THE "GHOST,"
You're so cute when you get mad!
Aw c'mon!
IN ONE WEEK,
I FELL IN LOVE
THE END

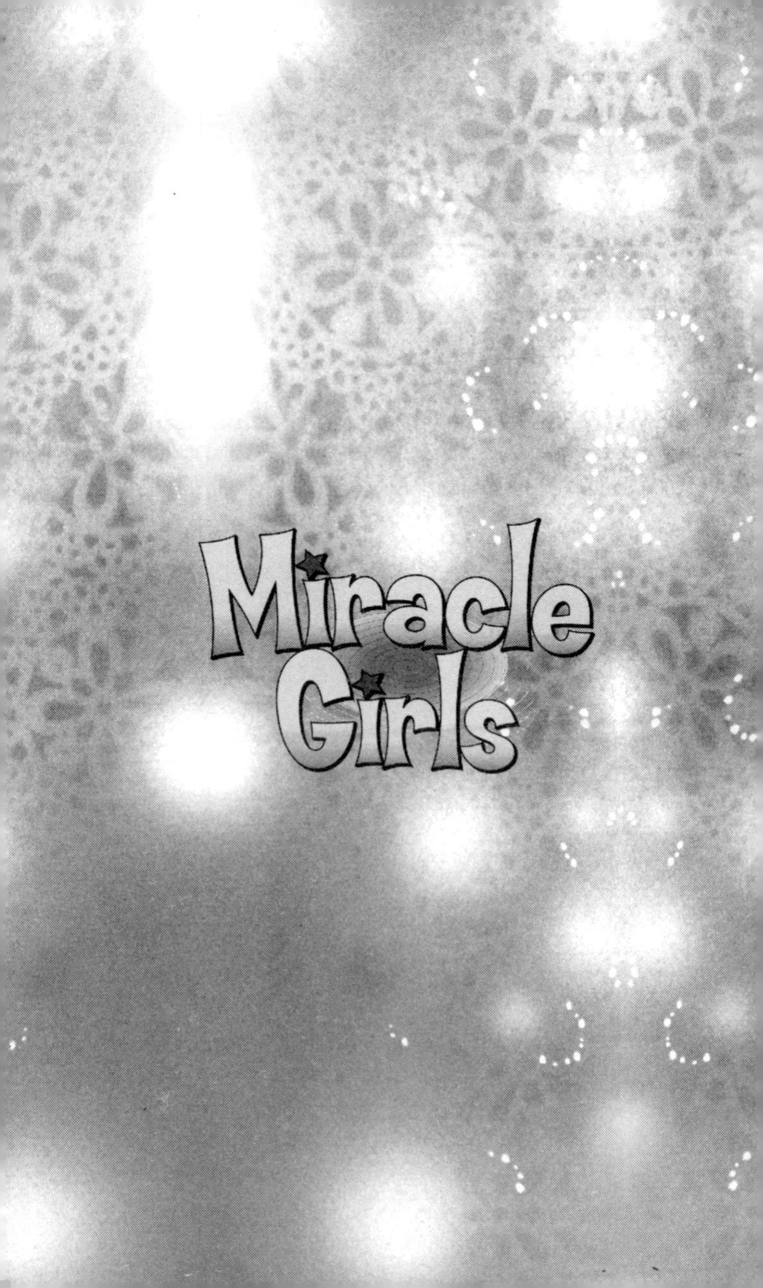
Miracle
Girls